POPULAR CATHOLICISM
IN A WORLD CHURCH

FAITH AND CULTURES SERIES

An Orbis Series on Contextualizing Gospel and Church

General Editor: Robert J. Schreiter, C.PP.S.

The *Faith and Cultures Series* deals with questions that arise as Christian faith attempts to respond to its new global reality. For centuries Christianity and the church were identified with European cultures. Although the roots of Christian tradition lie deep in Semitic cultures and Africa, and although Asian influences on it are well documented, that original diversity was widely forgotten as the church took shape in the West.

Today, as the churches of the Americas, Asia, and Africa take their place alongside older churches of Mediterranean and North Atlantic cultures, they claim the right to express Christian faith in their own idioms, thought patterns, and cultures. To provide a forum for better understanding this process, the Orbis *Faith and Cultures Series* publishes books that illuminate the range of questions that arise from this global challenge.

Orbis and the *Faith and Cultures Series* General Editor invite the submission of manuscripts on relevant topics.

Also in the Series
Faces of Jesus in Africa, Robert J. Schreiter, C.PP.S., Editor
Hispanic Devotional Piety, C. Gilbert Romero
African Theology in Its Social Context, Bénézet Bujo
Models of Contextual Theology, Stephen B. Bevans, S.V.D.
Asian Faces of Jesus, R. S. Sugirtharajah, Editor
Evangelizing the Culture of Modernity, Hervé Carrier, S.J.
St. Martín de Porres: "The Little Stories" and the Semiotics of Culture, Alex García-Rivera
The Indian Face of God in Latin America, Manuel M. Marzal, S.J., Eugenio Maurer, S.J., Xavier Albó, S.J., and Bartomeu Melià, S.J.
Towards an African Narrative Theology, Joseph Healy, M.M., and Donald Sybertz, M.M.
The Earth Is God's: A Theology of American Culture, William A. Dyrness
The New Catholicity: Theology between the Global and the Local, Robert J. Schreiter, C.PP.S.
Mission & Catechesis: Alexandre de Rhodes and Inculturation in Seventeenth-Century Vietnam, Peter C. Phan
Celebrating Jesus Christ in Africa, François Kabasele Lumbala

FAITH AND CULTURES SERIES

Popular Catholicism in a World Church

Seven Case Studies in Inculturation

Edited by
Thomas Bamat
Jean-Paul Wiest
Center for Mission Research and Study at Maryknoll

ORBIS BOOKS

Maryknoll, New York 10545

The Catholic Foreign Mission Society of America (Maryknoll) recruits and trains people for overseas missionary service. Through Orbis Books, Maryknoll aims to foster the international dialogue that is essential to mission. The books published, however, reflect the opinions of their authors and are not meant to represent the official position of the society. To obtain more information about Maryknoll or Orbis Books, please visit our website at www.maryknoll.org.

Library of Congress Cataloging-in-Publication Data

Popular Catholicism in a world church : seven case studies in
   inculturation / edited by Thomas Bamat, Jean-Paul Wiest.
        p.   cm. — (Faith and cultures series)
    Includes bibliographical references.
    ISBN 1-57075-252-4 (pbk.)
    1. Christianity and culture.   2. Catholic Church—Doctrines.
I. Bamat, Tomás.   II. Wiest, Jean-Paul.   III. Series.
BX1795.C85P67   1999
230'.2—dc21   98-55523

Contents

Foreword

ROBERT J. SCHREITER, C.PP.S.

It has long been known that a gap of varying dimensions has existed between what elite professionals purport to be the proper and complete way to live and believe in a religious tradition, and how that acting and believing happens among other strata of the population. These latter ways, usually referred to as "popular" (i.e., coming from ordinary people) religion, were often seen as deviations from the official norm. From the perspective of elites, such deviations were to be overcome either by stricter discipline, or better education, or some combination of the two.

Popular forms of being religious occur not only in Christianity, but in all the translocal forms of religion, such as Judaism, Islam, Hinduism, and Buddhism. Each of these traditions has taken a variety of stands within their ranks regarding popular practice and belief, ranging from toleration to periodic waves of reform. Christianity began, at least from a sociological point of view, as a reform movement within Judaism. Perhaps its reformist beginnings, with preoccupations about purity of practice and of doctrine, have given Christianity a greater concern about apparent disparities between official and popular practice than has been the case in other translocal traditions. The waves of reform that have come throughout the history of Christianity (such as iconoclasm, reform movements in the Middle Ages, the Protestant Reformation, and the Second Vatican Council) can be read, at least in some measure, as trying to come to terms with disparities between official and popular belief and practice.

The focus on culture and local place in the study of Christianity which has arisen since the 1970s has permitted a new way of looking at popular forms of Christianity. Popular religion no longer needs to be dismissed as deviations brought on by psychological need or lack of proper evangelization. It can be seen as an authentic way of living out the message of the Gospel. To be sure, these ways are open to exaggeration and heterodoxy; but history shows that official forms of Christianity have not been immune from such charges either.

A closer look at popular forms of Christianity has been teaching us much about what conversion means, how people construct their lives and live in their religious worlds, and how they find resources to adapt to challenges and changes in their environment. Such closer examination also helps us to see that practices and beliefs are never as tidy as we might like to believe: people can engage in the same practices out of very different motivations, can profess the same faith while drawing different conclusions about how one should then act, or see in the same religious world very different possibilities for living in the world. This has allowed us to move beyond a simple-minded approach that does not do justice to complexities that Christians face in different environments in their efforts to be faithful to the Gospel and to the Church.

The growth of interest in inculturation since the 1970s, and its implications for faithful witness in a Church that bridges many cultures and, in principle, can find itself at home in all of them, has provided an important framework for evaluating popular religion. That evaluation involves not only a greater understanding of what is at play in popular practices and beliefs, but also the challenges and limits of what official practices and beliefs can mean in any given context, given the constraints of the social and cultural environment. As a result, we have the making of a far richer understanding of the texture of Christianity as it is incarnated in a World Church.

The seven case studies in this book represent an important reading of where we have come in the understanding of popular religion—in this instance, focusing upon popular Catholicism. The editors are modest in their claims about what is and is not implied in these studies. They provide an empirical view of popular Catholicism in Latin America, Africa, and Asia of a kind that has heretofore not been available. Not only are these studies important in and of themselves, they have profited from intense reflection on site in each of the studies, and also from the researchers having come together to discuss one another's efforts and findings. While this book has not included studies on North America and Europe (and the studies on popular religion among Hispanic/Latino peoples in North America have already made a significant contribution to how we think about popular religion elsewhere in the world), it has mapped out for us important insights from that part of the world where Christianity is growing most rapidly. That alone yields considerable information and food for reflection about ways of being Christian about which we knew relatively little before.

In retrospect, it becomes clearer that the Second Vatican Council's efforts to confront the problems of the Church in the modern world were insightful in addressing some of those issues in Europe and North America. Here issues of modernization, secularization, and atheism were dealt with in ways that continue to serve us well four decades later. What the Council was less able to achieve lay in questions arising in other realms—particularly "non-Western Catholicism"— integral to "World Catholicism," partly because those issues were at that time only dimly seen. To be sure, the signals were there about the need for adaptation, for openness to other great religious traditions, and for dealing with specific issues arising in so-called "mission territories." And that was perhaps as far as the Council could go in 1965. Today we find ourselves in a situation where those one-time "mission territories" now command greater attention and respect. Some of the findings that emerge in these studies point to where we now need to go—

not only in the countries of Latin America, Africa, and Asia, but in the North Atlantic sphere as well. Let me note four sets of insights that this book sets before the World Church from its study of popular Catholicism.

First, *modernization*: it has now become apparent that modernization does not occur in the uniform fashion that had been predicted by Max Weber and others at the beginning of the twentieth century. These studies show in abundance that modernization (and its current form, globalization) does not sweep away premodern cultures, leaving only individualism and secularization in its wake. The agency of peoples in local cultures to select, to resist, to refashion, and to recreate their worlds when modernity and local cultures meet is an important lesson we have been learning in the last decade and a half. This very capacity to create new worlds on the part of peoples in Latin America, Africa, and Asia helps us sort through the reforms of Vatican II that have become the newest form of official Catholicism. In this connection, what is sometimes touted as return to authentic sources may have more to do with coming to terms with modernity in the North Atlantic and its specific conditions than maintaining the breadth of authentic teaching. Movements that have easily been dismissed as "pre-Vatican II" can now be seen as having a greater complexity than they were sometimes accorded by enthusiastic reformers who were unaware of the limits of Western modernity.

Second, *politics*: the reforms of the Second Vatican Council coincided with a time of great political and economic optimism in the 1960s. The end of the 1990s finds us in a more sober state of mind. While we should never abandon the hope that *Gaudium et Spes* and other Vatican II documents instilled, we have also come to realize that some of the grand political and economic projects that were born in that period did not address conceptually all the complexities of the world or overcome practically the deeply entrenched forces of evil that resist and undermine transformation. The studies in this book touch on how people in their locales address the political and economic realities in which they live. Sometimes the disappointment of the researchers with local responses to those realities shows through; but more importantly, these researchers have struggled to discern respectfully and carefully what James R. Scott has called the "weapons of the weak" (Scott 1985). This is important, since it allows us not to become beholden to one or other political model for transformation and liberation. What these researchers have found in their local settings reflects a larger rethinking that is going on in the world today.

Third, *ritual*: this motif comes through in many of the studies as vitally important. Ritual, nevertheless, has been discussed in Freudian terms in modernity as the obsessive behavior of the impotent. These studies, by contrast, all point to the importance of ritual in world-building and the creation of solidarity. These studies may not draw out all the implications that ritual has for these and other situations in the world today, but they do point to a burgeoning area in religious studies that holds out promise for studies in popular religion in general. They are particularly important for gaining insight into how people sustain hope in what may seem for outsiders to be hopeless situations.

Fourth, *the problem of evil*: as a number of the theological reflections at the end of this book point out, the religious worlds created in these locales bring us face to face with the problem of evil in our world. The emphasis on spirits and demons may make many Westerners uneasy, but this aspect should underscore the message transmitted in Western postmodernity, namely, that high modernity was far too optimistic about how reason would overcome evil in the world. Evil turns out to be more than shortcomings that education, political reforms, or a better social environment could repair. Its intractability needs to be faced squarely. This is surely an important message at the end of a century that has seen at once dazzling advances in science and technology, and at the same time incredible and brutal savagery.

The study of popular Catholicism, then, is not just an interesting ethnographic excursion into the exotic or a more refined way of diagnosing ecclesiastical deviance. It is precisely where we as a Church need to be at this time—exploring how Catholics struggling to be faithful deal with their world in their successes and in their failures. Popular Catholicism is not just a mirror for the exotic "other" for Westerners, but the source of fundamental and important questioning about how a World Church encompasses its diversity and its unity as it enters a new millennium. The Center for Mission Research and Study at Maryknoll is to be congratulated for having conceived of and coordinated such an important study. It bodes well for future projects that they will undertake.

Acknowledgments

This volume is the product of an international, interdisciplinary, and cross-cultural partnership. We are deeply grateful to all those whose insights, energy, commitment, and perseverance have brought it to fruition. First among them are the researchers and consultants who have labored with us on this project since 1995, and whose studies and essays are presented in these pages. It has been a great privilege and pleasure to work with them.

Additionally, we want to thank all those who participated in the 1993 Inaugural Consultation of the Center for Mission Research and Study at Maryknoll (CMRSM). Their insights and indication of critical issues for research provided the seedbed for the project. They included Virginia Fabella, Marie Giblin, Stephen Judd, Smangaliso Mkhatshwa, Anne Nasimiyu, Judy Noone, Mercedes Román, Paulo Süess, and John Waliggo.

Our sincere thanks as well to those who funded this study. The Pew Charitable Trusts made possible the Inaugural Consultation through the Overseas Ministries Study Center's Research Enablement Program, and then provided a substantial grant for the research itself. Dr. Christopher Smith, then at Pew, was exceedingly encouraging and helpful.

The Maryknoll Fathers and Brothers provided the remaining funds. Our special appreciation goes to Kenneth Thesing and Raymond Finch of the Maryknoll leadership, who recognized the importance of this project; to Wayman Deasy, who assisted with budgeting; to Curtis Cadorette, who provided some initial orientation; and to Stephen Judd, who served as a liaison and consultant, and contributed especially to the Peruvian case study.

We are deeply indebted to our fellow workers at the CMRSM for their support and participation in project gatherings: William D. McCarthy, Anne Reissner, Cathy McDonald and Mary Ann Cejka. Special thanks to Clara Araujo for the countless hours of global communication, logistical work with partners, and the almost endless secretarial tasks.

We want to express our gratitude to the able professionals at Orbis Books, especially Bill Burrows, who accompanied us from beginning to end and made valuable suggestions along the way. Thanks also to Joseph Maloney and John O'Donovan at the Maryknoll Controllers Office, who helped keep our accounting straight.

We are thankful for the painstaking work of all who helped with fieldwork around the world, including local community members who were trained for the task. Last but not least, we are deeply grateful for the generosity, openness, and enthusiasm of the people from the study sites in Chile, Ghana, Hong Kong, India, Peru, St. Lucia, and Tanzania. They allowed us to explore with them what we share now with you.

None of those acknowledged here, of course, should be suspected, or much less rounded up, for possible errors or omissions. For them, we the editors and the individual authors alone are responsible.

Introduction

The Many Faces
of Popular Catholicism

THOMAS BAMAT and JEAN-PAUL WIEST

"The Catholic thing is and has always been a 'popular' thing, a thing of the people, shaped and colored by the continuity of popular cultures." So wrote Rosemary Haughton some two decades ago in *The Catholic Thing* (1979). Her argument was that Catholicism, as a historical enterprise seeking to integrate the whole of human life in the search for the reign of God, could be neither the exclusive domain of elites nor excessively controlled by institutional interests. Her book celebrated particularly the development of Celtic Catholicism in Europe and ethnic Catholicism in the United States.

Today, there is growing awareness that the majority of the world's Roman Catholics are no longer located in the global North. Christianity's center of gravity has shifted dramatically during the second half of the twentieth century. As humanity prepares to enact the opening scenes of a new millennium, an estimated 70% of the world's Roman Catholics are living outside Europe and North America (cf. Bühlmann 1986). The Catholic thing, historically shaped and colored by popular cultures, is thriving in Latin America, in Asia, and in Africa. The "world church" that is emerging is stunningly diversified.

Most of those who identify themselves as Catholics today inhabit lands that were once colonized by European powers. Foreign domination, enslavement, and processes of cultural uprooting are part of their historical inheritance. Today, their well-being, identity, and security are affected by the diffusion of modernity and postmodernity, the dynamic of capitalism, and the growing "globalization" of social life.

Many of these people face the dire consequences of vast and growing inequalities of power and wealth. Some are simply superfluous in the cruel logic of the new world order. They tend to live under formally democratic but often oppressive or unresponsive political systems. Not a few are minorities, mistrusted or disdained by dominant cultural or religious majorities. Most are women, bearing the multiple burdens imposed by patriarchy.

Despite the hardships under which they live, they can resist adversity in creative ways. Within the popular cultures of the global South, many of these ordinary Catholics participate in familial and community "strategies" of survival, cultural revivals, or organized efforts to enhance collective well-being. And while their religious beliefs and practices are under siege from modernity's cult of the market, its processes of secularization, and the diversification of the religious field, their worldviews and values demonstrate a surprising resilience.

Among the people that call themselves Catholic, one finds a diverse array of cultural and religious expressions, much of it with roots that predate the arrival of Christian missionaries. The latter often landed with conquerors and colonizers, and brought norms and values that were too often more Western culture than Gospel inspiration. Today, the people combine beliefs and rituals from different traditions, and engage in what may seem to some like indiscriminate "syncretism" or parallel religious practices (cf. Schreiter 1985, 144-149). For them, however, there is seldom a sense of clash or contradiction. Their popular rituals are a response to everyday problems in the struggle for more abundant life or for life itself (cf. Pieris 1988).

Within this context, there is a growing conviction among Christian theologians that "Christian faith must be rethought, reformulated and lived anew in each human culture . . . and this must be done in a vital way, in depth and right to the culture's roots" (Bosch 1991, 55). Local faith communities and particularly the laity are often seen as the primary actors in such processes.

While much more is being said than done in official church circles, authentic processes of "inculturation" have been called for in numerous documents since the 1970s. In the Message of the 1994 African Synod, this was called a "demand of witness" for each local church and each Christian. And while discussions of popular Catholicism are often unconnected to discussions on inculturation, the Latin American bishops have called popular Catholicism a "privileged expression of the inculturation of the faith" (Santo Domingo Final Document, No. 36).

AN AMBITIOUS UNDERTAKING

This book is the product of a three-year interdisciplinary research project on popular Catholicism and the emerging world church, which we have had the privilege of coordinating. It was developed at the urging of the international participants in the 1993 inaugural consultation of the Center for Mission Research and Study at Maryknoll, was administered through the Center, and was funded by the Maryknoll Society and a substantial grant from The Pew Charitable Trusts of Philadelphia.

The overall goals have been to enhance understanding of vital contemporary expressions of popular Catholicism, particularly in the global South, and appreciation for the diverse ways in which Catholic identities are affirmed and constructed; to stimulate greater theological reflection on the significance of such phenomena; and to help clarify concrete challenges that churches must face with regard to Christianity, traditional ecclesiastical structures and patterns, and cultural pluralism.

At a time when religious fundamentalisms have been growing rapidly, and intolerance of those who are different is dangerously prevalent in many contexts, it seems important to explore, affirm, and celebrate Christian diversity. At a time when many church officials are fostering increased institutional centralization and seeking to impose greater uniformity, it seems important to take greater cognizance of the richness of popular religious expressions. It is worth remembering that popular Catholicism actually has a normative character in the Catholic Church and that there should be reciprocal and critical relationships between popular and official religion (cf. Süess 1986).

Popular Catholicism has been studied intensely in Latin American countries over the past two or three decades, and creative syntheses have been provided in recent years (Parker 1996; González, Brandão, and Irarrázaval, 1993). But as social analyst Daniel Levine has noted in surveying the field, there have been few truly comparative empirical studies (1992, 23). Outside Latin America and Europe, there are relatively few studies. One finds no more than a handful of works on popular Christianity or popular Catholicism in Africa or Asia.

This project has been an exciting undertaking. We have sought to examine simultaneously and with a common lens religious phenomena in seven sites, in locations as far apart and as different as northern rural Ghana and metropolitan Hong Kong. We have worked with local researchers from each of these contexts and sought to weave together a common project that also responds authentically to local needs. We have employed professional academic skills of analysis with a practical set of goals.

A few words are in order to clarify further the scope of the undertaking, its terms, and its limits. The seven sites selected comprised communities in Chile, Ghana, Hong Kong, India, Peru, St. Lucia, and Tanzania. Each case study was headed by one or two local scholars (the "study heads") who authored the chapters that follow. Together they provided the endeavor with a rich interdisciplinary mix—anthropology, sociology, and theology—as well as cross-cultural and ecumenical dimensions.

Each case study also had a national theological consultant. They met with the local researchers at the inception of each study and served in an advisory capacity thereafter. Some participated in small local ecumenical consultations on the results and their implications. The consultants were Manuel Ossa for Chile, Kwame Bediako for Ghana, Allan Chan for Hong Kong, David Carr and then Theophilus Appavoo and Gabrielle Dietrich for India, Gustavo Gutiérrez for Peru, Harold Sitahal for St. Lucia, and Laurenti Magesa for Tanzania. In addition, three renowned Christian thinkers, Kosuke Koyama, Ivone Gebara, and Lamin Sanneh, served as international consultants, providing guidance and overall interpretation and integrating missiological reflection. Michael Amaladoss worked with the researchers to develop the synthesis with which this book concludes.

The case studies that were chosen are not meant to "represent" regions of the world, but to give a significant indication of existing global diversity. We opted to examine specific communities as opposed to broad national religious patterns. Readers will also note that we have no cases from the sizable Catholic populations in Brazil or Mexico, the Philippines or South Korea, Nigeria or the Democratic Republic of the Congo. The selection of cases depended in part on our finding committed local partners in a relatively short period of time.

We were successful in assembling a very diversified sample of communities. Three are urban, three are rural, and one is a cluster of fishing villages. There are two from Africa, two from Asia, one from the Caribbean, and two from South America, one of which is comprised of indigenous people. Among the countries in which the communities are located, the United Nations Development Program lists two as having a high "human development index" based on income, health, and educational statistics; while two have a medium-level index, and three a low one. And the ratio of Catholics in the communities studied ranges from large majorities in St. Lucia, southern India, and Chile, to extremely small minorities in Hong Kong and northern Ghana.

Given the scope and novelty of the project, it would have been very difficult to formulate rigorous, global hypotheses to test or disprove. We operated instead with a set of working assumptions and a series of guiding questions. The assumptions included the notion that people's religious beliefs and practices are part of popular culture and are thriving despite secularization trends; that religious identities are in a historical period of great reconstruction; that there should be a critical and organic relationship between popular Catholicism and official Catholicism; and that most churches in the so-called "two-thirds world" are far from having achieved truly inculturated expressions of the Gospel.

The questions served to orient the work and keep it on course. The more social-science ones included:

—How is popular Catholicism being expressed, and how is it related/unrelated to the institutional church?

—How does popular Catholicism relate to popular culture? In what ways, if any, is it countercultural?

—Does popular Catholicism appear to help people respond to oppression or to strive for social change?

—How are Catholic Christian identities actually being forged and sustained in these contexts? What does it mean to be Catholic?

—Are identity conflicts being experienced which threaten either Christian or cultural/national identity?

—In the case studies of the project, what is common about being Catholic and what is different?

The more theological or missiological questions included:

—Is any significant progress being made in the inculturation of the Gospel?

—What are the principal challenges for local churches and foreign missioners?

—Which are the principal challenges (institutional, doctrinal, liturgical, ethical) for the global church?

The common foci of the researchers who carried out the local case studies were three: prayer and ritual, problem solving, and social change. These elements are only aspects of popular Catholicism, but they were not isolated from the totality. They were examined in the cultural context of the everyday lives of self-declared Catholics with little wealth, status, or power in their social milieus.

There was an effort in each of the case studies to examine local gender dynamics, historical developments, organizational patterns, and the relations between popular and official religion.

All partners used the same basic set of research methods for data collection: consultation of secondary sources, including demographic data and local histories; collection of personal narratives; observation; individual interviews; and group interviews or focus groups. It had been our consensus that a common questionnaire or common set of very specific interview questions was not feasible, given the vast differences of context and culture. Chile, Hong Kong, St. Lucia, Tanzania, and Ghana partners added surveys with structured questionnaires. Partners in Peru and India were more ethnographic in their approach.

Interpretation of data was left to the professional skill of the case study researchers. We agreed that each would be free to use her/his theoretical filters, and that interpretation could move in different directions within the framework of our common goals, assumptions, and questions. There was recognition that several levels and forms of interpretation would operate both locally and collectively.

The reader may wonder why there are no cases of popular Catholicism from Europe or North America. Their presence would have provided a more revealing window on the emerging world church, or—to transpose the metaphor—would have broadened the horizon. Our focus was on the demographic center of gravity in the "two-thirds world," however, and resources were limited. We are by no means suggesting by the absence of cases from North America or Europe that popular Catholicism is not being expressed among ordinary Catholics trekking to Medjugorie, meeting in Base Christian Communities in Texas, organizing the charismatic movement in Brussels, running a parish soup kitchen in Montreal, or gathering around the Thanksgiving table in Topeka.

A mere glance at the table of contents makes it obvious that while the researchers come from many countries and cultures, ten of the eleven study heads are men (four laypeople and six priests). This gender imbalance was an outcome we did our best to avoid. Concerted attempts to find women partners were generally unsuccessful. Invariably those we contacted were committed to other tasks that made their participation impossible. The reality is one of far fewer women than men with the preparation needed for a research project such as this.

These women tend to be much sought after and more heavily "booked" than most men.

Among the three consultants-commentators we were able to include Sr. Ivone Gebara of Brazil, but hers was only a long-distance involvement. We were unable to schedule her participation in either the opening workshop or the concluding symposium of the research partners. She was thus unable actually to meet the research partners or to contribute in direct fashion to the development of the project. Her critical reflections on partners' articles are included here with those of consultants Kosuke Koyama and Lamin Sanneh.

TERMINOLOGY

Developing common working definitions of key terms was crucial to laying solid foundations for this project. How, for example, were we to understand "popular," "popular Catholicism," or "inculturation"? Achieving consensus during the opening workshop was no mean feat. Ultimately we determined that "popular" would mean *those sectors of society who do not enjoy much wealth, status, or power, those who are perceived as part of the "common people" in their own milieu.* This, we said, should be determined concretely in each context.

We agreed that "popular Catholicism" would mean *the complex of beliefs and religious practices of self-identified Catholics who belong to the popular sectors of societies,* though certain elements of such beliefs and practices may not appear to be particularly Catholic. We noted, furthermore, that popular Catholicism is a constantly evolving expression of people's life experience. It interacts with cultures and with actors in the socioeconomic and political fields. The institutional church—which may ignore, belittle, or seek to control it—helps to shape it, but it can likewise redefine and give new connotations to official, established symbols and rituals.

We agreed to define "inculturation" as *a theological term that refers to the dynamic interplay between the church (both as an institution and as a people of God) and a particular people as they strive for an authentic embodiment of the Gospel message.* We added that the relationship implies both that the Christian message transforms a culture and that it is transformed by that culture. Among the phenomena we saw as worthy of attention were the role of the local people as agents rather than mere followers; the attitude of the local institutional churches toward both the people and popular culture; the people's understanding of church; and the ethical or prophetic dimension of Christianity.

But defining these key terms did not domesticate them. Throughout the course of the project, the words kept raising their mischievous heads. We sometimes found ourselves using the term "popular" to mean *unofficial church,* as well as *nonelite.* One meaning sometimes overlay and simply reinforced the other. But "popular religion" was even used—though rarely— to refer to the unofficial beliefs or practices of the wealthy.

"Inculturation" was more elusive. Despite having agreed to our own working definition, we were drawn into employing some of the other meanings it has acquired in ecclesial parlance since it was coined in the 1970s. Beyond that, some of us grew disenchanted with the term in any guise. This was because it seems to place much more emphasis on initiatives of the official church than on the practices of ordinary communities of faith; and because it can suggest the existence of an "ethereal" Gospel above all cultures, when in fact the Good News has been presented in four Gospels that reflect the life of several different communities of faith, and has been conditioned historically by many cultures (cf. Amaladoss in this volume).

Gebara argues in her essay that the notion of "inculturation" is grounded in philosophical idealism and dualism, and that it can cloak forms of center-periphery religious and cultural domination. She adds that it seems to bestow an undue normative character on the church's patriarchal tradition. Both she and Amaladoss prefer to speak in terms of cultural encounters or dialogue.

The working definition of inculturation which our group had crafted and our group discussions of it were relatively free of "essentialisms" and ethnocentrism. The article from Chile explicitly notes that no one has access to the Gospel "in a pure state"; that all experiences are specific and culturally mediated. Several of the studies speak of inculturation as a dialogical process and critique historical impositions of the colonial and neocolonial church.

Some of our case studies and reflections give primary emphasis to the agency of the local people. The Tanzania authors see the Marian Faith Healing Ministry as an example of "inculturation as popularization" with its local merging of traditional African and traditional Roman Catholic cosmologies. The Chile and Peru studies both affirm the active way in which Catholic Christians welcome the Gospel in everyday life.

Other case studies put more emphasis on the role of the official church. Recent church initiatives in religious art and liturgy are applauded in St. Lucia. The church is seen as lacking any appropriate rituals for many cultural problems in northern Ghana and in need of developing them. At the same time, the local Christian Communities in Ghana are seen as embodiments of love, prayer, and dialogue; while the local people in St. Lucia are said to be engaged in liturgical innovation and to be challenging the institutional church. In general, the case studies treat inculturation as involving interaction between the official church and popular Catholicism.

The overall results of the study suggest at any rate that despite official endorsements of its importance, the churches are doing little in the field of "inculturation" or Gospel-culture encounter (cf. Schreiter 1997, 116 and 126-127). Furthermore, as argued by the authors from Tanzania, the post-Vatican II Catholic Church, in opening itself to the modern world, has simultaneously turned away from the cosmovision and cultures of traditional indigenous peoples around the world.

EPISTEMOLOGICAL CONSIDERATIONS

A project of this kind is replete with epistemological challenges, as Cristián Parker noted during the project's opening workshop. We have attempted to be conscious of them throughout. While acknowledging the subjective character of our enterprise, we have striven to enhance its objectivity by adhering to norms of social science data collection and analysis. While operating out of our own particular and professional worldviews, we have struggled to recognize and respect the differences between our constructions of reality and those of the people in the case studies. While observing what is strikingly unique in different people's religious convictions and practices, we have sought to reflect simultaneously on what appears to be common among them. While being attentive to the cultural differences among ourselves as researchers and consultants—as well as the distinctions between disciplines like sociology and anthropology, and between crafts like social or cultural analysis and theology—we have sought to bridge the divides and to work together as partners.

Like most research enterprises, this one was marked by questions that outsiders have constructed and employed to try to understand aspects of the lives and thoughts of others. In this project we have at least asked what Otto Maduro calls "real questions" (1992, 143-144): questions of seemingly deep importance for which we have no definitive answers, questions posed in the hope of coming to some provisional answers and to changing elements of the status quo. We are not using the answers to pigeonhole or dismiss groups of people, but returning to them with what we have discovered and sharing it with them.

The experience in St. Lucia provided an example of the issue of restricted access to the thoughts, words, and practices of historically subjugated peoples. The researchers there, including ordinary lay members of the Jacmel/Roseau parish, found their neighbors initially reluctant to talk with them about aspects of popular religion. They also found some suspicion about why church people were now so interested in practices which the church had historically condemned and driven underground. In situations like this, there is a need for great honesty and a slow building of trust. It goes hand in hand with the ethical requirement to treat with respect what may ultimately be communicated in trust.

All knowing is conditioned; our past experience provides us with both flashlights and blinders. It is not merely a matter of what we focus on; there are also different modes of understanding. Thus, while this predominantly masculine group of researchers affirmed the importance of gender dynamics from the beginning, while we sought female partners, while every case study included some examination of gender issues, and women were involved in most of the local studies, those of us who guided this project could not escape our skins or our socialization. The analyses touch on gender, but they do not perceive social relations and cultures from the vantage point of women's everyday realities and their struggles. And our theological reflections do not adequately incorporate the kind of stimulating challenges being offered today by Christian thinkers like Chung Hyun Kyung, Ada María Isasi-Díaz, Mercy Amba Oduyoye, Dolores Williams, and so many others (cf., for example, World Council of Churches 1996a).

In dealing with the challenge of relating theology and sociohistorical analysis, we opted for a turn on the now classic "pastoral circle" (cf. Holland and

Henriot 1983, 8). In other words, we first did the historical, sociological, or anthropological work; then did theological or missiological reflection. This was true both in the local sites, where theological consultations came after most of the social and cultural analysis had been done, and in structuring the overall research process and presenting the conclusions. The method is reflected as well in the order of this book and in its individual chapters. Kosuke Koyama lamented in our concluding symposium that social science and theology had not done more "walking together." Given their different epistemological and methodological bases, the two cannot be merged without transforming an enterprise such as this into theology alone. But our enterprise might have been enriched by more dialogue between them. To use the imagery of the hermeneutical circle, we might have moved back and forth between the analysis and reflection phases, before turning to the challenges for practice.

A word of caution is in order about our conclusions and about the comparisons between situations that are drawn here and elsewhere in the book. As readers can readily observe, this work is largely descriptive (ethnographic, sociographic) and exploratory in nature. The cases selected are by no means representative of a supposed universe of popular Catholicism. The study was not designed with rigorous hypotheses to be tested, nor has comparative analysis been done in depth.

On the other hand, versus the extremes of some contemporary postmodern skepticism about the validity of comparisons and meanings across cultures, we affirm human commonalities and our ability to perceive them, however dimly. We affirm our ability to communicate about them, however haltingly. In these case studies, we perceive not only human differences but also important points of convergence, many of which are pointed to by Amaladoss, Gebara, Koyama, and Sanneh as well. These include basic human needs, desires, emotions, and beliefs, as well as a sense of religious belonging that builds a certain unity out of diversity.

RESULTS

The fascinating articles which follow take us on a truly global journey. They introduce us to people and places that most of us could never imagine actually visiting. They offer a penetrating and sympathetic look at some of the many faces of popular Catholicism and of an emerging world church. They invite us to self-examination, to profound respect for the other.

Michael Amaladoss provides some synthesis of results at the end of this volume, and we do not wish to be repetitive, particularly of the ecclesiological and theological points he makes. We will merely highlight a few points here and add some of a more sociological nature.

One important question is to what degree—in spite of the aggressive inroads of modernity's market culture, mass consumption, and pragmatism—people are able today to maintain their own religious values and faith.

The results of this research attest to a marked *resilience* of popular Catholicism despite the undeniable global impact of modernity and secularization, a resilience that appears in a vast *diversity* of cultural-religious forms. In poor urban neighborhoods in Chile, for example, the research revealed not a loss of faith or religious beliefs, but rather a relative secularization which seems to move in three different directions: a pluralization of the religious field; an accentuated rationalization of beliefs among Catholics, accompanied by some aversion to institutionalized religion; and a growth of the rather diffuse beliefs and practices that are commonly referred to as "new age."

In Tanzania, on the other hand, where religious diversity is also growing, but in a context of dire poverty and failed projects for change, we found greater skepticism about modernity. There a novel Marian devotional movement harks back to pre-Vatican II Catholic practices and traditions, while simultaneously appearing to adapt a more African spiritual worldview and practices, including the celebration of public healings and exorcism. For the followers of the Marian Faith Healing Ministry, it is clear that the globalized social world is controlled by spiritual forces.

In vastly different and evolving hybridities, we found popular Catholic beliefs and practices to be an important aspect of many people's overall identity. They express a profound sense of the sacred and help sustain everyday struggles for life and well-being.

CULTURE AND IDENTITY

Cultural identity appears as one of the central themes in the debate about the capacity of modernization processes to assume the values of each culture, or conversely to destroy them. The overall results of this study suggest that most expressions of popular Catholicism in the global South are not fundamentalist, but open to the meaning and ecumenical value of different religious beliefs and practices. While by no means free of conflict, relations between Catholic and Adventist Aymaras in Peru or between Muslims and Catholics of the Dagomba tribe in Ghana are marked by considerable mutual respect.

At the same time, Catholic faith seems intimately connected with family and local community. In the face of a universalizing homogenization of consumer society and a promotion of individualism, popular Catholicism seems to provide countercultural expressions that question the pragmatic and instrumental logic of modernity, and promote —albeit subtly and indirectly—ties of solidarity and a sense of basic justice. The study in Chile is eloquent on these points.

An interesting set of results had to do with Catholic identity and the maintenance of local cultural traditions. In contexts where Catholicism has been established for centuries and enjoys majority status as a religion (St. Lucia, Peru, Chile, and the Mukkuvar region of southern India), local Catholics appeared to have little or no personal difficulty with performing traditional popular rituals or going to traditional religious specialists, neither of which enjoy the sanction of the official church. In Ghana and Hong Kong, where Catholicism is more recent and decidedly minoritarian, and where Christianity seems more identified with foreigners and modernity, stricter boundaries on the permissible and sharper breaks with tradition seemed more frequent. Indeed, we found Aymaras in Peru stating that being Catholic (as opposed to Evangelical or Adventist) meant freedom to be faithful to their indigenous cultural traditions; while Dagomba or Hong Kong Catholics faced troubling accusations by others that as Christians they were no longer truly Dagomba or truly Chinese.

The maintenance of local cultural identities does not appear to imply a slavish attachment to tradition nor hostility to modernity. Tradition-rooted Aymara Catholics value schooling, new building materials, electricity, and urban jobs, and even seem to adopt the hectic pace of modern life as they bus to and from the markets of the Peruvian altiplano. Dagomba Catholics in Ghana appreciate "Western" schools and medicine, community development projects, and water sanitation—and have adopted much more egalitarian gender relations than their fellow Dagombas. Hong Kong Catholics, proud of their Chinese identity, are firm believers in modern technological conveniences, individual rights, and representative democracy. Living within and between the old and the new, people make distinctions, sort out what appears to be valuable, select what is useful and within their reach, and seek to forge their own (still spirited) versions of modernity.

RITUAL AND PROBLEM SOLVING

In reviewing the results of the case studies, we were struck by the degree to which rituals, sometimes quite elaborate rituals, are linked to people's efforts to find solutions to their everyday problems. In the design of the study we chose three foci for each of the case studies to examine: prayer and ritual, everyday problem solving, and social change. While people's modes of handling a wide gamut of problems certainly included actions that would be considered highly practical by Western moderns, what were defined as significant problems and what people did to remedy them sometimes tended to erase the distinction we had drawn between problem solving and ritual. The studies from Ghana, St. Lucia, Peru, Tanzania, and India are replete with examples, but one finds them as well in Hong Kong and Chile.

SOCIAL CHANGE

The ordinary Catholics of our case studies are all relatively deprived. Most are oppressed and some are very marginalized people. They strive for good health and seek healing from physical and emotional as well as spiritual afflictions. They want to overcome poverty. They long for personal and collective well-being. Their prayers and rituals are often focused on tangible goods like a decent wage, the successful sale of a cow, or an abundant harvest; and on protection from natural as well as social or political catastrophes.

These people are not unaware of social and political injustices. The majority of the community leaders surveyed in Santiago declared that there is no justice in Chile. The farmers on the island of St. Lucia decried a lack of government support for their banana production. The parishioners in Hong Kong annually commemorate the massacre of democracy protesters in Tiananmen Square. The *wanamaombi* of Tanzania regularly denounce the blatant corruption of national government officials. Popular religion in these cases does not appear to have had alienating influences on sociopolitical consciousness. People are not oblivious to domination, duped into seeing their social subordination as right, or actively complying with their oppression or that of their compatriots.

Yet despite the people's plights and their awareness of injustices, we found little organized action for structural or historical change in the communities studied. This was true even in areas of the world where there has been notable political mobilization in recent years, like the Chilean capital, highland Peru, Dar es Salaam, or Hong Kong. This is perhaps a sign of the conservative times in which we are living, marked by the current triumph of liberal capitalism, a globalized disarray of the political left, and a retrenchment in the social engagement of the Christian churches.

What was generally encountered were local social service efforts, community self-help, and small-scale development programs. Participation in them was sometimes very self-consciously linked to a sense of Christian solidarity, as in Ghana. On the other hand, where limited struggles for enhanced rights or greater justice were occurring, as among striking St. Lucian banana farmers, popular consciousness and organizing seemed to be relatively detached from religious faith as such.

It may be tempting to conclude that the official churches have not successfully wed a prophetic Gospel-inspired sense of social justice to the vitality, rituals, and everyday ethical norms of popular Catholics. But it is not a simple matter of ideology. There appear to be specific, practical reasons for the lack of religiously rooted social or political action.

In the Peruvian and Tanzanian cases, researchers reported a prevailing skepticism about social and political projects of any stripe. Past frustrations make the current state of affairs, however distasteful, appear inevitable for at least the time being.

In Ghana, Catholic Dagombas are mostly young adults without influence in a tribal culture that is dominated by Muslim elders. And in both Hong Kong and Ghana, Catholics are an infinite minority of the population, concerned about the consequences of assuming controversial positions in potentially volatile social and political situations.

Hong Kong is enmeshed in a momentous historical conjuncture, given the 1997 transfer of control from Britain to China, and economic uncertainties. Religion has been a relatively privatized phenomenon for most ordinary Catholics there, and the official church, as discussed in the article in this volume, is looking for definitions and new directions.

While organized action for structural or historical change was absent in the communities under study, these grassroots Catholics did not exhibit passivity, fatalism or a hopefulness simply projected to the afterlife. In many cases we encountered forms of the "everyday resistance" which is characteristic of weak and relatively powerless segments of society (cf. Scott 1985).

Most of the populations in our case studies, either because of considerable autonomy in their routine work as peasants or fishermen, or because of the heterogeneity of their modern urban employment, do not confront a large landowner or a common boss in their everyday laboring lives. Government officials, wealthier fishermen with motorized boats, and commercial middlemen were the objects of their frustration or wrath, but were not necessarily converted into targets for "off-stage" ridicule; and most people do not march to an imposed pace of labor in which they can "drag their feet."

In these case studies, the weapons wielded by the weak are predominantly in the realm of ritual. There is symbolic protest in ceremony, prayers, and healings in which the powerlessness of the poor is transformed into active agency. These rituals appear to heighten personal and community worth, enhance self-esteem, and maintain relationships of mutuality—without implying resignation to the current material conditions of life.

If social and political action for change is not now present in most of these situations, this hardly implies a permanent or ubiquitous state of affairs. As Levine (1986) and others have noted, religious belonging can generate values and experiences of solidarity and self-reliance with effects in other realms of social life and in new historical circumstances. A political crisis or a mass social mobilization can transform a social landscape, and popular religious dynamics can greatly change in such a context.

OFFICIAL AND POPULAR CATHOLICISM

Just as popular Catholicism cannot be adequately understood apart from a people's broader cultural matrix and their history (cf. González et al. 1993), it cannot be comprehended apart from its "official" religious counterpart. Throughout the seven case studies we found grassroots Catholics affirming officially promulgated beliefs, participating in church ceremonies, and employing—though often in novel ways—its sacraments and sacramentals. Clear affinities were also evident between popular cosmovisions with their spirits, intermediaries, and miracles and the traditional Catholic cosmovision that prevailed before Vatican II.

At the same time, serious tensions between popular and official Catholicism were manifest. Despite more positive evaluations of it in recent church documents, some officials and pastoral agents still tend to look upon popular Catholicism as a complex of superstition and ignorance, if not outright idolatry. Others seek to affirm only what they paternalistically perceive to be "acceptable," or attempt to control popular manifestations in the interest of religious orthodoxy. There are rifts within the churches themselves between those who perceive in popular religion a wisdom directed at meeting concrete needs or who readily participate in popular rituals, and those who will have nothing to do with such things. Whatever their theological or practical positions, however, few pastoral agents and even fewer Catholic officials actually share a popular cosmovision. The official church is a modern Western institution.

Ordinary Catholics for their part may rightly be wary of a church that was a colonial import and that continues to lack deep local roots. Accustomed to ecclesiastical charges that certain of their beliefs and practices are illegitimate syncretism or worse, they may hide their actual beliefs and veil practices like their traditional burial rites in Hong Kong or visits to the obeahman in St. Lucia.

In the case study we carried out in Tanzania, the principal axis of tension between popular and official Catholicism seems much simpler: power and authority. The hierarchy is threatened by a charismatic leader and a novel movement that it cannot control. The response is to forbid the leader to celebrate the Eucharist and to ban members of the movement from normal participation in parish life.

In some countries, sectors of the institutional church have taken seriously the need for profound liturgical "inculturation." In St. Lucia's Jacmel/Roseau parish, for example, a huge mural depicts the holy family as Afro-Caribbean and colorfully affirms the everyday life of the islanders, while the annual Easter Vigil is celebrated in the Kwéyòl language, is accompanied by enthusiastic dancing, and follows the local traditions of a wake. In most places, however, Catholic liturgy is far from local culture and the collective psyche. In the article from Ghana, it is argued that the church has no ritual solutions for traditional Dagomba problems like "bad death" or witchcraft, but that Dagomba Christian communities are drawing attention to their needs and that more creative and responsive rituals are beginning to appear.

The deepest challenges for official Catholicism seem not to be in liturgical innovation, however, but in the fundamental pastoral and theological stances with respect to popular religion and ordinary people's own agency in the realm of the sacred. In popular Catholicism, the people generally forge a spirituality adapted to their own basic needs, grow roots in an uprooting world, and find a life-giving vitality.

DAUNTING CHALLENGES FOR THE CHURCHES

Issues of Gospel and culture have challenged and bedeviled Christians from the beginning. The Council of Jerusalem, in the very first decades of the Christian movement, struggled precisely with cultural differences between Jewish and non-Jewish disciples of Jesus, and affirmed that to embrace the Good News people need not do violence to their culture.

Issues of culture are no less important today. They figure prominently in theological debates, in Catholic episcopal Synods, in mission conferences of the World Council of Churches, and in discussions of ordinary believers around the world.

Popular Christian modes of understanding and living the Gospel present a particular set of challenges to Christian elites and to the official church. As historian Eduardo Hoornaert (1997) recalls, there has been a long and sometimes even tragic history of church opposition to popular emotional, mystical, and devotional expressions of faith that the church has not been able to control. In the reflections at the end of this book, Lamin Sanneh urges us to be converted to a bottom-up view of the world, Ivone Gebara to take the whole of creation and the experiences of women much more seriously than we usually do, and Kosuke Koyama to appreciate the necessary reciprocity between official and popular Christianity.

The reflections of Michael Amaladoss stress the importance for the church of truly recognizing and honoring what the bishops of Latin America have called "the Catholic wisdom of the common people," a wisdom that affirms human dignity, establishes fraternity, shows people how to relate to nature and work, and allows for celebration even in the midst of hardship (Puebla Final Document, 448). The church needs not only to appreciate the importance and vitality of popular Catholicism, but also to learn from its bonds of community and from its holistic approach to life. A modern, Westernized church needs to take stock again of the power of symbol and sacrament, and to reconsider its approaches to the world of spirits and to the communion of the ancestors. It needs to value diversity as part of a true catholicity, and above all to focus on the kind of conversion Jesus called people to, the conversion from mammon to the reign of God.

In this context, cross-cultural missioners are challenged to be critical of their own cultures and open to others. They are called to a *kenosis* or self-emptying of their prejudices, sense of superiority, and tendency to impose. Western Christians, often quick to wield charges of "syncretism," should be generous in listening to their sisters and brothers, more circumspect in speaking, slower to judge, and conscious that precious treasures are borne in mere vessels of clay (Schreiter 1997, 83).

González et al. (1993, 234-237) propose a missiological and pastoral-theological approach to popular Catholicism that implies personal insertion in the world of grassroots Catholics, and seeks not the "purification" of popular Catholicism but rather its enhancement and growth. Such a methodology begins with a recognition of the wisdom of the people and of their conviction that their religion helps them to live better lives. It attempts to understand popular cultures and their symbolic universe both historically and existentially. It takes seriously the notion that ordinary Catholics are protagonists of their own evangelization rather than mere recipients. In it, missioners and local people together affirm traditional spiritual richness, community life, and sacramental creativity. They explore relevant biblical and doctrinal issues. And they reflect on sociocultural vacuums, ambiguities, or problems with an eye on praxis in ever-changing circumstances.

A key challenge for missioners is that of facilitating dialogues of life and faith in which local communities are truly subjects. As affirmed at the most recent World Council of Churches conference on world mission and evangelism (World Council of Churches 1996b, 7), dialogue is a vital mode of developing relationships, cultivating understanding, and growing in unity.

In their local faith communities, people should be encouraged to grow in relating the Gospels to their own reality, history, and culture, including their experience of the divine. This is not interreligious dialogue but rather *intrareligious* dialogue among Catholics with their diverse cultural and religious heritages.

Such intrareligious community dialogue is also profoundly intrapersonal dialogue for many individuals as they deal with Christianity and their traditions. Korean theologian Chung Hyun Kyung (World Council of Churches 1996a, 31-32) expresses this dramatically when she says that she herself has shamanist bowels, a Buddhist heart, a Confucianist right brain, and a Christian left brain and mode of speaking; that she is a Christian who lives out the reality, power, and dangers of the Buddhist, shamanist, and Confucian traditions which are alive in her and in her people's long and multilayered history.

While dialogue is key to authentic evangelization, it cannot be "open-ended," as Amaladoss puts it. There must be an effort to discern Gospel imperatives. The point of reference is the Gospel and the values of the reign of God, a vision which radically challenges all cultures and societies. Mission and Christian practice today should therefore be guided by core "teloi" such as the struggle for the full dignity of all people, shalom, and a new creation (Schreiter 1997, 131).

THE PROMISE OF THIS ENTERPRISE

We are thoroughly convinced of the value of the kind of research that has led to the production of this book. It has been cross-cultural and interdisciplinary in nature. It has combined social-cultural analysis with theological reflection. It has been shaped and led by local professionals. It has incorporated ecumenical dialogue. It has had important practical as well as theoretical aims. Such are the norms for the projects of the Center for Mission Research and Study in and out of which we labor.

It has been an extraordinary pleasure to work with the group of scholars and human beings who have participated in this endeavor. While together for only a short period of time, we grew into what Peter Senge (1990) calls a "learning community": a team with common goals, trusting one another, complementing each other's strengths, compensating each other's weaknesses. We yearn for opportunities for similar undertakings in the future.

We trust, finally, that this volume will be a useful contribution to explorations of popular culture and religion, and of the dynamics of Gospel and culture in our world. We hope that it will lead to greater appreciation of popular Catholicism, and that it will be a welcome stepping-stone in this field for the forays and journeys of others.

Part One

CASE STUDIES

1

Chile

Identity and Diversity
in Urban Popular Catholicism

CRISTIÁN PARKER G.

"Now if you ask me whether I believe in the evil eye, well, they put the evil eye on my son about four times. I used to say I didn't believe in the evil eye: 'That's nonsense,' I'd say. But you have to go through it yourself. You go into a room, you know, the room where the child is, and you get this odd feeling. I got that feeling: he cried and cried, and he had a fever. I mean, you didn't know what he had; but you went into the room and felt something very odd, something dense, it was like . . . there was no explanation for it. But you have a sort of sixth sense that tells you something's wrong. Like, you look at the roof and have a funny feeling; you turn around and you have the sense that something's smothering you. 'Ah,' I said, 'they've given my son the evil eye again! Bring me that piece of paper my sister-in-law gave me, the one who knows about praying to the saints.' It's full of prayers, all right, and some really nice ones, too: it's kind of a family thing with us. You lay the baby down on its back and you pray the prayers you know best; then you make several crosses with a silver crucifix on its forehead, its back, its chest. And finally you say, 'Spirits (of the person you're healing), go out of him and let him come back to his senses!' And you know how you feel afterward:

This text was written by Cristián Parker G., bearing in mind the contributions of the Permanent Pastoral Agents' Workshop, the Local Theological Consultation, and of theologian Manuel Ossa. It was translated into English by David Molineaux. The author wishes to express gratitude for the help of research assistants Ana Urmeneta and Mauricio Palominos.

you absorb all that. The person who does it, they can't be weak in character. It's tricky: I didn't even believe it and it happened to me three times. So now it's something I believe in: I've been through it. There are spooks abroad, as the old saying goes. I believe in it because it's happened to me. All these curses fall on the weakest people or animals in the house. A child can get sick on you, or some little animal can. Anyway, after the healing rite you end up with your arms hanging down this way ... you're simply drained. Also, there always has to be somebody waiting outside. Afterward you give the child oregano tea to relax, and the child sleeps well all night long. And after you get done praying you have to pay somebody for the prayers. Even if it's only ten pesos, you have to pay. Anyway, when it's all over the person who's been waiting outside comes in and yells, 'Hey, what the hell's going on here? What's all the fuss about? Get out of here, all you good-for-nothings!' That's the way it has to be. And then it's all over, just like magic."
(Interview with M.H.)

A major sign of our times is the complex and often profoundly contradictory process of globalization (Robertson 1992). This process is first of all economic, a result of the creation of an integrated worldwide market. Another key aspect of the process is the communications revolution; and finally there is the fact that throughout the world people have become aware of their planetary identity, their belonging to something far larger than their local region or their nation.

Globalization is a process that is spreading modern culture throughout the entire world. At the same time it is shrinking time and space. Often, however, the globalization process is paralleled by an opposing process in which local cultures and traditions are taking on new life. The interaction between global and local realities has not been a simple reproduction of Western modernity: it "has indeed generated plural modernities that may resemble the Western variety, but nonetheless remain distinct" (Schreiter 1997: 12). This process has brought about changes throughout Latin America that are having a major impact on the Church and its evangelizing mission.

Here we will observe, albeit in a partial way, how this process is taking place within the Chilean urban context. Among these changes, the prevalence of the market as the entity that regulates not only economic but also social relationships has taken on special importance. Another change is the fact that public attention is focused not on political life but on the economy. Finally there is the internationalization of communications brought about by the dizzying scientific and technological changes that mark the end of this century.

All these changes go beyond the economic sphere. We are faced not just with a new economy but also with a new culture that is being born out of the transition to a postindustrial society. And Latin American societies, while they are being subjected to deeply contradictory processes and continue to endure poverty and social inequality, are not exempt from the influence of the globalization process imposed by neoliberal development models.

In order to deal with this reality, the Catholic Church faces the need to design an appropriate strategy for carrying out its mission of inculturated evangelization within the emerging global framework (Arroyo et al. 1992; Bosch 1991; Shorter 1988).

THE CATHOLIC CHURCH, GLOBALIZATION, AND MARKET HEGEMONY

Faced with these sociocultural changes, the Church, like so many other organizations, is forced to deal with a new situation. Since its basic mission is the evangelization of the world, it has understood for several decades that it needs to face the challenge of cultural change. Ever since *Evangelii Nuntiandi* it has spoken of the evangelization of culture, and more recently of the inculturation of the Gospel as a way of updating its mission in history.[1]

For this reason, it is essential to understand what we mean today by "cultural dynamics." In carrying out the New Evangelization, the Church will not be dealing with a cultural "tabula rasa," either in our countries or anywhere else. Rather, it will be involved in a dialogical process in which, relying on the Spirit's mysterious intervention in history and building on previous evangelizations, the evangelizers will be evangelized and the evangelized will also be evangelizers. Hence it is necessary to examine the double dynamic involved in the process of evangelizing culture:

a) Sociocultural diagnosis and a theological-spiritual discernment of seeds of the Gospel already present and active in the people's cultures; and

b) The evangelizing action of church institutions and communities, which should be carrying out appropriate cultural mediations through missionary action.

A highly significant question then arises, one that marks all case studies in this international study: to what degree is Christianity, and specifically Catholicism, inculturated in popular sectors, in different settings, within this emerging global context?

The theoretical assumption that makes the above question possible is related to secular cultures' own dynamics. A dominant official culture never eliminates the most essential values harbored by members of dominated cultures or subcultures. In other words, no globalization process is capable of totally destroying local, private identities and values. We can go so far as to affirm that the dynamics of globalization, as we observe them today, encourage and spawn local values and identities in reaction to itself. Having said this, we need to analyze the degree to which cultural confrontation and/or interaction occurs in each specific society.

Within every society we need to acknowledge the existence of a dominant culture, the one that exercises hegemony; today this culture is clearly linked to the logic of the market, both in Chile and in Latin America in general. At the

---

[1] See the reflection on inculturation in Center for Mission Research, 1994. See also Shorter, 1988.

same time, every society has many internal cultural dynamics that are independent of it and act as subcultures or countercultures.

If the dominant culture that emerges from the globalization process and market supremacy is one in which pragmatism and consumerism reign, the questions
we need to ask are: To what extent, despite the presence of this dominant culture,
do people hold onto their Christian values and identity? And how, in recent times,
has this consumer culture coexisted with the people's religious spirit?

Is Catholic Identity Being Challenged by These Cultural Changes?

The theoretical framework used in our international research has defined
broadly but rather precisely what we understand by Catholic identity.[2]

Considering that every identity makes itself known as soon as it is challenged
by an opposing one, we could ask, within the Chilean context, to what extent
Catholic identity is challenged by religious diversity and by new cultural norms
that emphasize the market above everything else.

A key factor to consider, in the light of Weber's analysis (Weber 1958 and
1964), is the fact that Catholicism, as opposed to Protestantism in general, is not
well matched with capitalism. Its attitude toward accumulation is not built on an
austere and individualistic foundation; instead it develops a communitarian ethos
centered on sharing and "festive squandering" (see González et al. 1993; Parker
1996). Is our Catholicism changing as a result of these new cultural norms? Is it
becoming privatized? Is it losing its communitarian, festive, and life-sharing character?

These questions lead us to inquire into the urban popular[3] Catholicism that is
present in slum areas and tenements in the working-class neighborhoods of
Santiago's most populous districts.

We understand popular Catholicism as a dynamic form of religious expression that evolves with the people's lived experience. It revitalizes the traditions
out of which it emerges. It has an ambivalent relationship with official Catholicism. As it has been regarded by the Puebla and Santo Domingo meetings of the
Latin American bishops, popular Catholicism is "a privileged expression of faith's
inculturation" (Santo Domingo Final Document, No. 36; also see Johansson 1990).

Other questions arise. Is popular Catholicism in urban, postindustrial, under-
developed society threatened by secularizing[4] influences? What seeds of the
Gospel are carried by this expression of popular Catholic identity? What other
Catholic identities are appearing in popular urban settings?

---

[2]See "Theoretical framework for the study," in CERC-UAHC 1997.

[3]"Popular" in Latin America refers above all to poor and marginal people: the working class,
urban slum dwellers, and the rural poor.

[4]By "secularization" we mean a historical process in which beliefs are rationalized and
diversified, and sectors of social life are removed from the control of religious institutions, rather
than the loss of religious influence in societies. See Parker 1996.

A STUDY WITHIN THE FRAMEWORK OF AN INTERNATIONAL RESEARCH PROJECT

The present article describes the essential elements of a case study carried out from 1995 to 1996 in the municipality of San Joaquín in Santiago, Chile (CERC-UAHC 1997). The municipality of San Joaquín is a district (or borough) of 114,000 total inhabitants in the national capital of over 5 million inhabitants. It is a mixed urban sector where you find services, industries, and lower-middle- and working-class neighborhoods, together with urban slums where a significant number of poor and marginal people live.

Ecclesiastically, San Joaquín is comprised of five parishes of the Santiago archdiocese which are located in the jurisdiction known as the Zona Sur (southern zone). The Church is very active pastorally. There has been considerable development of Base Christian Communities, and the Church was known for its commitment to the defense of human rights during the period of military dictatorship which began in 1973.

In this municipality we interviewed 147 popular secular community leaders[5] on their religious practices and beliefs as well as on other forms of cultural expression. The study used a multifaceted triangulation method whose central axis was a survey. The poll's quantitative material was complemented by qualitative methods that included a permanent reflection workshop with pastoral agents working in the sector,[6] in-depth interviews with selected leaders, on-site observation, and secondary sources such as previous studies on popular religion (especially Parker 1992a and 1992b). The study focused on leaders who identified themselves as Catholics, though the data presented here will be for all of the leaders, except as otherwise indicated.

The Chile case study was designed to focus on the changes brought about by rapid modernization and globalization processes in a totally urban and popular context. It focused on the cultural changes brought about by the market-centered economy and the globalization process, and their impact in the religious field.

---

[5]Of the 223 community leaders in the district we studied, 56% were women and 44% were men. A random sampling of this total was polled: 66%, or 147 leaders. For statistical reasons, in order to ensure sample representativity, only 117 leaders' responses were considered for statistical analysis: 55% from neighborhood councils and 45% from the Comités de Adelanto or "Progress Committees" of fourteen "neighborhood units," seven of which had a high percentage of poor residents while another seven had a low percentage of poor residents (i.e., lower-middle class). Our sample is 59% female and 40% male. It comprises a group of experienced and relatively well educated leaders. Forty-three percent are 40-55 years old, 34% are 56 or over, and 23% are under 40. Forty-seven percent have completed secondary school and 39% have finished primary school; the remainder have gone on to study a specialized technical subject or have been to college. In terms of personal income, most are in the lower stratum, earning less than US$250 (100,000 pesos) a month. Only 37% earn more than US$450 (180,000 pesos) a month, which places them in the lower-middle-class category.

[6]Throughout the stage of fieldwork and data analysis, a Permanent Pastoral Agents' Workshop met with relative frequency. Participants were Sister Marie Aimé and the following priests: Mariano Puga, Carlos Coopman, Oscar Berger, S.V.D., James Weckesser, M.M., and Eugene Toland, M.M.

How do these shifts challenge the inculturation of the Gospel? Does popular Catholicism still have a vibrant identity? How is it changing in the face of modernizing trends?

RELIGIOUS IDENTITIES AND BELIEFS

We worked with urban popular community leaders, assuming that their beliefs and religious identities would differ from those found among the great mass of the faithful. Still, we should note the common features shared by both leaders and followers. When it comes to sociological dynamics, no reality or popular group can be understood in isolation. "There are no leaders without followers, at least not for very long. By the same token, popular groups, beliefs, and practices do not spring full-blown 'from the people' " (Levine 1992: 23). These should be understood as historical creations that emerge out of complex relationships between the masses and their leaders; and between these masses and their leaders, on the one hand, and the dominant institutions, among them the churches, on the other. This has been called the dialectics between official and popular religion (Amaladoss 1989; Dussel 1986; Lanternari 1982; Vrijhof and Waardenburg 1979).

On the other hand, community leaders are more directly influenced by sociocultural change: it is they who are most affected by the processes of modernization, globalization, and secularization; and this is reflected in their mentalities. A study of the influence of these processes on the beliefs and practices of urban popular Catholicism will therefore give privilege of place to popular Catholic leaders. In all probability, what affects them will in time affect the wider population they lead. For this reason, our study will focus on Catholic leaders; but these leaders will be observed within the context of the beliefs, rituals, and values shared by all the municipality's leaders.

RELIGIOUS AFFILIATION

We began by analyzing respondents' religious affiliation. The following list shows their distribution according to religious convictions:

Category	Percentage
Catholics	70.9
Believers without religious affiliation	15.4
Protestants	7.7
Atheists	5.1
Other Religions	0.9

More than 70% of respondents called themselves Catholics. This figure concurs roughly with the results of Chile's 1992 national population census.[7] In con-

---

[7]The figures of the national population census of 1992 for San Joaquín district are 77.6% Catholics, 10.9% Protestants, 6.6% indifferents and atheists, and 4.9% other religions.

trast to earlier trends, however, it appears that today there is an ever more significant presence of a type of noninstitutional religious belief classified in our poll
as "believers without religious affiliation." In this sample they outnumbered even
Protestants. There is a trend toward increasing numbers in this sector at the expense of traditional, church-affiliated religious practice. It is a new phenomenon
that we have been able to corroborate with the conclusions of several other empirical studies in popular urban settings (Parker 1992a). Here we see the emergence of an interesting new religious category that constitutes a challenge to
inculturation in modern urban settings, even popular ones, in a society that is
under the influence of the globalization process.

Besides believers without religious affiliation, there are "self-styled Catholics" who say they are Catholics "in their own way." For example, one respondent
told us:

M.H.: "I'm a Catholic and my wife is a Pentecostal Methodist. My
father-in-law is a Protestant. Spirituality goes beyond all religions and
all materialisms. The reason my wife and I got married is that while I'm
a baptized Catholic, I don't give a damn about the Catholic religion. I
believe in a God and I respect everybody's ideals and political views . . .
I believe in a God, but to believe in a God you don't need a religion. All
you have to do is to think and believe that there's a far greater person
who's in charge and who guides your whole life."

Our studies indicate that the trend toward secularization in these popular settings appears to move in three directions:
   a) A tendency toward religious diversification, that is, toward the loss by
       Catholicism of the monopoly it once enjoyed in Chilean society. Tradi-
       ionally, Catholicism was part of Chile's heritage of "colonial Christendom."
       In these urban popular settings, the movement toward an emergent plural-
       ity of religious options is very clear.
   b) A notable rationalization of beliefs accompanied by institutional estrange-
       ment (that is, a certain aversion toward religious institutions or institution-
       alized "churches") rather than by the relinquishing of basic belief in a tran-
       scendent realm. Only 5% call themselves atheists, a figure that is much
       lower than in other social classes and strata. We have been able to corrobo-
       rate this conclusion in the present survey. All those who call themselves
       "believers without religious affiliation" believe in God, and the great ma-
       jority also profess their belief in Jesus Christ. To the category of the insti-
       tutionally estranged we would have to add the above-mentioned "self-styled
       Catholics" who report that they are Catholic "in their own way"; in using
       this phrase, they show their estrangement from the institutional Church.
       We should also add Catholic believers whose basic practices do not in-
       clude the observance of Church precepts and official rituals (the 50% of
       Catholics who report that they "almost never" or "never" go to Mass, for
       example). These respondents adhere to "popular Catholicism," the prac-

tice of a folk religion that is more or less independent of clerical control (cf. Tables 1 and 3, Official and Popular Beliefs).

c) A tendency toward an increase in "diffuse" noninstitutional beliefs that have been characterized by contemporary sociology as "new age" (Valveçius 1995; Soneira et al. 1996: 269 ff.; Pace 1995). This category comprises a heterogeneous collection of mysterious and magical beliefs combined with esoteric and nature-based traditions, many of them influenced by Oriental perspectives. These are found in syncretistic combinations with Christian, Gnostic, and indigenous traditions.

The data obtained by correlating beliefs and educational levels reveal that the higher the individual's educational level, the greater the tendency toward both institutional estrangement and the rationalization of beliefs: saying, for example, that one is a believer without any religious affiliation. The lower the educational level, the greater the degree of adherence to institutionalized religion.

Comparing Catholics and Protestants, we find contradictory trends. In the former group, church affiliation diminishes as educational level increases; while in the latter, church affiliation increases with educational level. The number of atheists and believers without religious affiliation also increases with formal education. This suggests the hypothesis that people distance themselves from Catholicism as their educational level rises. This could mean that the educational system tends to influence the religious sphere by acting as a transmitter of secularizing trends in modern urban society, opening up a greater number of religious options.

Looking at these urban settings, we are able to conclude that Catholicism is still a component in the religious identity of the great majority of the people. This is true despite what we have said about the ongoing influence of modernization and globalization on the attitudes of the community leaders interviewed. There are varying degrees of alienation from Catholic beliefs and rituals; but as we shall see, there is still an adherence to the basic tenets of Christian faith and of Catholic doctrine.

The religious identity of popular Catholics studied is neither closed nor intolerant. Respondents were asked about their views on whether members of Christian religions that are not their own are "sisters and brothers in the faith"; 72% of the Catholics responded in the affirmative, while the overall mean was 65%.

When asked what is the difference, in faith terms, between Protestants and Catholics, and why we distinguish between Catholics and Protestants, two respondents answered:

G.T.: "I think Protestants aren't ashamed of their religion. They actually have to go out and preach their religion in the streets, they go right out there . . . Some of their pastors don't have college degrees, but still they have more time to talk with you. I've seen them in the hospital visiting sick people, for example, but when I was in the hospital I never saw any priests. I think Protestants are really more present among the poor, and it's like they help one another more."

L.V.: "I've never discriminated against people from a particular political party or from another religion. If they invite me, I go . . . with Protestants . . . because I like to listen and understand and get an idea what it is, what it's about, so I'm not talking about things I don't know about."

This kind of openness toward "sisters and brothers in the Christian faith" indicates tolerance rather than agreement with others' beliefs. The interpretive hypothesis we would need to verify is that Catholics feel less threatened by religious plurality than Protestants. Because they are a minority, Protestants would tend to be more wary of Catholic hegemony. In the workshop too, we saw that Catholics historically show a more tolerant attitude toward different leanings, groupings, charisms, and options within their own church than do Protestants. In the latter churches, the emergence of diversity quickly leads to the formation of new denominations.

Religious Beliefs

Regarding religious beliefs, the leaders were asked about their faith in a variety of supernatural beings. They were given a list that included sacred entities found in Christian doctrine, others that appear in popular beliefs, and still others that coincide with new age ideas, several of which have magic or superstitious connotations, that is, specific modes of relating to the supernatural world, and where no pejorative connotation is implied.[8]

The overall results can be seen in the three tables below.

Table 1: Official Religious Beliefs

	Sample	Catholics
God	93.3%	100%
Jesus	92.2%	97.6%
The Bible	88.8%	97.6%
Holy Spirit	80.2%	80.2%
The Virgin Mary	74.8%	88.9%
The Devil	65.2%	69.5%
The Saints	59.6%	78.8%

Examining official religious beliefs, we can see that the most widely accepted are those that are part of the dogmatic creeds of the institutional churches, both Catholic and Protestant: God, Jesus Christ, and the Bible.

---

[8]For a more elaborate discussion see Parker 1996, especially Ch. 10.

Table 2: Traditional and New Age Beliefs

	Sample	Catholics
Herbs	75.9%	78.0%
Horoscope	52.2%	61.3%
Aliens	46.9%	43.2%
Reincarnation	42.1%	39.5%
Spirits	42.1%	46.3%
Telepathy	40.7%	37.5%
Iriology	38.2%	36.2%
Yoga	38.1%	40.0%
Acupuncture	36.9%	32.1%
Astrology	36.8%	40.7%
Selfknowledge	30.7%	39.6%
Hands healing	30.4%	29.6%
Gnosis	28.8%	24.7%
Spiritism	26.5%	30.0%
Palmistry	26.3%	28.4%
Phantoms	21.9%	24.6%
Tarot	21.4%	26.6%

Table 3: Popular Religious Beliefs

	Sample	Catholics
The other life	64.4%	66.6%
Paradise	61.4%	71.6%
The end of the world	57.4%	62.4%
Hell	53.0%	59.2%
Souls in Purgatory	45.2%	54.3%
Intercessory Spirits	41.7%	53.1%
Curses	33.9%	39.5%
Aromatic herbs for Purification	28.0%	36.3%
Witches	27.0%	30.8%
Dwarfs	20.0%	23.4%

All Catholics said they believed in God and almost all in Jesus Christ. Contrary to what could be expected from the results of earlier studies, there is a greater percentage that says they believe in the Bible (98%) than believe in the

Virgin Mary (89%). The latter devotion remains very common, however. Examining respondents' emphasis on belief in the Bible, we can suggest two hypothetical explanations:

a) Traditional belief in the Bible as Sacred Scripture, as the Word of God, as sacred, as powerful and untouchable, and as evoking magical associations; and

b) The renewed importance of the Bible in postconciliar Catholicism.

When we observe the distribution of percentages regarding traditional and new age beliefs (Table 2 above), we see that the majority of community leaders believe in medicinal herbs and in horoscopes. Looking at the next highest percentages, we see that they coincide with perspectives that have begun to prevail in Western culture in the current transition to a postindustrial society (which some have mistakenly identified with "postmodern" culture). The latter include beliefs in natural medicine, horoscopes, parapsychology, and unidentified flying objects, all of which are characterized by the conviction that trans-rational mysteries and energies impinge on individual, collective, and planetary life.

There is a tendency to understand the sacred as a diffuse energy and to see God not in personalized form, as Christian theology does, but in terms of cosmic energy, often flowing from within the individual:

M.H.: "To me, God is an interior power I carry within me and project toward others. It's like a power, and I know it's not just inside me; it's also outside me. Don't ask me how I feel it: it's something intangible. But I can feel it."

It is interesting to note that some of the "Oriental beliefs" that, along with the above-mentioned convictions, make up what Western and North American sociology of religion has called new age beliefs, have similar percentages—from 36.8% to 42.2%.

In the in-depth interviews with Catholics, some curious new age elements appear, especially the ideas of reincarnation, the transmigration of souls, and extraterrestrials.

"Do you believe in reincarnation?"
"Yes."
"How do you think reincarnation takes place?"
G.Q.: "You can turn into an animal or you can go on being the same person. You don't know what you'll end up being . . . I imagine you'll go up and then come back again reincarnated as another person, or as a plant, or as an animal: we move on eternally in circles . . . I imagine we meet all the people we know who have died."
M.H.: "I don't know what's going on with me, but when I go to certain places I have the impression I've been there before. I don't know how to explain it: let's just say I might be some kind of reincarnation."
L.V.: "At this point, psychologically speaking, I don't know whether the

spirits exist or not; I don't know about reincarnation and all that, but people have seen there's such a thing as reincarnation."

Belief in ghosts and in "Gnosis" is much less common among the leaders interviewed: 21.9% and 28.8%, respectively.

In all this we note a trend toward more cosmological visions of religion and religiosity, featuring a syncretism that brings together elements from traditional Catholicism, indigenous religions, Eastern religions, current science and technology, and new age practices. There appears to be a secularization process that relativizes traditional, orthodox Catholic beliefs and appears in conjunction with religious diversification and the relativizing of all beliefs. In other words, there appears to be a process of secularization without secularism.

Regarding those beliefs that fall into the category of popular religiosity (Table 3), we would underline some interesting observations about responses given by the community leaders polled.

First of all, the data indicate that among all the popular religious beliefs mentioned, the leaders have the strongest faith in the end of the world, "the other life," heaven, and hell.

Regarding traditional magical-religious beliefs (Table 3), a large percentage (42%) believe in intercessory spirits (*animitas*); spells and curses (34%); and the burning of aromatic herbs to chase off evil spirits (28%).

A significant percentage also believe that a baby can be affected by the evil eye (33.3%).[9] The baby that has been "eyed," or looked at by a person with "heavy blood," is affected by a spell that causes a serious, life-threatening illness. The only cure for the "evil" that provokes this illness is a magical-religious healing rite called a *santiguamiento* or *santiguerio* that is carried out by a popular healer, the *santiguadora* (see interview that opens this chapter).

Besides the one-third of persons who really believe in the possibility of the "evil eye," 36% doubt its existence. When the latter say they are not sure whether a baby can be "eyed," they are giving tacit credence to the possibility of extranatural intervention by evil forces, and consequently to practices such as healings, amulets, and incantations.

The overall data on religious beliefs offered by this study allow us to affirm that there is a relative (and not strong) secularization process among a significant segment of the leaders polled. This process shows two tendencies: one toward the rationalizing of belief; and the other toward an increase in new age beliefs. While the majority still adhere to the dogmatic teachings of the official churches, there

---

[9]Belief in the evil eye or *aojo* is traditionally related to a sickness found among the Latin American and Chilean poor; its main symptom is severe diarrhea, and it can occasionally bring about the child's death (Parker 1992b). The idea of the evil eye is widely held; it is passed on orally and goes back to the most ancient roots of religious history. It was present in the Old Testament and in classical Greece, and it is also spread widely throughout Africa (Plath 1981; Read 1966). Its etiology has clear magical-religious connotations, and there has never been an empirical-rational explanation for the phenomenon (Grebe 1971).

remains a very significant proportion of magical-religious beliefs typical of traditional popular religion. The latter beliefs have been reshaped in the urban setting, and are different from the traditional religiosity of peasant communities, in that they are no longer shaped by the regular cycles of nature.

TYPES OF POPULAR CATHOLIC

In the light of our study's objectives, based on the indications provided by the statistical sample, and using the qualitative data generated by the interviews, we created different types of Catholic leaders: a first type who would be closest to the official Catholic Church; a second type who would more often practice rites associated with traditional folk Catholicism; and finally a third type who would tend to be closer to some new age beliefs. We discovered that all of them, for reasons we will analyze, can be validly classified as "popular Catholics." We proceeded to do in-depth interviews with those leaders who seemed most representative of each type.

We should keep in mind that these people all call themselves Catholics. And in fact, if we analyze their religious beliefs by type of Catholic, we will find that there are not great differences in their attitudes toward official teachings: they all share the basic Catholic beliefs in God, Jesus Christ, the Bible, the Virgin Mary, the Holy Spirit, and the saints. The differences are to be found in other areas, and it is these we will analyze.

First Type of Popular Catholics

These are "practicing Catholics," that is, people who go to Mass with a certain regularity and who basically believe in the dogmatic teachings of Catholicism: God, Jesus Christ, the Holy Spirit, and the Virgin Mary. They also believe in the intercession of the saints and in the afterlife. This last major belief associated with official Catholics is consistent with classic Christian faith statements about the Resurrection.

This type of Catholic is clearly closer to the doctrines of the institutional Church than to unofficial beliefs such as popular magical-religious tenets and new age ideas, both of which they criticize.

In general they have a more acutely formed ethical sense that can be attributed to their understanding of the devil, who is seen to be present in every person and above all in human activity in the form of sin.

Second Type of Popular Catholics

These Catholics believe in and practice popular magical-religious rites that have grown out of rural settings and are reproduced or reinvented in the urban world: promises to God through the intercession of the Virgin Mary or of the saints (*mandas*); the evil eye; spells and curses; ritual curings; and herbal medicines linked with traditional healing rituals.

This type is distinguished by its great belief in Chile's folk religious tradition, which is marked by *animitas* or intercessory spirits, to which we will return below.

It also practices ancient Catholic ritual traditions that have become popular in urban settings, such as the celebration of Mary's Month and Palm Sunday.

Members of this type keep a certain distance from the official Church; nonetheless they go to Mass rather frequently.

Consistent with its popular magical-religious beliefs, this type of Catholic sees God, Jesus Christ, the Virgin Mary, and the saints in very concrete terms and makes use of traditional iconography.

Third Type of Popular Catholics

This is a new kind of syncretism within popular Catholicism. It combines elements from traditional folk religion with some of the new beliefs and spiritual sensibilities of the new age movement.

Catholics of this type, together with traditional beliefs, make use of yoga and believe in astrology and horoscopes, as well as in reincarnation and healing through the laying on of hands. They also believe in spiritism, Gnosis, extraterrestrials, and astral bodies.

Their spirituality sets the spiritual against the material, opting for the first but recognizing that the second is functionally necessary.

They identify themselves as Catholics, but they are not identified with the Church as an institution and they are critical of the churches, but still say they are profoundly influenced by Catholicism.

These leaders' image of God is more abstract, resembling a kind of energy that can take on different forms.

Members of this type display a comparatively greater range of "beliefs," colored by certain superstitious traits. They have a comparatively greater belief in the devil and in almost all the things we saw in Tables 2 and 3. They are more "credulous": they are more likely to believe in hell, the "souls in purgatory," spells and curses, and witches and elves.

Open or Closed Identity and the Various Catholic Types

Finally, an aspect that is of special relevance for our study is the degree of adherence by Catholics to their own "Catholic identity." The question "Do you think yours is the only true religion?" yielded various outcomes. Clearly, the third type shows the greatest openness to other religions; this is quite consistent with the diffuse and deinstitutionalized faith that characterizes these Catholics. The first type, on the other hand, remain most closed to religions other than their own: they regard their faith as the only true one. The second type's openness is greater than that of the first, but far less than that of the third.

RITUAL IN POPULAR URBAN CATHOLICISM

As descendants of peasant groups that immigrated to the cities generations ago become more settled in the urban setting, and as new generations are born into this world, popular piety is shaped by the urban way of life. This phenomenon can be observed in San Joaquín. We can begin to speak of a "popular urban Catholicism" that has grown out of experiences in the city. This type of Catholicism is far less drawn to typical folk rituals or massive public expressions of devotion than it was in the countryside. Its life becomes more privatized, but the religious dimension is still present in daily life and in certain parish celebrations. As we will observe, it becomes a less ritualistic and less "practicing" piety.

"Practicing" Catholics and Popular Catholics

An analysis of the data from our study reveals that Catholics are generally less observant of their religion than Protestants, but they are far more devoted than "believers without religious affiliation." Protestants participate much more frequently in their own religious services than do Catholics in theirs. Reflecting on these data, we propose two hypotheses about "nonpracticing" Catholics:

a) Catholics do not see going to Mass as essential to their life: they see it as less important than how they live.
b) Nevertheless, they tend to persevere in the practice of certain popular rituals; this could be because they find meaning in popular devotion despite all secularizing trends, as well as to the deep rootedness of Catholicism in Chile's national culture.

Looking at the popular Catholic types we can observe that Catholics of the first type are more likely to be "practicing Catholics," but that they do not necessarily practice very intensely. Only 20% say they always go to Mass, and 80% say they go "rather frequently." The third type are the least "practicing" group: 54% say they never or almost never go to Mass. Still, a certain level of Sunday observance does exist among these Catholics: 15% say they always attend Mass and 31% say they go rather frequently. Finally, the second type of popular Catholics appear to be the most constant regarding Mass attendance, perhaps because of their traditional Catholic sensibilities: 57% say they always go to Mass, and only 22% say they never or almost never go.

Ritual Practice: Rites and Traditions

As shown in Graph 1 below, which lists the ritual practices in which respondents said they participated most frequently, there is a very wide range of rites that mark different moments in the lives of these community leaders. Graph 1, "Ritual Practices," tallies responses to the question, "In the last year, have you participated in . . .?"

Clearly, the practice of attending baptisms and funerals is widespread. Forty-five percent of respondents attended one of these during the last year. Nevertheless, only 30% engaged in "popular religious" practices such as *mandas* (promises to the saints, the Virgin Mary or to *animitas*) during the last year. Only 4% admit having attended practices such as divining the future, and only 2% had participated in spiritist sessions.

Graph 1: Ritual Practices

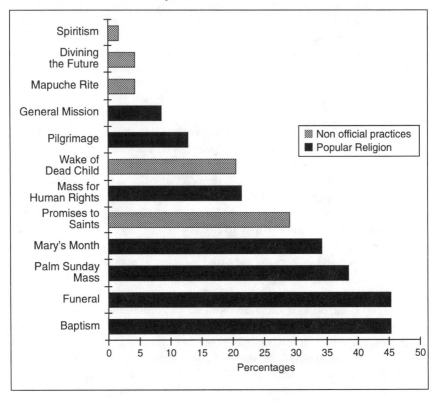

Mass attendance is low, while participation in baptisms and wakes is high, perhaps because there is a lack of deeper motivation in the former case, while in the latter they abound:

"You told me you're a Catholic?"
C.Q.: "Yes I'm a Catholic, but only halfway. If I go to Mass it's to participate in a wake or when there's a first communion or a baptism. I'm lazy about going to Mass . . . I get bored, and I find priests very boring."
"What does Baptism mean to you?"
C.Q.: "You don't know anything when you're baptized; you're becoming a Christian, because nobody is a Christian until they're baptized. What happens is that if you're not baptized, you're a pagan [literal translation: a Moor]."
"What do you think happens to them?"
C.Q.: "I've seen older children who aren't baptized and they're sickly; it's like they don't have any defenses. All kinds of things happen to them, and they've always got problems; that's the difference."

The frequency of religious practice is not determined within a social and cultural vacuum. It reflects the variety of needs, values, and aspirations of people who live in the context of poverty and social and cultural oppression. What can certainly be affirmed is a kind of "spiritual warfare" involving certain symbols of popular faith. This "spiritual warfare" separates popular Catholics who are closer to Christian Base Communities from those who display a "popular" faith deformed by the sociocultural exploitation that defines their whole context.

In 1992 a young San Joaquín man was run over on an avenue in his working-class neighborhood. Immediately his friends built an *animita* for him, a tiny temple erected by the roadside near where he was killed. According to popular tradition, the soul of the victim of a tragic death "dwells" there. The *animita* becomes a consecrated spot where people go to pray and to offer *mandas*, promises to the soul of the departed, just as they do to the Blessed Virgin Mary and the saints.

So it happened in the case of this particular *animita*, which became the object of an odd symbolic conflict between a group of Catholic women, members of a Christian Base Community, and the young man's own group of friends. To complicate matters, the victim's mother belonged to the Christian community. The young man had been a member of a working-class street-corner gang that gathered to drink and use drugs. They liked rock music, and their religious beliefs had drifted ever closer to those of a satanic cult, which probably grew up within the group itself. The curious thing is that, with macabre syncretism, the young people included among their "satanic" beliefs the ancient and traditional popular faith in *animitas*. While usually this roadside *animita* would be adorned by an image of the Virgin Mary and by many decorations and flowers, in this case the only thing to be found in the tiny temple was a black throne; the idea was that it would be used by Satan. Around the temple there were no flowers or pious images; the only image was the austere and foreboding darkness of the black paint that completely filled the tiny space.

When the women who belonged to the community saw what had happened, they immediately set out to give the *animita* a "Christian baptism." They painted it in lively colors, adorned it with several images of Jesus Christ, the Virgin Mary, and various saints, and inundated it with flowers.

Here we see how Catholics from a church community turn to the symbolic weapons inherited from the deepest of their popular faith traditions in order to take action and attempt to overcome the influences of the "powers of evil" incarnated in the confusing religious influence of the new youth subcultures, which mix hard rock, drugs and satanic notions—subcultures that are characteristic of the small but very degraded "postmodern" atmosphere found in the lower-class neighborhoods of a large metropolitan area.

This story points to the survival of older popular faith traditions in the heart of the city, but it also shows how these traditions are reappropriated by new religious groups that are under the influence of a globalized culture, moved by a diversified religious field, and diluted by multiple influences—including new age culture on the one hand and a renewed Catholic pastoral practice on the other. The simple and direct reproduction of the traditional manifold of peasant folk superstitions and religious traditions is no longer found in these urban conditions.

In contrast to what is a frequent practice where traditional rural culture is the norm, these urban popular Catholics do not appear to seek solutions to their problems through magical-religious practices that reflect a dependent, fatalistic mentality. Instead, what seems to prevail is the attitude of people who, far from seeking the tutelage of heteronomous forces, take the initiative and believe in human action. This stands in paradoxical contrast to their religious beliefs, where, as we have seen, the influence of magical-syncretistic beliefs is significant.

In any case, it is important to note that most respondents made it clear, in answering other survey questions, that they did not have much regard for classical State paternalism. They opted instead to encourage collective actions in which the community organizes to solve its own problems in conjunction with the State or the municipal government. Observing their style of social action, it is apparent that they believe in organized community action. Let us look now at what happens in the area of health care.

FAITH AND PROBLEM SOLVING: HEALING AND HEALTH

What we have been saying becomes clearer when we look at the alternatives available in resolving health problems. While our study did not focus on the poorest and most marginal of the slums, we know that the life of the urban poor is lived out in constant tension because many of their basic needs go unmet. Chile's public health indicators are somewhat above the Latin American average, but it is still not an exception in the region. Because of social inequality, poorer sectors have deficient access to health services and do not always have job situations that guarantee adequate medical benefits. Public health facilities lack adequate resources and are chronically deficient.

Our question aimed at getting respondents' view of modern medicine and the health services it offers, as well as their opinion of the types of healing that characterize traditional popular medicine, dispensed by popular healers or "wise women."

Informants were asked about the way they proceed when a sick family member is abandoned as incurable by modern medical practitioners. The alternatives they had were as follows:
    a) Take the person to the priest or pastor.
    b) Take them to a popular healer or "wise woman."
    c) Take them to a priest or pastor *and* the popular healer.
    d) Keep them home, because if the doctor couldn't do anything nobody else will be able to cure them.
    e) Other.
Because the popular healer or "wise woman," a typical practitioner of traditional medicine, is mentioned in two of the possible alternatives (b and c), we have combined both in order to carry out our analysis. In this way we have set up

a comparison between those who trust only modern medicine and institutionalized religion and those who have some degree of openness to popular medical practices that have magical-religious components.

While the average community leader is inclined to leave the ailing family member at home, it is significant that slightly more than 30% turn to the popular healer, or else to the healer and a clergy representative at the same time. Only 18.6% say they would go only to a priest or pastor.

It is interesting to analyze this attitude in terms of community leaders' educational level: we learned that the lower their educational level, the more frequently they turn to healers. Those with more education prefer to leave the sick person at home or find some other solution, such as persisting with modern medical treatment.

Among community leaders with only a grade school education, most prefer consulting the healer to other alternatives. Leaders with a background in higher education say they would leave the person at home or find some other solution. Leaders with a high school education are distributed close to the mean.

In any case, the reason for turning to the popular healer is faith related. It implies faith in healing power, faith in the healer, and faith in the possibility of a miracle:

> **R.P.:** "My husband had been operated on for a kidney stone, and one day I spoke to the gentleman who sells herbs in the market. 'Listen,' I said, 'they operated on my husband, you know, and now he's got gall bladder symptoms.' 'Take along some *llantén*, some *matico*, and some *pangüe* and make him a tea out of it: it's a sure cure,' he said. I believe in herbs because they're natural things, they're from the countryside. Iridologists have a look in your eyes and they know all about you. They sit you down and have a look at you before you tell them anything at all. And everything they say turns out to be just what you have—"
> "But they're not doctors . . ."
> **R.P.:** "According to them they're doctors. They call themselves doctors. Of course they've been accused of things, of giving out prescriptions; but people have faith in them, and in the long run it's faith that counts."

But this is not blind faith; it doesn't arise from a mentality that depends on blind powers, on providentialism and miracles. Rather, it is a faith in the power of God that does not rule out pragmatic attitudes in seeking concrete ways of overcoming health problems:

> **M.H.:** "I'll go out and look for other solutions—not the ones that are easiest, but the ones that will work as quickly as possible. That's what everybody looks for now; it's what either of you would look for. Something that offers me a satisfactory solution and makes me feel I'm playing to win. Winning is not always possible, but you ought to at least

feel satisfied because you did your very best. If there are no other
solutions, then may God's will prevail. If God wants your family
member to die, then great; but at least they won't die because nobody
made an effort. You have to knock on every single door."

When we analyze the responses by type of Catholic we find that the first type
leave the sick person at home (46%) or take them to a priest (36%); none of them
simply takes the person to the popular healer. The third type, however, are the
group who turn most frequently to the popular healer to treat an incurable patient
(50% do only this, and another 25% go to the priest as well as the healer). This
shows a very high level of faith in spiritual healing (75%). No one of them would
take the sick family member only to a priest. The traditional type would leave the
person home (31%), take the person to a healer (25%), to a priest (25%), or to
both (19%).

Looking at belief in the evil eye, which we have already described, we asked
the three types of Catholic whether a baby can receive the evil eye. Most second
or traditional types said yes (61%); 46% of the third type also agreed; while only
38% of the first type answered affirmatively.

Since the evil eye is cured by means of a ritual procedure called a
santiguamiento, we asked about people's familiarity with this type of healing
ritual. Responses, by type of Catholic, were as follows:

The first type of Catholics "have heard talk about it" (almost 70%), while
close to 40% of the other two know exactly how the ritual is conducted. This
indicates that family members of the latter types have direct experience with this
magical-religious procedure. It is significant that there are no second type of
Catholic for whom *santiguamientos* are totally unknown.

Overall, the data we have collected on the role of faith in dealing with health
problems show that it is important for a significant proportion (more than 50%)
of popular Catholics, although its role varies for each specific type. The priest is
the most important healing figure for the first type, while for the third it is the
healer or the laying on of hands. The second type of popular Catholics have a
variety of alternatives: they may turn either to the priest or to the healer or to the
laying on of hands.

RELATIONSHIPS WITH THE INSTITUTIONAL CHURCH

We have seen that the different types of urban popular Catholics have different
relationships with the institutional Church. The first type of Catholics are closest
to the institutional Church, both in ritual observance and in participation in church
organizations. The second type of Catholics, while they participate in other aspects of church life and do not share some official beliefs and sacramental rites,
are also close to the institution. The Catholics who appear to be most estranged
from the institutional Church are the third or new age type.

One reason people of Catholic background give for feeling estranged from the

Church is the search for a more liberal, less authoritarian religion. The reasons most often given by the third type or "self-styled" Catholics is the sense of obligation they perceive in a church whose preaching seems demanding and authoritarian:

> **M.H.:** "I don't want to feel obligated to do things. I believe in God, in Jesus Christ, and in the saints, for example; but I just believe, you know? I don't want to feel I have to. If I feel I have to then I won't go, but if I want to then I will . . . The churches, religions, are too rigid."

On the other hand, those who feel close to the Church say they go precisely because of the Catholic Church's relative openness compared to the fundamentalism of Pentecostals or neo-Pentecostals.

> **M.M.:** "I'm attracted to the Catholic religion because it's the religion that gives you the least trouble: if you want to go to church, then you go. There are other religions that give you a lot more problems—the Jehovah's Witnesses, for example. They can't drink tea or coffee, they have to fast, and I don't know what all."

We will now look at two factors that are important in analyzing the relationships and interactions between the official institutional Church and the various popular Catholicisms. These are the contexts in which people have received their formation in the faith and the more or less critical attitudes of the various informants with regard to the institutional Church and its role in society.

The Importance of the Institutional Church in Religious Socialization

Regarding their religious socialization, all respondents were asked: "Where did you get your religious formation?" They were given several alternative replies.

While "the family" is an important locus of basic religious socialization for all, it is most important for Catholics: 90% of respondents mentioned it.

Next in importance is "school." (This can mean having attended religion classes in public school or having gone to Catholic school.) Almost 65% mention two other very relevant contexts within the Church's pastoral life. The first is the "Month of Mary," which is a traditional, widely attended Catholic parochial celebration in November; and the second is "catechetics," which generally refers to a post-Vatican II system of presacramental instruction that is required for all Catholics in their respective parishes. Another significant source of instruction, mentioned by 40% of Catholics, is the Sunday sermon.

Less widespread sources of instruction in the faith, such as Christian Base Communities, study days, workshops, courses, retreats, and participation in apostolic movements, have less influence on Catholics in general—that is, on those we have called "popular Catholics." Hardly any of the informants mentioned them, though they are decisive in the formation of lay Catholic leaders and active members of the postconciliar Church in popular sectors.

In general terms, then, the Catholics we studied had not had the exclusively traditionalist religious socialization that characterizes folk Catholicism, as would have been the case had they mentioned only the family: they have also been exposed to more contemporary forms of instruction that include a more nuanced theological, liberating, and missionary content, imparted in formal contexts devoted to the instruction of the laity as part of a renewed pastoral strategy.

From a missionary point of view it is essential to recognize the continuing importance of the family, and within it undoubtedly mothers and grandmothers, in the religious socialization of children in the popular classes.[10] Next, it is important to underline the significance of two activities that constitute privileged conduits of interaction between official Catholicism and popular Catholicism in modernized urban settings: the Month of Mary and parish catechesis.

EVALUATION OF THE CHURCH'S CURRENT ROLE

In general, the Catholic Church's image among the leaders polled is positive; this coincides with national public opinion polls, which identify the Catholic Church as one of the Chilean institutions that has the highest credibility. The high regard enjoyed by the Catholic Church in Chile is in large measure a result of the key role it played in defending human rights in the face of the repression and authoritarianism of General Augusto Pinochet's military regime, which governed the country from 1973 until 1990.

These community leaders believe the Catholic Church is playing a more positive role than it did in earlier periods. San Joaquín leaders were asked to respond "Yes" or "No" to the following statement: "I'm pleased with the Catholic Church as it is now; in former times it was more traditional."

Most Catholics (62%) agreed with the statement, while 31% of non-Catholics (Protestants, no religion, and atheists) agreed. Only 17% of Catholics said they disagreed, showing a degree of critical distance from the contemporary Catholic Church. The Catholics who expressed strongest agreement with the affirmation were the first type, but the results among the others still show strong agreement.

Turning to another issue, the community leaders think the Church should play a role in "social issues." These Catholics overwhelmingly agree with the Church's position on drugs and on AIDS. There is not the same consensus regarding the way the hierarchy deals with problems such as divorce and abortion: dissidents number one-third of respondents.

It appears that a key variable in differences of belief among Catholics is their

---

[10]"Latino Popular Catholicism is fundamentally dependent for its existence on the entire community, on the families within the community and especially on the older women within the families" (Espín 1997:4).

relationship with the institutional Church. Those who are the most accepting of dogmatic beliefs and sacramental practices we have classified in the first type. Still, it is important to point out that strictly speaking, members of this group are not the practicing Catholics and Base Community members who have the closest relationship with the official, post-Vatican II pastoral life of Catholicism. The sample was not focused on them.

Those we have classified in the second type have easy, familiar relationships with the various sacramental, theological and educational dimensions of the official Catholic Church, but they hold to their own beliefs and practices. Their degree of attachment to the institutional Church is varied.

Those we have classified in the third type continue to be popular Catholics, but they adhere to syncretistic, magical-religious and esoteric beliefs and practices. It is they who are the most sharply critical of the official Church and its hierarchy, and feel the most alienated from it.

CATHOLICISM, IDENTITY, AND LOCAL CULTURE

Cultural identity emerges as one of the central themes in the debate over the ability of the modernization process to relate to or destroy values that are intrinsic to each specific culture. Our concern here will be to see how religion—especially popular Catholicism—interacts with the dynamic of identity-modernization.

The modernization process has often been questioned because in its efforts to overcome backwardness and tradition it tends to overlook individuals' sense of identity and to uproot them. They find themselves in an unpredictable environment where they are subjected to deep and accelerating social changes brought about by the globalization process. There is a tendency, then, for the boundaries of our societies' symbolic identities to become fuzzy: all differences are subordinated to the "homogeneous universalization" imposed by the market and by scientific and technological progress.

However, the modern sense of identity is a matter of interiorization, a reflexive act that responds to the basic notion of a thinking-acting being as the center of the world. This notion, which results from the secularization of consciousness, is radically different from the kind of vision that conceives of the human while mired in traditional and religious atavisms.

Our sense of personal identity is linked, first of all, to a sense of belonging; and later it is associated with representations of our bonds to our surroundings, which become ever more evident and familiar to our common sense. The latter make up all that constitutes our familiar, everyday world, the place where we were born, where we grew up and became independent.

For this reason, a sense of identity built on the rational and utilitarian patterns present in highly modernized societies tends to favor an individualism that rests on a totally secularized foundation. That is to say, it favors a sense of the absolute autonomy of each individual, an identity detached from our primary bonds and relationships. The "self-made man" is sufficient unto himself and no longer needs the community in order to govern his life or get along in the world. In traditional societies, however, the individual relinquishes individuality in the name of tradition and forms an attachment to the events, circumstances, relationships, and interactions that "have always been there" and therefore cannot be changed or questioned. It has been said that religion in premodern societies functioned as a key component of this "tradition," which comprises and sustains collective identities.

The globalization process, then, generates a personal identity that is individualistic, pragmatic, and geared to the market; it is highly competitive and tends to deny traditional bonds. And once it does that it denies its specific local and religious roots.

With this frame of reference in mind, then, our study asked the following question: In what way is these community leaders' sense of identity "modern," and how is it related to the Christian faith?

It is beyond the scope of the present study to offer a final or definitive answer to this question. Nevertheless, we believe that the analysis of our data provides enough information to offer a clear picture of the direction in which our informants are moving with regard to religious-cultural models.

Our goal is to offer a detailed look at the three types of Catholics, regarding factors that are especially relevant to our study: the construction of personal identity and perceptions regarding specific cultural values.

IDENTITY AND A SENSE OF BELONGING; THE IMPORTANCE OF PRIMARY, LOCAL BONDS

Those interviewed were questioned about what they "felt to be most truly their own" (Graph 2). They were offered a series of alternative categories of groups or collective entities with which they identified to a greater or lesser degree. The responses in terms of their primary preference show that for all types of Catholics, the family is undoubtedly what they "feel to be most truly their own."

In the case of the first type of leaders, we can conclude that their faith and the areas in which they live constitute secondary identification factors. This situation is repeated in a very similar way among the second type.

However, the third type of Catholics do not consider their faith to be a significant factor forming their identity. This fact may be related to the diffuse kinds of beliefs that predominate among this type of Catholic. Members of this group mention the nation and the neighborhood as their secondary identification factors.

It is worthy of note that those interviewed generally did not list their birthplaces as factors in the construction of their identity. This traditional sense of identity, so closely linked to closed, rural, and isolated societies, was of primary importance in earlier times; but today it appears to be irrelevant. The place where one was born, so essential to *campesino* identity, is no longer so crucial among the urban popular classes.

Graph 2: What you feel most truly your own, by type of Catholic

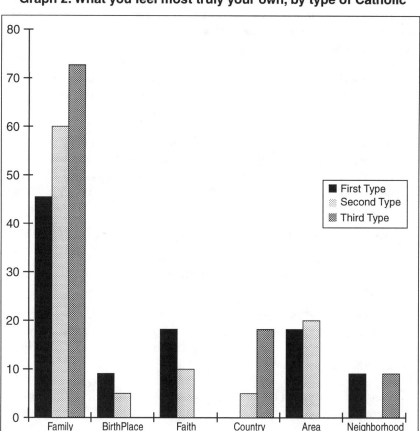

The spatial axis—by means of which territorial identity was expressed in traditional rural societies—has been replaced by a sociological axis made up of "the family." "Where I was born" and "where I grew up" are deeply marked by communitarian rather than sociostructural bonds. In terms of the typology of Tönnies (1955), the privileged place of the family points to the predominance of community over society. Perhaps we can find here an explanation of the lack of spontaneous or outstanding identification with one's social class or nation.

Another identification factor that in past decades was very important—that of belonging to a political party—has today been relegated to a low standing. Indeed, in many cases this identification factor seems to be rejected out of hand.

The faith, both for Catholic leaders and for ordinary slum dwellers, appears to be a secondary factor in defining identity. It is important to point out that both the family and the neighborhood in which one lives refer to social relationships of a private and/or local kind. In contrast, identification with the Catholic faith constitutes a factor that refers to a more universal type of relationship. In the in-depth interviews, we verified the fact that identification with the local community was generally associated with identification with a faith lived out in the midst of the local community. Popular Catholicism thus constitutes a significant element that is generally associated with primary and local relationships.

Some excerpts from the interviews will help us appreciate this sense of identity with the community:

"We used to have a great time [laughter] and at the end of the year we'd participate in the graduation from the workshop and celebrate with champagne . . . but we had a great time and we were happy . . . This is the sort of thing I've done in my neighborhood, and I love it; if they told me I had to move, I wouldn't do it."

I love my neighborhood " because I've lived here all my life and this is my world."

". . . I think this is my own: I've made my whole life here and I'll live out the rest of my life here too . . ." in the neighborhood.

I've participated in "catechetics and organizing workshops . . . I've organized workshops throughout my neighborhood; even as far away as La Legua . . . I took a course in sewing: God has given me a lot of ability to work with my hands."

A semantic analysis of the answers of some of those interviewed can be done, as below, by categorizing their responses as belonging to *one's own space* and a space *outside oneself.*

One's Own Space	Space Outside Oneself
lived-in	(dehumanized)
commitment	no commitment
organization	discord
artisan work	(industry)
partying	(having a tough time)
security	violence
a good atmosphere	a bad atmosphere
persons	power
FAITH	DISBELIEF
IDENTITY	UPROOTING

One's own space is associated semantically with the community: the sense of identification is not with a geographical place (a specific territory); rather, it is with a network of interpersonal relationships and with a life-giving, existential commitment. As one woman interviewed expressed it, her experience is "what I've gone through with the folks, that's all [laughter]."

In this communally lived-out experience, affective relations with family, with the community, and in faith sharing have been decisive.

We can now characterize "one's own" communitarian space as the place where there is commitment and community organization (artisan workshops and catechesis); the place where there is artisan work and artistic work; the place where things are shared and where one "has a good time" (there is a playful sense); and finally, the place where Christian community is lived out.

This *space of belonging* is contrasted semantically with *alien space*, which is tacitly associated with urban metropolitan life: it is semantically referred to as an empty place without life or vitality and without commitment; it is a depersonalized place, a place of hostile relationships, a place of crime and violence and of insecurity; it is a strange, "politicized" place, a place of territorial power and of efficient but divisive relationships.

Moreover, this alien space is the workplace, above all the industrial and functional workplace, opposite in connotation to the artisan occupations carried out in small workshops.

For these reasons, alien space is the antithesis of a sense of identity; it is a threatening space associated with being uprooted, a space where "no one cares" and where "there's a bad atmosphere."

A SENSE OF LOCAL IDENTITY IN THE FACE OF INVASION BY THE MARKET

Chilean society has undergone and continues to undergo major changes marked by the neoliberal capitalist model, which is characterized by a market economy that has brought about (a) the eclipsing of the state's regulatory role in the area of socioeconomic relationships, and (b) a growing preponderance of the market and its logic. The corporate pursuit of increased profitability has depended in large measure on companies' ability to increase their productivity and competitiveness in national and international markets. The prevailing logic promotes a "competitive" attitude marked by selfishness and individualism. At the same time, the relationship between producer and consumer has come to be measured exclusively in terms of money, on the one hand, and to be mediated by the advertising industry and by "marketing strategies" on the other. The economy's growing commercialization and market orientation exhibit an inner logic that tends to disrupt social solidarity systems: their expansion is threatening traditional, time-honored patterns, norms, and lifestyles.

We will now analyze the responses of community leaders affected by this commercialization of Chilean society and its reorientation to the market, and see how their faith influences those responses.

First of all we looked at the commercial establishments where people generally make their purchases, from the closest at hand (the corner store) to an extremely modern, consumer-oriented mall (the Plaza Vespucio, a few blocks from the local neighborhood).

While virtually all the leaders have been exposed to the consumer society through the constant influence of TV in the home, a variety of more traditional practices still persists; and to some degree these practices challenge the newer consumer patterns.

Shopping alternatives run the gamut from traditional neighborhood "farmers' markets" to ultramodern "malls," temples of the consumer society patterned on the U.S. model, which have recently been introduced in a variety of Greater Santiago settings. These alternatives represent two types of social networks: the first embodies face-to-face relationships featuring strong collective bonds; while the second is characterized by impersonal relationships that are mainly individualistic and that promote a "U.S.-type" lifestyle.

The data from our survey show a clear tendency: rather than favoring the impersonal mall, these local leaders still tend to prefer spaces that allow the traditional "face-to-face" relationships found in the "farmers' market." This is clearly the case among all of the different types of Catholics.

Graph 3 compares informants' degree of adhesion to values that tend to reaffirm a shared identity with those that are more in line with modernizing tendencies. The graph summarizes the loyalties of the different types of Catholics in terms of these two kinds of value orientation.

We regard certain values as being associated with the reaffirmation of cultural identity. These would include the items referred to as "the need to do things that revitalize the neighborhood's cultural identity" (summarized in Graph 3 as "identity") and preferring "Chilean TV programs" to foreign ones, which is a way of affirming "things Chilean."

In general terms, as we can see, informants value activities that revitalize community identity. We can interpret this tendency, as we have in the case of preferences regarding places to shop, as the natural result of the weak influence exercised by the consumer society on the mentality of the Catholic leaders polled. If that influence were stronger, then the market, with its pragmatic and individualistic code of values, would tend to break down habits of social solidarity and bring about a decline in concern about issues such as neighborhood identity.

To track values associated with modernization, we asked questions about informants' view of foreign technology. We also asked questions designed to measure whether advertising promoting "consumerism" was understood as something negative, as a manipulation; or whether "advertising" was seen as positive, as necessary information that safeguards consumer sovereignty.

As we can see, for the first type of popular Catholics the most important thing is to engage in activities that revitalize neighborhood identity. At the same time, this group clearly rejects consumer-oriented TV advertising. They are divided in their level of openness to foreign technology.

Graph 3: Agreement with cultural values, by type of Catholic

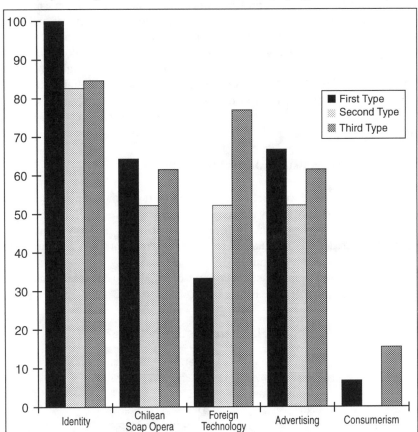

More traditional Catholics (second type) affirm neighborhood identity and "things Chilean"; but their level of openness to foreign technology is greater. They reaffirm their identity by totally rejecting the consumer society, which they say "promotes individualism and selfishness" and clearly militates against the notion of community and of a popular culture marked by solidarity.

Of the three groups analyzed, the third were the most heavily influenced by a modern consumer mentality. They wholeheartedly favored foreign technology, and the level of their rejection of consumer-oriented advertising was relatively low compared to that of the other two groups. As in the previous cases, they reaffirm neighborhood identity and prefer Chilean TV programs.

Given the results of this study, we can see very clearly how the dynamics of the relationship between global and local realities work in this popular urban context. It is not so clear that the introduction of modernizing tendencies has led to a decline in values that reaffirm cultural identity. Identification with what is "our own" is reaffirmed, but a degree of openness to modernization associated with "things foreign" is also present—whenever it does not tend to break down social solidarity systems. When models that promote individualism and self-centeredness are introduced, they tend to be rejected.

In general, popular Catholics' profession of religious faith does not seem to decisively influence the affirmation or negation of modern values. On the other hand, religious faith can indirectly favor a range of cultural values that reaffirm community and local identities and (using critical analysis to varying degrees) reject the individualistic and competitive values of the consumer society.

POPULAR CATHOLICISM AND JUSTICE IN CHILE

Those interviewed were polled on a value that research into popular culture has indicated is deeply felt by the people: justice.[11]

In response to the question, "Is there justice in Chile?" the answer was clear: 52.6% answered that there is not; 38.6% answered "more or less"; and only 8.8% believed there is justice in Chile.

If we compare the opinions of men and women, we see that it is women who most clearly affirm that there is no justice (60.3% vs. 41.3% for men).

Table 4. Is There Justice in Chile?

	Men	Women
Yes	15.2%	4.4%
More or Less	43.5%	35.3%
No	41.3%	60.3%

A clear sense of justice and a critical attitude toward the national situation are present among all the types of Catholics; this shows that popular Catholicism, faith, and popular piety among grassroots leaders—whatever expression that might take—are not an "alienating" element or an "opiate of the people," either in the classical Marxist sense (Marx and Engels 1979) or in the way that Weber's theory looks at popular religiosity (Weber 1964).

We can verify what we have affirmed on earlier occasions (Parker 1996: 219-246): that in its logical and symbolic constructions and in its syncretistic style of thinking (Marzal 1986), the popular mentality accepts different levels of reli-

---

[11]In Spanish, *la justicia* can mean either "justice" or the judicial system. Thus, when informants refer to "justice," they may be referring to the unjust distribution of income or to the "unjust structures" of society. In general, however, research has shown that when people speak of "justice" they are talking about the judicial system (Correa and Barros Lezaeta 1993).

gious and social representation and does not see them contradicting one another. The presence of magical-religious elements—especially among the second and third types—does not prevent them from showing a critical sense in their representations of society. None of those studied manifested a religiously reinforced sense of fatalism or social alienation.

POPULAR CATHOLICISM AND SOCIAL PROGRESS

Let us now analyze how popular Catholics perceive individual advancement, social privilege, and competition.

A good indicator of the way in which informants represented personal advancement within the framework of competition in a liberal capitalist society is their response to the following affirmation:

"Only the most capable manage to move upward in the world. The rest end up losing, and nothing can be done about it."

This statement is a loose translation to everyday language of the Darwinian ideal extolled by the market. It exemplifies the supposed "natural selection" process that inspires people's access to and success in the market by means of a vicious competition in which only the most competent survive; those unable to compete are left behind and excluded. Some 41% of those interviewed said they were in agreement with this affirmation, revealing perhaps an acceptance of the value of competition as we have described it, or perhaps a fatalistic or cynical outlook on contemporary economic life, or even the respondents registering their frustration or a sense of impotence.

On the other hand, they were asked whether they considered the following saying to be consistent with Christian teaching:

"The rich get to heaven more easily than the poor."

It was clear that the vast majority of those interviewed (84%) rejected the idea that the wealthy are privileged by divine design and will be rewarded with a life in heaven beyond the grave. Approximately 50% do not agree that only the most capable manage to succeed in life or that this legitimates the exclusion of the rest.

In my own interpretation these answers reveal the following implicit logic:

a) The rejection of the exclusionary elitism implicit in the idea of the predestination of the wealthy.

b) The denial of the underlying fatalism contained in the idea that the poor are doubly excluded.

c) The affirmation, not made explicit but nevertheless implicit, that wealth and poverty are not situations predetermined by divine design. Rather, they are caused by a status conditioned by social structures.

At the same time, the denial of (a) or (b) implies:

d) The belief that wealth and poverty are products of a social structure of opportunity and must not be guided by elitist or exclusionary criteria.

The fact that the majority rejected the statement should be interpreted, therefore, as the implicit rejection of an elitist conception of social advancement. It affirms a more egalitarian perception in which the values held by modernity (and often contradicted by the modernization process), whether democratic or mesocratic, prevail over social values identified with an oligarchic (traditional) or an elitist (modern) society.

The model of social modernity implicit in the mentality of these leaders seems to be more inclined toward a modern, anti-elitist, more or less democratic understanding that at the same time recognizes the value of solidarity. But a minority of these leaders would also accept a model of social modernity in which individual interests prevail over collective ones, in which the idea of an exclusivist competition reigns, and in which utilitarian thinking holds sway in the pursuit of individual social advancement.

BY WAY OF SYNTHESIS: GUIDELINES AND CHALLENGES FOR INCULTURATION

It is difficult to formulate an overall synthesis of this study's results.[12] Nonetheless, there are certain elements in the cultural and religious situation of the popular leaders interviewed in San Joaquín, especially in the light of other studies carried out in similar popular settings, that allow us to offer the following general hypotheses:

Popular Catholicism, which historically has been an important element in the Chilean people's religious, social, and national identity, continues to be a vital factor in the identity of people within urban popular settings that are going through processes of increasing modernization and globalization. In fact, popular Catholicism continues to accompany most members of the popular classes throughout their entire life cycle.

The neoliberal economic development model is quickly integrating Chile into the transnational capitalist market. In countries where this is happening, popular Catholicism as an evolving religious expression of people's life experience is influenced by an array of sociocultural transformations, among the most important of which are the growing influence of the market in social life.

Despite the disintegrative impact of the above-mentioned processes, urban popular Catholicism, as an expression of urban popular culture, contributes to

---

[12]The following remarks offer a brief synthesis of theological reflections offered by Manuel Ossa and by the Local Theological Consultation carried out in Santiago, Chile, in January 1997. Participants were Doris Muñoz, Pastor Juan Sepúlveda, Cristián Johansson, María José Caram, O.P., Julián Riquelme, O.P., Pastor Osvaldo Herreros, Bridget Cook, Eugene Toland, M.M., James Weckesser, M.M., Mariano Puga, Pastor Juan Salazar, Hernán San Martín, Ana Urmeneta, Mauricio Palominos, and Cristián Parker.

processes of resistance and to countercultural forms that are not in contradiction with modernity. In fact, these processes must be regarded as a conflict-ridden encounter between global and local realities. "Local situations are not powerless either. They work out all kinds of arrangements, from syncretic borrowing to living in subaltern or dual systems" (Schreiter 1997: 12).

While it does not do so explicitly and consciously, popular Catholicism offers a structured resistance to, transforms, or simply reproduces many elements of these processes. As we have seen, popular Catholicism generates a very strong sense of local rootedness. At the same time, however, the form of identification it establishes includes a sense of global belonging, given the universal character of Roman Catholic symbolism and practice and its presence throughout the world.

Among the processes of symbolic orientation and transformation that are made possible by urban popular Catholicism, the following deserve mention:

a) It resists and transforms the processes that are globalizing urban popular life and orienting it toward the market:
— by sustaining and reinforcing the sense of community and local identity that is already present in popular urban cultures; and
— by calling for the sense of solidarity and justice that is integrating values, both inborn and constitutive, for the majority of those living in popular sectors.

b) It resists and transforms modernization and its secularizing tendencies by altering them in various ways and by continuing to offer religious meaning and identity; it does so:
— by increasing its internal plurality, as we have seen in this study regarding the various "types of urban Catholicism," which certainly constitute a challenge to any inculturated pastoral strategy; and
— by a limited rationalization of beliefs; in fact, we have seen the revitalization of magic and superstition among some types of popular Catholics.

It is important to add that urban popular Catholicism does not constitute an alienating influence. It tends to favor or at least not to contradict democratizing trends; and it questions elitist tendencies. While we can observe traditionalist attitudes (especially in some types), urban popular Catholicism does not appear to be an obstacle to progress or to modernization processes. At the same time, it is to one degree or another critical of these processes' negative and dehumanizing effects.

Finally, we have said that all popular religion develops within a dialectic interplay with official religion. This dynamic is very meaningful and necessary in the case at hand, since it permits this complex relationship between local and global realities in terms of the reproduction of traditions, the revitalization of beliefs and rituals, and the forging of new syncretisms. Without the Church, urban popular Catholicism would lose its universality and would risk falling into localistic fragmentation or the alienation brought about by the hegemony of the dominant global culture. In fact, however, the Catholic Church continues to be an important reference point for urban popular Catholicism, despite the ambivalence of relationships with it. As we have seen, all these types of urban popular Catholicism do in fact interact with the hierarchical Church; and these interactions are not contradictory but rather complementary and complex, to different degrees depending on the particular types of Catholicism.

THE SENSE OF CHRISTIAN IDENTITY IN POPULAR CATHOLICISMS

The first thing we need to recognize is that the responses of popular community leaders polled offer some guidelines and starting points for deepening the process of inculturated evangelization.

In the face of their socially subordinate situation, which includes poverty, unemployment, hunger, social and psychological insecurity, and the threat of violence in many forms, members of the popular classes turn to Christianity in search of a hope that helps them to go on living. Among the poor majority of the Latin American people there is a shared feeling, a secret reliance on supernatural powers. These constitute a symbolic hope of survival, a form of cultural resistance, and a wellspring of meaning and security not found in the secular symbolic referents generated by official and globalized culture (Parker 1996).

Based on what we have learned in this study, we can affirm that there are numerous signs that point to a genuine search for God, as well as a spirituality that is made present in daily life by religious beliefs and practices, even those we have classified as influenced by some new age beliefs.

All Catholics, however estranged from the institutional Church they may feel, identify themselves as such. Here we can see a foundation, a seed on the basis of which to preach an inculturated Gospel: all these people profess their faith in Divine Providence, in Jesus Christ, in the Holy Spirit, and in the Bible; and almost all believe in the mediation of the saints and the Virgin Mary.

Indeed, faith emerges as a vital element in one's identity; it is not just a matter of accepting traditional doctrine. It is more an aspiration to life than an adherence to the content of the Christian faith as defined in church teaching.

For this reason, the lived faith of these popular leaders still assumes concrete expressions that require theological and missiological discernment.

A legitimate question would be: What experience of the transcendent Christian God who is revealed in history do these people have?

In the case of the third type and even of "believers without religious affiliation," what is the vacuum that leads many of them to seek answers in astrology, tarot, talismans, and the search for extraterrestrials?

It seems that all spiritual quests arise out of a sense of meaninglessness—a meaninglessness that may have to do with existential situations such as societal oppression or with a feeling of being smothered in the materialism of the consumer society. But while this search does not find an answer in secular society, neither does it seem to be satisfied by the institutional Church.

The defects of popular Catholicisms are, in this sense, a critical mirror held up to the defects of a faith lived out within the institutional Church. A central challenge for inculturated mission, then, is the recovery of a fuller sense of community and of its center, Jesus Christ, alive in the hearts of its members.

At the same time, the challenge is how to empower this privileged role of popular Catholicism as a significant factor in articulating local identity and at the same time encourage a critical openness to global and universal realities within the context of the globalization process.

INCULTURATION WITHIN A CONTEXT OF RELIGIOUS PLURALISM AND SYNCRETISM

Our study shows that as secularization has advanced in Chile, religion has diversified and been transformed. Nevertheless we see that religion still plays an active and important role in personal and communal identity.

The in-depth interviews show that people's beliefs are even more widely diverse than the official Church had imagined. Does this attest to the pluralization of faith?

We must remember that biblically and theologically there has always been a plurality of ways of understanding and living out the Christian message. If they recognize the fact of religious pluralism, theological reflections on inculturation will necessarily be different from what they are within the framework of Christendom, however vague or diffuse this latter concept may have become. When evangelization seeks to restore or to create a "Christian culture," it ends up denying the reality of cultural diversity in our societies.

Indeed we need to consider at least two factors:

a) Anthropologically speaking, every culture is the sum of a complex and dynamic process of social production. If the inculturation of the Gospel is a cultural process, then it must be understood as the active way in which Christian subjects (persons or communities) creatively welcome the Gospel within their history, their geography, and their local social and cultural context.

b) We never have access to the Gospel in a pure state. What we really have are specific, incarnate, and culturally mediated encounters with the Gospel. And every mediation both reveals and hides the Gospel. The theological consequence of all this is that the spreading and proclamation of the Gospel make it necessary by definition that it continually undergo processes of incarnation and syncretism.

RITUAL: FROM SUPERSTITION TO THE WORSHIP OF THE LIVING GOD

As we have observed, a certain percentage of popular Catholics participate in official ritual expressions, while others join in more popular rites.

Many of those interviewed sought, through religious practice, a more palpable access to God and a worship that relates better to their daily lives. Indeed, their style of resolving their problems appears to be less magical than that of traditional peasants.

The popular Catholicism we observed has a tendency to make symbols more concrete and objective, preventing them from becoming abstractions. It expresses itself in a symbolism that shows a need to link concrete, tangible objects to divine powers.

The interviews show that popular Catholics use sacramental symbols as well as nonsacramental ones, but that they are not aware of the full meaning these symbols and rites are intended to convey. Also, the Catholic Church's official sacramental practices do not appear to have a vital linkage with people's daily lives; this tends to discourage their participation.

Looking at this overall picture, other questions come to mind. For example, to what extent is participation in worship an indicator of true religious faith in the Christian sense of the word? Furthermore, where Christian religious life is concerned, is participation in nonofficial worship always a negative indicator?

It is not ritual in itself, or the frequency of our participation in it, that constitutes the best indicator of religiosity in the Christian sense, but the content of ritual as it relates to life. For example, participation in a wake for an *angelito* (a baby or small child who has died) can be an expression of very close association with family and neighbors at an extremely painful moment. Participation may have a highly Christian character even though this is not classified as an "official ritual practice." On the other hand, going to Palm Sunday Mass could totally lack this Christian character and resemble the self-interested participation of a few people in a spiritist session.

The high level of participation in wakes for *angelitos* and of belief in *santiguamientos* (the burning of aromatic herbs for purification or to ward off evil spirits) leads us to ask whether the thing that makes them endure is not their ability to deeply touch the concrete lives of people, accompanying and reinforcing networks of solidarity.

Adherence to some of the new age practices shows that even in modern societies, with their high level of economic and technological development, there continues to be a felt need for a space that is both transcendent and immanent (concrete and incarnate). These practices permit a certain contact with "the beyond" while offering a sense of community and of belonging.

Those engaged in the task of inculturation need to be familiar with these poles and to value them in their very specific life settings (those that involve women or men or the poor or the rich).

We could also ask ourselves whether the institutional Church itself (and not just enlightened modernity) has not provoked, within the people, a certain level of self-deprecation regarding their popular faith. How do we distinguish between a faith that respects community traditions and draws us closer to God, and a faith based on superstitions that can end up being harmful?

JUSTICE AND THE COMMUNITY OF GOD'S REIGN

As we have seen, it is the perception of the overwhelming majority of informants that justice is not done in Chile, whatever way the term is understood. On the other hand, there is a clear option for values related to solidarity: our informants value commitment and criticize both social Darwinism and the logic of the market. In general, there is an appreciation of cultural values such as family, community, one's own neighborhood, and one's own culture.

These values, which are part of the mentality of popular Catholics, lead us to reflect on justice and on the community of God's reign.

If God's reign, as Jesus proclaimed it, begins here and now in history, then the Johannine and Pauline ways of understanding justice offer a substantial and critical contribution to the formation of the criteria by which income is distributed and wealth is accumulated (distributive and social justice), and also to criteria for the administration of justice in the court system. And identifying and naming injustice, above all if it is accompanied by coherent action aimed at bringing about justice in the different realms, is an action that, in Christian terms, is on the road to God's reign. It appears that an important challenge for the inculturation of popular urban Catholicisms such as those studied here is to link more explicitly its vital faith and rituals to a prophetic, Gospel-inspired sense of social justice.

2

Peru

The Shape of Catholic Identity among the Aymara of Pilcuyo

MARÍA JOSÉ CARAM, O.P.

WALKING WITH INTEGRITY AND HARMONY

Silvia Ticona is a young Aymara woman from the community of Cana Maquera near the district town of Pilcuyo. Like thousands of other Aymara women of her generation she is caught up in the processes of a culture in transition. At any moment of a typical day, she crosses the boundaries of many cultures. Hers is a worldview shaped by ties to her ancestral Aymara ritual life and the demands of survival in a global economy, as susceptible to the whims of the market as her counterparts in other parts of the world. In Silvia, modernity and a cyclical concept of time and sacred space intersect.

Like so many in Pilcuyo, her day begins long before dawn, fetching water from a well at a distance of one kilometer from home. Next she prepares breakfast but not before she has led the cattle out of the family corral for pasture. Strapping her youngest child to her back, she tends to additional chores such as getting the other children ready for school. During this cold winter season when agricultural activity is minimal, her husband, Casimiro, is off in the coastal city of Tacna in search of odd jobs to supplement the meager family economy.

One of the chief chores that consumes the bulk of her day is to provide forage for three head of cattle, the family's sole source of capital and its savings account. If it is Thursday, she walks to Pilcuyo for the weekly market at which she sets up a small stall to sell a few potatoes and onions. Other days may find her out on the highway waiting for transport to any one of the regional markets that stretch all the way to the Bolivian border on one side and to the larger cities of Puno and Juliaca. There she will attempt to sell a few items of clothing, but she will also enter into contact with a wider world of commercial activity and exposure to the latest gadgetry from around the world.

Back in Cana Maquera she participates in the weekly community meeting. As one of the growing number of women who have finished high school, she often acts as secretary. Late afternoons and early evenings provide a short respite, but she always has one or two weaving projects to keep her busy while she prepares the evening meal. The recent arrival of electricity has brought television, so one can soon imagine her weaving to the accompaniment of a Brazilian soap opera. Silvia carries within herself the memory of the family and community, the connection with the outside world, and a deep sense of her nurturing role in a time of rapid change. One cannot help but wonder how she manages all of these different worlds. Yet, she demonstrates a remarkable resiliency, stubborn determination, and a contemplative attentiveness to her surroundings that would be the envy of any homemaker in the postmodern world. Even in the busyness of all this activity Silvia speaks openly of how prayer permeates her life. Hers is a life of integrity and harmony under far from optimum conditions.

A SEARCH FOR HARMONY IN ALL OF LIFE

The present study attempts an immersion into the realm of mystery. Because the reality of God is so inscrutable and because it touches the very heart of men and women, language to describe this experience is often inadequate. Challenged by God's word, people search for God's presence in their own unique personal and social histories and interpret this presence in the symbols, myths, and language particular to them.

The Aymara people from the area of Pilcuyo, Peru, in the southern Andean department of Puno where our study took place, carry within their memory a long history of a continuous search for the presence of God in their lives. From their ancestors they have inherited a tradition of wisdom and a way of encountering God; they have learned how to recognize his footsteps and to relate with God in a way uniquely their own. The history of evangelization by the Catholic Church, and more recently that of new religious movements, have introduced new elements into this process which they have discerned and made their own in the hope of being able "to go on living well in harmony with all of life."

On this journey, they have undergone a kind of ongoing course in discipleship, an apprenticeship that has allowed them to nurture their ancient sources of wisdom and incorporate new sources and insights from Christianity and from the dominant cultures. At the same time, they have a capacity to comfort those afflicted by life's travails. There are "seeds of the Word" present in Pilcuyo's history, seeds that contain a universal vocation destined for sharing with all peoples. With a spirit of humility and a heartfelt connection to God, the people open their ears to listen to how the Spirit speaks to them in this Aymara corner of the Andes.

If Catholic in its broadest sense signifies universality, the term corresponds to those people in Pilcuyo who readily name this identity. They open themselves up to others and welcome them into their world through a philosophy of *andando bien* which conveys the sense of "walking through life with integrity and harmony." We understand these words, so easily used by the people, not in a utilitarian or conformist sense, but as an expression of the ongoing search for the universal dimension of life. Happiness and fulfillment are achieved, not only by shaping creation, but also by contributing to the establishment of a political, economic, and social order of service to people that enables everyone to cultivate his or her own human dignity (*Gaudium et Spes*, 9).

It would not be correct to interpret the above as a naive and acritical vision of the culture. Like every human reality, Pilcuyo is not exempt from ambiguities and shortcomings. However, in order to discover the truths this people offers us and to allow ourselves to be challenged by their faith understanding, we need to dispossess ourselves of any ethnocentricism and attempt to understand what goes on in their world. The problems, defects, or mistakes of a people are not what define them, but rather the ways that they overcome and transcend them. To approach a people and its culture otherwise, or to judge them on the basis of what we perceive as correct, is to commit a great injustice.

By taking off our shoes and knowing that we tread on "sacred ground" (Exodus 3:5), we adopt a posture of humble listening. But, we approach this study with the realization that we are only going to hear part of the great secret that nourishes the people of Pilcuyo from the depth of their ancestral roots and historical experience. To them I extend my gratitude for having shared with all of us in this research effort their great treasure of life and faith.

PROFILE SKETCH OF THE DISTRICT OF PILCUYO

The site chosen for this research is found in the District of Pilcuyo, in the southern Peruvian department of Puno, an area roughly equivalent to the size of a large state of the United States, and located in the southern part of the Andes around the Lake Titicaca Basin. According to the 1993 census, the population is 17,227, of whom 37.9% are below the age of 15 years.

The research focuses on the people who identify themselves as members of the Aymara indigenous nation, a people who preserve the distinctive features of a culture that dates back to a few centuries before the birth of Christ. As a result of the impact of outside influences on the culture over the past five hundred years, the people are involved in an ongoing process of reshaping their identity. It is generally known that the Aymara people were politically conquered by the Inca

Empire in the fourteenth century but were never fully absorbed into its sociocultural matrix, thus preserving their distinctiveness as a people and culture. In daily discourse and ordinary social transactions alike, the Aymara language remains the norm. Spanish ranks as a second language for usage in official and commercial dealings. A relevant factor is the high percentage of illiteracy, 31.4% of those above 15 years, which affects the district's full insertion into the outside market economy.

According to the same 1993 census figures, Pilcuyo has other indices of widespread poverty. For example, in 63.1% of the households, one can find a range of unsatisfied basic needs such as inadequate housing, lack of sewage, children not attending school, and a high level of economic dependence. For every 100 persons who are employed there are approximately 382 people dependent on them for support.

From the standpoint of religion, there is no organized indigenous religious movement with official status. Building on the peoples' original religious structure dating back to pre-Conquest times, a process of ongoing syncretization with Christianity began with the first wave of evangelization in the sixteenth century. But this syncretization is more like an ongoing interreligious dialogue that has gone on quietly within the Aymara people as they shape a Christian identity compatible with their religious worldview.

Since the second decade of this century Catholics and Seventh-Day Adventists have coexisted in Pilcuyo and other areas of Puno. Several generations of both creeds have grown up alongside each other within one cultural matrix. This reality of religious diversity allows us to become acquainted with the differences among them, the mutual influences, the ways they interrelate and recreate their religious identity. What emerges is the profile of a distinct way of being Catholic that does not yet enjoy official recognition.

The district capital is without its own Catholic church building, although dispersed around many communities are a multiplicity of small chapels dedicated to the veneration of different patron saints. The institutional presence of the Catholic Church derives from a pastoral team of missionaries from the different branches of the Maryknoll community who live a simple lifestyle in modest rented dwellings among the people. They have chosen to represent the Catholic Church without the usual signs of official church identity such as a parish office or regular church services. The pastoral team supports the Pilcuyo communities with agricultural assistance and programs in organization, health, and Christian formation as well as frequent religious services for the entire community when the occasion arises.

The Adventist Church, on the other hand, enjoys a highly visible presence and recognition with its own church building located in the district capital. Regular church services are held on Saturdays in line with Adventist practice. Adventist influence is quite evident in the field of education, since the first school in the district was created by them. Everyone considers the school a noble achievement. A well-known fact is that at the time of the arrival of the first Adventist missionaries the Catholic hierarchy acted in concert with local landholders to keep the indigenous peoples marginated from the educational system.

Although Pilcuyo depends in great part on agriculture and cattle raising for its subsistence, it has developed a unique range of entrepreneurial activities and strategies that connect its people with nearby urban centers for commercial interchange. In this way, it has the advantages of being inserted into the market economy and, consequently, into a daily encounter with modernity. Aspirations deriving from this insertion contrast sharply with the precarious conditions in which the majority of the people live. Factors that point to this insertion are a weekly market for food products and other basic materials, along with a cattle market; the paved highway connecting the department capital city of Puno with the town of Desaguadero on the Bolivian border, the site of a twice-weekly market of great importance for the area; and migration of both a temporary and a long-range nature.

With a 6% yearly out-migration rate Pilcuyo contributes to the statistics that place Puno among the first four departments with the highest rates of migration in the country. In almost every family interviewed for this study, at least one member has migrated to one of the coastal cities without breaking totally with Pilcuyo. Migration is accepted without any feelings of disgrace. One community member remarked that "every misfortune has its benefits like the floods in 1986 that necessitated many families buying lots in cities like Tacna, Arequipa, Puno, and Ilave" (Interview #46). Such fluid mobility in and out of the area is due to the lack of arable land for cultivation, which necessitates other sources of income.

From a political standpoint, Pilcuyo is a relatively new district whose creation came about through the struggle for self-determination and recognition. At the beginning of the century it comprised a large extension of land on a peninsula stretching to the lakefront, dependent on the political administration of the larger nearby town of Ilave. The authorities of Ilave abused their power by demanding services in kind from the people of Pilcuyo and exploiting state-owned lands for their own benefit. In reaction, the campesinos of Pilcuyo, trying to free themselves from this oppression, invited the noted Adventist missionary and pastor, Fernando Stahl, in the town of Platería, to establish a school in 1917. From this time onward several attempts were made to separate from Ilave. These efforts culminated on November 24, 1961, with the creation and formal recognition of the town of Pilcuyo.

At the official inauguration of the town the process of urbanization of the district capital began in earnest. Lands were acquired for a central plaza around which were built spaces for commercial interests, health and educational facilities, and a police station. Recently, an imposing monument was built in the center of the plaza that can be seen for several miles around. Sculpted onto the monument are murals depicting representative scenes from the area's history and struggles, mixed with Aymara mythological themes. The monument stands as a source of pride to the people of Pilcuyo as well as a recognizable landmark.

METHODOLOGICAL CONSIDERATIONS FOR AN APPROACH TO RELIGIOUS DIVERSITY

Our critical question throughout the present study has been how Catholic identity is shaped in Pilcuyo in a context of change and confessional diversity. The analysis centers on the very self-identification of the informants achieved through certain characteristics that they readily identify in each other. These point to self-recognition as well as to an awareness of distinct religious identities. The people continue to give shape to this differentiation through various outside influences and their own world of experience. On the one hand, everything is wrapped up in the cultural baggage of a belief system, worldview, and customs inherited from their elders. On the other, there are the different ethical and doctrinal principles proffered by the Catholic Church as well as by the amalgam of different religious groups, chiefly the Adventists.

The methodological approach in the research is a qualitative one. We have utilized an open interview type of research instrument, leaving room for spontaneous responses and considerations the interviewees deemed important. In order to carry out the interviews we selected two areas of family life as a focus: health and illness, and the process of building and roofing the family dwelling. We also chose a more public activity, the processes associated with the buying and selling of cattle. In none of these areas do pastoral agents or missionaries enter as the principal actors.

The interviews were conducted in the Aymara language by young people from the area with secondary school and university-level education who then translated them into Spanish. In all, there were 108 interviews, 90 in the sector of Pilcuyo known as "18 de enero" and 18 in Cana Maquera, among a wide range of people. Copies of the interviews are located in the library of the Instituto de Pastoral Andina (IPA) in Cusco. In this publication, only the number of the interview is given in most cases.

We also used focus groups, conducted in the Aymara language, with the idea of more sharply defining some of the elements of religious identity to obtain clearer data on the relationship that the people establish between their faith and the daily problems they face.

For interpretation we followed the logic of the arguments in the collected testimonies. Similarly, for purposes of exposition, we selected representative quotes of a commonsense nature. Finally, to complete the analysis we reviewed previous studies conducted on popular religion in the Aymara areas of Peru and Bolivia.

During the entire research process we relied on the advice and guidance of a group of experts in the field of popular religion in Peru like Horténsia Muñoz, Manuel Marzal, Diego Irarrázaval, Carlos Flores, and Luis Mujica. We consulted with them on the design of the research instruments and received feedback and suggestions for the elaboration of this report. Peruvian theologian Gustavo Gutiérrez graciously offered us his comments and opinions.

The study is organized in the following way. In the next section we develop the theme of religious identity guided by the question of what it means to be a Catholic in Pilcuyo. Then, we investigate how one constructs, deepens, and celebrates this identity in the context of building a house and in the manner in which problems are solved. Next we examine the way Catholic identity is shaped amid the sociocultural changes that take place with an exploration of how Catholic identity is subject to transformations as they become manifest in an organized set of ritual practices.

Given the fact that our perspective is a theological and pastoral one, we will indicate in the final section how our understanding of the Gospel has been expanded and enriched by the findings of this research. Similarly, we will point out those areas that need further development before we can espouse them as uniquely Aymara contributions to shaping a truly inculturated Catholic Church and identity. We will also address the challenges the Church faces in drawing closer to the life of the people in contexts like those of Pilcuyo so that the Gospel will reach its fullness in particular indigenous settings.

For the elaboration of the final section we gathered data and input from members of different Christian churches during an ecumenical consultation organized in November 1996.

UNIQUE FEATURES OF CATHOLIC IDENTITY IN PILCUYO

Prior to their specifying or naming a distinct ecclesial identity, be it Catholic, Adventist, or any other, we discovered in the people of Pilcuyo a profound religious identity evidenced in an all-encompassing religious sense of life that connects all facets of it. For them God does not pose a problem, but is an ever present reality with whom they relate on an everyday basis. For many of us their way of naming and relating to God may seem strange. Even those aspects of life that might seem entirely secularized, such as trading and business dealings, are imbued with a strong religious sense that the people readily and naturally call faith. Variables in their lives like formal schooling, migration, and contact with the media of social communications act as secularizing influences without diminishing that religious identity.

Religious life in Pilcuyo is characterized by a concrete, dynamic, and integrating worldview that presupposes the construction of a unitary vision of the world. Faith expresses itself every day in the constant search for harmony in all relationships. Moreover, it has great bearing on the stages and passages of life, the family, the community, the education of children, working the land, the raising of animals, travel, and business undertakings.

Significantly, in Pilcuyo there is no official Aymara religion. What we discovered are a coherent belief system, customs, and a unique way of perceiving the world permeated by the Christian message which is constantly open to new interpretations. The decision to integrate onself into one or another group comes after the a priori acquisition of a religious sensibility toward life to which everyone is enculturated from an early age. Testimonies reveal the fact that people are free to choose the church to which they want to belong. Observing participation in neighborhood or community assemblies as well as in religious celebrations, one recognizes how people of different churches participate with the same level of interest and work toward the same objectives with identical fervor. Initially, this situation seemed strange to us, and not finding satisfactory explanations for it in the interview surveys, we looked for an answer through dialogue with the people and with the pastoral agents of the area.

Our conclusion is that there are several interrelated reference points that help to define the identity of the inhabitants of Pilcuyo. One is the neighborhood or communal organization, which, without necessarily having a religious character in itself, embodies an element of religious identity insofar as it contributes to making sense out of human existence. It is interwoven into the fabric of everyday life. There are also group referents centered on religious sensibility that flow out of the conviction of the existence of a single God.

The combination of these referents reveals high levels of religious coexistence and tolerance between Catholics and Adventists, which is vital in an environment where the daily struggle for survival is so strong that it requires collaboration among everyone. Recognition of a single God and a unified community are essential elements that hold the people together in a common life. These values relativize religious differences, especially when the churches are attentive to interpreting and supporting the just aspirations of the people. Bear in mind that the Adventist Church accompanied the people very closely in their demands for autonomy from the authorities and people of the more powerful town of Ilave, a fact that remains imbedded in the people's collective memory. Most Adventists, like the leader Gabino Flores, do not place any restrictions on participation in Catholic rituals, since "we respect all the churches and sects and we have no problems with them" (#27).

For Adventists as well as Catholics the Bible is the fundamental religious text. People perceive its teachings as a source of wisdom in their orientation for a more holistic life. No faithful Adventist or Catholic would deny this. However, the Bible in the life of Pilcuyo becomes a mark of differentiation, more closely tied to Adventism for being a central element in the formation of its faithful. One informant allows that "for me to be Catholic is not to be reading the Bible a lot" (#85).

For the people of Pilcuyo religion is necessary for its humanizing effect. It regulates relations, impeding the giving of free rein to one's more destructive impulses. Besides, they find in it protection and security. Religion provides a kind of guarantee for "being good." That aim of keeping things in balance and harmony becomes the primary reason for human existence, whether an Adventist Aymara is building a house or attending to a sick relative or friend or whenever a Catholic Aymara is making a ritual offering to the *Pachamama* (Earth Mother) or lighting a candle to a patron saint. What is most important is the prevention of illness, accidents, and fights in the community. Every explanation given in the interviews was accompanied by similar expressions of the need to *andar bien,* to live with integrity, to be on good terms with everyone and all of creation. In the rational world of the informants, religion occupies an important place in the generation, restoration, and promotion of life in its totality. A Catholic respondent claims that "without religion we would act like savages" (#14).

DIFFERENTIATION

By means of comparison specific religious identities are shaped and distinguished. In this way, coexistence in an environment marked by heterogeneous creeds brings one to affirm the difference of one's own religious identity over against the other person's. Recognizing the distinct characteristics allows people to affirm themselves in their particular choice of religious affiliation.

Identity traits refer more to particular beliefs and to ritual and ethical conduct than to dogmatic concepts or constructs. The Catholic Church is perceived by those who adhere to it as a space of freedom where it is possible to practice the customs of their ancestors, to celebrate the patronal feasts, drink liquor, dance, and eat all kinds of food. The Adventist Church is perceived and characterized by Catholics by the rigidity of its norms, dietary restrictions, and prohibitions based in its interpretation of the Old Testament. "Above all we are Catholics so that we don't forget or for being able to follow our customs of blessing our livestock, to remember our ties to the earth, to raise up the incense so that it will bring us a good harvest. When we go over to be with the brothers and sisters of the Seventh Day we forget those customs which they consider as unnecessary in their religion" (#79).

The concept of death also differentiates Catholics from Adventists with consequences for the ways one expresses oneself in the face of death. Catholics believe that the souls of the dead live on and that they need the support of our prayers. Beliefs like this enable the people to maintain reciprocal relationships on every level. On the other hand, Adventists deny that there is life after death since, according to their doctrine, human life ends totally until "after 1,000 years, the Holy Spirit descends and God allows all the pure ones from every generation to resurrect" (#28). For this reason, a relationship with departed loved ones would be, for the Adventists, an illusion and a prayer for the souls an effort in vain.

The fact that in Pilcuyo the people differentiate themselves is not indicative of closed religious identities. On the contrary, the boundaries that separate Catholics from Adventists are fairly fluid. We already said that it is possible to participate in one another's cult and rituals with a degree of ease and flexibility, not seeing any contradiction. This extends even to the point where Adventists think nothing of having their children baptized Catholic.

However, the diversity of the two principal religious alternatives raises doubts in both Catholics and Adventists. Increasingly, it was found that young people hesitate to identify themselves with any religious group in particular, although they do profess to believe in God and classify themselves as religious people.

Fears about being mistaken in one's choice of religion appear in not a few of the testimonies like this one: "Now there are several religions around and I'm not sure which one would be best, I can't make up my mind" (#51).

Daily interaction gives rise, through comparison, to the elaboration of a raison d'être for each of the two major churches. In this way, the proof or guarantee for religious authenticity is given fundamentally in the capacity to provide a coherent meaning for life, to maintain or reestablish relationships, or to contribute to the common good of the community. Every religion that helps to maintain and cultivate these values is considered valid and good.

In spite of this fundamental opening to religious diversity, daily conflicts give rise to sentiments of mistrust and aggression toward that which is different. Catholic informants judge the behavior of Adventists as inconsequential with comments like this: "I think that the Adventists only proclaim their belief in God on Saturdays, but when a conflict over land ownership arises they act worse than when one of us gets drunk. They always look in the Bible, but they don't live up to what the Bible says. With us Catholics we always can repair a relationship that goes bad, but the Adventists don't look for ways to repair it" (#63). Conversely, Adventists view their Catholic neighbors as inconsistent in their drinking behavior, in aggressive acts, and for unwisely investing all of their resources into religious celebrations.

In spite of the fact that both groups recognize common traits, Catholics express the need to underscore specific characteristics of their religious identity, motivated by the presence of the Adventist church building as well as the formation classes and meetings that are so visibly a part of Adventist identity. Catholics in Pilcuyo lament the absence of a church building and seek out opportunities from the pastoral team for more formation and instruction in the Catholic faith as a way to make them feel different from their Adventist brothers and sisters.

In the construction of the whole complex set of sacred times, places, and relationships, religious rituals play an extremely important role for everyone. When someone in Pilcuyo says that he or she practices religious rituals like "our ancestors did" or because it "is the custom here," he or she is making a strong claim for Catholic religious identity. In fact, Adventists for their part sometimes attack and satanize Catholic ritual practices, which they attribute to the work of the devil on earth. In order to be a good Adventist, in the opinion of one of their leaders, "one has to leave aside vices related to drinking liquor and flirting with members of the opposite sex," actions that they believe are an integral part of Catholic ritual life (#42).

The Catholic Church in the southern Andes region of Peru, especially since the 1969 founding of the Instituto de Pastoral Andina (IPA), has developed a theological reflection and pastoral practice around the conviction that the Andean people "are not far from having discovered God by a way far different from ours" (Campredon 1992, 180). Such a change of attitude enabled campesinos of Aymara and Quechua extraction to incorporate their own traditions and customs as distinctive traits of their Catholic identity.

Like the acceptance of Andean traditions, the celebration of the Mass as a communitarian experience is a recurrent characteristic of Catholic identity. Many informants stated that Catholics are those who attend Sunday Mass, but also noted that many do not. Among the Aymara, Masses for the dead, for health, and in the wake of natural catastrophes are the most sought after Catholic celebrations.

One characteristic of Catholic identity that is in a process of development is the Feast of Corpus Christi. Before Pilcuyo achieved its political autonomy from Ilave, the nucleus of its popular expression of Catholic faith was celebrated on this patronal feast in the month of June. Once the community underwent this transformation, however, the feast day and its devotions lost a considerable degree of their unifying force. Now civic celebrations have replaced such feasts as moments to unite the whole community, although they don't fully respond to the religious needs of Pilcuyo's Catholics. For them Corpus Christi continues to be a source of religious differentiation, and its celebration binds Pilcuyo to other communities of the altiplano with its array of processions, offerings, blessings, and dances. It was very difficult for the people to fully explain the meaning of Corpus Christi before the pastoral team presented the community with the gift of a picture of the image of the Sacred Heart. The image provides a symbolic representation to which the people make offerings and light candles.

Faith is a recurrent topic of conversation. Faith, associated with certain beliefs, carries with it a profound conviction and an interior attitude that permeates all of life's key moments, giving them meaning, strengthening the ties between people, and encouraging them to carry on with a sense of hope in the face of difficulties. Faith is not necessarily identified with the content of one particular religious expression. Rather it encapsulates the fervor with which a person prays to *andar bien,* a deep-seated faith that one's prayers will be answered if only "the person put all of his or her will power into it" (#5).

So that things in life "go well," faith is an indispensable factor. To lack faith is to fall into shame and suffer misfortune. Faith is very related to a sense of coherence that goes beyond a feeling of individual intimacy. It always has a communitarian and familial dimension in its intention as well as in its expression. Here is also where we see the practice of one's faith as a further sign of differentiation between Catholics and Adventists.

Prayer or "raising up the name of God" is conceived of by everyone as an act proper to faith, but Catholics hold out the possibility of expressing it with a wider range of symbolic actions, resorting to a multiplicity of mediations that have been nurtured throughout many years. Thus, Catholics pray to the saints, make offerings to the *Pachamama,* light candles to accompany their supplications, seek out *yatiris* (local religious practitioners with shamanic powers) to perform their rites or solicit the services of a priest to celebrate a Mass. For some these are ways to access the divine and are practically indispensable. For others this is not the case.

Such faith expressions, be it a prayer or an offering, carry with them something of what is known uniquely in the Aymara world as *ayni,* a central feature of Aymara culture and relationships that connotes reciprocity in daily interchanges and a set of mutual obligations that regulates life in the altiplano. It also signifies a sense of personal sacrifice offered up to the divine. What distinguishes an act of faith from ordinary reciprocal transactions is that the person seeking an answer to prayer throws himself or herself totally into the prayer in the hope of receiving a favor. This transcends any other act based on reciprocity or mutual obligations by its relationship to an absolute higher power, according to our informants.

Through the different faith expressions people experience God as a companion on the journey, a protector and a defender against adversity who helps them overcome loneliness and makes it possible for everything to "turn out well." Faith is an all-encompassing and permanent state of mind out of which they relate to God.

Catholic identity in Pilcuyo, then, takes shape in the course of everyday life within a cultural matrix that has a strong religious point of reference, and with a level of self-understanding that surpasses any doctrinal formulation.

Diversification of religious identities places one's very identity in crisis and provokes doubts in the people that often lead to conflicts among family members and neighbors. However, awareness of the precarious nature of life that all share strengthens the consciousness of unity, rendering apparent differences of relative value. An effort to bring together everyone's different contributions to overcome conflicts and live in closer harmony remains an unfinished goal.

To belong to a particular religion implies having a bedrock faith which makes possible divine protection and more humanitarian interpersonal relationships. A coherent, holistic lifestyle is considered a sign of religious authenticity. The most important quality, from a religious standpoint, is not that people belong to this or that church, but that they are believers and feel themselves a part of the same community and race of people. This does not detract from a desire among Catholics for certain visible symbols like a church building or a center for religious formation that would contribute to shaping their own identity.

SHAPING CATHOLIC IDENTITY IN THE EVERYDAY LIFE OF PILCUYO

THE CONSTRUCTION OF THE FAMILY HOME

To have one's own house implies a new mode of insertion into established social networks for a newly married couple and carries with it a set of mutual responsibilities and obligations. The building and roofing of a house constitute a ritual process that culminates in the transition to adulthood for the Aymara. As one man of a nearby community stated bluntly, "While I didn't have my own house, I was a nobody. But when my wife and I built our house, I knew finally that I was the head of my family" (#91).

Parents play an important role in encouraging a young couple to embark upon a new life together, thus ending the stage of moral and economic dependence and responsibility for them. Building and owning a house constitute the ideal expression of human maturity in the culture. It is common for the parents of both young people to provide resources for their children when they are starting their life together. The parents of the bride ordinarily contribute a heifer, while the parents of the groom donate a bull, the economic and symbolic basis for the couple to begin their own family and educate their children. Significantly, the roofing ceremony and not the marriage rite celebrates this status of a new kind of incorporation into the community (Albó 1996, 137).

The daily routine of the people of Pilcuyo does not transpire, however, within the confines of the house but on the cultivated lands, pastures and grazing areas, in the marketplace and the far-off cities where they migrate in search of temporary employment. The house is where one begins and ends one's different journeys, the point of departure and homecoming. All of the informants underscored the importance of the house and family dwelling as a place of protection and security. The metaphor most applied to the house is of a nesting place for birds, especially in terms of the frequent migrations. One Pilcuyo resident accepts migration as a fact of life, but for him "home is still the best place and an anchor in an otherwise hostile world of instability" (#103).

The house also takes on importance as a temple or sanctuary. One of the first things that a child learns from his or her parents is that their home and the area surrounding it constitute a sacred space occupied by protector spirits called *uywiri*, which are akin to guardian angels (Albó 1996, 130). On the basis of the interviews themselves it is difficult to determine whether these protector spirits refer to God or the Earth Mother *Pachamama*, but what is certain is that they convey a sense of the nearness of God and are not multiple deities. For the people of Pilcuyo and the Aymara there is but one God, whose mediation and action are seen more clearly through the presence of these spirits.

Rituals utilized in the construction of a house reinforce the importance of the family in a time when community and district structures are often weak and transitory. More and more, the family home takes on significance in the life of the people of Pilcuyo as an enclave out of which one extends himself or herself into the network of relationships with the outside world, and as a point of connection with the past and the future.

A new house represents a rootedness in the past and a bond with one's ancestors and their traditions and customs, cementing a distinct identity. There one recognizes the millenarian wisdom upon which the future is to be built, a storehouse of knowledge that allows one to adjust constantly to new situations. Custom is not merely a servile reproduction of the past, but rather a recreation of the tradition in the present.

Affirmed in the ties to the land and rooted in tradition, the house becomes the place for building identity and tying together the network of social relations. Our informants confirm that among both Adventists and Catholics the construction of a house is a deeply religious experience, although there are variations in the rituals due to changes brought about by the influences of migration or education outside the community. Housebuilding is an ongoing process open to periodic transformations and modifications. New rooms are added as needs arise, but ritual practices remain constant, especially with reference to laying the foundation and placing the roof.

The land where the home is to be built has a name: the *Pachamama,* benevolent and dangerous at the same time, the source of life and a threat. Therefore, before pouring the cement for the foundation, offerings are made and the borders of the house are carefully designated so as to mark the limits between the threatening chaos of the outside world, where the struggle for life takes place, and the place of rest, where the recuperation of forces, fecundity, and intimate communication that constitute a home takes place. Those who come to lay the foundation ask permission and pardon from the *Pachamama,* present their petition, and make offerings. The *despacho* or offering, often called a "Mass," is made up of sweets, coca leaves, amulets of several kinds, strings of brightly colored thread or yarn, alcohol, and incense, which represent the *ayni* relationship described above. All this is performed by the *yatiri* in the presence of the entire family and their neighbors.

Besides the "Mass" offering and the demarcation of the limits separating the house from the outside world, *ají* (a hot pepper), onion, and salt are placed by the cement workers in the four corners. They serve as reminders for the family of their customs.

The moment of the roofing is marked by another ritual ceremony called the *wilancha* that consists of an offering of blood in honor of the *uywiri,* or house protector spirits. A lamb, llama, or alpaca is beheaded and its blood is poured into a basin mixed with paper confetti to be splashed on all the walls of the house by both spouses, who are owners of the house. The *mixtura* of finely chopped paper of bright colors signifies both joy and prosperity. The *wilancha* is a type of *ayni* in which protection for the family against accidents is requested. But, according to one informant, "We have to make this blood offering and blessing so as to communicate better with God" (#13). The meat of the animal is shared by everyone in attendance to further seal the bonds of community.

Roofing the house with straw, as opposed to the more common practice today of using tin sheeting, conveyed a greater sense of collaboration with the entire community, since it involved more people working together. It was followed by a fiesta at which those who didn't participate were severely criticized and later ostracized by the community. Tin roofing does not require as many helpers, but whether with straw or tin, a roofing ceremony is replete with a joyous outburst of celebration followed by an abundant meal shared by everyone.

House construction with its attendant ceremonies is important for everyone, Catholic and Adventist alike, as it signifies the beginning of one's entrance into life as a full-fledged adult. The central place of the tents in Adventist initiation rites coincides perfectly with the house construction rituals, with the different layers of meaning easily transferable. Therefore, converts to Adventism do not have to renounce one of the most deeply felt Aymara customs. Many of the ritual offerings and symbolic gestures of the Catholic adherents, however, are replaced by prayers, usually pronounced by an Adventist elder.

Thus, in spite of the unifying elements present in the construction of the house, there are significant marks of differentiation that allow Catholics and Adventists to distinguish themselves from one another. These characteristics do not find their source either in Catholic doctrine or in the Gospel, but are part and parcel of everyday religious practice.

CHRISTIAN FAITH AND LIFE PROBLEMS

Generalized poverty and the precarious nature of life in the altiplano make the problems of everyday existence stand out sharply. In this section we will offer an approach to some of the difficulties that the people of Pilcuyo face every day, describing how their Catholic faith helps them to deal with problem situations.

Family Relationships

To speak adequately of gender relationships among the Aymara people requires the researcher to take care not to use Western categories that do not easily transfer to Aymara cultural paradigms. Pilcuyo is an example of a place where social relations have been affected by multiple change processes and *mestizaje* (the encounter between Aymara and the dominant Spanish culture). Interaction with the modern world gives rise to new problems and the shaping of a changed worldview.

In the relationship between spouses, there is an ideal of complementarity and reciprocity that should result in shared decision making in the family. In fact, the interviews point to a common practice of consultation and deliberation between spouses when making decisions such as the choice of a site on which to build the family home.

Interpreting the data at hand, we tend to think of this practice as more of an ideal than the norm. More often than not, we concluded that there is a subordination of the woman to the man, although this is not as extreme as elsewhere. This fact is borne out in the high level of illiteracy among Aymara women, which keeps them in a state of unfulfilled potential. Moreover, this is a cause of a great deal of suffering; many women lamented the fact that they had to remain at home while their male counterparts were sent to school.

Another proof of persistent subordination that is the source of conflict is women not being recognized as full participants at community meetings but only as "representatives of their husbands." On the part of many women there is a tacit acceptance of this, although they are beginning to become more conscious of the limited role assigned to them. In the interviews women often expressed the pain of being excluded from having a full voice and voting at public gatherings.

We hasten to add that gender status in Aymara society does not constitute a mark of religious identity. However, men's behavior affects women's freedom to decide on whether to affiliate with the Adventist Church. One woman bemoaned the fact that when her husband was chosen as a community leader he had to hide his Adventist identity. Consequently, she was also expected to refrain from Adventist religious practice as long as her husband held this authority position in the community.

Alcoholism is one of the most serious problems affecting the relationship between spouses and is notably more present in those households that call themselves Catholic. Although both men and women drink often, excessive drinking is more pronounced among men. This leads to spouse abuse with the woman suffering the consequences in most cases. In the words of one woman, "When my husband comes home angry and drunk, he hits me rather than the one who made him angry. After some discussion, however, we pardon each other" (#33). In the face of these conflicts the Adventist Church requires strict adherence to prohibitions against drinking and spouse abuse.

The common pattern of resolving conflict in family relations and among families is through pardon and reconciliation, motivated, to a great extent, by a basic feature of the religiosity found in the Aymara culture. Underneath this practice of pardon and reconciliation is the need to ensure harmony in this life and the hereafter. Prayer, or the oft used expression "raising up the name of God," is an important recourse for those who face any kind of problem situation, including problems within the family.

In the resolution of interpersonal conflicts, at the family as well as the communal level, religiosity has a very important role to play. The Aymara paradigm of the need to build harmony in every aspect of life is strengthened and encouraged through the pastoral accompaniment of the churches which encourages ritual gestures of pardon. Prayer, likewise, serves as a way to foster reconciliation.

Health and Sickness

Illness is an accepted fact of life among the people of Pilcuyo and is understood as both an organic and a psychological disturbance, with a multiplicity of manifestations that place people in limit situations. Among the causes for illness mentioned in the interviews are the harsh climate of the altiplano that mainly affects children, insufficient nutrition attributed to scarce economic opportunities, contamination of water and food, epidemics, the lack of hygiene, and even holes in the atmosphere's ozone layer. But, above and beyond every other factor, illness is explained by imbalances and disruptions in relationships within the community, in nature, and with God. And, it is perceived as a warning sign "that things are not going all that well" (#41).

The means employed to restore order and balance are intrinsically religious. In practice, we can distinguish two areas of approach in the fight against illness. The first and more traditional one is based on the application of natural medicines, which underlines the need for divine intervention in the therapeutic process of recovery. The second means, derived from conventional modern medicine, cannot be separated from religious motivations since the interviewees speak constantly of the need to set oneself right with God to prevent illness, and make frequent appeals to prayer.

In the face of illness the people of Pilcuyo proceed in the following manner. If the case appears ordinary, it is treated in the home with herbs or other natural elements. If the sickness persists, one is likely to consult a local *curandero* or healer. This specialist in traditional medicine undertakes a diagnosis to determine if the solution to the problem falls within the scope of his or her competence, or if the person should go to the local medical station or hospital.

The healers are called *qolliri* (modern medicine men and women), but many refer to them as *yatiri* (literally "one who knows"), the same name given to Aymara ritual practitioners and specialists. The healers exercise a true religious ministry at the service of the health of the people. Almost all, men and women alike, are elderly people who have accumulated a vast experience on which their credibility and prestige are based. They exercise their vocations of healing bolstered by the wisdom and authority of tradition and enjoy wide confidence among the people.

Generally, the healers are self-identified Catholics with a clear awareness that they carry out a sacred mission granted by God, who both guides them and calls them to accountability. Therefore, they exercise this ministry as a voluntary service to the community without expecting much payment. There is usually a voluntary offering of money or food products. Since for the people of Pilcuyo health is so closely related to the religious worldview, and given their modest economic means, resorting to *yatiris* or healers is a very natural course of action.

The *qolliris* or specialists in herbal medicine follow prescribed procedures and rituals. In order to find out the origin of an illness they utilize the sacred coca leaf, which serves not only as an offering but also as a way of consulting with the divine being. Through reading the coca leaf they also determine what rituals and offerings are required to restore the patient to full health.

Among all the illnesses two in particular call especially for the intervention of the *qolliri* because their cure involves a prescribed ritual. One is the *katja* or seizure. The other has to do with a *susto,* which means falling into a general state of fright or shock.

During the months of December, January, and February the altiplano is afflicted by strong electrical storms. While the rainy season is propitious for agricultural production, it is a fearful time because of potential damage to homes and crops by lightning. Places where lightning strikes are called "Calvary" and are considered accursed sites related to the devil. They pose a constant threat of illness for those who unknowingly pass their way. Such places are like a "deep well possessing powers that can capture an unsuspecting person," according to one interviewee (#95). Seizures of this kind can result in the loss of appetite, weight, and strength, and in high fevers and convulsions.

An affliction of this kind calls for the offering to the *Pachamama* of a *despacho* of herbs and coca, during which God's name and the names of the places where the lightning struck are invoked. Reading the coca leaf one can find out the names of these fearful places. Often a Catholic priest is asked to celebrate Mass in an affected home; the liturgy is attended by family, friends, and neighbors. Following the Mass the house and its surrounding areas are blessed and a reconciliation rite takes place in which everyone participates. This is done in the hope that people have adequately responded to this sign, and to pay attention to real or perceived wrongs that were committed in the community.

According to Adventist custom, people pray in the place where lightning strikes, but without employing the same traditional ritual practices. They do attend them when invited by family and neighbors.

The *susto* or scare is a type of malady that especially affects children. It is commonly said that "a person's spirits have sunk" and that he or she begins to lose weight. Other symptoms of the *susto* include the grinding of teeth, sleepless nights, and waking up frightened. Healing cannot occur unless the spirit is reunited with the person.

The healer sets out to determine through reading the coca leaves how and when the person was seized by fright. Then all of the person's clothes are washed. Articles of clothing next are wrapped around a soda pop bottle, an improvised doll-like object in the shape of an infant. With the doll in hand the healer goes about the area to the places where the *susto* supposedly took place, often ringing a small bell and calling for the spirit to return. All the while the healer is in a prayerful state of mind. Several informants reported that a lost spirit often reappears in the shadow of a dog, a bird, or even a drunken man walking along the road, whereupon the spirit is called out of them. One of the signs that the spirit has reappeared is when the person starts to sleep peacefully again.

It is more common among Adventists to shun this traditional form of healing in favor of consultation with the doctors at a local medical station or the well-known and reputable Adventist Clinic in the city of Juliaca, two hours away. But Adventists readily admit their mistrust of the medical facilities and personnel in the case of the *susto*. In these situations they are more likely to rely on consultation with the community elders and prayers to plead for the return of the person's spirit.

Traditional medicine and reliance on healers and *qolliris* are the preferred form of treatment in the Aymara world and particularly in Pilcuyo, chiefly for the practical reason that conventional medical care is deficient and costly. Significantly, modern scientific medicine is also suspect for representing the alienation of the outside world and because of fear of the unknown. People are inclined to trust what is familiar and what they feel protects them in their own surroundings. Moreover, there is a certain intimacy that comes with the familiar touch and consoling words and prayers of the healers. It contrasts with the cold, impersonal styles of Western-trained medical professionals.

Treatment with herbs and plants from the area is preferred to the methods of modern medicine with its assortment of pills, injections, and the newer medical technology found in the local hospitals, though the prevention of diseases by means of vaccinations is generally accepted in the Aymara world. Cures are attributed to herbs applied in the confidence of a long tradition of use and the common wisdom of generations of local healers. They are believed to come from the *Pachamama* and are customarily gathered on Good Friday and brought to the churches for blessing on that day.

Whenever health is threatened, the religious sentiments of the people become more visibly present. They demonstrate the efficacy of tradition and the more cohesive aspects of the community with its vital connection to nature and the whole cosmos. Except for variations in ritual performance, there are few traces of confessional differentiation in the therapeutic processes we have described here. The realm of health is one where traditional healers and *qolliris* hold sway. While other elements of modernity are tenaciously pursued by the Aymara, medicine remains the preserve of ancestral beliefs and practices of a natural origin.

Difficulties Related to the Raising and Sale of Cattle

Cattle raising is the principal economic activity and source of monetary income in Pilcuyo. Almost every family possesses, or at one time possessed, two or three head of beef cattle, utilized for fattening, agricultural work, and eventually for sale. This activity provides families with a source of cash in case of emergency. For nearly every informant, cattle are considered a savings account. Money derived from the sale of cattle goes toward the purchase of food, school uniforms and supplies, to pay off debts, and for the costs incurred in building a house. Finally, cattle raising involves everyone in the family; children, except during school hours, assume equal responsibility for pasturing the animals.

Cattle are fattened using the forage of the area, including scant amounts of barley, but especially the *totora* reeds that grow on the shores and inlets of Lake Titicaca. Cattle raising is a difficult undertaking for a number of reasons, chiefly the scarcity of land to grow forage. There are also the harsh climatic conditions and the few resources available to families to buy the necessary feed.

The buying and selling of animals take place every Thursday in a large area on the outskirts of the town. The most propitious time for selling is during the rainy season, from January through April. Because of excess forage at that time of year, the cattle are likely to bring a better price. However, economic necessity makes a sale possible at any time.

If for some reason a family loses all of its cattle, the people of Pilcuyo have two alternatives. The first is for one of the family members to migrate to a coastal city in search of work to buy another animal. When this isn't possible, a family will ask another family with more cattle to share a cow with them. They, in turn, will feed it until it can give birth. Then a calf is given to the family from whom the cow was "borrowed."

Cattle raising also falls within the scope of living an integral life or of being on good terms with everyone. For Catholics, prayer for the health and well-being of animals is always mediated by set rituals such as lighting candles to St. Isidore, the patron saint of animals, or by making an offering to the *Pachamama*.

The raising of livestock in Pilcuyo provides only satisfactory results for the people. It requires many sacrifices not compensated for by the scant economic return. Inclement weather and a heavy investment in feed and forage during the dry season often lock farmers and their families deeper into the cycle of poverty. The demands of intensive labor and the role of intermediaries or middlemen lessen the chances for any kind of profit from livestock. Alternatives to the monopoly exercised by outside buyers are few. Most of our informants said that individual efforts are preferable to joining cooperatives or other associations. Organizations have been considerably weakened over the past several years in the southern Andes and have lost a great deal of credibility. Conflicts with neighbors over landownership and boundaries make cooperative endeavors all the more difficult. Pilcuyo is an area where many organizational initiatives have been tried in the past with few positive results, making people suspicious of state and nongovernmental organizations alike.

Among our informants there are some who believe it is important to pursue an organizational alternative. They are generally younger people who have had experience outside the community. Through an organization of cattle raisers they envision advantages such as better production, the ability to negotiate a just price, and transportation to more profitable areas for sale. They also claim a greater role for the government in regulating the sale of cattle and as a provider of credits, loans, and incentives for greater production. Most people interviewed realize the unjust imbalance that exists with rural people subsidizing better-off city dwellers. However, most feel helpless about changing the system even as they take pride in "raising cattle for high-quality meat." Many see the Church playing a role as a mediator in their favor vis-à-vis outside organizations and the government.

The world of commerce with its various pitfalls stands over against the secure world epitomized in the family dwelling. Religiosity is lived out in different ways in each area. If the sphere of familial relationships in the home is permeated by a religious spirit that sacralizes many aspects of daily life, another spirit rules the sphere of the cattle market. There the rules and whims of the competitive market reign supreme. One must abide by them to gain a modicum of success. At the same time, religion has its place in the commercial arena as evidenced in the common practice of prayer in the home on Thursday mornings before going to market to sell animals.

APPROPRIATION AND ELABORATION OF CHANGE

Given the harsh climatic conditions of the altiplano, with its great differences of temperature between night and day, and its alternating periods of drought, frost, and floods, we can appreciate the great adaptive capacity of the people. Despite the range of natural adversities, they have been able not only to survive but also to continue, against all kinds of odds, to give shape to a life project. Adversity in the altiplano is not limited, however, to the vagaries of climatic change. One cannot forget the suffering and margination throughout its history.

Neither can one erase the political violence, marked by the constant violation of human rights, that afflicted the country in recent decades, paralyzing any initiatives for development. Nor can one desist from considering the negative impact of current policies of economic structural adjustment.

All of this has generated, particularly among young people, an attitude of "confidence in no one" (Instituto de Pastoral Andina 1990). This is all the more understandable insofar as the state has not expressed or defended the interests of the majority of the people of the country. Older people in Pilcuyo point to "a dangerous and unstable future for our children. Before, education held unquestioned value. Now it has none. Today, everyone goes along his/her own path without concern for the other" (#56).

The campesino community, which until recently remained solid as a space in which to treat common problems, find solutions, and share responsibility, has declined in power and influence. A young man in the community, Vicente Alanoca, takes a dim view of the short- and long-term future of the campesino community. He points to migration, internal divisions, and a lack of cohesion as chief factors in its inviability as a place for problem solving. Traditional sanctions no longer hold people accountable. The economic demands of each family unit override common community projects. There is insufficient flexibility in the structure or social mores to allow for the participation of women. Finally, the emergence of a mentality that places individual effort over the needs of the collective unit deals a severe blow to a once tightly knit social fabric (#49).

The allure of modernity has reached the Andes through education, the media, migration, and urbanization, though in places like Pilcuyo, "the possibility of thinking about the world and society without recourse to external forces like God or transcendental principles other than human reason" has not penetrated to the core of the Aymara worldview (Urbano, 1992: VIII, 13). The majority of the people continue to explain life, the world, and what happens therein in a nondichotomous manner, showing evidence of a more integrated worldview that includes a normal relationship with the transcendent.

Temporary migration has contributed to a reconstruction of the rural campesino structure. The city is a model to imitate and an achievable goal. If young people finish their studies, their parents automatically assume that they will no longer have to suffer as they do and will have opportunities for better employment. Migration is not just an option, but an attractive aspiration shared by parents and children alike.

A consequence of migration is a new conception of the relationship between city and countryside. People in our study are more aware of the countryside's importance as a provider of food supplies and services that the city needs. Typical of this awareness is the remark of 29-year-old Juan Gilberto Caxi, who views the government as "a necessary mediator to regulate the exploitation of our people by city dwellers" (#4).

The tendency toward an urban mind-set is evident in how people in Pilcuyo proudly view the town as the district capital. This is all the more visible in the style of new buildings and in the way that space is organized. The altiplano countryside of open skies and wide horizons is now dotted by the mixed profile of adobe and cement houses, straw and tin roofs, small doors and wide glass windows coexisting within the same space and time. It is a kind of metaphor of the dynamic spirit of Pilcuyo's populace. This is a spirit that merges the old with the new, and moves toward the future with hope, although not without a critical attitude toward what the outside world may offer. Throughout the interviews one perceives a profound relationship with the past, which is recreated and reinterpreted in a dynamic fashion as a paradigm for the future. The desire for progress and integration into the modern urban world is not only a dream in the district capital but a worldview shared throughout the surrounding countryside.

The way of constructing a house is determined by the economic conditions of the family, but is equally influenced by a desire for progress and modernization and the advantages these offer. There is a decided preference for building a cement house rather than one with adobe bricks, since in the view of many informants, "it will last longer and we don't want people to think that we are backward" (#30). Iron rods rise up to the sky as the inhabitants of new dwellings foresee a second and even third floor in their future vision.

Durability and practicality are prime values and considerations in construction. Whatever the benefits in terms of heat afforded by a straw roof, the ease of placing a tin roof more than compensates for it. Still, for rooms or adjacent buildings to store produce and potato seeds a family will often choose a straw roof. All of this demonstrates a logic that combines the old and new in a synthetic way.

The main axis on which life turns in Pilcuyo is no longer agriculture or livestock, or even the land itself. Mobility, education, a money economy, and interchange with urban centers contribute enormously to the sense of life of the people and to the ways they construct their space and time. When the vans and buses that speed along the highways of the altiplano filled with people dressed in traditional garb stop to pick up others along the way, impatient passengers often yell at the driver not to delay and become quite angry when he does. The cyclical notion of time and an easy pace of life have given way to the hurry dictated by market concerns.

Confessional identities don't seem to bear too much relevance to this commitment to the dynamics of change for a people submerged in this process. People expect their churches to embrace change and modernity and still foster a spirit of harmony. The religious spirit so much in evidence and a reliance on divine intervention in every dimension of life, from illness to business dealings, the raising of animals, and the education of children, continue to hold sway among the Aymara of Pilcuyo.

THE ROLE OF THE CHURCH IN TIMES OF CHANGE

In this study we have examined everyday experience and have sketched the portrait of a people endowed with a form of Catholic faith in a process of histori-

cal development. Their life is unfettered by the control of the institutional Church
and is nourished by a dynamic tradition that unfolds through successive adaptations, reformulations and transformations, shaped by generations of ancestors.
The same dynamic of openness to the new is operative today with the phenomenon
of modernity.

We will reflect now on the mission of the Church in the midst of this people
undergoing vast changes with regard to their identity. The Catholics of Pilcuyo
are potentially co-responsible subjects and valid interlocutors in the dialogue of
salvation that constitutes evangelization today. In this sense, we speak of a missionary church called to convoke them to be and to recognize themselves as a
church of the People of God. This is a daunting challenge because the people of
Pilcuyo, by and large, do not yet see themselves reflected in these categories, nor
do they possess self-awareness as co-responsible agents for shaping their church
in the image of the Aymara culture and religious worldview.

Since the Second Vatican Council (1962-1965), a fruitful time for the workings of the Holy Spirit, a new theological language with a missionary focus has
begun to unfold. It has been developed in numerous documents that shape the
Church's magisterium. Such documents speak of adaptation, incarnation, dialogue, and inculturation, all of which presuppose an openness to the world as
their starting point. In recent years the southern Andes Church has placed much
more emphasis on the pastoral challenges of inculturation.

The kind of discourse present in these reflections signals a shift in mentality
as well as a retrieval of fundamental aspects of ecclesiology. Herein lies an invitation to pay attention to how the Lord is revealed in the "other," in the person
who is different—in short, to bless God's name in every language and within
every culture.

By allowing ourselves to be led by "what we have heard, what we have seen
with our eyes, what we have examined and what our hands have felt, the Word
that is life" (1 John 1:1) has become manifest in Pilcuyo. We will now touch on
four areas of the Church's mission as they apply to Pilcuyo: inculturation, ecumenical dialogue, social change, and ritual expressions. Into this reflection we
will introduce valuable elements shared by the participants in a November 1996
ecumenical consultation that took place in conjunction with this research project.

INCULTURATION OF THE GOSPEL

Throughout this study we have underscored in different ways the ability of the
people of Pilcuyo to define themselves in the face of influences and possibilities
for change from outside their culture so as to arrive at a synthesis between their
traditional values and new elements that they consider valuable. This capacity to
absorb change becomes particularly apparent in the process of constructing their
own religious identity. In inculturation, diverse actors and protagonists converge.
Among them is the people to whom the Gospel is addressed. This is precisely the
point that overturns the conventional missionary model in effect for centuries,

based on a tabula rasa approach according to which little or no role was given to the recipients of Christian mission. In fact, this was a one-directional model with little room for dialogue.

Inculturation involves a richer and more complex process. It presupposes the interaction of many subjects: God, the people of diverse cultures, and the missionary Church, all of whom enter into the process of dialogue in which they are subjects and equal partners. Under this model the objective of mission would not be limited solely to the transmission of doctrinal concepts and ethical norms, but to broadening and sharing the scope of revelation, guided by the Spirit, to enable every partner to grasp the depth of their own lives and traditions. The goal of evangelization in this scheme would be to learn about each other and the patterns of each other's history and to be instructed together into the "whole truth" (John 16:13).

Moreover, this paradigm of inculturation presupposes that the people themselves become the subjects of their own history and faith. It also presupposes that the Church is called to look into the depth of the lives of its members and discover there the signs of the presence of God, in order to proclaim them as promptings and guarantees of the promised Reign of God. The coming of the Reign of God within the human community demands the contribution of a multiplicity of charisms, the recognition of all the services and ministries that prepare us to receive it and calls us to lives of co-responsibility in the face of the challenges of history.

For some 30 years the Church of the southern Andes, made up of five dioceses and prelatures, has cultivated a spirit of contemplation and listening to discover the action of God in the lives of the people of this region. At the same time, the Church has redefined its role in terms of "accompanying the people" to become a prophetic voice against social injustice and an advocate for the defense of life. But it is still necessary to put aside the bad habits of a vertical, top-down approach and attitudes of paternalism and maternalism that impede us from contemplating the truth that "bursts forth from the earth" so as to traverse the road of history and cultures of the people, the places and times of salvation from the very moments in which "the Word of God became flesh and dwelt among us" (John 1:14).

This process involves learning how to discover in the "other" the presence of the Reign of God, the possibility of articulating a different version of history and a new meaning of the value of life in these times of change. It means leaving aside all pretensions of proselytization, imposition, and domination. In this search for an inculturated church the Aymara people of Pilcuyo contribute their profound sense of the sacredness of all of life. This is like a spring of water that runs its hidden course through the nighttime of history only to burst forth now in the present.

The people of Pilcuyo not only experience the nearness of God, but speak with and about God with surprising ease. Affirming life and searching for its fullness, they proclaim God present in the poorest of God's children. In this way they are shaping a theology based on the paradigm of the sacredness of life with their own unique language of images, gestures, symbols, and words and offer these to the rest of the human family. Insofar as the Church scrutinizes the "signs of the times" it is called to embrace this insight into the mystery of life and incorporate it into its patrimony.

In Pilcuyo the people say that to be religious and particularly Catholic one must *andar bien,* live a life of integrity and wholeness. With this ideal in mind, they "raise up the name of God" in prayer and practice their ritual life in this spirit. What instantly comes to mind is what Christians pray daily at the end of the Liturgy of the Hours: that "the Lord bless us and keep us from all evil and bring us life everlasting." If we relate this blessing with the ritual dismissal prayer of the Aymara that closes any religious ceremony—"que sea buena hora" or "may you leave now feeling good and whole"—we detect a continuous and common thread, namely, that a good relationship with the transcendent is, for them and for us, a source of life.

If the people of Pilcuyo have offered the institutional Church an understanding of mission in terms of dialogue, then, in all justice, we ask what the Church offers in exchange. In answer to that question I will point out some elements that, separate from the Church's evangelization project, are tacitly or explicitly recognized as such offerings by the people of Pilcuyo.

The first deals with the connection with the great tradition that begins with the historical Jesus, of offering all peoples a new understanding of the meaning of their histories. To make this connection with the lived history of the Church demands a good deal of creativity and a serious effort to create those spaces and opportunities for Christian formation in which the people have access to the knowledge of the Scriptures. The possibility of reflecting on Scripture in light of their own life experience allows new interpretations to surface and enables people to celebrate the originality of their way of living out the Christian message.

Authentic Catholic identity is defined primarily by a living relationship with Jesus Christ in which one is invited to follow him. In the testimonies we gathered one does not detect a clear reference to the person of Jesus nor to the demands he sets out for the community of believers. There is, however, among the people a basic disposition to welcome and develop a Christological and ecclesiological sense of the evangelical values of reconciliation, pardon, and solidarity and an identification with the suffering of Jesus so visibly present in their spirituality. It is up to a Church imbued with a missionary spirit to provide the necessary means so that the potentiality of this relationship be enabled to unfold in the fullest way possible.

The strong and persistent claim of the Catholics for their own church building in Pilcuyo is an aspiration motivated by Adventist influence. However, it touches on a more basic religious sensibility. Support for this endeavor could provide the incentive for a process of consolidation, whereby the Christian community would become that temple of "living stones" and a true place of encounter with God and each other (1 Peter 2:5).

As we have seen, the family home is conceived of as a temple. This is a concept that could be reinforced and strengthened with the presence of a church building in a town where the wider regional community congregates and where the Christian community shares and celebrates its common faith.

This theme also raises many other questions. Would the construction of a Catholic church reinforce localistic sentiments overshadowing the spirituality of a relationship with God "in Spirit and truth" (John 4:23)? Would such a place of worship encourage feelings of superiority on the part of Catholics in relation to weaker, minority groups in the community? Would a church block the way to the growth of a living church incarnated in the life of the people?

For an answer to these questions we turn to the practical wisdom of the people. Having recognized the presence of God in their lives, they search for ways to nourish their religious experience by frequenting places where they feel God has been manifested in a special way: sanctuaries, temples, or small chapels that house a particular patron saint. In fact, Catholic faith is built up in the area by identification with a church building.

Most important, the nexus of their spirituality is gratitude for the gift of life. At the present time Eucharist is celebrated in different homes. A church building as a common house of worship would provide the foundation to build a true community around the celebration of the Eucharist. But such decisions do not come from either the pastoral agents or the people themselves, but rather as the fruit of a long and profound reflection in common.

To speak of building a Christian community presupposes at the same time strengthening the personal dimension of each person's conscience, namely, the unique, free, and responsible character of every human being. To be sure, the campesino community offers a solid foundation on which to develop the communitarian dimension of Christian community, but we cannot ignore its limitations.

In the face of a hostile world the campesino community acts like a "clenched fist" and tends to submerge or dilute the personal realm into the communal. No doubt this mentality serves as an antidote against tendencies that would obscure indigenous identity from within or outside the communal context. It shows up in economic organization, in the division of labor, and even in the practice of religiosity, though this way of life is in crisis because of its encounter with modernity.

The personal nature of each individual's call to follow Jesus meets difficulties. Communal religiosity is of a "collective nature with communitarian fiestas, around certain pre-determined dates and very much related with a God of the natural world. To go from there to a personal living out of one's faith, of a personal relationship with a merciful and pardoning God as well as to a personal relationship with Jesus that calls for commitment and discipleship requires a process of personal growth into the life of the Holy Spirit. This is no easy task" (Instituto de Pastoral Andina 1996, 22-23).

Finally, if we accept the principle that "the identity proper of the Church is mission" (Conferencia Episcopal Latinoamericana 1992, 259), then the rich content in the faith life of the people of Pilcuyo impels them to become a "light for the nations." For this to occur it is necessary to develop that capacity of listening to the mystery that is revealed in the most intimate parts of our personal and community lives. That vocation, that basic irresistible impulse to become witnesses of God's saving action in the world through a life of service, with different charisms and ministries, flows out of the discernment of the Holy Spirit in community. In short, this is one of the strongest challenges for the southern Andean Church today. The Church will have its own Andean face only when the Quechua and Aymara peoples can overcome the tendency to identify the Church's origins in the white, economically powerful West. The tendency is reinforced by the almost exclusive presence of foreign missionaries who often unknowingly project a perceived superiority of the Western worldview.

ECUMENISM

The history of religious pluralism in the area of Pilcuyo has been marked by conflict, aggression, mutual distrust, and even persecution. However, the people have discovered some unifying nuclei: God, the Bible, and community. Along those same lines, one can place the practice of reconciliation, daily prayer, the celebration of rituals, and the common definition of diverse ethical prescriptions that see conflict as "differences among individuals and not among religions" (Focus Group No. 1).

In the course of daily interaction, it would seem that religious diversity can exacerbate existing tensions. From its very tradition the Catholic Church can rely on many resources for finding pathways to greater tolerance, dialogue, and collaboration with others. For its part, the Adventist Church, despite being locked into a process of redefining its identity, shows signs of a certain openness, though its position toward the traditional Aymara cosmovision continues to be mostly negative.

One factor standing in the way of ecumenical dialogue is a dualistic conception of the Adventist Church toward salvation. According to this conception, paying attention to socioeconomic necessities is superfluous (Instituto de Pastoral Andina 1996, 38). Nevertheless, in practice both Catholics and Adventists in Pilcuyo carry out their social responsibilities.

The greatest difficulty standing in the way of dialogue is the minority status of the Adventists over against the vast Catholic majority. According to the 1996 IPA study, the lack of acceptance as members of a full-fledged Church causes the Adventist no end to feelings of insecurity, and there are real or imagined threats of aggression from the Catholics. The Adventist looks constantly for legitimacy not only from Catholics but from the surrounding society (ibid., 37).

Aggression is reciprocal, often accompanied by a tendency of mutual disqualification, including a rejection of the public discourse of the other Church. The tendency to consider themselves the sole owners of the means of salvation "leads to attitudes of not wanting to leave anyone outside the fold and to pretending that everyone who joins either the Catholic or Adventist churches, enjoys the gift of eternal salvation" (ibid., 38).

In order to overcome these handicaps, one should seek to build an open community of believers and one that welcomes differences so that in a manner of concentric circles one expands outward from the smallest localized experiences toward one with wider and universal dimensions. The common experience of the people of Pilcuyo offers possibilities for this method. Family life is a natural place for dialogue and encounter, since families are often made up of people of different religious creeds. A good family pastoral plan would help to lessen the level of mutual aggression.

In Pilcuyo there is widespread participation in the liturgical celebrations of one and the other church from which no one feels excluded. These experiences of common prayer contribute to strengthening the sense of unity among the people.

The Catholic Church of the southern Andes, in its pastoral practice and public discourse, expresses an openness to being converted by the "other." And similarly, it strives to develop a consciousness of the necessity of leaving behind doctrinaire beliefs that impede it from truly becoming a servant of the Reign of God, present in all the values of the Andean cultures. An ecumenical spirit invites us to conversion and to break with the notion that one church is the sole proprietor of faith and salvation. For the people of Pilcuyo common ownership of the Bible is a potential unifying factor, allowing them to discover the common ground to overcome division.

Within a context of extreme poverty, the evangelical call directed to the churches is to join forces at the service of life, to search and discover the strategies to build a different kind of society together with the poor.

THE SOCIAL ROLE PLAYED BY THE CHURCHES

Since its arrival on the American continent the institutional Church has possessed not only religious but political and economic power through its close relationship with the state. As such, it has fostered profound structural change that has affected, for better or worse, the lives of the peoples of Latin America. The project begun in the sixteenth century by the Viceroy Toledo, in close collaboration with the missionary Church, substantially changed the structures and customs of indigenous society, its ways of relating, and even its work habits.

During this century, the Catholic Church and the Adventist Church have played extremely important roles in the altiplano, helping the campesinos to become aware of the situation of exploitation and margination, and to struggle for their rights. Through literacy training and education the Adventist Church made a great and lasting contribution to the quality of life of the people.

By the same token, the Catholic Church, initially through the work of the Maryknoll Fathers, Brothers, and Sisters, oriented its pastoral action toward raising the people's standard of living while revitalizing their faith. They designed a system of radio schools and various development programs that fulfilled an important role in adult popular education starting in the 1950s and 1960s. In the decade of the 1970s, inspired by the theology of liberation and breaking with the tradition that identified the Church with the higher social classes, Church leaders rededicated their efforts to support campesino organizations. In this way, the indigenous people were no longer considered the objects of evangelization, but rather active subjects.

In the interviews we discovered a certain disconnection between social change and the institutional Church. For example, there was only isolated mention and recognition of the support offered by the Pastoral Team with regard to agricultural and livestock technical assistance. The same was true of the role of the team in supporting small-scale community enterprises. This scant mention stands out all the more when one considers the work of the Vicariate of Solidarity, of the Parish of Ilave, and of the efforts of the Lutheran and Adventist churches in promoting small enterprises and various organizations in the Pilcuyo area.

This lack of expressed recognition of the social role played by the churches raises a question about differing views of what constitutes social change. As one of the members of the Pilcuyo Pastoral Team commented, "When the people of Pilcuyo hear the phrase 'social change,' their notion is of someone traveling to Tacna. We are still a long ways from responding to this reality."

In order to reformulate the Church's social role in times like these, it is necessary to overcome a generalized feeling of perplexity in the face of a complex sociocultural reality. Discernment with the people to discover the goals to be pursued would be more in line with the Church's social role. Principally, these are to nourish hope and to defend life and human dignity. To concentrate on the formation of people, enabling those without a voice to acquire one, and to create spaces for dialogue are other contributions the churches can make in carrying out their social role in a setting like this.

The people of Pilcuyo detest poverty and want desperately to overcome it. Their daily struggle for life and progress reveals an understanding of God's plan which condemns poverty as an affront to the project of love for all humankind. In their effort to overcome poverty the people instruct us how to become subjects of a history where God's presence is a given. They invite everyone, believers and nonbelievers alike, to share this conviction and join in their struggle for human dignity.

RITUAL LIFE

In Pilcuyo, everyday events and the occurrences of life are accompanied by different ritual practices. From a theological point of view, the mysterious dimension of life is present in the ritual practices of the people. Ritual actions constitute a highly dense world of religious experience and a web of relationships. Symbolically, the people express a relationship with the divine and are called to extend that relationship to the rest of humanity and the entire cosmos. Rituals, by their relational and communicative nature, speak for themselves and call us to make an effort to dispossess ourselves of our own mental schemes and mind-sets, so that we assume a contemplative stance to recognize the traces of God's presence there. A basic disposition of this kind is indispensable if the Gospel is to act as a critique of those aspects of a culture that are less than humane.

From the perspective of a missionary consciousness, understood not as a spiritual conquest but as a fraternal sharing of mutual enrichment, evangelization then becomes a reciprocal process. In the exercise of that process one learns to welcome differences, to respect mutuality, essential dimensions of any human relationship. Grace thus can carry out its transformative action, and the subjects who cooperate with it are the carriers of the Good News. All the more reason, then, to affirm that in the case of Pilcuyo the people have already received the Gospel. They are involved in the process of making it their own by welcoming and incorporating it into their own sociocultural matrix.

Ritual in the Aymara world contributes to reinforcing one's faith and reconnects people to the divine in an act of projection, affirmation and the multilayered world of meanings that shed light on life. Moreover, faith expands and prolongs itself to become an abundant source of life amid the dangers that threaten life. Under similar circumstances, we can better understand how people of every race and culture place their hope in God. It is no less than the limit experience that places people before the radical poverty of the human spirit, manifested in their intrinsic fragility and the contingency of every undertaking.

Perhaps in societies where the level of development achieved guarantees at least the security of survival one can cushion or even impede the experience of limit situations in all their crudeness. Not so in a place like Pilcuyo, where every day demands a gargantuan effort to survive without any guarantees because of the ever-present threats that accost the people, be they from natural disasters, structural causes, or internal strife. Therefore, in the search for solutions to a range of human problems as well as in the experience of social change, not one person thought of religion as superfluous. On the contrary, we discovered a multiplicity of signs that betray the overwhelming presence of a religious sensibility that includes a perception of life as gift.

Consequently, one participates fully in the ritual life of the community with the end of keeping alive a relationship with the God who provides life, health, nourishment, harmony, and peace. The people of Pilcuyo enjoy a level of self-understanding that assures them of their destiny as recipients of these gifts. Through the enactment of their ritual life people feel themselves in tune with God's presence. In recognition of that presence they make their offerings, rites, and prayers throughout all of everyday life in order to continue to receive the gift of life. Here it is possible to discover wider dimensions of gratitude as the fundamental core of every Christian spirituality.

Every ritual action constitutes a codified language by means of certain rules that express the sense of a people, their fears, values, their way of relating to nature and the ways they understand their role in human history. Therefore, it is necessary to enter into this world with respect. The Church, if it understands its role in the inculturation process, can be informed by the language of ritual action so as to discover the evangelical roots that are there. In this way, the missionary Church begins to understand the perspective of the subjects with whom it is called to share in the dialogue of evangelization.

At the same time that he criticized the external cultic celebrations of his time for their lack of a spiritual dimension, Jesus put into practice other rituals. Moreover, he recovered the deepest sense of their originality by showing wherein God was revealed. Authentic rituals contain the language of communion and are expressions of love.

BUILDING A LOCAL CHURCH WITH AN AYMARA FACE

We have grown close to the people of Pilcuyo by conversing with them and have observed key moments in their lives while searching for the face of popular Catholicism in times of great change. We have met a people of deep and abiding beliefs with a treasure house of wisdom, grown accustomed to struggling for life, of merging the old and the new. We have made contact with a unique way of being Catholic that is flexible, open, and truly universal with vast and creative potential. We have met and come to know a people with an innate capacity for making the Gospel their own from within the depths of their culture and for expressing it in their own language, rituals, and symbols.

All this wealth of insight, however, has a reverse side that must be addressed. In Pilcuyo the people do not identify being Catholic with belonging to the Church. They construct their own particular Catholic identity as best they can with what is at hand. Some are aware of the need for formation and accompaniment and make strong claims for it. Therefore, a huge task remains for the missionary Church. We firmly believe that the strongest challenge is to build a local Church with its own face so that it can become an open and fully developed servant of the Reign of God. This then will be fertile ground for vocations and for diverse ministries and services, a community whose members feel themselves fully identified as Catholic and feel as at home in that identity as they do in the houses they construct on the sacred ground of Pilcuyo.

3

St. Lucia, West Indies

Garden of Eden?

PATRICK A. B. ANTHONY

... the valley of Roseau is not the Garden of Eden,
and those who inhabit it, are not in heaven
Derek Walcott, *Sea Grapes*

INTRODUCTION

Dunstan St. Omer was born in Castries, St. Lucia, on 24th October 1927. From childhood he loved painting. As a boy he remembers admiring the beautiful Sacred Heart paintings in Belgrave's shop on the Chaussée Road in Castries, the capital of St. Lucia. He used to make cheap reproductions of them, selling them for a few cents in order to make the entrance fee to the movies on Saturdays. He loved art, especially religious art, but all he knew of art was from European art books. Then one day, the young Dunstan was introduced to the legendary St. Lucian artist and scholar, Harold ("Harry") Simmons. A silent revolution began. Along with young Derek Walcott and young photographer Leo "Spa" St. Helene, "Harry" introduced him to the St. Lucian landscape and experience, to the St. Lucian peasant as an artistic hero.

With elation St. Omer began to discover himself as a Caribbean artist and a black man. The experience impacted upon his spirituality and religious sensibility. Over the years he has searched and questioned relentlessly. "I cannot see my people developing, finding happiness, being secure, being free, being wonderful lovely people, if they must of necessity have a white God. It's contradictory to their nature, it's conflicting. It must create discord, terror, violence and so forth,

because the human mind cannot accept this . . . it means that in a few
years all black people in the world will have to abandon Christ as they
develop. "[1]

   St. Omer has now resolved the conflict for himself and his people: "I
feel that my greatest contribution as an artist in St. Lucia, my monument,
is that I've been able to start painting Christ, his mother, and Joseph in
the church as 'blacks.' Your God must be of you, and you of your God.
I live in God and God lives in me; and my God must be like me, like my
father, like my ancestors." This he magnificently illustrates in the mural
of the church at Jacmel [see cover of this book].

There are spaces and places that to passersby may seem starkly ordinary, yet
have extraordinary significance. Jacmel, in the Roseau valley, is one such place.
There two of the most creative spirits of the land have converged, the poet and
Nobel laureate Derek Walcott and his artist friend, Dunstan St. Omer. Out of the
encounter two of our most remarkable creations were born: St. Omer's mural of
the Holy Family as altarpiece for the parish church, and Walcott's poem on the
mural, the central part of the middle poem of his homecoming collection, *Sea
Grapes.*

St. Omer's mural is a masterpiece, recognized as one of the finest in the Caribbean. It is church art celebrating the life of the community. Walcott captures in
verse what the painter's brush has stilled from life:

> The chapel, as the pivot of this valley,
> round which whatever is rooted loosely turns
> men, women, ditches, the revolving fields
> of bananas, the secondary roads,
> draws all to it, to the altar
> and the massive altar-piece;
> like a dull mirror, life
> repeated there,
> the common life outside
> and the other life it holds
> a good man made it.
> (Walcott 1976, 52)

The "chapel" Walcott speaks of is the parish church for the community of
Jacmel/Roseau. "The common life outside" is bananas, the heart of the valley.
When sugar was "king" in the 1940s this valley was one of the three major estates around which the entire economy of St. Lucia revolved. People came from
all parts of the 620-square-kilometer island to work in Roseau, which then boasted
of one of the major sugar factories on the island. In 1949 fallen prices on the

---

[1]All quotations of Dunstan St. Omer are from personal interviews with this writer.

world market caused the owners of the Roseau and Cul de Sac estates and factories to discontinue production.

The government purchased both factories and estates and formed a local company, Sugar Manufacturers Ltd., to manage them. In 1961 Geest Industries Ltd., a Dutch multinational company, purchased the Roseau and Cul de Sac estates and factories from Sugar Manufacturers Ltd., and despite promises made to the government to continue sugar production, in 1962 abruptly stopped. Geest Industries Ltd. began to put most of the estates into banana cultivation.

THE STORY OF A VALLEY

The story of the Roseau valley is the story of bananas. Bananas have dominated the economy of St. Lucia for the past three decades, contributing significantly to socioeconomic changes in the society. By 1986 banana exports contributed 17% of the gross domestic product. Of the total value of exports that year, US$80 million, banana exports comprised US$53 million or 67% (Venner 1989, 80). Although the banana is a ready cash crop with a short gestation period, it is highly vulnerable to hurricanes, storms, and floods. It is also susceptible to price fluctuations and other adverse factors on the international market. By the middle of the 1980s, Geest Industries Ltd. began to sell banana lands to individual farmers.

If the story of the Roseau valley is the story of bananas, then the plight of the banana industry is the plight of the valley. In 1994 Tropical Storm Debbie ravaged St. Lucia, causing US$74 million in damage (Darmuzey 1994, 33). In Jacmel, the fragile walls of the parish church, which had shown signs of structural stress since 1991, began to give way. Daily Mass was a risk, and Sunday services a potential disaster. The celebrated St. Omer mural was also in danger.

The parish priest, St. Lucian-born Fr. Lambert St. Rose, mobilized architects, engineers, contractors, and officials from the relevant government ministries. They consulted and recommended immediate closure of the church building and reconstruction. Estimated cost was US$190,000. That decision could not have been more timely, says Fr. St. Rose. On the day demolition began, the outer walls of the building came crashing down at the very first touch of the heavy equipment. Thankfully, the inner walls and the mural remained intact.

According to Fr. St. Rose, when the old altar was finally pulled down, a large assortment of bottles was found beneath its walls. The workmen jokingly remarked in the native Kwéyòl language, "Sé la pwen tout gajé Jacmel té yé" (That was the *pwen* [power source] for all Jacmel's sorcerers). The story buzzed round the parish. Only then was the priest reminded that this was the third church building on that spot to have collapsed. But that was not all. People also told the priest that a woman noted for her sorcery (*gajé*) had publicly confessed (*dépalé*) shortly before her death that she had been responsible for the destruction of the two earlier churches. People believed she had such supernatural powers.

This is the Roseau valley, the parish of Jacmel/Roseau, where official Roman

Catholic doctrine and practice encounter a dominant African traditional religious milieu and popular culture. The results of this encounter are the content of this study.

CONTEXT AND METHOD

The parish of Jacmel/Roseau consists of a cluster of nine rural communities in and around the Roseau valley, on the western side of the Caribbean island of St. Lucia. With their respective populations these communities include Bois D'Inde (204), Jacmel (540), Millet (917), Morne D'Or (246), Roseau (238), Vanard (321), Marigot (552), La Croix Maingot (422), and Barre Denis (592), making up a total population of 4,032 (2,033 males, 1,999 females) living in 941 households.[2] There are a number of tiny villages in the area, such as Morne Ciseaux and Coolie Town, which were not included in this study.

The agricultural sector is the largest single employer in the area, providing 37% of jobs compared to 23% nationwide. The remainder of the labor force in the area is employed principally in crafts, service jobs, and elementary occupations such as fieldwork or casual labor. Whereas 70% of the agricultural labor force and 63% of the entire labor force of the district are male, women outstrip men as clerks (80%), technicians (67%), and legislators (61%). There are an equal number of male and female professionals and service workers.

The number employed in the agricultural sector varies considerably from community to community. In Barre Denis it is 24%, in Jacmel 31%, in Vanard 57%, Bois D'Inde 58%, Morne D'Or 64%, to a high of 71% in Millet. According to the last national census in 1991, the average annual income per person for the parish was US$3,375 for males, and US$3,135 for females. The community of Barre Denis had the highest income (US$3,735 for males, and US$3,420 for females), and Bois D'Inde (US$1,930 for males, and US$1,812 for females), the lowest.

There are no secondary or tertiary educational institutions in the entire Jacmel/Roseau area. There are four infant and primary schools: Millet Infant School, Millet Primary School, La Croix Maingot Combined School, and Jacmel Combined School. With regard to births and infant mortality, out of 176 live births in 1993 in the whole area there were 3 infant deaths.[3]

Originally the study was to be conducted in all nine communities, but various logistical and other problems limited the research to Millet, Jacmel, Morne D'Or, Bois D'Inde, Barre Denis, and Vanard. The people were initially informed of the project through the parish priest during regular Sunday Masses in the central community of Jacmel. A project committee was established, com-

---

[2]All statistics on population, labor force, and income are from the 1991 national census. For the purpose of this article all statistics have been rounded off.

[3]"Main Report: Poverty Assessment Report—St. Lucia," in *Final Report submitted to the Caribbean Development Bank* by Kairi Consultants Ltd. Tunapuna: Trinidad. Vol. 1 of 2 (April 1996), 43.

prising representatives of each of the communities. Those selected were known for their ability to mobilize, lead, and encourage others to participate in community activities.

General meetings were held in the Jacmel parish center following church services primarily to encourage receptivity, to solicit participation and to gain insights into the commonly held beliefs with respect to the research parameters. These meetings also provided the means whereby prior assumptions could be tested. Additional testing occurred in focus groups.

The methods of data collection included a quantitative survey using a 78-item questionnaire, focus groups, popular theater and oral history, employing in-depth interviews with persons noted for their knowledge of cultural practices and community history. All data collection was done in the local Kwéyòl language. Of the 617 households in the six communities, 211 households were surveyed. Households instead of individuals were chosen, based on the assumption that persons occupying one household would share broadly similar beliefs. Nevertheless, heads of households were interviewed, whether they were male or female. Interviewers were instructed to interview one person in every third household, alternating between male and female interviewees, with a 3-1 bias for interviewees between the ages of 47 and 62.

From the data obtained in the survey a selected sample (45 out of the 211 households surveyed) formed the basis for the analysis, but the other methods served to verify and validate the data obtained from the sample. The sample size was computed on the basis of data already available, from which such a priori assumptions as the homogeneity of the belief system could be made. It was established that popular beliefs and practices with respect to the study parameters of health, healing, death, burial rites, well-being, birth and birthing, baptism, power and protection, and protection rites were virtually the same throughout the communities. The parameters of the study were established after a number of focus group sessions on health, healing, evil, and evildoers in Jacmel/Roseau.

There were no marked variations in the belief system from one geographical location to another in the parish of Jacmel/Roseau. Responses to the questionnaire were similar from Vanard through Millet to Morne D'Or. Mixed focus groups in Jacmel, and with men in Barre Denis, as well as popular theater sessions with youth from Bois D'Inde and Jacmel, all confirmed the homogeneity of the belief system.

POPULAR CATHOLICISM AND THE INSTITUTIONAL CHURCH

For the purposes of this study, "popular" refers to those sectors or strata of the society which do not enjoy much wealth, status, or power, and which are perceived as part of the "common people" in their milieu. In the Jacmel/Roseau parish that's 83% of the working population. According to the 1991 census, only 2% described themselves as professionals, 3% as technicians, and 7% as plant and machine workers; 23% have either no occupation at all or are described as having "elementary" occupations. That would include such casual labor as cleaners, yard-boys, and domestics. The average income per person in the parish is US$3,205, compared with US$3,570, the average for the Anse-la-Raye district of which Jacmel/Roseau is an administrative unit, and US$4,688, the national average. Vis-à-vis the wider St. Lucian society as a whole much of Jacmel/Roseau would have to be considered "popular."

"Popular culture" refers to the self-conscious expression of the shared knowledge (folk wisdom, language, and meaning) and behaviors of the popular sectors, while "popular Catholicism" is the complex of beliefs and religious practices (sacramental, devotional, problem solving and social change related) of Catholics who belong to the popular sectors of society.

We shall first examine some rituals of popular Catholicism, insofar as they relate directly to the sacramental and devotional life of the institutional church. Then we shall look at some of the problem solving and social change-related beliefs and practices of popular Catholicism in their relationship to popular culture.

POPULAR CATHOLIC RITUALS AND THE SACRAMENTAL LIFE OF THE CHURCH

Baptism (Batenm)

Infant baptism or christening (*nonmen/lonmen*) is a community affair. There is usually a big party for the christening with music, eating, and drinking. Even printed invitations are sometimes sent inviting special persons to the christening party. The ceremony takes place on the last Sunday of every month during the 8:00 a.m. Mass. The sponsors or godparents are required to attend six preparatory sessions conducted by parish leaders and/or the parish priest before a child is baptized. Church regulations stipulate that the sponsors must be practicing Catholics whose marital status is not irregular. As people say in St. Lucia, "They must not be living in sin!" Rules concerning irregular marital situations applied not only to the sponsors but, in the past, also to the parents. As a result the children of unwedded couples were baptized on a weekday, while children of married parents were baptized on Sundays. This might explain why mothers absented themselves from the baptism ceremony and had a married woman "carry" the child to the church.

Besides the godparents, this other person (always a woman) who carries the infant to church for the baptism ceremony when the mother is unavailable is called the *da*. In popular Catholicism, there is the belief that people can "steal" a child's baptism (*volè batenm*). Since the *da* is the one who carries the infant to the church when the mother is absent, and holds the child during the baptism ceremony, she is usually identified as the culprit when it is believed that the child's baptism has been stolen.

Although only 37% of those interviewed said that they believed or had heard about *volè batenm*, only 17% did not believe in it and said it was impossible. Some of those who believed said:

"I have heard that you put a coin under the child's head before it is baptized. The baptism can then be captured in the coin or shilling. The child has no baptism then, because the baptism is in the coin."

"Put a coin in the child's hand during baptism and use the coin to do obeah.[4] The baptism is contained in the coin."

"They will put something in the child's clothes when the child is named, and the baptism is captured by whatever was placed on the child to take it."

One other element of popular Catholicism associated with baptism is belief in the phenomenon called *kokma*. When asked to explain what *kokma* was, only 10% of respondents said they did not know. Defining the phenomenon others said:

"*Kokma* is a child who died without baptism. Baptism can prevent *kokma*."

"*Kokma* is a child that died before it was christened. When a child is not christened it becomes a *kokma*."

"*Kokma* is when a baby dies before it is baptized. It is baptism that will prevent a child from being a *kokma*."

"*Kokma* is something that bothers babies who are not yet baptized."

"*Kokma* is something dreamlike. When you are asleep it grabs you in the throat."

"You see *kokma* in sleep, in dreams. It grabs you in your throat and I believe it can be seen as a small child. I believe it must be children who have died without baptism that become *kokma*."

"*Kokma* holds people by the throat. It is the same people who come to do black magic that hold you by the throat. That is *kokma*."

We shall explore the underlying theology of popular Catholicism evident from these remarks on the phenomenon of *kokma* in our discussion of the theological and missiological questions raised by this study.

First Communion (Pwenmyé konminyon)

First Communion is one of the biggest social events associated with the sacramental system of the Catholic Church in Jacmel/Roseau, and in the rest of St. Lucia as well. From the day of the baptism, people begin to talk about when the child will "make First Communion." The expression to "make First Communion" (*fè pwenmyé konminyon*) refers to the first reception of Holy Eucharist at the age of seven or eight years. This happens after a three-year period of weekly religious instructions.

Bringing the "First Communion paper" home is one of the happiest days of a

---

[4]The origins of the word "obeah" are unclear. Newall (1978, 29) quotes Cassidy and Le Page (1967, 326-327), who affirm that "its origins are African." In "Treatment of slaves in the West Indies and all circumstances relating thereto" which is Part III of *Report of the Lords of the Committee of the Council appointed for the Consideration of All Matters Relating to Trade and Foreign Plantations* (London, 1789), the report considers the origin of the word Egyptian because of similarity between the "ob" of "obeah" and the Egyptian "Ob," which means snake. Sereno (1948, 15) states that obeah is "a word of Gullah origin meaning witchcraft." Williams (1932) states that the origin is Ashanti.

child's life, and the first popular ritual in the immediate preparation for reception of the sacrament of Holy Eucharist. It signifies that the child is "in First Communion." The First Communion ceremony is preceded by a "First Communion retreat" (*witwèt*) for all candidates lasting between three days and one week. In the past, the retreat was a time of total seclusion from friends and games, a time of spiritual preparation. Today, although less rigid, normal activities are still suspended for the candidates and restrictions imposed until after the First Communion ceremony. It is during the retreat that candidates make their first sacramental confession.

On the First Communion day, candidates all wear their "First Communion clothes," an elaborately designed white dress and veil of the finest material for girls, and an equally special white suit for boys. First Communion clothes and apparel are always brand new, even in the case of the poorest child. It is one moment when there is a conscious attempt at social parity. After the ceremony, the "First Communion clothes" are used only on very special occasions.

Confirmation (Lakonflimasyon)

In the past the reception of the sacrament of confirmation followed a pattern similar to that of First Communion. Children were usually "confirmed" two or three years after First Communion, at about the age of nine to eleven years. After First Communion, the child would enter into a new catechetical program in preparation for confirmation within two or three years. In confirmation, the godparents play a role similar to that played in First Communion.

The same pattern of examination and retreat as with First Communion is followed for confirmation. However, confirmation has never generated the kind of total involvement, excitement, and participation of so many people. It is almost as though it were a repeat of what had already occurred just a few years before, even if this time it is the bishop who administers the sacrament. There is still a party for the occasion, but it is nowhere near as elaborate as for First Communion.

One of the factors responsible for the changing attitude toward confirmation is intense catechesis on the part of the official Church criticizing the excessive importance of partying associated with the reception of the sacraments. Moreover, the age for confirmation has been changed from ten to eleven years to middle or late teens. At that age, it is thought, candidates are better equipped to make decisions as adult Christians do. Despite great pressure and opposition from some sections of the congregation, who argue that the youth, especially the young girls, may "get to know life" or even get pregnant before confirmation, the Church authorities have stood their ground.

First Communion Jubilees and Anniversaries (Jibilé)

One phenomenon of popular Catholicism unique to St. Lucia is the celebration of First Communion anniversaries and jubilees. In Jacmel/Roseau it would not be surprising to hear a notice, at the end of the Sunday service, inviting all persons who made their First Communion in a particular year to meet to plan their anniversary. For an ordinary anniversary, a special Mass would be said on the actual date of the anniversary, depending on the availability of priests, or on the Sunday nearest to that date. All who are alive and able usually attend. These ordinary anniversary Masses would be followed by a group breakfast, brunch, or supper, depending on the time of the Mass. A Mass is also always offered later for the repose of the souls of those members of the original First Communion group who have died.

Although people will celebrate the tenth, fifteenth or twentieth anniversary of their First Communion, it is the jubilees, silver (25 years), gold (50 years), and diamond (60 years), which are very special occasions. For silver, golden, or diamond jubilees, people are known to have traveled from England, the United States, and Canada for the celebrations. For a silver jubilee participants will wear silver-colored dresses and suits, and gold-colored ones for a golden jubilee. An elaborate service is always planned for the date of the jubilee. At that service or Mass, baptismal promises are renewed. The church service is always followed by a lavish meal.

Giving of Masses (Bay lanmès)

One other area of popular Catholicism associated with the sacramental life of the Catholic Church in Jacmel/Roseau is the monetary offering for Masses to be said by the priest for various intentions. This is a custom sanctioned by universal church law, with very clear rules regulating the practice (Canons 945-958). For the people, this church practice has become a ritual for problem solving. Masses are offered for all kinds of intentions: in thanksgiving for favors obtained, for healing of physical, emotional, or spiritual sickness, to get a job, for the curing of an alcoholic or drug abuser, for protection from danger, for warding off evil spirits, to name a few.

Sometimes a Mass will be offered for one intention, sometimes for a combination of intentions. A person may request that several Masses be said over a period of time for one particular intention. That is usually the case when Masses are given for a solution to entrenched marital or domestic problems. Besides giving individual Masses, or a series of Masses over a period of time for a specific intention, persons sometimes request a novena of Masses (i.e., a group of seven or nine consecutive Masses) for one particular intention. Since it is usually impossible for the parish priest to honor such a request because there are already so many individual Mass intentions, the petitioner may arrange to have the Masses said consecutively in seven or nine different churches.

POPULAR CATHOLIC RITUALS AND THE DEVOTIONAL LIFE OF THE CHURCH

Baptism, First Communion, confirmation, jubilees and anniversaries, and the giving of Masses are a few examples of popular Catholic rituals in Jacmel/Roseau which directly relate to the sacramental life of the Church. There are other examples which are not directly related to the sacramental life but are rather connected with the devotional life of the Church.

Confraternities and Sodalities

In the parish, three confraternities help to sustain the devotional life of some of the people: the Sacred Heart, Our Lady of Mt. Carmel, and St. Isidore confraternities. Confraternities or sodalities are voluntary associations of the faithful established and guided by ecclesiastical authority for the promotion of special works of Christian charity or piety. The Sacred Heart Confraternity is based on devotion to the Sacred Heart of Jesus as recommended by Blessed Margaret Mary Alacoque. Every first Friday of the month, members dressed in white with the red scapular of the Sacred Heart around their neck attend Mass and make their novenas. The members are mainly women, although there are also a number of men in the confraternity.

Attending Mass for nine consecutive first Fridays and praying for a special intention is considered a most powerful tool for obtaining spiritual favors. The "Nine First Fridays" novena is a very common example of prayers as a ritual for everyday problem solving. The first Friday novena is used as an instrument of healing in case of illness, for guidance in terms of decision making, for success in business undertakings, for assistance to children during exams or even for rehabilitation of a son or daughter who is a social deviant.

The Scapular of the Most Sacred Heart of Jesus, a small piece of white woolen cloth, on which is embroidered or sewn in red a picture of the heart of Jesus, is believed by members to be a potent protection against all kinds of adversity. Some believe that if you are wearing this scapular, *gen gajé* (sorcerers), *lèspwi* (evil spirits), and *maji nwè* (practitioners of black magic) cannot harm you.

The confraternity of Our Lady of Mt. Carmel is another of those associations of the faithful that is part of popular piety in Jacmel/Roseau. Every first Saturday, the members attend Mass wearing white dresses with a brown scapular over the dress. The feast day for that confraternity is July 16, the feast of Our Lady of Mt. Carmel. Members also wear a smaller scapular around their necks all the time. They believe the tradition that the Blessed Virgin Mary promised special grace and protection especially at the hour of death, to those who wear the scapular throughout life.

Many of the members of the confraternity of Our Lady of Mt. Carmel are also members of the Legion of Mary. The Legion of Mary is an association of lay Catholics founded in Dublin, Ireland, in 1921. The movement came to St. Lucia in the 1930s and has been established in the Jacmel/Roseau parish for several decades. Members have a special devotion to the Blessed Virgin Mary and the rosary, and believe that great spiritual favors can be obtained through her intercession. For official "Legion" outings, members wear a white dress with a blue sash over their shoulders. There are very few men in the association. Once a month, legionaries from Jacmel/Roseau join legionaries and other pilgrims from all over the island for a Day with Mary. The Day with Mary is a recent phenomenon. All legionaries journey to one parish for a day of prayer and devotion, teachings on Christian living and the role of the Blessed Virgin Mary in the history of salvation, the celebration of Eucharist and benediction of the Blessed Sacrament.

A few women, who meet to celebrate his feast day (May 15) by attending

Mass and sharing a meal afterward, keep the St. Isidore Confraternity alive in the parish. Once, devotion to this saint was very great and the St. Isidore Confraternity very powerful. Today the patron of peasants and day laborers does not seem to have any great influence on the contemporary banana worker.

Jesus Day

Jesus Day is celebrated on the last Sunday of September. This parish festivity or festival is unique to Jacmel/Roseau parish. That Sunday, there is only one Mass in the parish, as compared to any ordinary Sunday when there would be two Masses in Jacmel, one other at either Millet or La Croix Maingot, and one at Barre Denis.

All activities that day take place in and around the main parish church at Jacmel. The day begins with the official Morning Prayers (from the Holy Office) of the Church, followed by a period of praise and worship; then a feature address by a well-known speaker. This is followed by a fellowship breakfast for the whole parish at the Jacmel Combined School. After breakfast, the community comes together in the church building for discussion of the feature address. The morning's activities culminate with the celebration of the Holy Eucharist, the only Mass in the parish that day, which is usually a very specially planned parish-family celebration. At the end of Mass, all the families of the parish, who had been fore-warned to bring along their family meal to be shared with the wider parish family, are invited to celebrate a great communal agape. People share freely with each other whatever they have, in a spirit of unity and conviviality.

The post-lunch session begins with more songs of praise and worship, followed by another feature address on the life and workings of the parish. After the address, parishioners are invited to join various workshop sessions, according to the area of ministry (catechetics, music, choir, etc.) in which they feel called to be involved. By midafternoon, workshop reports are presented to the entire parish in a plenary session. The day's activities conclude with benediction of the Blessed Sacrament.

Marian Devotions at Barre Denis

In the community of Barre Denis there is a very strong popular Marian devotion. Every night, a cross-section of the Catholics in the community, children, youths and adults, go from house to house praying in Kwéyòl for the particular needs of each home, and conclude their prayers at the Barre Denis chapel. They pray a variety of rosaries and prayers, using the problem or petition of the household as the actual ritual words for the prayer litany or chaplet. This tradition, begun by the people in the absence of a priest, has continued independently of the official Church.

Corpus Christi

The worldwide Catholic feast of Corpus Christi is celebrated in Jacmel/Roseau at the same time as the rest of the archdiocese on the Thursday after Trinity Sunday every year. Corpus Christi is a public holiday in St. Lucia. In each parish it is the traditional practice to have a celebration of Mass followed by a public demonstration of faith in the Blessed Sacrament by a procession through the streets of the communities. In Jacmel/Roseau parish, the procession with the Blessed Sacrament goes from the church building, down the main church street, up into Jacmel road and back to the church via Blackstone road. Along the way there are three temporary shrines or "altars of repose" (*répozwa*) at each of which the main celebrant stops for benediction. The altars are built of a wooden frame (usually bamboo) covered over with plastic or cloth sheets and decorated with religious images, fruits, cakes, and loaves of bread. Those who build these shrines or decorate them or have them located at their houses are considered spiritually powerful people.

All Saints and All Souls Day (Latousen èk Fèt lémò)

The feasts of All Saints and All Souls (November 1 and 2) are important feasts in the Jacmel/Roseau parish calendar and in that of the official Church in St. Lucia. Several days before the feasts the parish cemetery is cleared of all unwanted shrubbery, graves and tombstones cleaned, and some tombs freshly repainted. On All Saints there is a solemn Mass celebrated in honor of all the saints. The next day, All Souls, is a day to remember all deceased relatives and friends. As the day begins, families recall the memory of their loved ones who have died in family prayer. It is a day when there is a sense of the "presence of the dead" all around the house.

In the late afternoon the solemn Mass for the "repose of the souls of the faithful departed" is celebrated in the parish church. Parishioners attend, wearing white, black, or purple clothes, as is the custom for funerals. After the Mass, there is a candlelight procession from the church to the cemetery at the back of the church building. At the cemetery persons go to the graves of their loved ones, place lighted candles, flowers, and fresh wreaths on them, and remain there praying, until the priest, who visits every grave to pray a while with the families and bless the grave, arrives. On All Souls, people visit the cemetery all day long. Those who are unable to attend the Mass go straight there with their votive offerings of candles and flowers. That night, the cemetery becomes aglow with candles and activity. Usually at night, it is a dark and abandoned place, except for those visiting covertly for purposes of obeah. One such obeah practice is the burying in the cemetery of a bottle containing bits of items belonging to a proposed victim. Such items include bits of clothing, fingernails, or hair. Once the bottle is buried, the intended effect on the victim will continue until the bottle is removed. Intended effects may vary from ill health, misfortune, and failure in business to loss of a job.

SOME OTHER POPULAR CATHOLIC RITUALS

There are also a number of customs and practices in the Jacmel/Roseau parish which form part of what we have called popular Catholicism, but which may or may not be directly related to the sacramental and devotional life of the Catholic Church.

The Use of Blessed Objects

Many ritual objects which are used for everyday problem solving deserve attention. Primary among these is "blessed water" (*dlo benni*), especially the water blessed at the Easter Vigil ceremony on Holy Saturday night. The parish priest claims that no matter how much water is blessed there is never enough to satisfy demands at the end of the service. Individuals come with several bottles and containers to get their supply. The "holy water" is used for many purposes. Some sprinkle or bless around their homes and business places with it for protection against evil. Some drink it for healing of internal sickness or give it to their children to drink for protection. Others rub with it, or pour it over an open wound for healing; while still others wash their faces with it or bathe with water into which some has been poured for self-protection. Bathing with water containing "holy water" is a common remedy for "*lanmaway*" (the belief that someone's life has been malignantly "tied up," so that the person can make no progress or see any light/clear direction in their life).

The use of "blessed oil" has grown considerably since the advent of the Catholic charismatic renewal movement in St. Lucia in the 1980s. Bottles of olive oil are brought to the parish priest or to any other priest to be blessed. The oil is then used for such healing rituals as anointing of the head, rubbing of wounds or other affected parts of the body, and drinking in traditional medicinal potions. There is a strong healing ministry within the charismatic renewal movement in the Catholic Church, involving healing services, "healing Masses," and deliverance. Blessed oil is used in all of these rituals, and so persons who bring bottles of olive oil to the service can also have them blessed there.

The lighting of candles for various intentions is one of the most common features of popular Catholicism. People say they will "put a light," "light a light," or "light a candle" for a particular cause or situation (Anthony 1995, 108). For example, someone may "put a light" against an enemy, a troublesome neighbor, a rival at work or in a love affair, or an opponent in a court case. In the case of an enemy, people speak of "putting a light on his/her head." The candle would be lit and left burning either in the church or at the home of the complainant. Candles are also lit for good intentions, such as, to help a child in an exam, to assist someone going for a job interview, to protect someone embarking on a long journey, and for general protection in all dangerous situations.

Lighting of candles as a means of everyday problem solving is complemented by another popular tradition, the "virgin-lamp" (*lanmp lavyèj*). The virgin-lamp is a dish of oil (coconut oil or olive oil) with a floating wick. This is placed on an altar or shrine in the home (Kremser and Wernhart 1986, 87). It is lit at 6:00 a.m. and may keep burning all day and night. However, because of the high risk of fire in many wooden houses, some people light the virgin-lamp at 6:00 p.m. and let it burn until 6:00 a.m. Thus, the lamp would be extinguished during the day while people are at work reducing the risk of fire. One ritual associated with the lighting of candles or virgin-lamps, is the placing of a piece of paper beneath the candle, or in the case of the virgin-lamp, inside the oil itself. On these pieces of paper are written the names of those for or against whom the petitioner wants to pray.

Another phenomenon of the popular belief system of Jacmel/Roseau is belief in *lowizon*. *Lowizon* is part of the system of protection rites and symbols. A *lowizon* is an amulet consisting of a piece of parchment paper on which a special prayer or psalm for protection is written. The parchment paper is then folded and placed in a small pouch, which is then sewn. The sewn pouch is then carried around the neck on a chain or pinned onto the inside parts of the clothes being worn, or it may even be carried in the pocket or wallet. Thus many persons may have a *lowizon* without anyone being aware of it. Besides the *lowizon* there is another protective amulet called the *gad*. The *gad* is generally associated with the obeahman and evil. Religious medals approved by the Church and rosary beads are also a very popular means of protection. Like the *lowizon* and *gad* they are either worn around the neck, pinned onto clothing, or carried in the pocket or wallet.

Thus far, we have examined the relationship between popular Catholicism and the institutional life of the Catholic Church in the Jacmel/Roseau parish. We have looked specifically at popular Catholic rituals in their relationship with the sacramental and devotional life of the Church. We also looked at other Catholic rituals, which showed signs of the influence of popular culture. In our next section, we shall examine more closely the relationship between popular Catholicism and popular culture.

POPULAR CATHOLICISM AND POPULAR CULTURE

Strong ties to tradition and adherence to the collective knowledge (folk wisdom) of the community both characterize popular culture. We shall now examine a number of problems in the Jacmel/Roseau parish and see what problem-solving processes exist as part of the collective wisdom of the community. Conscious of the vast and rapid changes affecting popular culture globally through modernization, we shall test the impact of social change on the religious beliefs and practices in that community. With 90% of the population of the Jacmel/Roseau area of African descent, and over 80% Roman Catholic,[5] that context should provide an excellent opportunity for assessing the interrelationship between popular Catholicism and popular culture.

Everyday Problem Solving

Our discussion of everyday problem solving will focus on the following areas in this study: birth and birthing, well-being, health and healing, powers and protection, and death and burial.

---

[5]Figures obtained from the Statistical Division, Government of St. Lucia.

Birth and Birthing

The case of "Man Antèl" of Millet is well known in the Jacmel/Roseau community. Her brother relates the story thus: Man Antèl was several months pregnant. One day a gentleman told her he wanted the child she was carrying in her womb. Jokingly she replied, "Sure!" A few weeks later the child disappeared from her womb. There was neither miscarriage nor abortion. She never bore the child.

According to tradition in the community, a few years later a man was returning home late one night when he encountered two small children (*boloms*), a boy and a girl. He asked them, "Who is your mother?" The girl replied, "Man Antèl." He asked, "Which Man Antèl?" The girl snapped back in annoyance, "Man Antèl of Millet, how many Man Antèls you know?" That child, it is believed, was the same child taken as a fetus from its mother's womb and now turned into a *bolom*.[6]

One of the areas of everyday problem solving in Jacmel/Roseau is pregnancy and childbirth. With a high infant mortality rate in the district, one is not surprised at the vast number of beliefs associated with this basic biological function. Among the problems associated with birth and birthing in the communities are barrenness (*bwahayn*) and difficult pregnancies. Barrenness is seen as a natural phenomenon by some of the people, but a vast majority believes that persons through the powers of evil can cause others to become barren. One form of barrenness is the "tying of the womb" (*mawé bouden moun*). When asked "Ès moun sa mawé bouden moun?" (Can someone tie another's womb), 67% of respondents in the survey said "yes," 3% said "don't know," and 20% gave no reply. The high percentage of "nonresponses" would seem to be more of a case of cultural resistance to perceived intrusion by the institutional Church into the universe of popular meaning than a lack of knowledge. Political scientist James Scott's question is particularly pertinent here: "How do we study power relations when the powerless are often obliged to adopt a strategic pose in the presence of the powerful?" (Scott 1990, xii). When asked "Si bouden an moun mawé, koumannyè y sa démawé?" (If a woman's womb is tied, how can it be untied?), there were 24% nonresponses, 44% "don't knows," 16% suggested trying modern medicine, 6% traditional medicine, and 6% said "trust in God."

The "tying" of a woman's womb may help to explain barrenness, but it does not help to explain delayed delivery. Here again popular belief is that someone, especially a jealous rival, can "tie the child" in its mother's womb. Respondents describe graphic cases where someone threatened to tie the child in the womb of a mother, and the mother died without giving birth to the child. Of course one

---

[6]The *bolom* is a small fetus-shaped being with amazing powers. Although its feet are turned backward, its agility is legendary and its strength extraordinary. It feeds only on meat. The *bolom* can be either male or female. It is fiercely loyal and obedient, but only to its master. Upon the master's death, the abandoned creature can be heard wailing as it wanders about homeless. Those who know how can catch the *bolom* and become its new master. The *bolom* is capable of bringing great prosperity to its owner. There is a commonly held belief that anyone who is doing well in business owns a *bolom* working for him/her.

may be inclined to suggest that this was before caesarian sections were being conducted in St. Lucia. But even with all the latest gynecological developments people still die in childbirth! That, for some, only confirms their fundamental beliefs. When asked how one does "untie" a child from the mother's womb, 59% did not respond, but 39% knew of some kind of traditional medicine. The following is one response:

> In order to untie the child, take nine leaves of *malpouwi douvan jou* (name of an herbal tea which means literally, "not-well-rotten before daylight") and boil them. Take the broom that is being used to sweep the house, make a cross with it on the woman's womb. Take some dirt from the doorstep, along with four knots of pig droppings, boil along with three grains of corn and three pea beans and make a tea for the woman in labor. Mix this tea with the previous one and give it to the woman. After that, place a grain of coarse salt on her tongue and squeeze her navel. The baby will come flying out after that.

Beliefs surrounding birth and birthing reflect the many everyday problems associated with pregnancy. Of those interviewed, 56% claimed to have heard of a fetus being taken from someone's womb and planted in another's through magico-religious rituals; 20% claimed that a fetus could be taken from a woman's womb to be turned into a *bolom*.

Health and Healing

In the parish of Jacmel/Roseau there is widespread belief in the powers of traditional medicine and suspicion of modern medical practitioners whom the people find aloof and insensitive. People will go to a doctor but only for certain illnesses and to avoid an autopsy being done in case of death. Thus, they will visit the doctor to receive a "doctor's paper" (*papyé dòktè*) which they will need to avoid an autopsy in case of death, but are reluctant to buy or take the medication prescribed. There is an overwhelming perception (93% of those interviewed) that people today are less healthy than those of yesterday. The reasons put forward for poorer health today are unhealthy lifestyles of the modern times, the advent of refrigeration of food, and the extensive use of chemicals in food cultivation.

Good health (*bon santé*) is described as living well, feeling well, doing things to care for oneself, and doing health-giving things; 43% defined good health as the absence of illness, while 3% defined it as "living for God." From the study one finds an unquestionable belief that people must get sick and die. There is a strong sense of determinism because there are things people have had to learn to live with for which they could find no explanation. In the communities there is a deep-seated belief in the powers of good and evil. Good is associated with God (*Bondyé*) and prayers (*lapwiyè*), while evil (*mal*) is associated with wickedness, malevolent behavior, and harmful spiritual forces and powers. Evil is not directly equated with a personalized force, such as the devil (*denmou*), but rather with behavior which has its origin in such a force. The belief in "evil" helps to explain so many of the daily tragedies of life among the underprivileged.

Responses to questions on self-protection are instructive: 56% believe it is important to protect oneself from evil; 10% said, "God will protect you"; 4% said "yes" it is important to protect oneself from evil, if one knows what to do; 30% gave no response. The high percentage of nonresponse to the questions about evil and self-protection may signify the refusal to disclose information that is considered taboo or secret. Sometimes respondents would give nonverbal responses that suggest an answer without actually answering the questions. Other times they would ask to have the tape recorder turned off, or would simply reply "I do not know" or "I've heard this." When all these varying responses are combined, a much clearer picture of the belief system emerges.

For example, in reply to the question "Do you believe that people can do evil to others and as a result cause their death?" 63% said "yes," 7% said "I've heard this;" 7% said "I do not know," and 23% did not respond. This indicates a dominant belief in the power to harm someone, even to the point of death. Here again one should stress that evil is always associated with the supernatural. When asked, "Do you believe this is something that is common today?" only 23% said "not common" and 10% "not sure."

Although there is such an overwhelming belief in the power of people to affect others, common sense and human experience show that there are people who seem to prosper despite all the evil around. Traditional explanations continue to keep the belief system coherent. The explanation is that there are persons who are born with natural protections, for example, *kwéfé* or *magoté*. The belief is that if one is born a twin, a breach delivery, or with a sixth finger or toe, one is born *magoté* and so cannot be easily harmed by evil practices. To be born *kwéfé* is to be born with a veil over the face. A child born *kwéfé* will see spirits, and so must be treated. The solution is to take the veil from the child's face, dry it, and feed it to the child in its food. When asked whether they believed such things, only 7% said "no." Belief in such phenomena, one would think, would be impacted by changes such as hospital deliveries. Yet the beliefs persist. This is saying something about the resilience of popular beliefs and popular culture. Such resilience has great implications for evangelization.

Well-Being: Powers and Protection

One cannot speak seriously about health and healing, powers and protection in St. Lucia without examining the role of the "obeahman/woman" sometimes referred to as the *gadè*. We have seen how widespread in Jacmel/Roseau is the belief that people can harm others through the use of preternatural powers, and thus the need for self-protection. In the research on birth and birthing we have also seen belief in the power to "tie up a woman's womb" or even mysteriously to take a child from its mother's womb and turn it into a preternatural being called the *bolom*. Central to the exercise of these powers is the "obeahman/woman."

An obeahman/woman is a person who works for others through obeah. Obeah is a broad term covering a host of activities both malevolent and benevolent. These include causing someone to become sick (with an ailment that cannot be diagnosed); causing them to lose their job or be unable to hold on to a job; causing low productivity in farming or poor returns in a business venture. Obeah is also believed to be able to help with success in exams, and with the acquisition of riches. The obeahman/woman it is believed, can foretell the future, as well as "see" things affecting a person which neither the person nor others may be aware of. This function is called *gadé* ("to see"). This is why a distinction is sometimes made between a *gadè* ("seer") and an obeahman/woman. Some people, for example, will see nothing wrong in going to a *gadè* ("pou fè an hòtè"—to have a sighting/reading of their situation) but would have nothing to do with an obeahman/woman, whom they may consider an evildoer. Another important function of the obeahman/woman is that of a "healer," particularly through the use of herbal medication, such as baths, teas, and potions.

In the phenomenon of the obeahman/woman, the interrelationship between popular Catholicism and popular culture becomes very evident. Although belief in the powers of the obeahman/woman comes from popular culture, many of the tools of the obeahman/woman come from popular Catholicism: prayers, sacred images, statues, medals, scapulars, candles, holy water, blessed oil. Some informants claim that among the things some *gadès* require of a client is to make a novena of Masses, or have a number of Masses said before working on the client's behalf can be successful. It is also widely believed that the consecrated host from a Catholic Mass is sometimes taken away by the faithful for use in obeah.

From the data on well-being, and on powers and protection in this study, "prayer" emerges as the single most powerful agent. Questions of "well-being" revealed a strong belief in the spirit world, and a strong belief in the powers of those connected with that world. Self-protection was always principally defined in terms of protection from such power. Prayers can work, but some believe that the obeahman/woman can get you power faster than other agents. Most persons claimed that they relied upon prayers for self-protection and to help them with problem solving. One reason is that prayers are socially respectable and acceptable. However, people readily admitted that when prayers failed they resorted to traditional means. These would include taking bush baths (*ben fèyay*) and wearing protective amulets such as the *gad* and *lowizon*.

From the data there is a perception that evildoers prosper. This many admit, but are quick to say that things gained from obeah do not last, because they did not come from God. "Y pakay signifyé yo anyen," which means, such wealth will get them nowhere in the long run. It is evident that despite what people may say, survival is the primary instinct in what is seen as an unfair and unjust world. When misfortune comes their way people believe it is the work of evildoers, as it is difficult to accept that bad things can happen to good people. Where official religion does not provide a relevant explanation, people resort to primordial beliefs.

Death and Burial Rites

Konpwi was a man dealing with *tjenbwa* (obeah). He had "powers." He worked at the Roseau sugar factory. Konpwi knew how many animals and how much garden everyone owned without anyone ever telling him. He used to tell Augustine how many cows the latter owned, how many were "in young" (pregnant), how many calves they would bear, as well as when they would give birth, with unfailing accuracy. Konpwi was always right. Augustine eventually lost all of his animals. People believe it was Konpwi who caused it.

For the community, this was confirmed when Konpwi died. His coffin refused to enter the church building. The coffin had to be beaten so badly with manioc stick (*bwa manyòk*, the same stick that is used to kill venomous snakes) that it split open and had to be tied with ropes. The refusal of the coffin to enter the church is always perceived as a sign that the person in the coffin was dealing with evil.

Death and burial rites are perhaps one of the areas of popular culture and religion which has been most vividly impacted by social change. The coming of the funeral home has transformed an entire ritual process. A famous St. Lucian folk-drumming group called "Tanbou Mélé," noted for its biting social commentary, has dealt with that whole issue in a piece titled "Lavéyé sé blòko" (Wakes are blockoramas). "Blockos" or "Blockoramas" are open-air parties, with excessively loud dance music played through massive speakers. The following text, which is just one of the five verses of the song, is revealing:

> *An tan lontan lè moun té mò*
> *fanmi jan èvèk tout lézòt té ka sipòté*
> *bwè an ti kafé pou tjenn kò yo fwé*
> *bwè an ti wonm blan pou tjenn kò yo vivan.*
> *Mé apwézan,*
> *lavéyé sé blòko an plas pou fè roro*
> *sé brandy whiskey, labyè*
> *asou tèt mò- yo ka bwè . . .*

> Long ago when someone died
> family, friends, everyone would give support
> drink a little coffee to keep awake
> drink a little white rum to keep the spirit up.
> But today,
> a wake is a blocko, a place for roro
> it is brandy, whiskey, and beers
> they are drinking on the dead . . .

The writer berates the new attitudes that have come to be associated with death and burial. No longer is there the community support system ("Fanmi jan èvèk tout lézòt té ka sipòté"—family, friends, everyone would give support). It has been replaced by selfishness and greed. This is a consequence of modernization symbolized by the commercial icons TV and video of verse two: "Yo ka gadé ès kay ou ni TV, ès ou ni video . . . ès ou ganyen kapèt"—at the wake, they are looking to see whether you have TV or video or new carpet on the floor. The song goes on to contrast those new attitudes toward the rituals with traditional attitudes. It concludes with a public rejection of the new attitudes and an affirmation of the traditional. And so when a cultural carrier (*jan kilti*) dies, the song says, "we don't want any blocko," just:

ban nou an ti dansé	give us a little dancing
ban nou an ti timtim	give us a little *timtim*
ban nou an ti débòt	give us a little *débòt*
ban nou an ti listwa	give us some storytelling
ban nou an ti fawin	give us some farine
ban nou an ti jwé	give us some ring games.[7]

The funeral home has radically transformed the rituals associated with death and burial. Before its advent the body could not be kept too long before burial, and there were many rituals associated with washing and clothing the body, as well as purification rites for the household. There were also established norms of behavior in and around the home where the body was exposed. Those rituals bound families and community together at a critical moment and promoted social cohesion. They also had certain health functions such as protection of the community from communicable diseases. The inability of loved ones to return from distant countries for a funeral also gave added significance to the rites of departure at the time when the means of social communication were underdeveloped. Today with the telephone for instant communication, and access to airline flights, as well as the ability to keep the body for extended periods through freezing, death and burial are much more manageable.

When the body was kept in the home, it was believed that the dead person should not be left alone, but always needed company until the day of burial. This was one of the many functions of the "wake" (*lavéyé*), held for three days from the day of death, and then on the ninth day after death. Informants gave several stories of encounters with the dead person on returning home after wakes. Such tales are commonplace in St. Lucian folklore; Jacmel/Roseau is no exception. One of the leading local researchers in this study gave a personal account of how

---

[7]*Timtim* refers to riddles and proverbs; *Listwa*, to folktales. *Débòt* is a song-dance once condemned by the Catholic Church for being too sexually suggestive. *Fawin* is a common food product made from cassava. The song "Lavéyé sé bloko" was composed by Moses Jn. Baptiste of Vieux-Fort, St. Lucia.

he was once beaten by a "dead person" as he returned from the person's wake. Several others on the local research team confirmed their own belief in this phenomenon.

The belief in the active presence of the dead person is borne out in the research data. Several informants spoke of well-known cases where the dead person is alleged to have shown dramatic signs of displeasure and refusal to cooperate. At the time when there were no hearses, the coffin with the body was carried to the cemetery on the head, in the case of an infant, and on the shoulders by four men, in the case of an adult. Sometimes the "coffin would refuse to pass a certain route," especially if the dead person had expressed a wish not to be taken that way when he/she died.

What do these experiences described by informants say about their beliefs, as well as their understanding of life and death, and the relationship between body and spirit? Has the process of social change exemplified in the funeral home affected the underlying belief system about the nature of the body, the soul/spirit and their interrelationship in the parish of Jacmel/Roseau? How dominant is the Catholic Christian anthropology of the person being made up of body and soul? Is there a deeper understanding of the human person, a kind of native anthropology, which can help official Catholic Church theology better understand the relationship between spirit and matter? What are the possible theological implications of this for doctrinal issues such as the notion of purgatory? These questions we shall revisit in the conclusion to this paper.

SOCIAL CHANGE

The study of death and burial rites in the parish of Jacmel/Roseau illustrates how social change can impact on ritual practice. Earlier, the data on health and healing as well as birth and birthing suggested that modernization in itself did not guarantee changes in ritual. For we saw that despite the advances in modern medicine and the availability of medical facilities, the vast majority of informants believed that people were healthier in the past. There remains the nagging distrust of doctors and the reluctance to take prescribed medication. Many still resort to "bush medicine" and will consult the *gadè* (medicine man/woman) when in serious trouble. This alternative health service is cheaper than professionalized modern medicine and much more readily accessible to the poor. That probably explains why social change has not affected rituals associated with health and healing too significantly.

GLOBALIZATION: THE BANANA INDUSTRY

The most significant area of social change in the parish is related to the banana industry, which has now entered a period of deep crisis, leaving many without a decent or stable income. As we said earlier, the story of the Roseau valley is the story of bananas, and the plight of the banana industry is the plight of the valley. The banana industry was severely damaged by Tropical Storm Debbie in 1994, and even as the industry tried to recover, industrial conflicts developed. For some time farmers had been dissatisfied with the manner in which the government had handled the industry. They had resorted to strike action under the leadership of the Banana Salvation Committee. Two years ago such strikes by banana farmers had resulted in the shooting death of two farmers at the hands of the police. Farmers demanded an inquiry, but there never was one. That soured relations between the government and the farmers even more.

Weeks of strikes and clashes between Banana Salvation Committee supporters and opponents and the police came to a head during the first two weeks of October 1996. There were several arrests. The following weekend, heavy rains caused extensive flooding and damage to property. Infrastructural damage was estimated at US$3 million. The parish of Jacmel/Roseau, which basically sits along the banks of the Roseau River, was badly affected as all fields in the valley were under water.

However, the greatest challenge to the banana industry has been the forces of globalization. Until the early 1990s Caribbean bananas had a secure position in the European market through the operation of a strict licensing regime by the United Kingdom Administration. France, Spain, and Italy also had these national banana import regimes, by which their former colonies were guaranteed a market for their bananas in the former "Mother Country." In 1993, with the unification of the European banana market, these national protective regimes were replaced by a regime for the entire European Union commonly referred to as the Community Regime-Regulation 404/93, which continued to guarantee ACP bananas' preferential treatment in the European market.

The German and Belgian governments challenged Regulation 404/93 at the European Court of Justice and lost. However, the United States-based multinational, Chiquita Brands International, succeeded in getting the United States Trade Representative (USTR) to initiate action under Section 301 of the 1984 U.S. Trade Law against the European Union in October 1994. Chiquita also succeeded in getting the United States to lobby Ecuador, Guatemala, Honduras and Mexico to place the issue of Regulation 404/93 before the Dispute Settlement Body (DSB) of the World Trade Organization (WTO). The DSB ruled against the European Union. This ruling was appealed by the EU, but the WTO appellate body reaffirmed the original DSB ruling. The ruling does not affect duty-free preferences under Protocol 5, but it condemns the licensing system of Regulation preferential treatment once enjoyed in the European market. Many doubt that Caribbean banana producers will be able to retain their share of the EU market on trade preferences alone without the help of the licensing system.

The consequence for the banana industry, and the economies of small island-states such as St. Lucia, St. Vincent, Grenada, and Dominica, which depend heavily on bananas, is devastating. Small farmers in these islands must now compete in an open European market with multinationals like Chiquita, which can produce far greater quantities of cheaper bananas. All the governments of the islands can do is request a delay in implementation of the WTO decision, in order to give the islands and farmers a chance to diversify from bananas into another crop. Those farmers wishing to remain in banana production will have to be rapidly educated to produce only top-quality bananas that can demand a competitive price in the open market.

The future looks bleak for the farmers of Jacmel/Roseau. During a focus group session with young and old farmers in Barre Denis, the issue of bananas was raised. There was a sense of resignation among the older farmers. Although they were personally affected by what was happening, they saw it all through the eyes of faith. "Bondyé bon" ("God is good!") one said. In the end, God would take care of them. But that faith did not lead them to militancy. The younger farmers were more militant. They blamed the former government for the present situation of the banana industry. They felt a righteous indignation about the whole affair. Their sense of justice had driven them to strike and face the armed policemen. Did their Christian faith play any role in that militancy? One cannot be certain. The older farmers who participated in the strikes spoke of praying for protection from injury and harm. Some of them performed other protective rites. The younger farmers claimed that for them it was a matter of standing up for what was right.

The Roman Catholic Church nationally was involved with the St. Lucian Christian Council in mediation between the government and the Banana Salvation Committee. These efforts failed. Many farmers thought that the official Church should have been more overtly supportive of the farmers' cause in the name of justice.

IMPACT OF MODERNITY: TOURISM

Tourism is the second most important sector of the St. Lucian economy after agriculture. In 1993 it was the biggest foreign exchange earner, bringing in some US$213 million (De Backer 1994, 26). There are some positive impacts that the tourism industry has had, especially on those directly involved in it. The industry has engendered greater efficiency, higher standards of performance, and a more customer-oriented approach to business. It has also promoted a greater consciousness of our natural and cultural heritage, as well as of an environment to be conserved.

Despite the contribution of tourism to the economy, there has been an ongoing debate on the real impact of tourism. Some question, for example, as to what percentage of the tourist dollar remains in the country, especially with the present emphasis on "all-inclusive" packages of travel, accommodation, and tours. Then there are the social change considerations. Whereas tourism opens a people to the world, to other nations, customs, traditions, and values, the question remains "at what price?" The price has been the destruction of the fishing industry in certain parts of the island, in order to make way for the construction of new hotels; the loss of access by the public to certain beaches which have become virtually private; and the desecration of certain areas of natural, cultural, and historical significance to the nation, through hotel construction, as was the case with the location of the Jalousie Plantation Resort between the famous twin mountain peaks, the Pitons.

Among the other negative impacts of tourism as practiced in St. Lucia today is the institutionalizing of a negative self-image: making people feel that they must always be servants of white people; that they must learn to speak with an acquired accent to be acceptable; that they must abandon their Kwéyòl language to speak affected English; that the only value in their cultural traditions is that they can be performed on stage for the consumption of the guests; and that in order to be somebody one must imitate the habits, values, and lifestyles of the tourist.

In Jacmel/Roseau the actual numbers of persons directly involved in the tourism sector are very small, varying from about 2% in Millet and Morne D'Or to about 8% in Bois D'Inde and Jacmel. However, the impact of tourism goes far beyond those directly involved in it.

IMPACT OF MODERNITY: THE MASS MEDIA

Rose is 17 years old. She is a secretarial student at the island's only community college. A good student, she loves the computer and loves to watch MTV. She wears the latest styles of her generation. For a time Rose had a serious problem. At nights, while asleep in her room, she would feel a presence, not physical though, wanting to have sex with her. She would have to struggle fiercely in order to ward off the being. Sometimes she would awake to find herself stripped of her nightdress and her body covered with scratches. This occurred for several weeks before she told her mother.

Her mother told her that it was *magi nwè* (black magic) coming after her. She should take a special "bush bath" and, before retiring to bed, make a cross with mustard on the soles of her feet. She should also sleep wearing a black panty turned inside out. According to Rose, from the time she began doing this, nothing has troubled her.

Rose's story is a true story from one of our popular theater sessions. Only the student's name was changed for anonymity. A young person like Rose would experience all the effects of the mass media on the society. With 24-hour cable TV, and some 30 channels to choose from, the whole world is literally in any house in Jacmel/Roseau. Soap operas portraying the fictitious lives of the rich and glamorous are fiercely popular. Consumerism, violence, and immorality are all glorified, seducing people to abandon their values and culture in quest of the illusion. It is television undergirding the tourism industry.

The mass media become an instrument working on behalf of tourism, preparing people to receive the tourist, to understand what country they are from, their customs and tradition. It is the softening of a people. Although the mass media contribute to modernization through exposing people to new ideas, approaches, methods, and styles, the media cannot force change. As in the case of Rose, there will be changes in behavior, attitudes, and lifestyle. However, changes in beliefs will only come within the intimate dialogue of the process of problem solving. If the solutions offered by modernization work, just as if the rituals of the Church work, people will use them. If they do not work, people will reject them. Rose will continue to watch the "soaps," love MTV, and dress in the latest fashion for the disco; however, unless she can find another more effective solution, when she gets home, she will continue to make two crosses on her feet with mustard, and put on her black panty inside out, in order to have a quiet night's sleep.

INCULTURATION

As we explored the popular beliefs of the people of Jacmel/Roseau, vis-à-vis the teachings and practices of the Catholic Church, it was evident that we were witnessing the drama of the tension between faith and culture. This drama is played out wherever Christians in a particular context try to be Christian in a way peculiar to that situation. In theological terms, this drama or ongoing dialogue between faith and culture is called inculturation.[8]

Missiologist Paulo Süess, writing on the polarity between popular and official religion, observes that "popular religion is not just a degraded form of official religion" but that "official and popular religion are mutually dependent on their reciprocal reception" (Süess 1986, 125). For Hervé Carrier, secretary to the Pontifical Council for Culture, that principle of reciprocity is an important element of inculturation (Carrier 1993, 156). The dynamic is neither oppression nor domination, but rather one of mutuality and dialogue. As he says, "The term inculturation includes the notions of growth and mutual enrichment for the persons and groups involved in the encounter of the Gospel message with a social milieu" (ibid.).

The relationship between institutional Roman Catholicism and popular culture in St. Lucia has generally not been one of growth and mutual enrichment, but rather one of domination of the indigenous culture by an oppressive colonial theology. As we have illustrated elsewhere (Anthony 1977, 191), a large number of popular rituals have come under fire from the Church.

Harold Simmons, St. Lucia's leading folklorist, explains why popular culture and the folk tradition is an "underground" tradition: "Its songs, dances, festivals, beliefs and customs manifest an unceasing attempt to create forms of expression for a way of life which is at variance with established authority, orthodox religion, upper class morality, law and other cultural forms having the sanction of

---

[8]For the purpose of this study, "inculturation" is a theological term that refers to the dynamic interplay between the Church (both as an institution and as the people of God) and a particular people as they strive for an authentic cultural embodiment of the gospel message. This relationship implies both that the Christian message transforms a culture and is transformed by that culture. As a result, the message is formulated and interpreted anew.

authority" (Simmons 1963, 41). He asserts: "It has been under constant attack from the pulpit" (ibid.). These attacks by the official Church on popular religion have driven popular culture underground.

According to Idris Hamid, the father of Caribbean theology, "it would seem that God had to do a lot of work underground." Noting the close alliance between the expansionist politics of the colonials and the colonial theology of the mainline churches, Hamid posits a thwarting of God's work in these churches, and puts the question, "Where then did God work if his work within the mainline churches were thwarted?" His reply: God "worked in and through the cultural fragments that were there among the oppressed. Cultural fragments would include the religious practices at the time, however crude and primitive these may be to 'moderns' "(Hamid 1973,123).

THE ST. LUCIAN EXPERIENCE

Official efforts at inculturation in St. Lucia began with the liturgical reforms initiated by Vatican II. The then bishop of Castries, Monsignor Charles Gachet, F.M.I., vigorously promoted the use of the vernacular in the liturgy, which at that time in St. Lucia was perceived to be the English language. A number of local hymns were composed based on the model of the "folk hymn" from North America. Bishop Gachet was the one who encouraged the artist Dunstan St. Omer to begin painting murals in various churches in St. Lucia in the 1970s. St. Omer's approach was genuinely radical. He not only painted the murals in bright Caribbean colors, but more important, he depicted traditional biblical persons and Catholic saints looking like St. Lucians. For the first time Christ and his disciples were being painted in a shape and a form with which people could identify.

St. Omer went even further. At the church of St. Rose de Lima in the parish of Monchy, he depicted the La Rose flower festival, the same festival that had been banned and its followers excommunicated in 1860. The La Rose flower festival, and its rival, the La Marguerite flower festival, are two of the best examples of what one might refer to as inculturation-from-below in St. Lucia. These popular festivals, whose origins are unknown (Anthony 1985, 1), are rooted in the Church, but are outside the ambit of official Church power. Despite the action taken by the Church in 1860, the Church has neither real control nor influence on the day-to-day organization of the floral societies. Yet, the very structure of their main celebrations (the grand fete) revolves around the traditional feast days of their respective patrons, August 30, the feast of St. Rose de Lima in the case of La Rose floral society, and October 17, the feast of St. Margaret Mary Alacoque in the case of La Marguerite floral society.

When St. Omer portrayed the La Rose flower festival in a church mural he was doing something with implications for inculturation that went beyond liturgy. He was making a statement about the ordinary life of the people and challenging traditional notions of the "holy." He was affirming that the joys and celebrations of ordinary people were holy and needed no authority to designate them as such.

St. Omer has painted murals in five of the major Catholic churches in St. Lucia, including the Cathedral of the Immaculate Conception, Castries. However, the mural of the Holy Family in the parish church of Jacmel/Roseau is publicly acclaimed as his finest.

In this mural, St. Omer depicts the ordinary life of the people from the Jacmel/ Roseau parish. The entire mural is engulfed in the green of bananas, the gold of sunshine, and the brown of St. Lucian bodies. There is a fishing scene, where a woman dressed in full traditional wear of the *chantwelle* (folksinger) blows a conch shell, the local manner of publicizing a good catch of fish. There are two Madonnas, a black Mary, and the infant Jesus, counterpoised by an East Indian mother and child, representing the two dominant ethnic groups in the community. St. Omer includes a larger-than-life-size couple dancing the *débòt,* an African song-dance once condemned by the Church for its sexual suggestiveness.

The center of the mural is the child Jesus in his mother's arms holding the host. The face is that of a young stag, a symbol of divinity in some African cultures, according to St. Omer. Mary's face is an African mask. St. Omer deliberately employed the mask technique as he claims he did not want to repeat the centuries-old error of European artists who depicted Mary looking like their women. For the infant Jesus, he argues that since there was no photo to give a true appearance, the artist was safest in the realm of symbolism. His portrayal of the infant Jesus holding up the host to his mother has been a source of much theological debate. The question is one of orthodoxy. St. Omer affirms that it reveals the divine plan: this child, in the mind of God, is destined to be the life of the world.

St. Omer's work stimulated much interest in the relationship between Church and culture. In 1973, this writer established the Folk Research Centre, St. Lucia, in order to deepen the process of inculturation. Motivated by the challenge of Vatican II to study local culture in order to lay bare the seeds of the word that lie buried there, the center began systematic collection and analysis of St. Lucian cultural data. The Folk Research Centre has grown into one of the leading cultural research institutions in the Caribbean. However, conflict with Church authorities over the years has lessened the center's direct relationship with the Church. The center still remains an indispensable resource for any serious attempt by the Church at inculturation.

Along with St. Omer's mural, the work of the parish priest of Jacmel/Roseau, Fr. Lambert St. Rose, in attempting to inculturate the Easter Vigil ceremony of the Catholic Church was a cogent factor influencing the choice of this parish as the Caribbean site for the "Forging Vital Christian Identities" project. Fr. St. Rose's efforts were the fruits of both his own study and research, as well as the people's need for more participatory liturgy. In 1993 he wrote a master's thesis titled "Towards African-St. Lucian Liturgical Identity within the Roman Rite." In 1994 he attempted it for the first time in the parish of Jacmel/ Roseau.

The vigil was planned around the traditional notion of the "wake" for the dead in St. Lucia. Wakes are an occasion for keeping company with the dead and relatives of the deceased. Inside the house where the body is exposed (or if the body is in a funeral home, the place where the deceased lived) people pray and sing hymns until the early hours of the morning. Outside, another group tells stories, sings *konts* (special wake songs), and plays traditional ring games fortified by drinking coffee and white rum. The wake is a normal occasion for traditional storytelling in St. Lucia.

Using the "wake" concept, Fr. St. Rose tried to respond to the often expressed desire for more Kwéyòl in the liturgy, as well as for a liturgy more reflective of St. Lucian culture. For the Easter Vigil, the first part of the ceremony was done in front of the church building, where a huge bonfire provided light and warmth. This fire was later blessed as the "new fire" from which the paschal candle was lighted. Some elderly storytellers from the community proclaimed the scripture readings in story form using the Kwéyòl language. The people punctuated the delivery with the traditional "Quick-Quack" of storytelling. "Quick-Quack" is the stylized crowd response in the call-refrain dialogue between the storyteller and the audience. For the responses to "the proclamation of the word," the choir danced to the rhythm of guitars, drums, banjo, and shac-shac of the native folk orchestra. After the lighting of the paschal candle, the people followed it into the church with songs of joy in their hearts and on their lips.

In 1994, that Vigil was a moving experience. There were no sleepy and bored parishioners. The people were aglow and the church radiated vitality. Those who had longed to hear and understand the word of God in their own tongue were delighted. Some claimed that although they had heard or read the creation story innumerable times before, it had now become alive to them. "Never again," said one, "can we go back to the way things were."

Important lessons can be learned from this kind of liturgical inculturation. (i) Any attempt at inculturation, if it is not to remain superficial, must involve rigorous study of the particular ritual as well as the relevant local cultural correspondences. (ii) Such an effort must be a response to a felt need on the part of the people. It must involve the people in dialogue, listening to their views, accepting their suggestions, and facilitating their ownership of the activity. (iii) There must be adequate preparation. (iv) The event must be a communal affair, involving as many persons as possible. This shows respect for the many and varied gifts of the community and protects against elitism. (v) Any such undertaking must be done with good taste, and (vi) whatever is done must not distract from the spirit of prayer and worship. The Jacmel/Roseau Easter Vigil experience has been repeated each year since 1994, and continues to be a beacon for any serious attempt at liturgical inculturation.

CONCLUSION

The parish of Jacmel/Roseau can rightly boast of the boldest and most significant efforts at liturgical inculturation in the St. Lucian context. St. Omer's mural challenged the traditional Catholic iconography of the European-based churches, while St. Rose's attempt at inculturation of the Easter Vigil continues to be unique in the English-speaking Caribbean. However, the data from our study of popular Catholicism suggest major challenges for both the local Church and foreign missioners.

First and foremost is the undeniable fact that people are open to serious attempts at inculturation on the part of the official Church. This is important in the light of the constant assertion on the part of many that "the people are not ready!" In Jacmel/Roseau, acceptance of a church mural where members of the Holy Family are depicted as Black or Afro-Caribbean, in contrast to the usual Caucasian imagery, meant a deep mental and ideological shift. That did not come without pain. During one of the focus group discussions in Jacmel, some reacted angrily at "what the white priests had done," now that the same church was interested in studying the very traditions which had been so vigorously condemned before. There were many allusions to the predominance of Caucasian features in religious art and literature, with only the devil depicted as "Black."

In Jacmel/Roseau, the response to the changes in the Easter Vigil has been overwhelmingly positive. Now the entire parish liturgy is more responsive to the needs of people. Scripture readings, hymns, as well as the homily are done either bilingually or in Kwéyòl, with the people themselves doing translations when necessary. They are not only open to inculturation, but also actively engaged in the process. This is most strikingly illustrated by the annual Kwéyòl Day or *Jounen Kwéyòl*, which has become one of the leading cultural events of recent times in St. Lucia.

It is a day dedicated to the promotion of things local and St. Lucian. People are expected to speak only Kwéyòl that day, wear traditional dress, and cook local cuisine. Celebrations for *Jounen Kwéyòl* always begin with a Mass that must be in Kwéyòl. The people themselves make all the preparations for these Masses. This has forced the local Catholic Church authorities to come to grips with the need for an entire Kwéyòl liturgy. Once before, the community of Jacmel was chosen as one of the host communities for *Jounen Kwéyòl*. In 1997 it was chosen again.

One direct consequence of this phenomenon of popular culture is the initiative on the part of the Antilles Episcopal Conference (AEC) to develop a Kwéyòl Eucharistic prayer for the Catholic Eucharistic celebrations in the Caribbean. The "Kwéyòl Eucharistic Prayer Project," as it is called, is being coordinated by the bishop of Guadeloupe along with a group of regional collaborators. In its first report, the group has recommended that the AEC declare open a period of liturgical experimentation in the Kwéyòlophone Caribbean to facilitate the project. This recommendation has been accepted.

One other major challenge to the local Church and the foreign missioners coming out of this study is the need to recognize the vast differences between the official Church's view of the sacraments and the popular perception of their functionality. Let us take, for example, the issue of *vòlè batenm* (or "stealing baptism"). There are evidently two different universes of meaning operative here.

The parents, godparents, and others may participate fully in the official ritual, to the satisfaction of the celebrant, after having attended all the prescribed presacramental catechesis. However, during the official rite, other rituals are operative. More than that is the willingness of the participants to endure all the legal requirements of the official Church, in order to satisfy the important social function of being a godparent. What connection is there with the whole question of Christian faith? It is obvious that in this situation, while faith would be very important to the pastor, it may have little significance to the actors. If this principle is applied to the administration of all the other sacraments, the pastoral implications can be far-reaching.

Recognition of the differences between official and popular perceptions of the meaning of the sacraments has great implications for Church renewal and reform. Initiatives for reform on the part of the official Church are usually motivated by perceived needs of the institution or its inability to function effectively in some given contexts. However, the question is, how much of this renewal is in response to genuine problems and needs of people? Serious and meaningful reform can only come after a process of discernment of those needs and problems. Otherwise renewal will be self-satisfying and irrelevant.

Another important theological and missiological question raised by this study is the issue of native cosmology versus the dominant philosophical framework of western Catholic theology. If we return to the phenomenon of *kokma* described earlier in our study of baptism, one can ask, what notion of the universe underlies this belief system? If a world exists where unbaptized dead children can roam about, what are the other characteristics of that world? Whether one accepts this cosmology or not, it gives meaning to the problem that some parents have with children who cry at night or claim that they "see things." The giving of meaning is the first step toward the solution of the problem. More important, though, is the inadequacy of the explanation of mainline Catholic theology. Children who die without baptism are supposedly saved through "baptism of desire"—a theological construct—or "go to limbo," according to traditional catechesis. The notion of "limbo" does not help solve the problem of those affected by the phenomenon which they call *kokma*.

There are still other issues of cosmology arising from this study. For example, what does the belief in the ability of the dead to beat someone or effect the movement of a coffin say about one's understanding of the universe? Add to that the belief that the dead can communicate with the living through dreams and visions, and elements of an entire philosophical system begin to emerge. The important question is, what can official theology learn from such popular philosophy? Our informants from Jacmel/Roseau seemed at home with that universe of the living dead. They had learned to manage that world. How adequate is the response of official theology to such experiences? From the perspective of problem solving, efficiency is the litmus test. If people have a problem and the official Church has a solution, they will use it. If the official Church has no answer, or its solution does not work, the people will seek answers elsewhere.

This raises questions of ethics. The official Church may say that something is wrong, while people, through necessity or otherwise, will still do it. We do not refer here to persons who knowingly do what is wrong, but rather to those who genuinely do not see things the way the Church does. For example, if experience has taught people that a dog howling in the neighborhood, or a black moth flying into the house, or a picture falling from a wall and smashing to pieces on the floor, are all omens of death, the official Church may declare them superstitious, but that will not stop people believing in them. Likewise the Church may say it is wrong to believe in dreams, but people will trust their experience and ignore the Church. More important still is the case where someone has a very serious illness, be it physical, emotional, or spiritual, and cannot find the cause. If doctors cannot help and the priests cannot help, people will turn to the *gadè*. No amount of condemnation by the official Church will cause them to think they have done something wrong.

Here again we are faced with another positive influence which popular culture and religion can have on official religion. Popular religion can force official religion to become self-critical as it assesses its relationship to the everyday needs of ordinary people. Our study of the relationship between popular and official Catholicism supports the suggestion of writers like Amaladoss (1989) and Parker (1996) that notions of "spectrum" or "continuum" are more suitable tools to define such a relationship than the sharp distinction that others make.

The notions of continuum and spectrum as applied by Amaladoss and Parker with their respective qualifications are useful tools for reflection on the relationship between popular culture, popular Catholicism, and the institution of the Roman Catholic Church in the Jacmel/Roseau parish. From our study, it is clear that there is no sharp delineation between popular and official Catholicism. The notion of continuum or spectrum seems more relevant to the phenomena we have witnessed. People move freely from official to popular rituals. They reinterpret official symbols, utilize official rituals, but operate from their own cosmology and universe of meanings.

For both the local Church and the foreign missioner this poses formidable challenges. The local person must revisit his/her own heart in quest of honesty. How authentic is Catholic Christianity in St. Lucia today? Is the Catholic Christian a whole and integrated person, at home in the culture and in the Church? For the missioner, it is the challenge to humility; to be aware of how little one knows or even understands, and to become childlike in the eagerness to learn. As we have stated elsewhere, for the missioner,

the quest for understanding must involve the dialogue whereby an effort can be made to find correspondences within the missionary's experience for the reality in the other's experience. The missionary must come to appreciate that there will never be identity of experiences with the "other," but only a measure of understanding that will come from the back and forth movement of dialogue through which correspondences can be discovered. And yet, is this not part of what mission activity is all about? Not the complete identification which destroys either the missionary or the other person, but rather the mutuality of giving and receiving that comes from an understanding of differences and an appreciation of the fact that people are similar in that they are different (Anthony 1988, 299).

This study has opened new possibilities for the churches in St. Lucia, but there is still much work to be done. There is need for further exploration of popular beliefs and practices, and reflection on the philosophical system that undergirds them. This may have far-reaching implications for theology in the Caribbean today. As Harold Sitahal, the ecumenical consultant to this study asserts, perhaps here we are witnessing, for the very first time, the emergence of a truly contextual theology in the Caribbean.

4

Ghana

Popular Catholicism in Dagbon

VINCENT BOI-NAI, S.V.D. and JON P. KIRBY, S.V.D.

"My name is John Amadu Shaibu. I was baptized as a Catholic when I was attending school at Malshegu. When I completed school I went to Kumasi to help my father, who is a butcher. Since my father is a Muslim he immediately introduced me to his Muslim friends, who advised me to be a faithful Muslim. I could see that they were all nice to me, and so I followed them every day to the mosque to pray.

"With the help of my father and his Muslim friends I started preparing and selling kebabs by the roadside in the evenings. After two years I became tired of this and went back to my village near Tamale. Back at home I started farming and in no time I became sick. I went to consult a malam *and after giving me a certain 'medicine' to drink he gave me a talisman to put under my pillow. Since I was still feeling sick I went to a diviner who asked me to bring a chicken to perform a sacrifice for me. I did this but I still didn't feel well. In my frustration I asked the Catholic prayer leader in the village to come and pray for me. Indeed, he came with some members of the prayer group and they prayed for me. They also brought me to Dr. Abdulai's clinic, and members of the prayer group visited me there and brought me food.*

"After I became well I decided to become a member of the prayer group because I could see how Christians love and help each other. I know the Muslims in the village make fun of me and sometimes abuse me, but I am not disturbed by that. Also my relatives who are not Muslims are not happy with me and they say I have betrayed them by not following the way of the ancestors."

METHODS AND AIMS

This story of John Amadu Shaibu illustrates one of the reasons young Dagombas in the villages of northern Ghana become Christians. Many young people like John come to see that Christians are people who pray; they also love and help one another. In our research among Dagomba Catholics in the villages around Tamale we tried to verify this. We also wanted to find out if there were other reasons why Dagombas converted to Christianity, as well as how others see Dagomba Catholics and especially how they see themselves.

This article summarizes the results of a study of Catholic Christian Communities in fifteen villages around Tamale in the northern region of Ghana. A wide range of local leaders, groups and individuals were interviewed both formally and informally,[1] and, in addition to participant-observation, a two-part survey was given to a sampling of the population. The first part probed Christian identity in terms of three areas: faith, modern life, and traditional life. The second part focused on typical Dagomba problems and problem-solving processes involving spirit-agencies and traditional rituals. Altogether, 320 people were interviewed, including 106 Traditionalists, 90 Catholics, 19 Protestants, and 105 Muslims. There were six Catholic interviewers and one Muslim; each covered two villages and a total of some 45 people.

The study addressed popular Christian identity, especially in terms of prayer and ritual, problem solving, and social change. Our survey findings will be discussed in response to these foci after a brief historical and ethnographic background situates them. In the latter part of the chapter we will discuss ritual and problem solving in terms of three traditional problematic areas of Dagomba life with suggestions for appropriate Christian prayer and ritual solutions.

DAGBON

"Dagbon" refers both to the kingdom of the Dagomba, a subgroup of the Gur-speaking people of northern Ghana with a population of about 600,000 (cf. Barker 1986; Ghana 1964) and to its geographical area of roughly 10,000 square kilometers. Dagombas are quite closely related, both historically and cultural-linguistically, to three other Mole-Dagbanli, chiefly peoples of northern Ghana: the Mamprusi, Nanumba, and Mossi (see Staniland 1975). All fit the model of West African traditional "states" (see Goody 1971) in having a hierarchical social structure consisting of a lower stratum of commoners incorporated from the surrounding acephalous or chiefless peoples and an upper stratum or royal estate (Goody 1973) who are closely associated with Muslim clerics (see Levtzion 1968). Outside the structure are all the unassimilated acephalous peoples whom even now

---

[1]We wish to thank all who participated and especially the experts who helped us to sharpen our interpretation of the data and to test resulting conclusions and theories.

are often referred to as "our slaves." With the aid of superior weaponry and horses, or control over "the means of destruction" (see Goody 1971), each dry season in the period from the 16th to the early 20th century Dagomba warriors made forays into the surrounding countryside, especially among the Konkombas (see Tait 1961), capturing enough slaves, foodstuffs, and domestic animals to keep them for the rest of the year.

GOD AND THE *NAAM*

In God, *Naa wunni* (sky god), the rulers of Dagbon had a satisfactory religious solution to their thirst for conquest. It articulated what seemed to them a self-evident truth: that the world is hierarchical. Just as God had authority over the lesser gods, rulers were naturally superior to commoners or conquered peoples. The discovery coincided with the fact that raiders and traders need a geographically broad-based God, a movable God, not limited to one place or to one territory-bound people. The interests and activities of the lesser deities of the earth were necessarily limited to their well-defined precincts and to the fertility and harmonious existence of those who inhabited them. But the interests and activities of the "sky god" were as expansive as the heavens.

Dagombas took their success in war as a sign of God's favor. So, although their notion of God was broad and fit well within their transcultural politics, this "sky god" (*naa-wunni*) retained a quite narrow moral code for a supreme being. In practice, it was the "spirit of the chief" (another translation of *naa-wunni*) that guided and protected them as they raided their way across the Voltaic basin. Now a new understanding of God and the *naam* (system of chieftancy and power) is emerging. Under the influence of a worldwide Islamic expansion *Naa wuuni* is becoming "Allah," and, in response to democratization, the *naam* is finding new modes of exploitation through land tenancy and political elitism.

RESPECT

"Respect" is the mortar holding the *naam* together. Everyone has a "place" in Dagomba society and must know how to show it in relation to everyone else. "Respect" is the demonstration of one's rank. The giving and receiving of "respect" are shown in hundreds of everyday greetings and responses that change and adapt themselves in a bewildering array of contexts—in the compound, the chief's court, the farm, the market, at funerals, namegivings, and dozens of ceremonies. All the bowing, squatting, lying prostrate, the obligatory concern about the well-being of the house, wives and husbands, fathers and mothers, friends and children, and all the praising and blessings are occasions for demonstrating, stabilizing, and reinforcing hierarchical relations. The ranks of power are also ritualized in the many sumptuary symbols and trappings of authority.

In Dagbon, hierarchy makes for stability: "It's when one is greater than the other that the world is stable" (Plissart 1983: 173, #1306).[2] Dagombas live in larger, more complex communities than their acephalous neighbors. They must be equally at home in a number of languages and accustomed from their youth to different laws and traditions, many of which can easily come into conflict. Their system of kinship blends with and supports these rules. Succession is patrilineal, and a chief cannot rise above the status of his father. Those at the bottom also feel that they have a stake in the system. Commoners have access to lower-status chieftaincies by being fostered in a chiefly household. Status is acquired gradually over generations through kinship ties. These rules of respect must be heeded by all for internal peace, harmony, and order. They let one know who defers when strangers meet along the path or in front of a compound and how quarrels are to be settled. They prevent wars; but when infringed upon, they also cause them!

CHANGES

Faith in the old political-religious formula of the *naam* and the ideals embodied in "respect" are now being challenged by Christianity, parliamentary democracy, and modernity in general. One can now become rich and powerful without chiefs, without "respect," and one can have access to God without Muslims. Former slave peoples are discovering the importance of their own ethnicity. Rulers and the ruled are fighting over land, not as a source of life and fertility, but as a commodity, a source of wealth and power. All are coming to see the importance of development. But many are using it to benefit only themselves. There is a quest for a new "sky god." It is leading many to a new Islam, more fundamentalist and obsessive, but worldwide in scope. But it is also leading some to Christianity.

In order to understand popular Catholicism in Dagbon it will be necessary to look at a number of major changes affecting Dagomba life: in education and politics, in the concept and use of land, and in Islam.

The rest of the world has finally reached Dagbon. It is a world that requires education. The many development projects that we find in northen Ghana, the Western jobs, the need for cash, and the modern conveniences that improve the quality of one's life, all require education. It is the key to everything, including power. Education fosters democratic government. The traditional feudal system that was kept in place by the British and by subsequent governments is now breaking down. The Dagombas rejected Catholic missionaries and their schools, but the low-status, nonchiefly peoples accepted. Now the more educated "minorities" are challenging the old feudal system by force of arms and democratic politics.

During the colonial period from 1900 to 1957, the British ruled through the Dagombas. Under the policy of "indirect rule" the constitutions of the Dagomba chieftaincy (*naam*) became the political model throughout the North (see

---

[2]All proverbs have been quoted from Plissart (1983).

Ladouceur 1979). As a result of this, the more than 30 ethnic groups of the "Northern Territories" who had no chiefs were put under the control of the slave-raiding Dagombas, Mamprusi, and Gonjas, who had chiefs. After Independence the apparatus of "indirect rule" was kept intact in order to control the North's illiterate masses. It was only in the most recent elections in November 1996, when some "minority" candidates won out over chiefly ones, that this pattern was broken for the first time.

The British initially provided education only for the sons of chiefs. By the 1950s Christian missionaries, who finally gained access to the North, brought education and development to all. After World War II the North was gradually opened to Christian missionaries but Dagombas for the most part resisted their efforts. With the churches came education and development. Catholic missionaries, who had already been long present among the peoples bordering the French colonial countries like the Dagarti and Kassena, spread southward, building mission houses, schools, and clinics, especially among the less privileged nonchiefly groups where their preaching was well received (see Dery 1989). After Independence the Ghanaian government greatly expanded northern services and development. Chiefs tried to control this development and expansion in old ways but increasingly found themselves at odds with the principles of a parliamentary democracy. Gradually tensions escalated, especially between the chiefs and the educated "minorities." Chiefs' sons became lawyers and politicians while the educated "minorities" formed "youth associations." A militant new spirit of ethnic identity and unity arose among the "minorities" which challenged the old order and nurtured a desire for their own chiefs and laws. Because of its key role in education, the Catholic Church is perceived as the author of many of these changes so unpopular with Dagombas.

Another major change in the Dagomba traditional world concerns land tenure and the need to find new ways for rulers to extract goods and services from their clients—especially by controlling the use of formerly open lands. During the colonial period the Northern Territories were illegally claimed by the British Crown. After Independence the "North" was "handed over" to the Republic of Ghana. In 1979 the contested lands of the Northern Region were constitutionally vested in the Dagomba and Gonja chiefs, where they remain to the present time. This was viewed by the nonchiefly tribes as a compounding of injustices, and the so-called "ethnic conflicts" began. Over the past fifteen years there have been more than fifteen such conflicts, bringing death and untold misery to tens of thousands. The latest and most serious of these in 1994, referred to as the "Northern Conflict," accounted for over 20,000 deaths and has made 100,000 homeless (see Katanga 1994). Now the fighting has abated, and the recent elections provide hope that a more peaceful political solution may be in the making. But despite early promptings from the Catholic Church (see Catholic Bishops Conference 1984), the deeper issues of inequality and injustice have not yet been seriously addressed (see Gonja Traditional Authority 1984) by either the government or the chiefly peoples themselves.

During the colonial era Islam was fostered and Christianity suppressed. Not wanting to upset the stability of local politics, the British government banned Christian missionaries with their schools and clinics, and kept the North a source of cheap labor for southern mines and cocoa farms. When northern laborers went south they were not accepted by the Asante, who regarded them as their "slaves," and so they turned to their fellow northerners in the predominantly Muslim strangers' quarters or "Zongos" for companionship and accommodation. They also converted to Islam. In the North thousands of rootless slaves freed from their servitude to the chiefly estates also sought status and employment by becoming Muslims and joining the ranks of Nigerian merchants. Gradually the percentage of Muslims rose but it was still a foreigner's religion. In 1969 Busia's Aliens Compliance Order expelled thousands of Nigerians from Ghana and along with them went two-thirds of Ghana's Muslims (Dretke 1970). But the gap of Muslim leadership was soon filled by indigenous Gonja and Dagomba Muslims, who together with northern chiefly politicians used their new influence and authority at the national level to cull the favor of Gulf states and other oil-rich fundamentalist Muslim nations. The early 1980s saw the first wave of foreign-sponsored Muslim missionary activity throughout northern Ghana. From this time onward most Dagomba chiefs, politicians, and businessmen, even those baptized with Christian names, found it necessary to identify with Islam. Today it is taken almost as an undisputed fact that to be a Dagomba means to be Muslim.

TAMALE

Tamale is the most important center in the North, controlling trade, commerce, transportation, politics, and the military. With an estimated population of 350,000, it is made up of mostly northern ethnic groups, of whom about 65% are Dagombas. It is also the most important religious center in the North, being the seat of the Northern Ecclesiastical Province of the Catholic Church with a resident archbishop, the northern ministerial outreach for most of the mainline Protestant churches, and the Muslim center for the North.

Catholics are about 1.5% of the Dagomba population. The other main Christian denominations around the Tamale area, both with higher percentages, are the Assemblies of God and the Baptists. There are also a few Presbyterians and members of Independent Churches. According to the Ghana Evangelism Committee (GEC 1988:24), the Dagomba Protestant groups, at 3,543 members, greatly outnumber their Catholic brethren of 571 members. But in the villages we surveyed the Catholics were dominant. The Christians in any given village generally form one congregation. In the villages surveyed the dominant group was Catholic, but in other villages other groups are more active.

Tamale has the highest percentage of Muslims in Ghana, about 65%. As many as 85% of the Dagombas of Tamale would claim to be Muslims, though only 60% of these would actually attend Friday mosque. The Tamale Muslim community is influencing the surrounding villages, and converts are increasing rapidly. They are now about 40% Muslim. One of the prayer leaders explained the growth

in his village: "In 1962 there were only three or four Muslims in Malshegu. Today the majority are Muslim." In most of the villages Christians get on well with
the Muslims. But some of the Christian Communities (CCs) complain of difficulties. In the last fifteen years as the Muslims have begun competing for followers in the villages, and as fundamentalism increased, relations have become more
and more strained. Here we must distinguish between two important Muslim
factions. One is strongly influenced by Iranian Shi'ites and is very antagonistic,
while the other maintains cordial relations with Christians.

THE VILLAGES SURVEYED

The 15 villages surveyed in this study (Appendix, Figure 1) are almost all
within a 10-mile radius of Tamale. Most of the villages are small, averaging about
1,500 inhabitants, or 150-200 "houses" or compounds—enclosed clusters of 6-
10 round huts (rooms) of mud walls and grass roofs. The residents, often as many
as 20, are basically a nuclear family unit consisting of a man and his wives and
children, including fostered dependents. Villages along the Dalon road where the
pipes run have access to Tamale's treated water. None of the villages have electricity; one has a health center with an operating theater and dispensary run by
Dr. Abdulai, a prominent Dagomba Catholic. Like other villages in the Northern
Region, those surveyed have a high annual growth rate of about 3.8% (GEC
1988:15). The population density is less than the national average of 51 per square
mile, but it is rising steadily, and people complain of less farmland and firewood
than before. Almost everyone still depends on subsistence agriculture, but unlike
the rest of the North, where only 24% of the people live in towns, the villagers
around Tamale regularly go there for market and meetings, and they have been
strongly influenced by urban thinking. There are no industries, little trading, and
only a few full-time specialists like teachers. All other specialized persons like
bicycle "fitters," butchers, brewers, weavers, seamstresses, grinding-mill operators, "bush" masons, and carpenters work part-time. Some sell provisions out of
their homes. All the villages studied are minor chiefdoms. One has a female
chief. In addition to the chiefs, each village has an educated "assemblyman,"
who is these days even more powerful than the chief in matters involving village
development. The literacy rates, levels of income, and health services are lower
than the national average but slightly higher than in villages farther from Tamale.
All but a few of the villages have primary schools (there are 30 Catholic primary
schools altogether in the parish), and three have junior secondary schools. Many
of the villages have adult education and literacy programs under the direction of
Christian leaders.

DEVELOPMENT OF THE CHRISTIAN COMMUNITIES

According to Father Olivier, parish priest of Holy Cross Church, the total number of adult Dagomba members in the village communities are between 400 and
450. "There have been more than 600 baptisms since the early 1960s when it all

began. But now there are only about 400 attending services, and of these only 30% are baptized." These village communities developed gradually over the last 30 years in response to the efforts of the "White Fathers." The early missionary approach was through schools. A great many like Shaibu were baptized almost as part of the school curriculum. Some priests tried to make it more personal with children's prayer groups and by instructing a few prayer leaders in the early 1960s. Those first baptized would be elders now but very few still live in their communities. "School children were less reliable than farmers," says Fr. Olivier.

> "Instead of remaining in the community they drifted to Tamale. Most of these subsequently became Muslim. The same was true of Malshegu. By 1970 we changed evangelistic strategies and began to focus primarily on the young farmers. This was better than the school model which was neither self-propagating nor village-based."

By the early 1970s another missionary priest began to organize Small Christian Communities on models borrowed from Latin American churches. As a result, Christian Communities were begun in Kumbuyili, Chirifuyili, Gurugu, Chesie, and Tampe-Kukuo. They started with young farmers and a few converts were made. Small churches were built at Gurugu and Yongduni. More recently, from the 1980s to the present, the work expanded to Nwodua, Garzeigu, Dobogshie, and Kataraga. But they have found that there is no perfect method for evangelization. "Sometimes even farmers 'deserted.' Many of the baptized leave when they become adults. They take a second wife, become wealthy, or get disillusioned" (Fr. Olivier).

Nowadays, both the community and education are stressed, communities have expanded, and the work has increased dramatically. But they are lacking leadership. Olivier explains that "in over half our communities there is no catechumenate because there is nobody trained to teach."

The CCs are small, averaging around 30 members each, although in some villages there are only 10 regular participants. They are composed of all the members of the Catholic community and also include many nonbaptized undergoing catechetical instruction. They meet for daily morning and evening prayers like their Muslim neighbors. On Sundays the communities of the smaller villages walk to the nearest larger village where they have mass or combined prayer services in a school classroom or small mud-block church. They regularly meet to discuss and organize activities related to Christian outreach in their villages, which includes visiting the sick and helping widows, the handicapped, and the destitute. They are also active in development. In most of the villages the CC leaders are involved in community-based projects of nonformal education in which literacy is taught along with basic hygiene, home economics, and childcare, along with some practical economic ventures like soapmaking.

Each of the CCs has one or a number of "prayer leaders" whose basic duty it is to conduct the morning and evening prayers and Sunday services. But they are highly influential in their villages and organize and lead the CCs in all the communal activities which they do together as Christians. Some have gathered the Christians to defend old women unjustly accused of witchcraft. They help the Christians to organize themselves for special celebrations like namegivings and communal labor projects like house building. They represent the group in official matters before the chief and elders, and give catechetical instruction. They inform the priest of special ministerial needs of the community, and they act as translators for the priest when necessary. Some may offer special services such as translations, although all of the Sunday readings have been translated by a special team chosen for this purpose. They are also involved in village-level self-help and development projects like pig and poultry farms; they teach literacy and adult education classes; and they help the community to organize for larger-scale improvements such as piped water, electricity, better roads, and schools.

Normally someone who is interested in joining the CCs simply begins to attend morning and evening prayers. After a year or so of this when the neophyte comes to gain a certain "feel" for Christian life, he or she is enrolled in a four-year catechumenate program which involves both instruction and activities. Each stage has clearly defined objectives and requires new understandings and commitments from the neophyte to various aspects of Christian life, such as to monogamy and Christian marriage without divorce, to dependence on the power of prayer and God rather than on divination and shrines, and to Christian service with acts of love and concern in their local communities. After completing a stage the neophyte is given a token such as a medal to mark his or her progress and new status in the community. Finally the neophyte is welcomed into the community with baptism in a village ceremony at Easter.

A TYPICAL PRAYER SERVICE

The chapel is a rectangular structure of mud and grass, small, about 30 feet by 15 feet, very similar to the simple mosques. The Christian community meets there each morning about 5:30 and in the evenings around 7:30. The evenings are better attended as the evening meal is over and women and children are able to come. The prayer leader usually begins with a simple song, often a passage from a psalm or a simple prayer put to well-known traditional melodies such as: "Jesus loves us, Jesus loves us" and repeated many times antiphonally. The prayer leaders have had singing workshops at Holy Cross where they were taught to make up simple songs, and they improvise quite well. The singing often attracts non-Christians who wish to join in.

After the opening hymn the prayer leader prays or reads a biblical text from the portion of the Bible that has been translated already or from the Sunday lectionary prepared by the Fathers at Holy Cross. The reading is followed by a short reflection and commentary about its application in daily life. Following this is the part everyone likes the most—the general congregation is invited to offer their spontaneous prayers. The prayers are offered in Dagbanli; they are fervent and often quite long, lasting three to four minutes. Some of the charismatics imitate the style of the Assemblies of God or Baptists by raising their voices, almost to the point of shouting. They sometimes behave as though they were possessed and make frequent repetitions and encourage confirming remarks like "Amen" or "Jesus" from the rest of the congregation. The prayers are mostly petitions for good health, success in farming, for individual sick persons, for more rain or for the rain to stop, for people going on journeys, or for protection from evil. There are also prayers of praise. Most of the adults take their turn to pray. The spontaneous prayers are followed by the Our Father and Hail Mary, which are led by the prayer leader. This is followed by another song and a concluding prayer which sums up the main current of the spontaneous prayers. After this the atmosphere changes as the congregation relaxes in their places and the leader makes the announcements for the evening. Typical announcements include invitations to a "communal labor" to weed or make corn rows on the farm of one of the villagers. Often the leader exhorts the members not to be lax in their commitment, saying, "We Christians must try to help." Other items might include helping someone build a house or coming together to help the Muslims celebrate one of their feasts, contributing to the needs of the poor, an accident victim, a disabled person, or someone who needs a medical operation. It is also an occasion to offer some catechetical instructions, announcements about the night school, local development projects, or some activity program at Holy Cross.

TAMALE PARISHES

The village CCs are extensions or "outstations" of Holy Cross parish. One of the priests at Holy Cross regularly visits them, and priests from the nearby seminary say Sunday masses in the larger ones. In Tamale itself, both at Holy Cross Church and at the cathedral, Dagombas are few. Most of the Catholics belong to more northerly "minority" tribes evangelized earlier on in the 1930s. Other large contingents, especially at the cathedral, include the Ewes and Asantes from the South. Most of the indigenous priests, including the archbishop, are Dagartis. There is only one Dagomba diocesan priest (at the time of the survey away at studies).

Since the character of the services depends on the languages and the cultures of the people attending, the parishes have tried to give each group an opportunity to worship in their own way, to pray and sing in their own language and styles. But because the majority of Dagomba Catholics are in the villages, church affairs in Tamale tend to be less visibly "Dagomba" in character. At times this has been the source of some friction, and more recently there has been a policy to give more attention to the Dagomba Catholics than their limited numbers would seem to require.

THE LACK OF WOMEN IN THE CCs

The lack of women and wives in the communities has severely hampered their growth in the past, though this is now changing. At first there were no women at all.

"Remember we only started with young boys; no girls. In Dagbon, religion is the realm of the men, not the women. Women started to come as a result of encouragement from their husbands and even then only after the birth of the third child when they didn't go back to their maternal homes anymore. All of this takes years and years. Now more women are coming. These are girls that have been influenced by the 'Fathers' and the CCs since they were children. They often married Christians. Somehow they saw Christian women as having a better life than non-Christians" (Fr. Olivier).

Over the last decade many of the youth have married and are raising families of their own. The communities are more balanced now, and, although they are not attracting many new converts, they are expanding by the natural growth rate.

OTHER DIFFICULTIES OF THE CCs

It is still a youthful Church. The members themselves are mostly young single men and in the words of the parish priest they have much to learn:

"Whether it was the lure of money, or other advantages it is hard to say. The truth is there is not much materially to be gained from conversion. Is it education and a higher standard of living? Perhaps. There are more converts now, but just how 'Christian' they are is another matter. I wonder how many of them would really distinguish themselves as Christians if an outsider were to be caught as a thief, or a woman under accusation of witchcraft ran to them for help, or they caught a Konkomba and were beating him to death. It is not easy being a Christian in this milieu" (Fr. Olivier).

Members of the CCs do not have high status. They are usually the poor. They come from Traditional, or like Shaibu, from Muslim religious backgrounds. Many have mixed motives for becoming Christians. One of the priests explained: "Initially I felt that people joined the church for religious reasons, but now I have come to see more and more that often it is for money, security, jobs, etc. For most of them, motivations are gradually purified in the long process of conversion which follows their initial joining the Church." At times there are quarrels, disagreements, misunderstandings. Lacking the support they need, they often fall away as they grow older, leaving the upcoming youthful ranks without mature leadership.

"What is there to show for 50 years? Only 400 adult Christians! It would not be so bad if they were very strong. I wish they were more exemplary. There are a few outstanding ones among them like Dr. Abdulai, but on the whole their faith is still weak. Yet, hearing confessions, sometimes you are surprised by the depth of their understanding and sorrow for their sins" (Fr. Olivier).

Islam is not the only serious obstacle to conversion among the Dagombas. CC leaders in the field have commented on the lack of commitment and of witness: "Some of them are addicted to drink and to the lottery." The strength of the commitment is not what it should be: "There are great differences among them. Some only come to church on Sunday to be with their friends." Many converts have been disappointed by the fact that they did not receive the benefits and support they had expected. One of the priests pointed to an embarrassing "Memorandum"[3] to the Archdiocese from a number of Dagomba Catholics in the aftermath of the tragic "Northern Conflict" in 1994 as an example of this kind of disappointment:

> "The 'Memorandum' of a few members of the Dagomba Catholic community to Archbishop Dery was scandalous . . . They were disappointed that they did not receive money, security and advantages . . . so they condemned the Church and they called upon the larger Dagomba non-Christian (mainly Muslim) community to further condemn Christians."

A DAGOMBA CHRISTIAN IDENTITY

What distinguishes Dagomba Christians? In their everyday activities and lifestyle, they are identical to their Muslim and Traditionalist brothers and sisters: they live together with them shoulder to shoulder in the same houses, eat the same foods, share the same taboos, wear the same clothes. The men perform all the various seasonal activities of subsistence farmers: cultivating farms, hunting, repairing compounds, weaving mats, and raising domestic animals. Likewise, the women collect firewood and fetch water together, process and cook food together, maintain small gardens, and care for each other's children. If there is any difference at all it is in how they do this.

In order to understand the Dagomba Catholic identity we directed our survey inquiries to three general areas: faith, modern life, and traditional life. In this chapter we will limit our discussion to the "faith issues" and some of the "modern" or "traditional" issues that touch on faith and identity. "Faith issues" treat aspects of Christian faith especially as differentiated from traditional beliefs, values, and practices. Included here are the concepts of love, knowledge of God, God's care for us, the Christian notion of prayer, the problem of what to do about important traditional beliefs when they conflict with modern life, and the most important personal reasons for conversion. Modern life issues include the changes

---

[3]In the immediate aftermath of the "conflict" the "Memorandum" evoked a greater response from Church leadership than was perhaps warranted. Later the document and its authors were condemned by a more representative group of Dagomba Catholic leaders.

that are required for living one's life in modern society: the need for more education, jobs, a spouse, access to Western medicine, the desire for wealth and prestige, and the lure and excitement of the modern world. Under the title of "traditional life issues" are the Dagomba customary practices and beliefs such as those related to "respecting" the Muslim customs that have become part of their life, the ancestors, and beliefs in witchcraft and unseen agents.

CHRISTIAN LOVE

As we have seen in the case of John Amadu Shaibu, Christian life seems to appeal to some Dagombas. To some the appeal is in the access to European things. To others it is money, education, success. Still others see Christians, especially Catholics, as powerful, with worldwide connections and influence. When asked why they converted, some just say "it is good for them" or "it is what God wants of them." But the two most often heard responses are "because of love" or "because of prayer." Christians, especially Catholics, are perceived as persons who care for others—including Muslims and Traditionalists. The men treat their wives and children better and "they pray." They seem to have greater access to God.

This led to our first survey question: "Do Christians help each other more?" The answers (see the Appendix, Table 1) show clearly that Dagombas think they do. The help they give is not limited to fellow Christians (mostly commoners), but it is freely offered to all—to chiefs and princes, to Traditional believers and Muslims, to the high and the low of society, to Dagombas and non-Dagombas. People see that they actively help one another and give each other support. The response also underscores the fact that Christian men love their wives. This is unheard of in Dagbon. One must love one's family, but women are strangers—to be suspected rather than loved. Women's lot has improved as a result of their life in the Christian Communities. Children's lives, too, have improved. People see that Christians are living a better life, that God seems to be blessing them with success.

It is especially surprising that Traditionalists and even Muslims were also of the opinion that Christians help each other more. Such love is something new in Dagbon, where "if a person bothers you, you should bother him" (371, #3335). The response, however, is ambivalent. Some despise Christians for being "weak." Love makes one vulnerable. It is better to seek power and one's own self-interest. "Something which is nice, the strong-hearted person gets it" (254, #2060). Others say they are not able to live a Christian life. Most feel that it is just too different from their present life to change. Christian men have been accused of spoiling their wives and endangering peace in the community. It is not that one should do evil to others, but good must be reserved for one's own family or community. Furthermore, like politics, love should be hierarchical. It is to serve power. "If you cut grass for a donkey, then come across a horse, you will give it to the horse" means: "Generosity to the lower comes only after due respect is paid to the higher" (45, #26).

But against all these arguments Christians are demonstrating their special kind of love, and, following the testimony of John Shaibu, some are coming to see and value it. Joseph, one of the CC leaders explains how this is happening:

> "They see that we Christians help each other. By helping everyone, including the Muslims, we Christians relieve the tension, and many are slowly coming to see Christianity in a new way. This gives encouragement for others to become Christians."

One of the major negative assessments of Christians was that they are "children." They have no status and therefore deserve no respect. The "school strategy" has brought about the notion in the popular mentality that "Christianity is a religion for children!" But the activities of the CCs are slowly changing this view. The day-to-day involvement of a few Catholics has already proven to be a powerful witness to the faith and has made them a forceful influence in public affairs going far beyond their mere 1.5 % representation. Even Muslims, for example, often call upon them rather than their fellow Muslims when they are in trouble.

THE IMPORTANCE OF PRAYER AND KNOWLEDGE OF GOD

Because of the CCs, Christians are gaining the reputation of being "people who pray." The Christian idea of prayer differs from that of other Dagombas, not in its basic concept as communication with or petition of God, but in who can presume to do this. According to Dagomba etiquette one cannot approach a great person on one's own but must be introduced by a mentor. Traditionalists invite Muslim clerics to "pray" for them on important occasions because, as they say, "they know God." On the occasion of the mass conversion of the Dagarti peoples in northwestern Ghana, a missionary named Fr. McCoy had to lead his Dagarti petitioners in prayer because as they told him: "But we don't know how. We have never talked to Him before. He is too big" (McCoy 1988:114).

Dagombas would agree that one cannot "pray" without also knowing God, and one cannot know God without revelation. But for illiterate peoples the "book" itself provides access to both God's revelation and power. In the popular mentality, Muslims have God "inside" their book, and they gain access to this by writing Qur'anic texts and then washing them and drinking the inky mixture, by burning the texts and sprinkling the ashes in food, or by sewing minute passages into amulets to be worn on a garment or about the waist and neck. Dagombas realize that unlike sacrifices to lesser gods, prayer to God must be noncoercive, but in practice they get around this. According to Muslim-influenced Dagomba custom, prayer makes power and goodness accessible in the form of *lada* or merit which can be applied to life's many problems.

Christians too are taught to pray "in spirit and in truth," not by such supposed controls as sacrifices, special formulas, or by "capturing" the word in talismans. Yet they too need assurances and ways to catch the whirlwind, as is demonstrated in the all-night vigils of the Catholic charismatics in the diocese, which one of the chiefs criticized as "trying to wear God out." Dagombas are curious to know if Christian access to God is in any way greater or more reliable than that of the Muslims, and they are watching closely for signs of God's presence and power. The most important one is success; if God answers Christian prayers, then it can only be because "they know God and God knows them."

The survey results show that many Traditionalists and Muslims are judging Christians positively in this regard. It was surprising to find such high percentages of Traditionalists (72%) and Muslims (43%) believing that Christians are able to "know God" more than other Dagombas (see Table 2). Along these same lines (see Table 3) we can see that a surprisingly high percentage of Traditionalists and almost a third (29%) of the Muslims (39% of Muslim women) report that God answers the prayers of Christians more. This probably relates to their perception of Christians as more successful and prosperous, and to the betterment of women's lot among them.

DAGOMBA IDENTITY AND ISLAM

One often hears that "all Dagombas are Muslims." Some of the members of the Christian-Muslim dialogue in Tamale explained that this is said because so many of the traditional customs have been influenced by Islam. They went so far as to say that all the most important aspects of Dagomba life are in some way managed by Islam. "If you are not a Muslim and you die you will not be given a proper burial. Even the Traditionalists depend on the Muslims for funeral ceremonies . . . If you are a Christian you will never be allowed to be the head of your extended family group." The Muslim leaders summed it up thus: "Christians are looked down upon by their fellow Muslims and Traditionalists alike because by doing this they are not true Dagombas. They do not really value their customs and life as Dagombas." It is no wonder that Shaibu found his fellowship with his father's Muslim friends in Kumasi "nice." He had very little choice!

Perhaps the biggest issue in becoming a Christian is that of ethnic identity. The elders ask: "Can one learn to pray like a Christian and still truly be a Dagomba?" No matter how much Christian principles are valued, for a Dagomba to become a Christian, as things now stand, means becoming an outcast. Muslims actively contribute to this misunderstanding by preaching that Christianity is European and foreign while Islam is indigenous. Even the members of the Muslim-Christian dialogue were firm and unapologetic on this point:

"Christianity came from the White man. When one becomes Christian he is becoming like the White man. This is going against our own Dagomba traditions. The pressure against Christians is therefore quite natural. When a Dagomba says he is a Christian, people are surprised. Can you choose to turn your back on your own people, your own traditions? When Christians move into Tamale and want a room, won't the Muslim owner of the compound demand that he be a Muslim? Muslims eat the same way, dress the same way, pray the same, have the same taboos and activities. They are always together. The Christians, on the other hand, are not together with them. When a Muslim has a Christian in his compound it causes difficulties. It is better that everyone is Muslim."

Unlike Islam, Christianity has not entered Dagomba custom. Christian prayer services are held in Dagbanli, but they are still peripheral to Dagomba life. The mass and other services have been translated, but the contexts, the occasions, the actions, postures, and clothing associated with the prayers still seem stilted, strange and foreign. Dr. Abdulai once shyly admitted to the authors that he "enjoyed our chapel so much because everyone removed their sandals and sat on the floor like the Muslims." Although the prayer of Christians is evident and recognized as powerful and important, the formal Church has not given it "a Dagomba feel," nor made it a part of Dagomba life.

Consequently, conversion to Christianity seems to involve a certain feeling of betrayal. We wished to verify this and asked the question "Are most Dagombas Muslims?" Interestingly (see Table 4), more Traditionalists than Muslims or Christians reported that they are. This would seem to confirm that the Islamic proselytization over the last decade and a half has indeed had its effect. But the discussion did not evoke many feelings that Christians are disloyal. Some of the Muslims were at pains to show that many who say they are Muslims are in fact not really Muslims because "they do not pray" or in any way "show that they are Muslims," except in their names and in the observance of superficial customs. The majority still believe (correctly) that the number of Muslim Dagombas is the same as non-Muslims. Still on the question of loyalty, however, one of the CC leaders mentioned with reference to the massive violence of 1994: "The conflict had both positive and negative influences. Christians were accused of having divided loyalties or siding with the enemy. But the conflict also convinced many that Christianity was the true religion."

DAGOMBA IDENTITY, GOD, AND THE NAAM

These days one often hears Dagombas say, "We are Dagombas, the land is for us!" But their relationship to the land is being defined in new ways. The Dagomba identity as "owners of the earth" did not originally refer to private ownership as it now is being interpreted. "Ownership" referred either to direct ritual jurisdiction over the land—access to the "earth" shrine—or to conquest of the people of the "earth." But now land has become a commodity. The assemblymen who mediate the sale of land around Tamale often have more power than the chiefs or the "earth" priests.

In the recent "ethnic conflicts," the underlying issue was power, not ethnicity. The *naam* aimed at controlling the people and their gods. Control of the people required weapons, and control of the spirit world required access to God via

Islam. The final objective was to achieve supremacy in both the visible and invisible worlds, which required keeping the hierarchical order intact. Now that hierarchy is being threatened by Christianity and modernity in general.

Now, too, Dagombas are redefining their identity in relation to God. The God of Islam is no longer an option solely for the royals but is also accessible to commoners. Even those at the lowest levels, the nonchiefly peoples, are acquiring access to God without going through the Muslims, or the "proper channels" as it were, but through Christianity.

DAGOMBA IDENTITY AND THE ANCESTORS

Christians are called upon to reject the sacrifices and rituals at the various traditional shrines, including those of the ancestors. It might be expected, then, that most would characterize Christians as being less involved with the traditional spirit world. The responses to this question did not bear this out, however (see Table 5). In the view of most Dagombas, Catholics continue to hold on to the ancestors. Most of the Traditionalists and Muslims volunteered stories about Christians who made sacrifices to the ancestors when in difficulties.

Why should Christians remain so attached to the ancestors? Most Christians are commoners for whom the ancestors are all-important, as opposed to royals for whom *Naa-wunni* is more important. Perhaps, too, the ancestors become "more" important as young Christian men become elders and are called upon to perform the traditional practices for others in the household. Related to this is the fact that Christianity does not offer suitable answers to the problems for which people go to the ancestors. Some Christians indicated in our survey that the traditional rites and the ancestors are not as difficult to part with as certain traditions, for example the necessity to have more than one wife (one can cook while the other is taking her two years' "maternity leave").

REASONS FOR CONVERSION

Fr. Olivier remarks that now there seem to be more conversions to Christianity than ever before: "After 40 years of evangelism there is a big change. Christianity is now in greater demand in the villages. People now realize that it is not just for the children. It is to be taken seriously. Is it because they are disillusioned with Islam?" The essay-type question "Why are you what you are?" was an attempt to find out what the people themselves say about their own religion, and their conversions where applicable (Table 6). It yielded three important answers: "Truth," "Heaven," and "Forgiveness." The Traditionalists naturally opted for "Met it" (82%), that is, they are Traditionalists because they were "born into it"; while Christians opted for "Truth" (25%), "Heaven" (21%), and "Forgiveness" (17%) as reasons for conversion. Muslims opted for "Met it" (35%), "Heaven" (20%), "Truth" (17%), and "Forgiveness" (13%). Also notable among the Christians was the importance of personal preferences, empathy, and the influence of priests and of friends.

It is very difficult to know what exactly is meant by these options or even by the word "conversion," but here are some culture-based interpretations: "What I came to meet" ("Met it") means born into the system. It emphasizes the status quo, no change. "True" religion refers to a lived truth rather than an intellectual one: "what God really wants of us human beings." It is often determined by external appearances such as the lifestyles of Christians or Muslims and the "feeling" that it is good and satisfactory, and it emphasizes something hard earned. "Heaven" (Hausa: *alazanda*) refers to the belief in an eternal reward in an afterlife and is commonly contrasted with "fire" or "hell" (*bugum*). It is also given by Muslim converts from Traditional religion as the most basic and acceptable reason for converting. But Muslims need not strive for "Heaven" but are rather assured of it in the mere verbal proclamation of the *shahada*, the assent to the one God in faith. For Christians it involves a way of living as well as faith—although this seems not always to be fully grasped by the Dagomba converts. "Pardon," reconciliation, and "forgiveness" are only important in Dagbon among converts to Catholicism and Islam. There are few examples of a Christian type of forgiveness in traditional culture. A gracious chief may forgive but will expect more in return. A husband may forgive an errant wife, but not often, as he stands to lose the esteem and the respect of his peers. It would be very unusual, indeed, even for Muslims, to forgive enemies. The need to feel forgiveness is important because it implies the admission of guilt and the need for change.

All three of these indicators of conversion, Truth, Heaven and Forgiveness, are not mere formulas but involve everyday life. Besides these indicators there are the personal stories of converts which are important even though they don't fit these models. In spite of all the criticism of Christianity, Traditionalists seem to see it as a step forward. Paul, another of the CC leaders, speaks about the support his parents gave his choice to convert: "My family even wanted me to be Christian. They are Traditionalists but they saw the Christians to be good and they approved of my wishing to join them." Some saw in the choice to become Christian a change from the old way of doing things, a move toward "truth" as experienced in a fuller way of life. Joseph, one of the CC leaders, describes his conversion experience:

"I became a Christian because it was for me. People will tell you that they feel it is the true religion. This means that it is really what God wants for us human beings in this life. Most do not become Muslims because they feel it is what God wants of them. They do it for other reasons. They want money, or power, or respect of the community. But the Christians love everyone. And now the Muslims are starting to see it."

Some, like Shaibu, seemed impressed with Christianity and disillusioned with Islam:

"If God was not with the Christians how could they succeed? Their projects are not done by the Muslims. The Arab countries are now giving lots of money to the Muslims. But when the Muslims get money they 'chop' it [keep it] for themselves. Their schools only promote Islam, not learning about the world. The schools aim to make all their students Muslims. In fact, they will not accept students unless they are Muslims" (Moses—CC leader).

Not all the Muslims oppose Christianity as this experience of Steven, another of the CC leaders, bears out: "I came from a Muslim family. My father, my grandfather and his grandfather before him were all Muslims. But I decided to move with the Catholic Fathers." Some have experienced the flaws in Islam and are looking for a more just and equitable system of beliefs as we find in the experience of Joseph:

"My family was all Traditionalists. In the 1950s most Dagombas were Traditionalist. I decided to be a Muslim when I was young. I was attracted to the religion. But when I went to a Malam to be instructed about Islam I found that he discriminated against us converts. We were all taught with his children. He taught us some of the prayers but didn't explain very much to us. He said that it wasn't for us. But when we left he explained things to his children. We were only given the prayers and the prayers were in Arabic, so there was no understanding. I wanted the understanding as well and I couldn't get this in Islam."

WOMEN

Women in the survey included 32 Traditionalists, 28 Catholics, 3 Protestants, and 26 Muslims. It is commonly believed that Christian women have it easier than Traditionalist or Muslim women. Related to this, Christian families are perceived as being more industrious and prosperous than their neighbors. The survey results (Table 7) confirmed this. Christian men are also perceived as more helpful to their wives and more caring. This was also confirmed by the survey (Table 8). Christians nevertheless have great difficulty in obtaining wives from their predominantly Muslim neighbors. If left to the women, it seems that Christians would have little difficulty in this regard.

But Dagomba women have tasted greater participation and want more of it. They are now more active in all areas of life, including religion, as one of our CC leaders describes:

"At first only the men were Muslim. Now you even see elderly women going to the mosque to pray. Before it was not like that. It is the same with traditional religion. It is the men who perform the sacrifices and libations. This is the reason why the women like Christianity. It gives them a chance to enter more into the religious life of the community."

CONVERSION TO ISLAM EASIER THAN TO CHRISTIANITY

Some of the CC leaders explained that most Dagombas would prefer Islam to Christianity. It is too hard to be a Christian. Less is required if one becomes a Muslim:

> "If you are a Muslim you can carry on with the traditional beliefs and practices. You can be both a Muslim and a Traditionalist at the same time. If you stay a Traditionalist people will look down upon you and if you become a Christian they will despise you even more" (Thomas).

One of the CC leaders had this to say: "People say that Dagombas are supposed to be Muslim. Those who become Muslim do so to gain the respect of others. They only want to be accepted, but Christianity is better."

The Muslims also make the point that Muslim practices have become part of the Dagomba way of life and that life just does not seem the same, not as good, not as "sweet," not as Dagomba without them:

> "Mothers prepare their daughters to marry in the Muslim way. They look forward to it, to the ceremony, to the dancing and feasting and especially to the gifts. This will be an economic aid in getting started in their new life. Therefore Muslim girls do not like to marry into traditional houses unless of course they are the houses of chiefs. Like traditional marriage, Christian marriage is not appealing. There is no feasting, dancing, celebrations, and above all no gifts.[4] Traditional girls, however, like to marry Muslims" (a Muslim-Christian dialogue committee member).

> "It is true that it is much easier to be a Muslim than a Christian. It is because of respect and materialism. This is what draws most Traditionalists to become Muslims," says Joseph, "but this is not what I wanted."

> "People want respect. When they become Muslim they are respected by the Traditionalists and by the Muslims as well. They are Dagombas, true Dagombas. It is easy for a Traditionalist to become Muslim. He need only begin to 'pray' with his friends. There is no formal ritual of acceptance, nothing to give up as with Christianity. He may have as many wives as he wants as long as he can support them. He may become a chief and perform traditional rituals. Islam is a very materialistic religion, so it is attractive to traders and those who go to the towns and cities are attracted by the materialism. It is the youth especially who find Islam very attractive."

---

[4]The Tamale archdiocese has for many years emphasized the importance of the sacrament by stressing "simple" celebrations, without the gifts or fanfare that characterize the practices among Ghanaian elites.

Some of the other notable survey findings are as follows: With regard to "respect" it was found that Christian elders are at least as "respectful" as their Traditionalist brothers or the Muslims (Table 9) and Christian youth show the same respect (Table 10). Christians are themselves respected more (Table 11), which goes against what is often heard and it was confirmed (Table 12) that Christians do relate differently to their neighbors after conversion. Most agree (Table 13) that it is more difficult to be a Catholic than a Protestant.

THE MUSLIM-CHRISTIAN DIALOGUE

A healthy Muslim-Christian dialogue is essential in Dagbon. In many ways this dialogue is making progress through the dialogue committee of the archdiocese, whose objectives as stated by one of the members are "to foster understanding, elaborating mutual interests, and to encourage and develop projects that can be done together. This will help mutual understanding and bring Muslims and Christians together and encourage peace and harmonious living." Another member added a practical observation: "We can appeal to these committees when trouble comes." From the perspective of the Muslims, however, the most important reason for such dialogue was development: "Such committees are important because through them we can share with our Christian brothers, gifts, etc., and mutually benefit." Aside from the "official" channels the real dialogue is taking place right in the villages, in households of mixed Muslims and Christians, in mixed marriages, and wherever Christian converts from Islam continue to interact with their Muslim friends.

But the nice words of the dialogue committee are not always found in the real world. "Some of the Muslims are fanatics and strongly anti-Christian. They will not even sit down and discuss with us." Religious prejudices carry over to everyday life. Christians are looked down upon as "lost" infidels. It is hard to gain the respect of such Muslims. A CC leader tells of his experience: "Dagombas don't really regard you as human if you are not a 'Muslim.' When you are a Christian they call you 'a person of the fire!' You are even worse than a pagan." One of the CC leaders tells us of his battles with the Muslims: "I remember once that I went to preach Christianity in Tolon. We went to the Tolon *Na* and got his permission and a day was set. But when the Muslims at Tamale heard of it they decided to hold a Muslim preaching on the same night. Then we knew that if we came there would be war." This case is not unusual.

As the Muslims increase in number, becoming a Christian in Dagbon becomes more of a risk:

"When you become a Christian the people of the village will tell you that you are no longer one of us, we will have nothing to do with you. This is very hard on the person because the whole community will make things difficult for him and they will never come to his aid. Nobody will come to any outdooring at his house, to a funeral in his house, nobody will help you in any way. They even refuse to eat with you. You become an outcast in your own community. They will say they have nothing to do with you again. You will have to endure much criticism. For example, they used to say to me, 'You only converted so that you could get free food from the Fathers.' But in reality they, the Muslims, get more than we ever get. The Muslims will do everything in their power to stand in your way and to get rid of you, to expel you from the community if you become Christian" (a CC leader).

In contrast to the "official" dialogue and in spite of the insults of the real world, the village dialogue is real and encouraging. Muslims are changing their attitudes about Christians. Joseph sees this as resulting from the way Christians offer help to everyone. "By doing this," he says, "we Christians relieve the tension and many are coming to see Christianity in a new way." This gives encouragement for others to become Christians. As Christian Dagombas become more common and as more of their village-level efforts accumulate, their witness becomes stronger: "Now it is not as repressive. There are more Christians now and Dagombas are getting used to them. They see that the Christians respect everyone, even the Muslims who abuse them." Another of the prayer group leaders pointed out: "They [the Muslims] see the Christian schools, clinics, day care centers, water projects, and agricultural projects. We build churches and schools, we have literacy classes and print literature in our own language."

One of the less noted positive effects of the Christian presence in local communities is the increase in trust. There is a strong degree of trust among Dagomba Christians themselves, and this is touching the non-Christians in the community. As a result, many of the CC leaders are also leaders within the community. In particular, their influence is felt in village development. So even though they are small in number, Dagomba Christians are becoming models for their communities and the villagers trust them to carefully lead them down the unfamiliar paths.

CHRISTIAN SOLUTIONS TO AFRICAN PROBLEMS ARE MORE SUCCESSFUL

Christianity is clearly seen as having an advantage in solving "White man's palaver" and this advantage is equally clear when it comes to problems and issues related to such Western-influenced areas of social change as healthcare, jobs, schooling, treatment of women and access to money. However, we were surprised at the relatively high endorsement of Christianity as being successful in dealing with "Black man's palaver." We expected that the majority would deem Christianity less successful when about half of them responded that it was more successful (see Table 14). The fact that the churches do not actually offer any concrete ritual or practical solutions for these problems aside from the elusive ideal of "prayer" seems to indicate a strong belief among the people (especially the Traditionalists) that Christianity has great potential to offer such solutions.

Most of the "African problems" are simply ignored by the Church. In a moment of frustration, Thomas, a former voluntary catechist, had this to say:

"Nevertheless the problems remain. When people go to our African priests the problems are not mentioned. Priests will not take them seriously. Furthermore there is nothing that the priest can prescribe to help the people deal with their problems outside of simple prayers and telling them not to believe. But the people do believe in these things like the power of witchcraft, the ancestors, and the need for divination. They need something from the Church to help them to make the power of Christ, which we speak of, visible and real."

Joseph, a CC leader, responded that Catholics in the villages must look both to the larger Church and to their own communities for the support they need. One of the most important factors here is communicating their real needs at the levels of parish and diocese. How much does the official Church address the question of witchcraft, for example? Joseph's experience on this is typical:

"The influence of the Christians in their local communities is still very small. If there is a witchcraft accusation, for example, we Christians would like to protect the woman accused of the witchcraft, but this is not acceptable. If a woman is accused of being a witch the matter will be taken to the chief and judged there. If she is found guilty she will be sent away from the village [to a witch village]. No Christian or anybody else can interfere with this. The only thing the Christians can do is to pray that the people don't kill the woman and to encourage the community to help her."

CONCLUSIONS

In spite of the survey, Dagomba Catholics remain a puzzle. Their Christian identity is at odds with their Dagomba identity at almost every turn. They are not the ideal Dagombas of their warlike history, nor are they ideal Christians. They are a weak lot. At times they seem to lack commitment. But it is noticeable to all that they "love one another" and "they pray." Both of these features are attractive to Dagombas. It is unusual for Dagombas to love one another without a good utilitarian motive, and while the Muslims "pray," they do it to obtain *lada,* which can be turned into an antidote for whatever difficulty they might be in. Access to God is power but the Christians try to leave God at the controls. This is both puzzling and attractive to their neighbors. They know that God cannot be controlled. But if God really loves them, God will respond with power to meet their needs. This is a strong expectation of all Dagombas but up until now it has not been made as clear as it could be. The CCs could make it more visible and palpable with the help of the formal Church.

When the elders ask, "Can one learn to pray like a Christian and still truly be a Dagomba?" they have issued a direct challenge to the Church, and the response must not be just with words but with demonstrations. Such demonstrations are already present in the CCs. Even in the limited ritual ways now available to them in their simple prayer services, and by blending their traditions as best they can at the village level with Christian love and prayer, the CCs are already meeting the challenge. However, the formal Church too must be involved, must come to understand their problems and come to their aid with direction and support.

Today Dagombas are searching for some new integration of their lives to meet the challenges of modern times. Christians are demonstrating a new way of living that involves a special kind of love. Many find this attractive but cannot give up the customs or support of their communities or families and friends. It also draws an ambivalent response because it seems so different. Dagombas feel they can't really live it for themselves. Their Muslim-influenced customs and traditional needs stand in the way. Becoming a Christian effectively excludes converts from full participation in Dagomba society and leaves them with little to face life's many problems.

Why should this be? Can the formal Church not help Dagombas to feel at home in their CCs as Dagombas? The Church must think on this and act on it. Jesus reproved his disciples saying, "not one dot, not one little stroke, shall disappear from the Law until its purpose is achieved" (Mt. 5: 18). Throughout Africa the ancestors and other unseen agents of the "Kingdom" are that "law," and they are going to keep coming back until the Church finds a place for them in the African economy of salvation. The Church must let the CCs take the lead here. They are living out the gospel in love and service in their local situations. They are trying their best to meet the African as well as Western problems—without much help from the larger Church. The Church must remember that it is Dagomba ethnicity and Dagomba culture that will form the solid base for a Dagomba Christianity. They are not to be cast aside in favor of any other cultural base—European or African, no matter how advanced or "Christianized" these are. Similarly, the Muslim-Christian dialogue that has already begun in these communities is a lived dialogue. It is real and at its core, joining both faiths, are the real lived problems of the people—like witchcraft, children crying in the night, the need for divination, and the need to placate the ancestors.

There are many blocks to becoming Christian. Dagomba Christians are believed to have access to great wealth, whereas in fact they exercise very little wealth or power. There are prejudices from fellow Dagombas, prejudices from Southerners, from Muslims, and even prejudices from fellow Christians of other tribes. Nevertheless there are still some who choose to convert, and the three reasons they give for converting—"Truth," "Heaven," and "Forgiveness"—dip deeply into the Dagomba religious psyche. All involve an assent in faith, a response to "Who do you say I am?" Their choice for "Truth" has to do with living a life that blends Dagomba traditions with gospel values and the Church's teaching. The "true" path is a path already present in the ways of the ancestors, already present in the traditions—including the *naam*. "Heaven" is a faith commitment to life after death, but it also means a piece of God's kingdom here on earth, a tangible experience of God's power and glory right here among the living. "Forgiveness" is faith in the unconditional love of God. It is the portal to a new sort of world—one accessed not by conquest but by submission; one in which there is admission of guilt and the possibility of pardon. All three affirm the hope for a "new *naam*," a new revelation of God's power. This new kind of power is discovered, not in triumphalism, but in service; not in militancy, but through love that overrides even the desire for life itself. Dagombas join the Church for many reasons, but they stay on for only a few very good ones. These are the foundations to Dagomba spirituality, and they must be nourished appropriately by the formal Church.

Politically, Christians are a threat to the old order. But not from the outside— not a militant or violent threat. Threats from the outside, such as those that aroused the "ethnic conflicts" in northern Ghana will not bring about the new order— they will only reproduce the same inequalities with different figureheads. The land tenure issue, the ethnic issue, the inequality issues can only truly be resolved from the inside. The reason the recent war was so shattering to Dagombas was that they were not victorious. Neither side actually "won," but Dagombas suffered great casualties and even greater humiliation. Their faith in themselves is being questioned, and so is their faith in their relationship to God in the old *naam*. If the other side was more powerful, they must say to themselves, it is because their God is powerful. Does this mean more receptivity toward the Christian God? Perhaps, but only if the Christian faith, if Christ himself becomes more recognizable as a Dagomba villager. And the Church must recognize Christ there first.

There are many parallels between this and what the International Monetary Fund and the World Bank are doing to Africa on the world stage. Here too Africa's model for "recovery" will have to come from, or at least be incarnated in, small communities who rediscover a more equitable basis for sharing the resources of the earth among themselves.

Dagombas crave "respect" as much as food, as much as life itself. The identity of the Dagomba Christians is most misunderstood in the accusation that they "don't respect" traditions or the chiefs and that they are traitors to Dagbon. From the Christian perspective, it is precisely here—in reshaping the *naam* in the image of Christ the king and eternal high priest—that they have the greatest say. Christians do "respect" the Dagomba traditions, they do respect the chief and his elders, they do everything required by tradition except that which goes against the Church's teaching. They try to give a new interpretation to such institutions as family and marriage and to rituals such as funerals and namegiving ceremonies. Above all Christians try to love everyone, not just their fellow Christians. In this way it is becoming clearer to all that they do "respect."

The "Truth," "Forgiveness," and selfless love which the CCs witness is the Holy Spirit in action, and the results, the fruits, are the new kingdom already beginning to be present in the community. In the end, love (not the old *naam*) conquers all. One can almost feel the expansion of this new reality as these communities become real families and begin to demonstrate the living family of Christ's Church. After all, we cannot know what the Church as the "bride of Christ" really is in Dagbon until we can see Dagomba Christian brides. Perhaps the greatest force for women's liberation locally can be found within the CCs, yet there are so few Church projects to help them. The voice of women in the community could be amplified by the Church's support—sending Religious sisters to work with them, sponsoring women's community development projects such as weaving, shea nut processing, tree planting, hygiene training, and many other possibilities. The Church must get more involved or their growth will continue to be stunted. On the larger scene the Church could get more involved and assist more the activities of such organizations as the International Federation of Women Lawyers (FIDA), Ghana branch, who have fought to establish the law on inheritance which gives widows some security, and to abolish female circumcision.

CHRISTIAN PROBLEM SOLVING

For the most part Dagombas still see the power of God only in Christian material success and prosperity. This is not enough. They need spiritual and ritual assurances. The old *naam* involved all of Dagomba life and so must the new *naam*. As in other areas the Muslims have a head start here. Christians are already recognized as people who "pray," but how much they really "know" God is still to be demonstrated. Rituals are necessary for demonstrating God's power. The power can only truly be experienced when it is successful in finding solutions. Can Christianity, too, demonstrate the power of God in the tangible forms the people need? The Church has much to learn from Muslims here. The first step involves listening to the problems, then taking their problems seriously, and ultimately it will involve a total rebuilding of the sacramental and ritual life of the Church on their worldview, directed toward their problems.

How is the Church to respond to the needs of Dagombas—especially to African ritual and problem solving needs, such as those described as "Black man's palaver"? As part of the larger study we examined some 58 traditional problems within the culture involving traditional ritual solutions with spiritual agencies, shrines, and sacrifices. Due to limited space we will only treat three of these problem complexes here, along with suggestions toward a Christian ministerial solution involving rituals. These may be taken as practical guides of what the formal Church together with the popular Catholics of Dagbon can do ritually to experience a Dagomba Christ in their midst. Each problematic area is described, then reflected upon theologically and commented on in terms of the suggested pastoral and liturgical/ritualized solutions.

Divination and Spiritual Causation (Spiritual Direction and Discernment)
Description. Although people believe in the natural causation of various difficulties and problems like illnesses, victims normally also ask for the root cause and the personal cause—not just how the problem came about but what the unseen force behind the visible causes was, and "why the thing came to me and not to someone else." It is through divination that they reach these deeper levels. In seeking a solution, recourse is usually made to the unseen world through various shrines and sacrifices, by means of offerings, libations, and invocations, as well

as by prayers and supplications directed to the ancestors, the divinities, and God.

Theological reflections. In Ex. 20: 3-6 and Dt. 5: 7-10, loyalty to the "One Living and True God" is stressed to the exclusion of all other natural, or supernatural powers. These injunctions have been followed in the New Testament as well as in Lk. 4: 8, Mk. 12: 24-30, and 1 Cor. 8: 6; 10: 6-9. Thus there seems to be a fundamental conflict between our Biblical doctrine of God and their therapeutic sacrifices to spirits and ancestors. In the ecumenical consultation that was part of this research project, the position of the Protestants on this point was clear:

> "Christians must not go to diviners. The book of Exodus gives us clear direction here . . . Christianity offers a new way of living without depending on idols and false gods. We have only one God who is our savior Jesus Christ. The old way needs divination and diviners to deal with its problems but Christians do not need such things" (Henneke Awimbilla, Ghana Institute of Linguistics and Bible Translation).

In the Old Testament, consultation of the spirit world through divination and spirit mediumship were considered evil aberrations to be avoided (Dt. 18: 10-12; 1 Sam. 28: 3-9; Lev. 19: 31; 20: 6, 27; 2 Kings 21: 6). But it is not bad to seek direction and assurances in times of difficulties or severe illness. Indeed, the tendency to ask about final causes could be interpreted as a direct link to God built into such situations. Nor is there anything theologically unacceptable about the diviner trying to derive some meaning from an unfortunate situation. What is wrong is to project meanings that are not there and to stifle creative and loving responses as a result of the misinterpretation.

Dagombas know that God is more powerful than all of the other spirits, but they are not used to going straight to God for help. They need to know that God welcomes this. Although, as Christians, we cannot know the whole reason for misfortunes and evil in the world, we know we can count on God's love. Dagombas need to know that the evil that befalls us is not a sign of God's disfavor but, often, the opposite. If God did not spare the sufferings of Jesus, we will also receive our crosses. But our burdens will be made light because God helps us carry them. In the end God's love overcomes all. People need to hear and experience this, both ritually and in daily life. All of this is new, fresh, and startling to Dagombas. Finally, God does not want blood sacrifice but self-sacrifice, for every act done to our neighbor is done to God.

Christian ritual and pastoral implications. These days Christians seem to be going to diviners along with non-Christians even more than in the past. "We've seen that soothsaying is a big problem," says Fr. Olivier. "But we are only now starting to address it by becoming more involved in their problems. In the past we presumed that the converts knew they shouldn't go to the diviners, that it was against Christianity. I guess that we presumed too much." Ideally, Christians should go to their priests instead of their diviners. But as one of our prayer leaders pointed out, "Nobody goes to priests with such problems." The Christians of the CCs say that they have no choice: "They are going to them. They can't help it. They are living among pagans. Even the Muslims go to the diviners. It is a way of life. The only way it can be solved is for priests to take a more active role in solving the traditional problems."

Many of those in Church leadership positions interpret these needs as a sign of weakness: "They go to diviners because they want immediate results. Those whose faith is mature are different. They do not need such solutions." What is the Church to do? Some say be more strict. "I admire our Assemblies of God brethren in this matter. They do not compromise their principles" (Olivier). But what about the people? What about their frustration when they are left with problems having no solutions? The people need rituals. They need something to fill the gaps and make the power of Christ visible and real.

The issue of "immediate results" comes up often. Many priests have said that is the reason Dagombas go to diviners, but this needs further clarification. Actually diviners do not give immediate results (cf. Kirby 1992). All their remedies are validated by trial and error. The "white offerings" advised by Muslim diviners provide a good example of the kinds of advice that could be given by Christian diviner-priests. Here in Dagbon some priests are already filling the role of diviner, whether they call it that or not, as they direct the faithful to appropriate prayer, ritual, and action in the light of the gospel and their problems.

The fact that the Muslims have "solutions" to most of the Dagomba problems encourages Christians to believe that the Church should have its own solutions, too. One of the prayer leaders expressed his hopes in this regard: "We Christians have the one way, but the Muslims have solutions to many of the problems which we do not address. People would all like it if we too have solutions."

Unlike traditional diviners a good pastor must lift people's eyes upward. Traditional diviners often played upon the worst fears and suspicions of the people. Muslim diviners have been able to emphasize the positive (see Kirby 1993) and "Christian diviners" can do the same. Research (Kirby 1986) into divination among the Anufo, whose beliefs and practices are very close to those of the Dagombas, helps us to see that the language of divination is neutral. Instead of going to a traditional diviner, troubled Christians could go to an acknowledged Christian healer or priest-diviner (with a charism for the discernment of spirits) who understands the thinking of the people and their need for counseling as is prescribed in 1 Cor. 12: 4-11. Or in the absence of a priest-diviner the CC itself through communal prayer becomes the living presence of Christ in the midst of the people and the proper source of discernment.

Death and Funeral Rites and Bad Death (Closing the Life Cycle, Humankind, and the Ancestors)

Description. All across Africa certain types of death are so polluting that in themselves they prevent any possibility of becoming an ancestor. In Dagbon these include death in childbirth, by drowning, suicide, in an epileptic fit, being struck by lightning, or having no one present at the moment of death. In some cases, like drowning, a special purification rite is made before the funeral. In others, such as death in childbirth or alone in the bush, no funerary rites are allowed but rather the purification rites are in themselves a form of "nonfuneral." The victims of such deaths are forgotten, their names are never again repeated, and they cease to exist in social consciousness. Thus they do not become ancestors. If the person dies in a room, the corpse cannot be taken out through the doorway but a hole is knocked in the wall to remove it. The body is unceremoniously taken to the bush where it is "thrown" into a shallow grave hemmed about by powerful medicines that are believed to incarcerate the wayward spirit, preventing it from doing any harm to the people of the area. Both body and soul are cut off from human contact, and it becomes another fearful "thing of the bush." After the corpse is disposed of, the house must be cleansed with the sacrifice of a sheep (Islamic influence) and its blood sprinkled about the whole compound. Finally the compound is again doused, this time with purifying medicinal water concocted from special herbal roots, barks, and leaves. A diviner is consulted to discover the cause of the abominable death. The possessions of the deceased are so polluted that they can only be taken away by a very powerful "medicine man" who has been called upon to perform the various rites. Fear of bad death also leads to many inhuman practices. For example, if a woman experiences a difficult delivery she will be harangued by the midwives to tell the name of a presumed secret lover, and if it becomes apparent that the woman may die, the child is forcibly pulled from her womb along with the placenta and uterus, thus killing the woman outright and usually the child as well. As they say, "Then at least it is not bad death."

Theological reflection. Christians must be taught the meaning and dignity of a Christian death. No kind of death is so abominable that it lessens this dignity. The kind of death a person dies is not as important as the kind of life the person lives. Death is only a temporary separation of the soul from the body, and the soul returns to God. The matter of the body returns to the earth until the day of the resurrection of the dead when it will be reunited to the soul for its eternal reward or punishment. Christians cannot die alone because Christ is always present. Therefore Christians bury their deceased with the dignity that befits a "temple of the Holy Spirit" (1 Cor. 3: 16-17). There is no bad death for the body, and only the death of the spirit is abominable. Jesus died a shameful death (1 Cor. 1:18). Roman pagans mocked Jesus' death by drawing him on a cross with the head of a donkey. But it was through this death that we were redeemed from the curse of sin and fear.

The Christian ritual and its implications. Muslims bury their "bad death" victims with a full funeral, and the people believe that the power of their prayers controls the contagion and reduces the effects of evil believed to be present. If Christians too insist on their own rituals in such cases, Traditionalists will allow them. There is already a precedent for this with regard to funerals for infants. "We Christians are responding more to the needs of the people in the new burial rituals for infants. Traditionally infants are given burial rites, or 'first funeral' but not made ancestors through the celebration of extended mortuary rites called 'second funeral.' Traditionalists do not have anything special for them but the Muslims do and now we Christians do as well" (a CC leader). While Christians must treat the deceased with dignity they must also assure the community, through their mortuary rites, that God has power over all evils, including death. Ministers must be at pains to eliminate any dehumanizing traditional customs. At each step the Christian funeral should overtly express God's presence and power over death. Scriptural readings and prayers addressing the fearful antisocial nature of the death and the fact that the person is specially blessed by the imitation of Jesus' own death should be a part of this. The priest and Christian Community must be present for support in this time of bereavement. They may be called upon to perform various secular and ritual functions, such as bathing and anointing the corpse, in place of the traditional specialists. The family and the house should be blessed with holy water and prayed over. After all the mortuary rites, a final ceremony should be performed, accompanied by readings from the Psalms with a short homily of encouragement, in which everything and everyone should be purified by holy water.

Witchcraft and Sorcery (Problem of Evil within Society and Its Structures)

Description. Witchcraft is universally believed in by Dagombas. Witches can be of either gender but are usually thought of as troublesome old women. Social neuroses within Dagomba society tend to produce an abnormal number of such women. A woman's security rests almost totally in the strength and support of her son. This causes many tensions and conflicts. When the child is small, there will be much rivalry between a Dagomba woman and her co-wives, who are each promoting their own sons. Later on tension will arise between her and her son's wife or wives, who are each competing for the man's limited attention and re-sources, with ambitions for their own children. It is in these situations that suspicion and envy, the seeds of witchcraft accusation, begin to take root and grow. If a woman has no son or if he is weak or unstable she is virtually defense-less. If she and her son are strong, the wife may end up the "witch." There are whole villages in Dagbon that are refuges, or rather "prisons," for these unfortu-nate women.

In Dagbon social harmony is cherished, and disruption, especially from inside one's own extended family, is utterly unacceptable. The family heads are ever vigilant against frictions and the threat of witchcraft. Protection is regularly sought through divination or special witchcraft oracles. Formerly, whenever persons were declared witches they were killed outright by stoning or beating. Now the women are consigned to "witch villages" whose chiefs are believed to have special powers to control them. Over the years since Independence the problem has not abated (cf. Tait 1963), and nowadays it is the Christians who are frequent targets of accusation. Can the Christian community hope to provide an answer to witchcraft? Certainly not without the overall support of the Church. Like the Muslims, the Christian Communities must come to the defense of their members.

Anthropological interpretation. The phenomenon of witchcraft is growing in Africa today. Witches are believed to be people who work in concert with evil forces or who have magical powers within themselves to bring about evil and selfish ends. In Dagbon witchcraft is both a spiritual and physical force and witches must choose to practice their nefarious activities, which always end in death. They can transform themselves at will into wild animals, black cats, snakes, birds of prey, and horses. They can choose to kill by invisible means such as slowly sucking the life from their victims, or they can work through natural means such as poisons or even car accidents. They sit together at night on desolate escarpments and on treetops, as red lights visible to passersby, to chat, attract new members, and plan new destructive activities on humankind in general but, in particular, on their own family members. They are the personification of the greatest threats to society itself.

Those accused of witchcraft are mere pawns, not the ultimate causes. These are built into society as a whole. The various means used to dispense with the evil—murder, incarceration, or banishment without trial—merely serve to further victimize the victims and the perpetrators in a never-ending cycle of jealousy, suspicion, and hatred. In the end, society itself is victimized and rendered helpless. Social sin is most deadly, and exorcising the demon requires more than just rituals, though they, too, are necessary. It requires the application of Christian social justice to all forms of subjugation and coercion.

A basic social factor underlying all this has to do with an appropriation of status that is perceived as illicit. In the past and even now, women are taken from the former "slave" minorities and low-status commoners. Any status they have is only acquired through their menfolk. A man can rise in status through his father, but just as the "slave" and commoner classes must always be subject to the ruling classes, a woman is always a "slave" to her husband and son. The dilemma is that it is only here that a woman can be secure. The problem is made more severe by the changing economic conditions. Dagomba women are a prestige symbol for their men. They are put on a pedestal, and they do not work on the farms as do the women of the surrounding "minority" groups (cf. Tait 1963), yet the men have to work harder now than they ever did in the past when much of their income came from raiding the surrounding peoples.

Christian ritual and pastoral implications. Dagomba Christians strongly believe in witchcraft. One of the prayer group leaders had this to say: "Witchcraft is a fact. Women accused of witchcraft have been 'promising' to the earth shrines [*bugri*]. We have seen them doing it. We have caught them in the act." Another said: "I believe in witchcraft, but as a Christian I don't believe that it can harm me." Still another demonstrated that the mentality of Christian Dagombas is not far from that of their non-Christian brothers and sisters who are helplessly caught up in it: "Even the Christians are involved in witchcraft accusations. Recently the Christian community in one of our villages went to their chief and accused a woman, whom they wished to have removed from the village, of witchcraft." One can sense the hopelessness in this comment by one of our village leaders: "We have a proverb that goes: 'Women are like dogs—if you declare a dog mad and kill it, the dog has no choice but to accept it.' The same with women ac-cused of witchcraft. If they declare your wife a witch, that's all! She is finished!"

Christians are frequent targets of witchcraft accusation, so besides being theo-logically important, this problem urgently needs a unified Christian response. This case was offered by one of the CC leaders:

> "A Christian woman who had been suspected of witchcraft visited her brother in Kumbuyili. During the visit the son of her brother got sick and was sent to Dr. Abdulai. Then the woman went back to her village. The boy died and the woman was accused in her absence. The people said they would have killed her if she had been around. What does the Church say about the woman?"

The pastoral care problem in itself is complex and fraught with danger, for Christians are a minority. Father Olivier warns: "We must find a way of support-ing women accused of witchcraft! But we are so few. What power can we exert? If one of us is accused of witchcraft, what can we say or do to change it?" The fact that Christians stand out as entrepreneurs and innovators makes even the young men susceptible to accusation. When the accusations are supported by the chiefs there seems to be no recourse:

> "Recently a young man died in a lorry accident and when they went to diviners to find out the cause they discovered that it was caused by one of the young men of the village, a Catholic boy. He was publicly accused of witchcraft and driven out of his village. In protest the case was taken all the way to the Tamale chief, but he too supported the witchcraft accusation. What is to be the role of Christians in such unjust accusations? If you are accused there is nothing you can do to prove your innocence" (a CC prayer leader).

There are two issues here: the politics of witchcraft in the larger society, with all its implications for social justice, and the pastoral and liturgical response to mend the lives of those personally affected. We have pictured witchcraft as a by-product of the *naam*, and a transformation is needed at the heart of the society to address it. Furthermore, nowadays Christians themselves are especially at risk. Can Christian Dagombas take the initiative to bring about the transformation and defend themselves as well when they are so few? We believe the larger Church must firmly answer "yes." It is in Christ's own answer to slavery. But simply to preach against the treatment of those accused is insufficient. The problem will continue until the accusers are shown that they can't get away with it. This means taking the kind of strong stand that the Muslims take on it.

Christ took the form of a slave that we might be free. Nothing less than such radical service in love can transform the power of the *naam* and its unwholesome by-products. Only this gospel message can turn the contemporary power relations around where Church and State politics have failed repeatedly. But the profound reversal cannot be gained by external changes alone. Real freedom can only be attained by the redemption of the *naam* itself, by the transformation of an enslaving system to a system that frees through loving service. Dagbon needs a *sh'v,* a penitential rite, a turnabout at its core.

The pastoral solution to witchcraft most of the priests would advocate is too individual and too general: "Put yourself into the hands of God; pray with the person, and encourage him or her to trust God whose power is greater than that of witches or spiritual powers." Even priests can easily misunderstand the real issues and try to find the answer in protection or purification of the one accused. The problem is not from the outside but from deep within society itself. The weak CCs have the answer to it in the love that is shown for the community. It is this demonstration of love, rather than purification and protection from danger, that is the Christian antidote to witchcraft, although, as in the cases of deadly social sins resulting in "spoiled earth" and "spoiled house," there must also be ritual and communal fasting and praying which emphasize love in service. It is true that the small CCs run the risk of being accused of witchcraft themselves and of being cast out of the village, but this must not be allowed to hold them back. For it is only when Christian communities come to the aid and support of those accused, and love them along with their accusers, that Christ's redeeming love can be made manifest.

To Illumine the Path toward the "New *Naam*"

The possibilities for creating new and more appropriate rituals which we have seen here are small beginnings to be sure. But the seeds are being sown. In the case of Dagbon, and, indeed, northern Ghana as a whole, it seems clearer that it is in the heart of the *naam*, where the results now seem so meager, that we will find the really important work of Christianity in the near future, and perhaps the model Christian antidote for the politics of subjugation throughout Africa. For even the "minority" tribes among whom the Church seems to be enjoying such success at present do not deny the system itself, they only renounce their place at the bottom of it. Without the model of Christian love illuminating a new path, they will be ready to take up the process of subjugation as quick as or more quickly than those in power now. The gospel message asks much more of us than justice, it asks for unconditional love. "Even the thieves can love those who love them." Christians must love those who persecute them.

APPENDIX

Figure 1
TICCS Survey of Catholic Christian Communities
in Fifteen Dagomba Villages

Village	Leaders	CC make-up	Bap-tized	Year beg.	Popu-lation	No. Part.	% RC	% Mus	% Trad	Activi-ties*
Yongduni	Awul, Moses & Hosea, Samson	youth & elders	20	'68	1200	25	2	30	68	lit/ voc
Garzeigu	Mahama, Peter & Issah, Paul	youth only	3	'82	1200	20	1.6	40	58	lit
Napagyiu	Salifu, Simon	youth only	6	'64	1000	12	1.2	40	59	lit
Nwodua	Paul & John	youth & elders	12	'82	1000	20	2	40	58	lit/ voc
Gumo	Imoro, Moses & Alhassan, Charles	youth only	64	'64	1000	10	1	40	59	lit/ voc
Tampekukuo	Mahama, Charles	youth only	51	'64	1200	20	1.6	40	58	lit
Chesie	Issifu, Stephen & Sando, Cletus	youth & elders	62	'59	2000	15	.8	30	69	lit
Kumbuyili	Adam, Philip	youth only	62	'66	2000	20	1	50	49	lit/ voc
Malshegu	Nindow, Joseph & Naporo, David	youth only	79	'68	2500	45	1.8	55	43	lit/ voc
Dobogshie	Zakaria, Francis	youth only	5	'85	500	10	2	45	53	lit/ voc
Chirifuyili	Michael, Adam & Peter	youth only	40	'60	4000	25	.6	40	60	lit
Dalon	(none)	youth only	30	'60	7000	10	.1	30	70	lit/ voc
Kataraga	Karimu	youth only	20	'82	1500	10	.7	40	59	
Kukuo Yipalsi	Thomas	youth only	30	'64	1500	6	.4	60	39	lit
Gurugu	Emmanuel	youth only	45	'68	3000	20	.7	50	49	lit

*lit=literacy classes; voc=vocational training

Survey Table 1
Christians Help Each Other More

%	Trad	Xtian	Mus	Total
More	92	94	71	86
Same	4	5	28	13
Less	2	1	1	1

Survey Table 2
Christians Are Able to Know God

%	Trad	Xtian	Mus	Total
More	72	90	43	68
Same	27	10	51	29
Less	1	0	6	2

Survey Table 3
God Answers Christian Prayers More

%	Trad	Xtian	Mus	Total
More	59	72	29	53
Same	38	27	70	45
Less	3	1	1	2

Survey Table 4
Dagombas Are More Muslim Than Trad

%	Trad	Xtian	Mus	Total
More	42	27	26	31
Same	43	37	48	43
Less	16	36	26	26

Survey Table 5
Christians Fear the Ancestral Spirits More

%	Trad	Xtian	Mus	Total
More	26	20	17	21
Same	36	18	33	29
Less	35	61	50	50

Survey Table 6
Why Conversion? (partial list)

%	Trad	Xtian	Mus	Total
Heaven	2	21	20	14
Met it	82	9	35	40
Truth	6	25	17	16
Forgiveness	2	17	13	10

Survey Table 7
Christian Women Have Easier Lifestyle (Men and Women)

%	Trad	Xtian	Mus	Total
More	81	82	66	77
Same	17	10	27	18
Less	2	7	6	5

Christian Women Have Easier Lifestyle

%	Men	Women
Easier	75	82
Same	17	8
Harder	7	10

Christian Women Have Easier Lifestyle
(Women Only)

%	Trad	RC	Prot	Mus
More	81	93	100	69
Same	19	7	0	31
Less	0	0	0	0

Survey Table 8
Christians Treat Their Wives Better

%	Trad	Xtian	Mus	Total
More	82	84	65	77
Same	16	8	29	18
Less	2	7	6	5

Survey Table 9
Christian Elders Respect Traditions

%	Trad	Xtian	Mus	Total
More	42	27	26	31
Same	43	37	48	43
Less	16	37	26	26

Survey Table 10
Christian Youth Respect Tradition

%	Trad	Xtian	Mus	Total
More	34	34	27	32
Same	43	30	46	39
Less	23	36	27	29

Survey Table 11
Dagombas Have More Respect for Christians

%	Trad	Xtian	Mus	Total
More	78	80	58	72
Same	10	5	26	14
Less	12	15	16	14

Survey Table 12
Catholics Respect Traditions More Than Protestants

%	Trad	Xtian	Prots	Mus
More	88	97	95	90
Same	7	3	5	2
Less	5	0	0	8

Survey Table 13
More Difficult to Be RC Than to Be Prot?

%	Trad	RC	Prot	Mus
More	66	67	32	64
Same	34	32	68	36
Less	0	1	0	0

Survey Table 14
Christian Solutions to African Problems Are More Successful

%	Trad	Xtian	Mus	Total
More	51	48	49	49
Same	36	37	30	34
Less	13	15	21	17

5

Tanzania

Marian Faith Healing Ministry

CHRISTOPHER COMORO
and JOHN SIVALON, M.M.

POPULAR STRUGGLE AND FAITH HEALING IN TANZANIA

"My name is Helena. My husband, who was a civil servant, died about seven years ago and left me with two children. I have been struggling on my own all these years to care for myself and my children. I am a secretary/typist with a monthly salary of 25,000 Tanzanian shillings [US$40]. I always tried to solve my own problems, but I was always bothered by high blood pressure and my low income and wondering where the next meal was going to come from.

"One of my neighbors kept talking about 'Mary's Grace,' and about miracles that she had witnessed at Fr. Nkwera's services [he is the leader of the Marian Faith Healing Ministry]. So I decided that maybe by praying to Mary she would give me the means to solve my problems and get a better life. Now, I devote most of my free time to the group's activities. By praying, I feel close to God and feel the assistance of the 'Mother of God.'

"My problems have diminished and even my income has increased. People in the group have given me part-time work typing for them and people outside the group now see that they can trust me as a faithful person, so they too give me their work to do. You have to trust in God and God will help. Most of the wanamaombi *(petitioners) have been helped and had their problems solved. Because of this I see no reason to leave this group, no matter what the bishops say."*

It is hard for strangers to Tanzania to conceive how difficult life is for a person like Helena. According to recent World Bank development indicators (World Bank 1995), Tanzania is rated as the second poorest country in the world. Between 1980 and 1993 the gross national product per capita registered an annual average growth of 0.1%. During the same period the inflation rate soared to an annual average rate of 24.3%. In 1993, one study found that a household income of 54,950 Tanzanian shillings was necessary to maintain a household at the poverty line defined in minimum daily calorific requirements (Cooksey 1994, 59). This would mean that Helena's basic salary was half of what was required just to reach this basic minimum poverty level of simply surviving. Helena is not an exception. The same study indicated that 35% of non-Dar es Salaam urban households, 27% of Dar es Salaam households, and 60% of Tanzanian rural households are in this same position. The seriousness of this situation is further highlighted by a dramatic drop in life expectancy in Tanzania from a high of 54 years in 1988 to levels of 49 years for men and 50 years for women in 1993 (Tanzania Gender Networking Programme [TGNP] 1993, 98).

In this situation of hardship, people have developed various coping strategies. Helena is one of a number of people, mainly Roman Catholics, who have joined a group known as the Marian Faith Healing Ministry. This is a group who are followers of a healer-priest named Fr. Felician Nkwera. They have a strong devotion to Mary, the Blessed Mother, which is expressed through a number of traditional Roman Catholic pietistic practices. Popularly, they are called *wanamaombi* (the petitioners) or "the Marian Children."

As Helena indicates, this group has had a difficult relationship with the Roman Catholic hierarchy in Tanzania. In recent years those relationships have deteriorated dramatically. In June of 1991, the Roman Catholic Archbishop of the Dar es Salaam Archdiocese in Tanzania, Polycarp Pengo, ordered that all members of the Marian Faith Healing Ministry (MFHM) be denied the sacraments, including a Catholic Church burial, and that they should remove themselves from any leadership positions at the subparish, parish, and diocesan levels. This was the last step in a long line of measures taken by Roman Catholic Church officials of Dar es Salaam against the *wanamaombi*.

Prior to this, the group were insulted from the pulpit, being accused of fanaticism and fundamentalism. Some followers were physically beaten in church when they knelt down to receive Holy Communion. Now, some parishes have even denied the followers entrance into their church compounds. According to Archdiocesan Church officials, the followers of this group have a "holier than thou" attitude. Church officials claim that the followers of Nkwera portray their way as the only Roman Catholic way and judge others to be not quite Roman Catholic because they do not kneel to receive communion; they do not receive it on the tongue; or they do not have an adequate appreciation of the Blessed Mother and the Holy Eucharist. The Church officials add that the followers are disruptive of Church services, have a bizarre understanding of the sacraments, and threaten the unity of the Church by their disobedience of the Archbishop and the majority of the priests of the Archdiocese.

The tension between the official Church and the Marian Faith Healing Ministry is very real and in many ways affected this research project. On different occasions there were remarks made that the researchers had become members of the group. Church personnel who appeared to be cooperating with the study were questioned by parish leaders. A consultation at the University of Dar es Salaam had to be stopped early because of a growing argument between followers of the movement and Church officials. Finally, a Church-sponsored journal refused to publish a short article on the movement because of what they called "the sensitivity of the subject matter."

HISTORY AND DEVELOPMENT

The Marian Faith Healing Ministry has a long history of development which is closely associated with the personal career of Fr. Felician V. Nkwera. Fr. Nkwera was born into a large Catholic family in Iringa, Tanzania. His father was a catechist and strong supporter of the Church. Shortly after his ordination in 1968, as he knelt praying after Mass, Nkwera heard the words:

"Felician, my son, I am the Heavenly Mother speaking. I have chosen you to help my children who I will bring to you. You will pray over them and through your prayers God will heal them, and through your prayers they will receive my assistance. I will continue to enlighten you about this work as days go by" (Kalemera 1993, 13).

From that day on, Nkwera (called the "Servant of God" within the ministry) has dedicated himself to praying for the sick, leading to their healing, and receiving private revelations and apparitions from the Blessed Mother which guide his work and teaching.

In 1973, after graduating with a B.A. Ed. from the University of Dar es Salaam, he was posted to government service in Tabora for thirteen years, first as a school teacher and then as a "School Inspector." With permission from Archbishop Mark Mihayo, Archbishop of Tabora Archdiocese, Nkwera organized prayer services for the sick both on an individual and a group basis. In 1974, however, Archbishop Mihayo reversed his decision and ordered Nkwera to stop his services of healing and exorcisms.

After quietly continuing his ministry, in 1977, Nkwera formally requested recognition for his work from the Tanzanian Episcopal Conference. The bishops replied that they were unable to grant blanket permission but that each bishop was free to invite Nkwera to perform healing services in his diocese. Thus, the initial response by the official national Church was skeptical and cautious. From 1977 to 1980, bishops from seven dioceses, Dar es Salaam, Morogoro, Mwanza, Musoma, Same, Bukoba, and Mbeya, agreed to Nkwera's prayer services. While during this time very little formal organization surrounded the ministry, he had begun to develop particular centers, often the homes of followers, for the ministry in Tabora and the above-mentioned dioceses, and there were assistants who began to work with him.

Conflict and hostility within the clergy continued to grow during the above period. Finally, in 1980 the Tanzanian Episcopal Conference ordered Nkwera to stop performing his healing services. Against this order, Nkwera continued his healing ministry, especially in Dar es Salaam. Just prior to and including the "Special Marian Year" of 1987-88 announced by Pope John Paul II, the Marian Faith Healing Ministry experienced what its members call "a joyful period of peace and growth." During this period the ministry received special blessings from the Blessed Mother. These included divine working tools and symbols in the form of special holy oil, special consecrated hosts, and a holy ring (Kalemera 1993, 35-36). Ultimately, in 1990, Fr. Nkwera was suspended by his Ordinary, the Bishop of Njombe, and ordered back to his diocese. This act resulted from the growth of the movement in Dar es Salaam and the ensuing conflict that arose between the clergy of the Archdiocese and the followers of this ministry. The official reason given was that he was functioning as a priest in a diocese without the permission of the local bishop.

As part of his duties as a civil servant in the Ministry of Education, Nkwera has spent much time in Dar es Salaam. In 1976, he attended the ideological program at Kivukoni, the Ideological College of the nationalist movement that became the single ruling party of Tanzania, TANU/CCM. From 1986 to 1989, he did his M.A. studies at the University of Dar es Salaam. It was during these years that the ministry took root and prospered in the Archdiocese. Beginning with home-based services, Marian Faith Healing Centers were eventually built in Kibaha, the capital of the Coast Region and Riverside, an area in Dar es Salaam. In 1987, Nkwera formally installed four assistants (*watendakazi*). These people had the same charisms of Fr. Nkwera in terms of healing, apparitions, and private revelations. The four were Eledina Ntandu (Dina), Venant Pelekamoyo (now deceased), Agnes Biseko Nyamburi, and Derofina Magessa (cf. Kalemera).

Agnes and Derofina are no longer active in the ministry, having sided with the Archbishop of Dar es Salaam when he banned the whole ministry and all involved with it. In Kalemera's book, their defection is described as the "Oysterbay Demon's Resolution." A group of leaders of the *wanamaombi* met with the seer Derofina at the home of the deceased Salvatory Mosha, a general manager of a major public corporation. After praying together, the Blessed Mother began to speak:

> "A few days back, I gave you my message to suspend the Faith Healing Ministry . . . I passed this message to my seer Agnes, saying that you should not perform my work in public. Rather you should pray only for those patients who come privately to your homes . . . If you want peace with your Church leaders, then obey them . . . Obey them, counsel them; tell them with humility what they should do and pray for them" (Kalemera 1993, 47-49).

Citing directives such as these, this group of prominent leaders broke with the *wanamaombi*. The two seers Derofina and Agnes went with this splinter group who advocated obedience to the Archbishop.

The leaders of the breakaway group were known as *walezi* (guardians) within the Marian Faith Healing Ministry. The "guardians" claimed they had been directed by the Blessed Mother that the "seers" should be answerable to them, but Nkwera countered that this message came from the devil and he refused to listen to the "guardians," who eventually wrote a letter of apology to the Archbishop and stopped their involvement in the Marian Faith Healing Ministry. Of the other people interviewed who had left the Marian Faith Healing Ministry, many claimed that they left primarily because of the struggle between Church officials and the ministry. They said that their families also put pressure on them to leave and maintain a good relationship with the Church. Some, however, also claimed that they left after they saw no perceptible change in their problems, whether it was a sickness or some other problem. Finally, some left simply because they did not have the time to participate in all the services and activities of the ministry.

TANZANIA'S POLITICAL HISTORY AND THE MARIAN FAITH HEALING MINISTRY

At the time of the founding of the Marian Faith Healing Ministry, Tanzania had become a one-party state. TANU, the single party, had already begun the process of consolidating its power. In that process, civil society diminished in importance with trade unions co-opted into the state machinery, associations of all types needing to be officially registered under strict guidelines and religious organizations limited to those registered by the government. Thus, the party became the state and civil, including religious, organizations became subordinate to it.

The government, through the Arusha Declaration of 1967, had officially announced its socialist strategy for development known as *ujamaa*. There was a tremendous eruption of hope for the future at this time, and while Church officials may have been hesitant, a large number of Tanzanians, especially young, educated Tanzanians were very hopeful that *ujamaa* would provide a path for a better life. This enthusiasm was followed by a period of four years of more radical debate over the defining of *ujamaa*. One group of TANU leaders was trying to define *ujamaa* in a much more Marxist way, emphasizing class struggle and lobbying for a shift in external alliances toward China and Eastern Europe. Another group was trying to keep it defined in a much more democratic and voluntaristic manner. The Church itself then was very preoccupied during this period with that struggle. This preoccupation allowed a certain amount of freedom for other movements within the Church to develop.

After villagization (1972-1974), which saw the forced movement of most of Tanzania's rural population into "development villages," and until 1985, Tanzania went through a series of economic crises that led eventually to near economic collapse. During this period, religious institutions maintained their duty-free status and through their international connections were able to add to their already powerful status in Tanzania. At this time, whatever conflict had existed between Church and State in the earlier period was resolved, and the Church with other religious institutions became more and more partners with the government. Through this alliance the Church was able to control the registration of groups and use State apparatuses to help it control any dissident groups among its own followers.

Since 1985, the government of Tanzania has agreed to International Monetary Fund proposals for structural adjustments and the political and economic liberalization policies that form their core. These proposals have led to the reemergence of civil society and a new openness in society that has allowed groups like the Marian Faith Healing Ministry to become much more public and open. This has also led to the opening up of a number of possibilities for ethnic, religious, and civil strife. During this period, the Marian Faith Healing Ministry has been able to register itself as a not-for-profit religious organization protected under law. This could not have happened in the earlier period and remains an element of conflict between the MFHM and the officials of the Roman Catholic Church in Tanzania.

GOALS AND METHODS OF THIS STUDY

This chapter attempts to understand the Marian Faith Healing Ministry with three primary questions in mind: (a) Is it Roman Catholic? (b) Is it popular? (c) What can we learn from it about popular Catholicism in Africa? A number of commentators claim that the attractiveness of a group like the Marian Faith Healing Ministry is its incorporation of African culture and beliefs (Muzorewa 1995, 38-41). Some would even say that groups like this are more African than Roman Catholic. While a critique of this sort is often heard among Church officials, we found that Nkwera and the followers of the movement see themselves as very Roman Catholic. They describe themselves as a devotional group within the Roman Catholic Church. They claim to have no intention of becoming an independent church and their cosmology is a traditional Roman Catholic cosmology. It includes an explanatory element that has been lost in most modern European, secularized Christian expressions. Within this explanatory component, there are many elements like the stress on the devil, the fallen angels, and evil spirits which resonate with African cultures.

Furthermore, commentators have indicated that the healing ministry is an example of the Africanization of Christianity, specifically in terms of the meaning of salvation (Healey and Sybertz 1996, 291-336). They claim that Africans are very attracted to this concept in some Christian expressions because it is a part of their own culture. This study found, though, that while many people joined the group because of this, it was not the only reason that was given and even those who gave it as their first reason indicated a change in their attitudes as they became more involved in the group. Many cited the dominant reason for joining the group and staying a part of it as being the attraction of traditional Roman

Catholic prayer life and its facilitating followers to praise and worship God. Thus, the conclusions of this study support the claim that this is a Roman Catholic group with a traditional Roman Catholic cosmology that resonates much more with the African cultures of its followers than do modern Western expressions of Christianity.

In terms of whether or not it is popular, we define popular as those sectors or strata of societies which do not enjoy much wealth, status, or power and which are perceived as part of the common people in their milieu. Thus "popular Catholicism" includes those beliefs, symbols, and practices followed by Roman Catholics of the above identified sectors of societies. However, as Ron Kassimir says:

> Conceptual difficulties in defining the term (popular religion) go beyond issues of normative bias. Three basic variants can be recounted: (1) popular religion as belonging to a particular social group—i.e., dominated classes; (2) popular religion as deviations from a canonical set of beliefs, symbols, and practices; and (3) popular religion as a rejection of the authority of designated religious specialists and the institution they represent which claims a monopoly on the distribution of religious benefits (Kassimir 1996, 13-14).

It is the thesis of this article that "popular religion" includes all three elements and the Marian Faith Healing Ministry is popular in all senses. First, it is popular as an expression of the dominated, especially in its heavy stress on nationalism against Tanzania's extreme marginal status in the global politico-economic system. Also, while being a very mixed group in terms of class, gender, and ethnicity, this study found a strong correlation between class and how the followers perceive their membership in the group. Second, it is popular in the sense of reviving traditional practices and beliefs of Roman Catholicism against the dominant secularized explanations of Roman Catholicism presented by foreign missionaries. Finally, it is a rejection of accepted Roman Catholic authority placed in its religious officials (archbishops and bishops).

In his work, Kassimir further differentiates between "official popular" and "popular popular." The followers of the Marian Faith Healing Ministry claim to desire to be an "official popular" Roman Catholic devotional group. However, because of conflict with the hierarchy, they are being forced into becoming a "popular popular" group. The source of the conflict appears to center on the rejection of Church authority. As Laurenti Magesa says in his reflections on this ministry:

> Ecclesiology is the source of the conflict between the MFHM and the official Church. Looking at the issues, the real bone of contention between Fr. Nkwera and the Church authorities does not in the main concern theology or basically the healing ministry per se, or even the pious practices of Fr. Nkwera's followers. In terms of traditional Roman

Catholicism, which most bishops in Tanzania are espousing, Fr. Nkwera could not be more orthodox. The ecclesiological question involved relates to what model of Church should prevail. One cannot but agree that the real issue is one of power . . . Who possesses the power to define the belief and practice of the Church? Even though the MFHM professes full allegiance to the hierarchical structure of the Church, its interpretation of the practice of the faith does not quite agree with that of the hierarchy and most of the nation's lower clergy who have a stake in the traditional interpretation . . . Due to the material and psychological power the official Church wields in Tanzania, it has a big advantage over Fr. Nkwera in this respect. The fact that the ministry continues and claims the kind of numbers of adherents it does, is testimony to the spiritual attraction it has among the people (Magesa 1997).

While Fr. Nkwera emphatically denies that in the MFHM there is a rejection of Church authority, there is at least an implicit rejection based on the strong belief in private revelation. However, Nkwera continues to formally petition the hierarchy to recognize and bless his ministry.

This chapter deals only implicitly with that conflict. Its primary purpose is to report the findings of our attempt to understand the Marian Faith Healing Ministry with the above three questions in mind. The research was carried out over a two-year period. It included a short questionnaire of a nonrandom sample of 132 self-declared Roman Catholic followers of the ministry, focus group discussions with selected followers both male and female who were included in the "poor" category of our sample, 22 life histories, five interviews with Nkwera, participant observation by the principal researchers and six research assistants, and four consultations with interested academics, theologians, and Church officials. The sections that follow present a summary of the information gained by this research.

First, there is a section on the beliefs and rituals of the ministry. Then we look at the followers of this ministry and their perceptions of how they are helped by being members. Finally, in terms of social transformation, what, if any, contribution does this ministry make?

BELIEFS AND PRACTICES

The members of the *wanamaombi* have a deep belief and dedication to Nkwera as the center of this ministry. They believe that he receives direct revelations from the Blessed Mother and that through her intercessions, he has the power to heal. Through a series of apparitions and private revelations, the Blessed Mother has emphasized ten basic messages to the *wanamaombi*:

   a. Repent and pray with your whole heart, the entire Fatima Rosary and the rosary of the seven dolors.
   b. Pray for sinners, for the souls in purgatory and infants who die without baptism.

c. Pray for world peace and a deep faith in God.

d. Pray for the church and her leaders; pray for the *watendakazi* (Fr. Nkwera's assistants who also have the gift of healing) and all the Marian children with weak faith.

e. Keep God's commandments especially the 6th and 9th that are most violated today. Abandon all superstitions and symbols of superstitions. Be humble and avoid hypocrisy.

f. Faithfully observe the first Thursday, Friday and Saturday of the month in honor of the Holy Eucharist, the Sacred Heart of Jesus and the Immaculate Heart of Mary by fasting and attending the Holy Eucharist.

g. Observe prayer vigils on every first Saturday of the month for reparation and to console the sorrowful and Immaculate Heart of Mary.

h. Daily perform acts of charity and always remember to offer your sufferings to the glory of God.

i. Catholics who are not barred should receive Holy Communion in a state of sanctifying grace, i.e., confess your sins well and then kneel and receive the Holy Eucharist on the tongue.

j. Do not segregate one another on the basis of religion, but each one should strive to marry or to be married to a member of one's religion and denomination in order to perpetuate peace in the family and deep faith in God (Kalemera 1993, 36-37).

The central ritual of the group is the all-night vigil that takes place on the first Saturday of every month in the Marian Faith Healing Center in Riverside, Dar es Salaam. This service begins at around 10:00 p.m. and closes at around 6:30 a.m. so that people can go to their respective parishes for Sunday Mass. Estimates of the congregation at these vigils average around 2,000 people; however, officials of the ministry claim that membership nationally is over 14,000, including those with casual contact.

The vigil is divided into four major sections. The first is the opening, which includes an entrance procession, introduction, and evening prayers from the Roman Catholic Liturgy of the Hours. The procession includes the choir, servers, a Sister helper, Nkwera, and his assistant. Strikingly, there is little distinctive liturgical dress. Fr. Nkwera wears a simple Kaunda suit (short-sleeved African-style suit) with Roman collar. Sister and the assistant wear their normal street attire. They process from the rear of the Center, which is roofed but open on the sides. The service is led from a sanctuary with an altar, a small shrine to the Blessed Mother, a podium at the front, and a large container of water at the rear on the right side. The congregation have their own books and photocopied sheets with the Liturgy of the Hours and a schedule of the service.

The second section would ordinarily be the liturgy of the Holy Eucharist, but since the suspension of Nkwera it is similar to the Roman Catholic "Sunday Service without a Priest." This includes a Liturgy of the Word, including a lengthy homily; prayers of the faithful; and Liturgy of Thanksgiving for the institution of the Blessed Sacrament and its adoration. Father's homilies vary, but usually during the homily one or two people begin speaking out or shouting. This is understood by the followers as the devil speaking through them. It often turns into a dialogue between Father and the devil with Father commanding the devil to be silent. Nkwera has also explained that at these moments the power of God can move the devil to reveal some truths about its strategy and struggle with God here on earth. As a group, the followers of the Marian Faith Healing Ministry express a deep devotion for the Holy Eucharist. They resent deeply the Archbishop's ban on their receiving the Eucharist and Father's suspension from celebrating it for them. Their devotion is shown during the adoration of the Blessed Sacrament when a "special host from heaven" is displayed in a monstrance on the altar. At one service, a follower took one of the principal researchers to a particular corner of the Center to see how the host glowed like no other host, proving God's special presence.

The third section is dedicated to prayers of exorcism and healing. Once again the prayers of this section are taken directly from the Latin ritual, with some in Latin and some in Swahili. There is a general blessing through the sprinkling of holy water throughout the congregation. This is followed with the special healing rite for those who are possessed. This includes a generous washing with water and laying on of hands. For the washing and laying on of hands, people line up. There are leaders present to control the line and comfort the ones who begin to throw themselves around and onto the ground. Women helpers take special care to wrap sheets of cloth especially around the women in the line to maintain a degree of modesty as they writhe and struggle with the demons within. While this is going on, the rest of the congregation, which is the vast majority of the people, continue with the praying of the rosary, songs, and adoration of the Blessed Sacrament.

The majority of those being prayed over are women, and when asked why, some people have denied this is so. Others have claimed that it is only so because the majority of the followers are women. Some, including some leaders of the group, said this was how it has always been since Adam and Eve. Finally, in a focus group discussion, women explained:

Life is difficult and is especially difficult for women. We have to struggle against all odds to survive. That struggle opens us up to all forms of temptations and makes us especially vulnerable to the devil as our strength begins to lessen (Focus group discussion carried out in July 1996. Participants were poor women).

Members of a male focus group said:

Women are more vulnerable to attacks by the devil because the devil knows that mothers are the pillars of the family. If they can take over the mother, the devil knows that they have taken over the whole family (Focus group discussion carried out in July 1996. Participants were poor men).

Dorothy Hodgson offers a more theoretical explanation that seems very similar to what the women of this movement themselves said:

> Similarly, I have argued that the symptoms of the "sickness" spreading through Maasai women have embodied and expressed Maasai women's anxieties about their increasingly isolated, precarious position in "modern" Tanzania. *Orpeko* has emerged and spread alongside a particular historical, political-economic conjuncture between the increasing pressures and alienation produced by the intensifying economic, political and social disenfranchisement of women and the alternative possibilities for female community and solidarity provided by the Christian missions (Hodgson 1997, 124-25).

The final section of the vigil is a time of testimony when a few individuals witness to the healing they have experienced. They are usually people who have suffered for a long time with a physical ailment and who have attempted to be treated by various health facilities but with no success. However, when they were prayed over by either of the healers, they experienced a miraculous cure and are no longer bothered. This period is followed by announcements and directions that come to the group through the various seers, morning prayers from the Liturgy of the Hours, and then a closing procession.

The vigil is well coordinated and professionally done. The choir sings a variety of songs in both Latin and Swahili that are appropriate to the various sections of the vigil. Most songs are extremely well known by the general congregation, which allows for a great deal of participation and life throughout the vigil. As such, the vigil is an enjoyable service and while most people expect the service to be too long, in fact because of its structure and liveliness, it passes very quickly. A number of our research assistants expressed their own enjoyment of the service, especially the singing, and wished to join.

Besides the vigil, the ministry has a variety of other identifying characteristics and beliefs. First, they stress that the reception of Holy Communion should be done kneeling and only on the tongue in respect to the sacredness of this Sacrament. Secondly, all remove their shoes when they enter the Healing Center and, if they so desire, when they enter their parish churches. Thirdly, many have a shrine to the Blessed Mother in their homes and many wear the rosary around their necks. They believe that they have been given a special holy oil which is a mixture of Our Lord's blood and water from his side and the tears of the Blessed Virgin Mary that are shed out of concern for her suffering "sons and daughters on earth." Besides the holy oil they have blessed water which is used in a variety of ways. In the service itself people were observed going and drinking the water. Others filled bottles to take home. In subsequent interviews with the followers, they said they added a small amount of the water to their drinking water and sprinkled themselves and their houses as protection against the devil and as medicine for the sick. They also claim to have been given at different times three consecrated hosts from heaven. These are said to be signs of Our Lord's presence as healer in the Marian Faith Healing Ministry, even in times of conflict with Church officials.

The ministry has shorter services three times a week. They also meet in small neighborhood gatherings and are organized with a general council and a small central committee at the national level. While Nkwera is the central figure, the other seers also have a special voice in matters, and there are a number of lay leaders who have had a great deal of leadership experience within the Archdiocesan structure before being banned by Church officials. This experience is evident in how well organized not only the liturgies are, but also the other community activities like visiting the sick, attending funeral and wake services, and their efforts to protect themselves as an organization.

MFHM—INCULTURATED CATHOLICISM?

Since Vatican II, the word "inculturation" has entered into theological language by way of anthropology. In recent Church teaching and theological writings, there appear to be four very different understandings of inculturation. On the one hand, the four are related and can be seen as growing out of and complementing one another. On the other hand, they are distinct and different, which may be the source of some tension and confusion in the discourse over this concept. The first and maybe earliest understanding of inculturation was *inculturation as translation*. This is the process of searching for concepts within the culture of a people that will help make the message more understandable. In translation, then, we have the message and we have culture as two distinct realities. Culture is used to translate the message in a "credible and fruitful way" with the ultimate goal being the conversion of the individual.

A very closely related understanding is *inculturation as adaptation*. This understanding pertains mainly to the shaping and forming of the local Church in terms of its structure and practices. Again, you have the two distinct realities of culture and the structure and form of the universal Church. In adaptation, culture is used to discover forms and practices that can transform the shape and form of the universal Church, facilitating its becoming a local Church, which is an "intelligible sign and effective instrument" of mission. These two understandings of inculturation appear to be the most acceptable to the official Church.

With the growth of the Church a natural process takes place as the Ecclesial communities gradually express their own Christian experience in original ways and forms. This is *inculturation as popularization*. It is the process by which the Christians of a local Church take the message and Church in its form and structure and reshape them into a local Christian culture. Sometimes this is in opposition to official Church attempts at inculturation and is often referred to as "folk Christianity." It is the gradual and unconscious selecting, transforming, and molding of beliefs and practices by the people as they knead their culture and Christianity into one. For us, the Marian Faith Healing Ministry is an example of this form of inculturation.

The final understanding of inculturation makes a radical shift in its under-standing of the relationship of culture to the message and to the Church. In *inculturation as hermeneutics,* God is seen as being present in culture. Rather than simply translating or adapting two distinct realities, in this understanding, we are placed much more in the position of discovering the message, the mission, and the form of the Church within culture itself. There is very little difference, then, between inculturation as hermeneutics and the option for the poor. It is the affirmation that God is uniquely present in the cultures of the poor and innocent sufferers and that their voices will inspire the mission and form of an inculturated Church.

In terms of the Marian Faith Healing Ministry, our research revealed two very different understandings of the movement as an expression of inculturated Ca-tholicism. Fr. Nkwera himself says:

Demons in all their forms or names (majini, devils, Satan) are fallen angels; they are not part of human culture nor of African culture. Hence, neither being aware of their existence and the influence on humanity, nor all the practices of honoring them explicitly or implicitly, mean inculturation. Hence what I do, that is making people be aware of the demons' existence and their influence on humanity and teaching people how to combat the demons is not an example of inculturation. This is teaching them true faith in God, not culture. Refer to Jesus Christ's comment on Religion and Culture [Nkwera 1997a, 71]: Religion is not culture. Let it be clearly understood that true religion is the word of God which is beyond human comprehension. Religion is taught not by human wisdom, but by revelation of the Spirit of God. . . . Real and true culture is knowledge which every person can understand (Nkwera 1997b, 4).

Fr. Nkwera and most of the members of the Marian Faith Healing Ministry, as said elsewhere, insist that their ministry is purely Roman Catholic and in no way is it a Catholicism that has made an accommodation with African culture.

However, Fr. Laurenti Magesa in his theological consultation on this article raised three points about the MFHM which have to do with the relationship be-tween African religiosity and Catholicism:

The first is the unquestioned acceptance of spiritual forces as ever-present actors in the world. From the findings of this study it can be seen that all the members of the MFHM assume the existence of spiritual forces as actors in the world. Their belief is clearly that these forces are of two kinds: those for good and those for evil. They seem to be ascribed equal power over humans, although by the power of God through prayer, the evil powers can ultimately be defeated. This appears to be the central purpose, the reason for being, of the MFHM. It is significant that witchcraft and behavior like bribery and lies as causes of affliction are also taken for granted. This synchronizes well with the traditional

African religious world view. So, despite Fr. Nkwera's conscious effort to separate the two, the appeal of his ministry for the people lies precisely in this spiritual merger. This is important for African theology because it is an actual living example of true inculturation.

The second is the need for mediators between humans and God. The findings make it clear that in the MFHM, Mary takes the place of ancestors in African religiosity. She is a powerful ancestress of the faithful and of Tanzania, her family or clan before God. Thus, as also the Mother of God, she enjoys unsurpassed appeal for the people in whose controlling religious tradition God was as a rule approached through such good and influential mediators.

The third is prayer as free, communal expression of inner emotion. "To praise and worship God by praying together in enjoyable liturgies" bespeaks the fundamental African need for community and spontaneity and actual involvement in celebrations of joy or sorrow. Fundamentally, African prayer is an expression of the need for the fullness of life. So, people pray most in time of need (Magesa 1997).

Thus, we have this contradiction. Fr. Nkwera claims that the ministry is "true religion" and not a form of inculturation. Fr. Magesa posits that this is a perfect example of inculturation as "popularization." He says, "Here is a powerful example of unintended and unrecognized inculturation." We would say that both are right to a degree. The worldview and cosmology of pre-Vatican II Roman Catholicism were in fact an inculturated understanding based on a culture and consciousness very similar to traditional African culture. Vatican II, while marking an opening up to the world in fact was opening up to a world, worldview, and culture of modernity that are quite different from African culture. As the Church accommodated itself to scientific and secularized culture, it moved dramatically away from the cultures of indigenous people around the world. Thus it is not surprising that people looking from a particular perspective would say that MFHM is an inculturated form of Catholicism, while the followers of the ministry see it as the Roman Catholicism that they know and love. Thus, as we look at popular Catholicism and an emerging global Church, we should not be surprised to see a rejection of some of the understandings of the world present in Vatican II. Moreover, an intrinsic part of popular Catholicism in Africa may be the resurgence of a very traditional Roman Catholic cosmology with exorcism and healing being seen as central.

Other studies of African independent churches note that European mission Christianity largely abandoned its explanatory character for the emotional and relational dimension, leaving explanation to science. Independent churches' attractiveness, they say, results from Africans attempting to understand the world around them and their marginal position in that world. The devil, demons, and evil spirits are a part of that explanatory character. Fr. Nkwera, the "Disposer of Demons" (Davis 1994), offers the same explanation that Roman Catholicism offered before it abandoned that function to science.

PROBLEM SOLVING:
PRAYER, HEALING, AND MUTUAL ASSISTANCE

The Marian Faith Healing Ministry, in our survey sample, exhibited characteristics of a very mixed group in terms of gender, age, education, and class. One
of the unique attributes of this group compared to some other religious movements in Africa is that it has no clear-cut class basis. Even though the majority of
the followers are poor, there is a large portion of well-off members. The following classification is relative and subjective in that the research assistants were
told to use their own judgment, taking into account the prevailing economic and
cultural context. Their judgments have led to a classification of a small group of
people who were almost destitute, 70% of whom were women; a large group of
poor people, 61% of whom were women, which is representative of the average
of the general population of Tanzania (Helena from our introduction was included
in this group); and finally, a significant number of people with an economic
status above the average for the general Tanzanian population.

Table 1
Education and Gender of Respondents

Education/ Gender	Tertiary	Secondary	Primary	Total
Male	20	29	14	63
Female	13	29	27	69
Total	33	58	41	132

Table 2
Economic Status and Age of Respondents

Economic Status/Age	Well off	Poor	Destitute	Total
16 - 25	9	11	4	24
26 - 35	9	27	5	41
36 -45	3	15	3	21
46 -55	8	8	1	17
56 - OVER	2	2		4
Total	31	63	13	107

On the one hand, this mixture militates against this group being perceived as
popular. On the other hand, it was found that the poor within the Marian Faith
Healing Ministry have unique views on how they are being helped and why they
joined the group in the first place.

Nkwera claimed that the main reason for people joining the ministry, after
responding to the call of the Blessed Mother, was the counseling that people

received through direct private revelations, the homilies of the services, and through private counseling sessions. Nonfollowers of the ministry and especially Church officials claimed that most of the *wanamaombi* were people with problems, especially psychological problems, looking for a source of identity and belonging.

The followers themselves indicated in our survey that there were four main reasons they joined. The first (33%) was that people join "to praise and worship God by praying together in enjoyable liturgies." Second, 18% claimed they originally joined for personal or health problems. Third, 17% indicated that they joined primarily to "gain eternal life." Finally, a small group (11%) said they joined "to be helped materially." These findings were confirmed by another question that allowed people to list four reasons for joining. Interestingly, " personal and health problems" was significant only as a first reason and insignificant as a second, third, or fourth reason, indicating that there is a significant minority of followers who joined the group originally because of personal or health problems. However, the vast majority of people expressed more spiritual reasons, describing their original attraction to the group and their continuing participation as related to prayer and the liturgies themselves as lively and enjoyable means of praising and worshiping God.

However, these responses varied by gender and class. Sixty-seven percent of the respondents claiming "personal and health problems" to be their main reason for joining the ministry were women. Sixty-three percent of those indicating "to praise and worship" as their main reason were men. Furthermore, within the "personal problem" category the more highly educated tended to talk about personal problems while the less educated spoke more of health problems. Half of those in the sample categorized as "destitute" mentioned health problems as their main reason for joining the ministry.

This pattern was confirmed by findings from the life histories of poorer members of the movement and focus group discussions. What follows are excerpts from four life histories which show the variety of problems facing the poor and their testimony to the help they have received by belonging to the group.

> "My name is Eleanora and I am twenty-five and my husband who is slightly older is James. We were married in the Church and we are both *wanamaombi*. I was the first to join the group. For years, I was bothered by pains throughout my body to the point that I couldn't even do normal kitchen chores. I went to a number of traditional doctors who did nothing for me. One day on my way to see a traditional healer, the pain was so severe, I had to sit down on the side of the road and I began crying. A man came by and asked me what was wrong and suggested that we pray together three Our Fathers, three Hail Marys and three Glory be to the Fathers. Then he advised me that instead of going to the traditional healers that I should go to see Fr. Nkwera.
>
> "I began to attend regularly and when Father was consulted about my

problems, he told me that I had a lack of faith and that God was reminding me not to forget God in my life. Also, that either I or my friend or relative needed to change our behavior and my suffering was meant as an invitation to do this. Therefore, I would suffer for a period but if I had faith I would recover. I became very committed to the group and began to experience relief from my suffering; later I recovered.

"The Tanzanian Postal Service was pressured into laying off a number of workers by the World Bank. James, my husband, was one of them. I convinced him to come with me to the prayer services and he did. Fr. Nkwera prayed over him and called him to pray for himself which he did. He was later rehired by the Postal Service."

"I am a Muslim woman named Nuru who was the first born in my family. After my father died, my mother was inherited by my uncle. My problems really began when I decided to move in with a man who was much older than myself and had six children of his own. After two years, I still had not conceived and I began to seek medical help. First I went to government clinics and hospitals, and after they failed to help me then I started visiting traditional doctors. In those visits it was revealed that my mother-in-law and her friend, a neighbor, had put a 'spell' over me and were trying to kill me. I went from one traditional doctor to another but instead of getting better, I only got worse. I was acting like someone possessed and started talking strange languages.

"Then, one day, my friend came and told me about Fr. Nkwera. At first I was hesitant to go because I did not want to associate with Christians, but later with a lot of encouragement from my friend I went to the services. The services are given free and Fr. Nkwera showed he had the power to chase away evil spirits. After only two sessions my problems started to disappear. Even though I have not conceived, my insanity has stopped. Also, my husband has now passed away.

"I would like to become a Christian, but right now my mother is sick and she would be upset if she heard I had changed my religion. I believe in the Blessed Mother and I believe that it is through her prayers that I have been healed."

"My name is Flora. I have been very sick from the time I lived in Moshi. My diseases were not able to be cured in hospitals. Then I tried to go to traditional healers but once again I received no relief. In 1981, I moved to Dar es Salaam and my condition continued to worsen until one of my neighbors told me that there was a Catholic priest who cures sicknesses like mine and without any charge, and this was when I decided to go to him.

"The day I went, there was a long line waiting to see him. When the person in front of me entered to see Father, I started to shake all over. Then when I went in Father looked at me just as I fell down and went unconscious. When I regained consciousness, my sister told me that I was filled with devils that started talking with Father and as he prayed over me they began to leave me one after the other. Father then told me to continue to attend the prayer services.

"From that time on, my condition has steadily improved. I have regained my health and these days I am eating like I used to before I became sick. I have gained weight and people who knew me when I was sick are surprised to see how healthy I am. From 1981, I have been a *mwanamaombi* and I will not stop."

"I am Daniel and I joined this group a few years back. I was in a bus accident and broke my leg. For a long time the bone refused to join together and I began getting sicker and sicker. Then one day one of my fellow workers told me that I should go to see the Servant of God. When I went, I was cured and I thank God that I was able to be healed both bodily and spiritually."

From the above, certain patterns emerge concerning the poor within this group. First, most of them are women. Second, a variety of problems appear open to solution for the *wanamaombi,* such as sicknesses, injuries, unemployment, and marital strife. Third, none of these problems are viewed by people as existing within a vacuum. They are seen as connected either to how one lives one's life, to evil spirits and people's control of these spirits, or to the behavior of one's relatives and friends. This is very similar to a general African understanding of sickness and death as opposed to biomedical theory. Even James's unemployment is seen to result from other forces in his life rather than the redundancy policies of the government, World Bank, or IMF. Fourth, through prayers and participation in the services of the MFHM, problems are solved.

PRAYER, HEALING, AND PROBLEM SOLVING

In terms of problem solving, one of our major findings was how deep the faith of the followers of this ministry is in the efficacy of prayer. While many respondents did not cite the strengthening of faith as help they received, the vast majority said that God responds to prayers in a real and pragmatic way, and that the major help the poor receive results from prayer. These findings were supported by a related question concerning how their faith has changed. Thirty percent of the respondents felt that the major change was that they had grown in their love of prayer and worship. Most of the followers interviewed said they had experienced real help in their lives through the prayers of the Ministry.

Focus group discussions confirmed that the biggest benefit received by the poor in the group is through prayer. People are helped tremendously by being prayed over by the "Servant of God," by one of his assistants, or by their fellow *wanamaombi*. It is normal practice for a *mwanamaombi* to ask other *wanamaombi* to gather and pray for him or her.

Repeating Magesa's observations, there is an unquestioned acceptance of spiritual forces as ever-present actors in the world, and, fundamentally, African prayer is an expression of the fullness of life. Problems of all sorts are seen as ultimately resulting from the workings of those spiritual forces and therefore can only be ultimately solved by prayer. This leads to one of the central features of the ecclesiology of the Marian Faith Healing Ministry.

THE CHURCH MILITANT AND THE WAR WITH SATAN

In the ecclesiology of the *wanamaombi* there is a return to an emphasis on the Church militant. The Church is seen as being involved in a war on earth. The competing sides are the forces of darkness centered on Satan and the forces of light centered on Christ through the Blessed Mother, Mary. The *wanamaombi* do not see this as a war of impersonal forces, but rather as a war between personalized forces who work through people. Therefore, not only does Mary speak to her seers, but the devil also speaks through people and can even disguise itself to sound like Mary. This idea of war with Satan was emphasized by research assistants evaluating the difficulties they encountered in doing this research. They said: "This group is like an army. No one will speak to you until Father gives his approval. They are very conscious of security and very skeptical about the motives of people who are asking questions about them. They are more security minded than the Tanzanian Army."

The war with the forces of darkness is being carried out in all spheres of life, including the Church itself. In the conflict with the local hierarchy, the *wanamaombi* claim that many of these church officials are being used by Satan to destroy the Church. In politics, they see many leaders as instruments of the devil, and when there were indications of religious unrest in Tanzania, they viewed these as signs of the devil's work. Followers of the ministry were asked to name the four major signs of the devil in the world. The major sign named by 60% of the respondents was war. Others included, in order of importance, fornication, domestic violence, new and strange illnesses, disrespect by children, witchcraft, religious strife, denying God, accidents, and famine. Women were the most prominent (83%) in selecting domestic violence and new illnesses (AIDS). The poor were also strongly represented (92%) in selecting these two. When asked how we can fight against the devil, the *wanamaombi* stress on prayer was once again evident. Almost all of them indicated prayer in the form of rosaries, novenas, and special services as the number one means. Fasting, being humble, making sacrifices, and doing good works followed in that order.

MUTUAL ASSISTANCE AND PROBLEM SOLVING

When asked how the poor were helped, the vast majority of respondents listed the following as the major help that the poor receive:

a. Charity in the form of clothing, housing, money and jobs.
b. Being prayed for.

   c. The counseling and comforting they receive from prayer, their leaders, and
the community.

   d. Being strengthened in their faith and perseverance.

Examples from people's life stories illustrated a number of people who had
been assisted by other followers through acts of charity. This help took the form
of housing for a widow who had been evicted from government housing after her
husband's death. Another widow was found a job, and an unemployed woman
was hired in the business firm of another *mwanamaombi*. Seventy percent of the
destitute group acknowledged that they had been helped materially by other
wanamaombi.

Focus group discussions showed that the destitute and poor of the Marian
Faith Healing Ministry do not view their poverty in terms of broader structural
dimensions. Rather, they see it as a real but not hopeless situation. It was stressed
that the only way to escape this situation was to work hard. They also said that
Father stressed in his homilies and teachings that each person had to live by his/
her own hard work and that he/she should only pursue legal ways of making a
living. Some cited the Bible: only those who work should eat. Working together
or organized cooperation in improving each other's lives is not an explicit part of
this group's ideology. Yet, as the story of Helena in the introduction and examples
above indicate, they do help each other in various ways. We observed that a great
deal of help is provided at the time of funerals and in the neighborhoods, especially through visiting the sick. However, materially, most said that little help
was actually available because the vast majority of the members are poor.

In all the interviews one major point that was made was that "Father did not
charge." The Marian Faith Healing Ministry is a free service. Traditional healers
end up being quite expensive for most people. Furthermore, during the late 1970s
and early 1980s there was almost a total collapse of government-provided health
services. And since the mid-1980s, again under pressure from the IMF and World
Bank, the government of Tanzania has been involved in a steady process of
privatization of social services and the implementation of "cost sharing" policies
in government social service provision. For some of the very poor, these policies
may have taken health services out of the realm of possibility. Thus, even though
it may not be the major reason for joining, the MFHM is one of the few free
services to which they can turn.

However, while Fr. Nkwera may present the healing center as another health
facility, very few of the people, no matter whether they are rich or poor, women
or men, highly educated or with minimal education, see the center as their only
medical option. Sixty-eight percent of the respondents said that they combine
prayer, the Marian Center, and other medical facilities in the treatment of themselves or sick relatives. People tend to begin with hospitals that mostly follow a
germ theory program of treatment. When people do not find relief, they then go
to traditional healers and finally they go to Nkwera. In terms of those who see
prayer as their only medical option, almost all of them identified the holy water
as the single most effective element of the rituals and sacramentals used in the

ministry. This water is used to bless oneself, to cook, to sprinkle on the home and to be drunk, in addition to its uses in the rituals of the vigil.

SOCIAL TRANSFORMATION:
A CHOSEN NATION, A BATTLEGROUND

NATIONALISM

As said earlier, Tanzania is the second poorest country in the world economy, according to certain World Bank economic indicators. It is marginal almost to the point of being insignificant. It has no strategic value for the dominant powers in the world. It has no major crop or mineral base upon which it can gain foreign exchange. It has a minimal industrial sector and therefore it is heavily dependent on imports for most consumer goods. Thus, from outside and from a dominant perspective in the world system, Tanzania is poor, insignificant, and marginal—a fact reinforced daily by the mass media.

In opposition to this view, Nkwera gives voice to the cries of many Tanzanians, claiming that their nation is a "Chosen Nation." It is a nation that is central to salvation history in that it was dedicated to the Queen of Peace and put under her protection by Pope John XXIII on its independence day, December 9, 1961. It is the Blessed Mother herself who has agreed to care for Tanzania and to purify it.

A major part of the services of the MFHM is dedicated to praying for Tanzania. Within those services is a special prayer rededicating Tanzania to the Blessed Mother. Much of Nkwera's writing and preaching is directed toward dispelling the idea of Africa being the lost continent by using various references to Africa in the Bible. Among the countries of Africa, he highlights Tanzania as the "Star of Africa and Mountain of Peace" and liberator of Southern Africa (Nkwera 1996, 2-13). Much of the praise given to Tanzania is implicitly directed at former President Julius Nyerere as Father of the Nation.

All this is indicative of Nkwera's own background as a civil servant during the Nyerere years and his own political understanding as it was shaped by his experiences under the ideology of TANU/CCM. For Tanzanians who lived under colonial rule and witnessed the peaceful transition to independence, the strong nationalism of Nkwera is very appealing and resonates well with their own position. They know the scorn that they have had to bear, being a colony and being African. For them, the devastation of poverty was not primarily economic but cultural—that they were not a people. In the struggle against the insignificant and marginal status of Tanzania, Nkwera proposes that Tanzania is unique as a "Chosen Nation," and Tanzanians as a "Chosen People" have a special role to play in carrying out God's will as communicated by the Blessed Mother. Different from other movements, the *wanamaombi* do not proclaim themselves as the "Chosen People" but rather Tanzania as a nation.

The force of his preaching is indicated by the answers of all the respondents who were included in the survey, case studies, and focus groups. Everyone, with no exception, expressed their knowledge that Tanzania has been dedicated to the Blessed Mother and is under her special protection. Some even clarified why this was so. The celebrations for the independence of Tanzania began on the eve of independence day, December 8, 1961. That is the evening of the feast of the Immaculate Conception of the Blessed Mother, and at midnight, independence was announced. Everyone also explained that they were reminded of this by Nkwera and his assistants, but they emphasized that it was not Nkwera who dedicated the country to Mary. As one said:

> "The news that Tanzania is under the special protection of the Blessed Mother has been given to us by the 'Servant of God' and his assistants. But more importantly the devils and evil spirits themselves have been forced to confirm this during the prayer services when the power of God, Mary, and the angels force them into submission and they begin to tell the truth through people. Tanzania is our hardest battleground because it is a Chosen Nation under God's special protection."

Another indicated the peace that Tanzania has experienced as a sign of the fact that Tanzania is under Mary's protection:

> "This country was dedicated to Mary twice. Once at the time of independence and then later when Pope John Paul II visited and he rededicated it to our Blessed Mother. A clear sign that our country is under Mary's protection is the fact that we have never experienced any disaster or turmoil like our neighboring countries of Uganda, Kenya, Ethiopia, Somalia and the Sudan. The presence of people like Idi Amin is a clear sign of the devil and Tanzania's ability to dispose of him was proof that Tanzania is under Mary's protection."

Many others affirmed the fact that the peace experienced by Tanzania is the clear sign that Mary is protecting it. Most of Tanzania's neighboring countries have experienced long periods of political and ethnic conflict. Mozambique has had a long civil war after independence. Burundi and Rwanda have had very recent violent eruptions of long-term conflict. Uganda has experienced a series of brutal military coups after independence, and Kenya's recent history has been marked by ethnic violence, student unrest, and urban rioting. In contrast, Tanzania has experienced over thirty years of relative peace and tranquillity.

PROPHETIC VOICE

Together with this nationalism, Nkwera also provides a strong prophetic voice against both the Church and the government. In an almost contradictory position, he forcefully proclaims that "Nchi imeoza" (The country is rotten) and claims that 99% of Church and government leaders are rotten. Most government leaders, he says, are unsatisfactory and respect neither God nor human rights. Corruption, misuse of public property, adultery, witchcraft, and total lack of justice characterize government leadership. A major problem, says Nkwera, is that both government and Church leaders do not want to listen to the truth. They only listen to lies and they themselves spread lies and witness to lies as being the truth. The nation has rotted because most leaders have rotted, and the few good leaders who remain are abused, shunned, publicly mistreated, and discredited (Nkwera 1996, 24-27).

Mosques are also called to conversion in Nkwera's writing and preaching. Muslim leaders are accused of advocating murder instead of preaching the word of God. They are also accused of spreading lies and becoming rotten. Because of this, he says that all three (Church, mosque, and government) are unable to defend the rights of people and speak out on behalf of justice. Followers of the MFHM themselves stressed that they are constantly reminded of the abuses of corruption of leaders. As one said:

"Concerning corruption and bribery, it is not a good thing and even the government has outlawed it. We are counseled to live by a legal means of living. Even though the economic condition is very bad, we should not look to illegal means to make our living. These include bribery, misuse of public property, stealing by use of a pen, and irresponsibility. We should live by an income that is legal according to the laws of the land and the laws of God."

In the transition to multiparty governance (Tanzania was a single-party democracy from 1964 to 1995) and campaigns leading to the elections of 1995, Augustine Mrema emerged as a significant figure. As Minister of Home Affairs he became popular as the defender of the oppressed, the weak, and the marginal. Gradually his popularity began to worry many of the old guard in CCM. While he was seen as a reformer and potential CCM presidential candidate by people of the grass roots, CCM leaders portrayed him as a dictator who acted as policeman, judge, and jury. Finally, he broke with CCM and became the presidential candidate of the opposition party, NCCR.

Nkwera's own emphasis on the need for reform seemed very much in line with Mrema's personal war against corruption and the lack of justice in Tanzania. At one time, Mrema asked that he be remembered in the prayer services of the *wanamaombi* and from that time on, he was mentioned publicly in the prayers of the faithful. The prayer was usually worded: "Let us pray for Minister Mrema and national security." The use of "national security" was emphasized in the context of the devil's use of religion to disrupt Tanzania.

It is claimed that Nkwera foretold of an Islamic demonstration against butchers who were selling pork. The demonstration took place and resulted in a certain amount of damage. It was Mrema who was then called upon to restore order, and his actions remained controversial throughout the presidential campaign. Thus, the prayers for him and for "national security" were aimed against all those forces who were being used by the devil to disrupt Tanzania's security. By implication, they meant Mrema was not a part of those satanic forces. This was only implied. Nkwera did not give a public declaration of support to any candidate. When CCM announced their candidate as Ben Mkapa, also a Roman Catholic and a former student of Nyerere, one influential member of the group remarked: "Now it does not really matter who people vote for because we have both the top candidates."

As the elections of October 1995 drew closer and the campaigns began, the *wanamaombi* responded by initiating a special weekly prayer service to pray for the elections, for Tanzania, and for peace and security. In a private revelation after the elections, the Blessed Mother gave an evaluation of them. She mentioned three basic evils of the elections:

a. Witchcraft—Leadership was not sought by depending on God but rather many candidates actually went to witch doctors and performed sacrifices of many types to win election.
b. Bribery—While the government claims to be bankrupt, hospitals have no medicine and people are suffering and even dying, a tremendous amount of money was used to buy the votes of people by the ruling party.
c. Lies—Falsehoods were spread about certain candidates and people were frightened by falsehoods about violence and how a multiparty system would turn Tanzania into another Rwanda.

Nkwera writes, how can the same people who were brought to office by corruption do away with corruption? How can the same people who were brought to office by lies do away with lies? How can a nation be led by justice when the leadership did not come to office in a just way? The Blessed Mother says:

> Until now, the hearts of many of her children are burdened and saddened by the lack of justice that was followed during the elections; they have despaired and see no chance for change in the near future (Nkwera 1996, 44-45).

At this point, though, this prophetic voice has remained just that: a voice. The MFHM have no explicit strategies for combating these evils. Rather, Nkwera continues to stress that what is left is to continue to pray for Tanzania, for God alone can conquer the work of the devil.

TANZANIA AND THE REIGN OF GOD

In the Marian Faith Healing Ministry, social transformation is not tied theologically to salvation in any explicit or pragmatic way. While some popular movements might see salvation as a process in which human history is a real part of salvation history, and action on behalf of justice is presented as an essential dimension of Christian life which contributes to that process, the *wanamaombi* tend to see the world as a battleground. Salvation is "eternal life" lived in a separate and unique realm. Entrance into that realm comes from the faith and commitment you have shown to God in the war with Satan.

While structural evils are perceived as signs of the work of the devil, faith itself is seen as a personal conversion that leads to a greater dependency on prayer and God. There is very little emphasis on faith as a communal commitment to struggle against those structural evils. We believe that this goes back to the African worldview and its understanding of problems as evil and their causes as spiritual forces who are active in the world.

This understanding is very different from a worldview that sees the social and physical world as being governed by laws and relationships that reside within those realities themselves. In that worldview, it is believed that those laws and relationships are knowable by human consciousness and ultimately controllable or at least changeable. Thus, human consciousness can transform reality, first, by gaining greater understanding of all the processes involved in creating a particular situation and, second, by devising strategies for changing those processes. This is not the understanding of the Marian Faith Healing Ministry.

CONCLUSION

Tanzania has been marked over the years by a high degree of regional differentiation. Two regions which are considered the richest are Kagera, especially the Bukoba area, and Kilimanjaro. These two regions were highly receptive to Christian missionary efforts and the education that accompanied those efforts. Thus, many of the earliest best-educated and wealthiest Tanzanians come from these regions. As such they make up a large portion of the well-off Roman Catholic followers of the Marian Faith Healing Ministry. As was shown by the data, they (well-off, highly educated, and older followers) are attracted to the ministry by the traditional Roman Catholic piety that was so much a part of their socialization into Christianity.

The poor and the destitute followers of the ministry are mainly women with the destitute being mainly widows. Most of them came to the group through an invitation by a follower to attain help for some long-standing problem. Many of them testified to the fact that through "prayers" their problems were solved. More pragmatically, a number of them received material help from other followers from the well-off sector of the ministry. In terms of their poverty, the group has a strong belief in the power of hard work. They stressed that the only way to solve their economic problems was to work hard and live by the sweat of their own labor. There is no conscious effort to attempt to organize people to help one another as a group to attack their poverty. This relates to what in this article was called a more spiritual worldview as distinct from a social science or secular analytical worldview.

They see the world as a battleground between the forces of the devil and the forces of God through Mary. All the evil in the world, whether it affects individuals, nations, or the world itself, results from the workings of the devil. The main signs of the devil's presence are war, violence, and unrest. As a country under the special protection of Mary, Tanzania has enjoyed decades of peace and tranquillity. However, according to the ministry, the devil is hard at work in Tanzania as exhibited by the corruption and the abuse of human rights by civil and religious leaders. The primary way of fighting the devil is through prayer. By the prayers of the ministry, people are cured, demons are expelled, problems are solved, and the devil is repelled. The followers are called upon to dedicate their lives to God and their whole life should center on the ministry in the war with evil of all forms through prayer.

In terms of their identity as Roman Catholics, it is clear that first they define themselves as Roman Catholic with a strong sense of allegiance to a certain tradition which includes its rites and beliefs. Within that tradition they see themselves as belonging to a devotional movement which supersedes even family ties. They call themselves Marian children, which reflects the low Christology and pneumatology of the movement and the central role of Mary. In their struggle against the official Church, there has been a tendency to demonize the leaders of the official Church, which for the movement apparently does not indicate a rejection of Church authority or a diminishment of their allegiance to Roman Catholicism. They see themselves as a reform movement calling the Church back to its foundations. The followers see their present estrangement from the official Church hierarchy as another sign of the devil's presence in the Church, and they are convinced that eventually, through the intervention of the Vatican, the ministry will be recognized and all suspensions will be removed.

In studying the emergence of a global Church and the role of "popular Catholicism" in the defining of that Church, this article highlighted two major findings. First, Vatican II, while marking an opening up to the world in fact was opening up to a world, worldview, and culture of modernity that are quite different from African culture. As the Church accommodated itself to scientific and secularized culture, it moved dramatically away from the cultures of indigenous peoples around the world. Thus, we should not be surprised to see a rejection by them of some of the understandings of the world present in Vatican II. Moreover, an intrinsic part of popular Catholicism in Africa may be the resurgence of a very traditional Roman Catholic cosmology with exorcism and healing being seen as central. Secondly, it should be expected that Mary will emerge as a central figure in the belief systems of popular Catholic groups. For Roman Catholicism in Africa, among a people with a strong belief in God being approached by mediators, Mary has an unprecedented appeal. She is our mother, the mother of our nation, the mother of our clan who is also the Mother of God. This is an ancestress with the closest of possible relationships with us and with God.

In concluding, it can be said that this group is a "popular" movement in all the senses of that term as described earlier. It has struggled to maintain the status of an "official popular" group within the Roman Catholic Church. However, Church officials have reacted strongly to the ministry and they appear committed to alienating the group from the Church. This reaction seems to be based on who has the role of defining the Church.

6

Southern India

Mukkuvar Catholicism

FRANCIS JAYAPATHY, S.J.

"Many years ago, Baslis's brother . . . you know the one who lived in the house north of Theesmas . . . died of cholera. My brother went along with my sister for his burial. Soon after the burial, my sister took ill and died. In those days there was no medicine . . . you see . . . my brother also became ill. People of the village fled in fear of contracting cholera and hid themselves. He was taken away to the next village. Only my elder sister refused to leave my brother's side. Pale Crone, an old woman, had the courage to be with my brother. She got ready a coffin, in case. . . . But then, at night she prayed: 'Mother Maariamma, take this illness away from him. Of all his siblings, this has happened to him! Give this kid back to us.' *At the very moment Pale Crone was praying, my Granny had a dream. She saw in her dream, a host of unfamiliar persons surrounding my brother. All of my family who had died, were shooing them away, shouting: 'You have taken one without our knowledge. We won't give you this one. We will pluck a bird and throw it to you.' At that instant, people in the village heard a bird cry. At that very same moment, my brother sat up in his bed and asked for something to eat! My brother was thus saved. How do I know, if the* souls *help us or not? I only know . . . that the dead don't return. But it is well known that when the* cholera spirits *came near the church, St. Anthony drove them away. . . . Only when we need help, we have recourse to St. Anthony."*

The concluding reflections of this chapter were prepared through the collaboration of Michael Amaladoss, S.J.

This snippet of a text comes from a 30-year-old Mukkuvar woman named Angilammal. She belongs to a world dominated by kinship. The Mukkuvar live their life in a unique collective representation, peopled with helpful ancestors and dangerous spirits. More things happen at night than during the day. Maariamma, a Hindu goddess, and St. Anthony, a Catholic saint, coexist comfortably in their world. This cosmology is as much a part of the world of the Mukkuvar as are their recognized fishing prowess, individual dignity, fighting spirit, and pride in being the oldest Catholics in the diocese of Kottar.

THE MUKKUVAR

The Mukkuvar are a traditional fishing community, living in 48 coastal villages in the southern part of the west coast of South India. The Mukkuvar villages stretch, contiguously, from the southernmost point of India, Kanyakumari, along the west coast toward Kollam (Quilon). Most of the Mukkuvar villages lie in the Kanyakumari District of the state of Tamil Nadu and the rest in Kerala. Those in the Kanyakumari district speak Tamil, with a unique intonation. Those in Kerala speak Malayalam. In both languages, a few corrupted forms of Portuguese words are also found.

According to the 1981 census of India:
* The Mukkuvar numbered 115,199, in 20,384 families.
* The male/female ratio is 51:48.
* 42.42% are illiterate.
* Only 9.15% have had college education.

The Mukkuvar are primarily traditional, artisanal fishermen:
* In 1996, 47.09% of the Mukkuvar used catamarans, made from three logs about twenty-three feet long tied together.
* 10.27% used mechanized boats.
* The most common fishing gear was gill and drift nets.
* 12.29% operated beach seines.
* Hook-and-line fishing was practiced by 7.1%.

There is a perceptible division of labor. Men go to the sea. Women manage the households. Women are not allowed to go into the sea, except on the Tuesday before Ash Wednesday—a local version of carnival. Women manage the finances of the house and the education of the children, save money for marriages of daughters, borrow money in times of hardship, and organize money-saving schemes. Men spend most of their time on the beaches and around the village shops. They spend little time at their own homes.

All the Mukkuvar villages in the Kanyakumari district and a few contiguous villages in the state of Kerala are almost entirely Catholic. To my knowledge there are no Hindu Mukkuvar in Kanyakumari District. There are, though, a few families who have, in the last two decades, become Pentecostal Christians.

Women encourage, coax, cajole, and even punish their men if they do not fish regularly. They compare their performances with other men and attempt to shame them into greater effort. The weapon they have is *aruppu,* a loud, acrimonious harangue spiced with swear words and name-calling. Men unable to withstand the onslaught succumb to the pressure and do attempt to give satisfaction.

Kinship is important to the Mukkuvar. An expansive claim among the Mukkuvar is that everyone is related to everyone else, either by blood or by marriage alliance. They have what is known in anthropological studies as the Dravidian system of kinship, which promotes cross-cousin marriages. Mother's brother and father's sister play crucial roles in the kinship system, ritually and economically. Kinship covers not only the living but also the dead. The opening text provides telling evidence of the ancestral spirits being involved with the living. The ancestral spirits are invoked during times of illness, marriage, and housebuilding, and for the import of new fishing gear.

Egalitarianism is a highly cherished value. Inequalities in social status are constantly contested. Decisions concerning the village as a whole *have* to be communally made at village meetings. Every adult male not only wants to have his say, but ensures that his point of view becomes part of the final agreement, if and when it is arrived at.

The introduction of mechanization of fishing, promoted both by the government and the Church, has resulted in inequality, which is most pronounced in port villages such as Colachel and Kanyakumari. This has also resulted in long-standing violent conflicts. Mechanized boats were destroyed. Boat owners beat up priests; loyalties were shifted to the Bharatiya Janata Party; the lotus flag of the party was hoisted.

THE STUDY

This study was conducted among the 31 coastal villages in Kanyakumari District. Though there are some settlements of the Mukkuvar in inland towns and villages, they were not included in the study. The study relied on standard anthropological techniques of data collection: observation and open-ended interviews. Most of the interviews have been audiotaped and transcribed. Five focus group discussions have been held. Interviews with priests and the bishop were also held. Six hundred and fifty structured questionnaires were administered, to gauge the epidemiological spread of beliefs and practices. A limited amount of archival work was also done in the diocesan curia.

There were sharp differences in the responses to open-ended interviews and structured questionnaires. In the open-ended interviews, the Mukkuvar talked freely about their beliefs and practices. But to the administered questionnaire their responses were formal. Very few acknowledged the presence of magical practices among them. One way of understanding the difference in responses to interviews and questionnaires is to acknowledge that magical practices are not common but are limited to a few; another is to ask if the responses to formal questions are or are not incidences of public discourse and matters of private thoughts. A factor that might have influenced the data is that the structured questionnaires were adminstered by educated young Mukkuvar men and women, involved closely with diocesan commissions on youth, communication, and the like.

THE CHURCH

In every Mukkuvar village in Kanyakumari District, coterminous with the Catholic diocese of Kottar, there stands a church, rising above the thatched huts and the few brick houses of the village and dominating it. Most churches boast stone masonry, tall towers, and a sufficiently large surrounding space. Village meetings and public functions are held there. The architectural dominance of the church building is the first clue one has of the dominant role that the Church plays in the Mukkuvar villages. From the mid-sixteenth century, the Church has had control of the coastal villages and has functioned both as the secular and the religious authority for the Mukkuvar. Given the geographical marginality and the Mukkuvars' innate distrust of caste Hindus and of outside political authority, the Church has filled the role of secular administrator for the coastal villages, with considerable ease and a great deal of local acceptance. Even today, more than 40 years after the foundation of the Indian Republic and the attendant processes of democracy, the Church retains vestiges of its functions as a state within the State, despite the inevitable attenuation of its power over the centuries.

The ownership of the common property of the village also resides with the Church. In a number of villages, even the tracts of land on which fishermen have built their huts and small houses belong to the Church. If the village has any common property, it is legally registered in the name of the bishop.

Every coastal village in the district has an imposing church building, a residence for the parish priest, and, in most cases, a school. The priest is the correspondent of the school, and in this capacity, he has a large say in the appointment of teachers. His signature is essential for the teachers to collect their salaries from the Department of Education. In some villages, there is also a community hall, crèche, and so forth. All these common buildings belong to the Church and are administered by the parish priest. No government official, be they police, civil or social administrators, will move into the villages without the support of the priest. The parish priest, as the representative of the Church, stands as the mediator between the Mukkuvar and the outside world. These multifaceted administrative roles endow a coastal parish priest with a complex set of interwoven powers that leave him peerless in the college of Catholic priests.

THE IDENTITY

Catholicism reinforces the separate collective identity of the Mukkuvar, setting them further apart from the caste society, of which they only occupy the fringes. Their relationship to it was more in the nature of trade than of rule-bound obligations and the marginality of the geographical location only serves to underline the ambiguous position they occupy in caste society. Anantha K. Iyer (1981, 275) notes that the Mukkuvar "occupied a low state in the estimation of the high-caste men, and were precluded from passing along the public roads. Being obliged to keep to the coast and unable to bear the social disabilities, many became Christians and converts to Islam . . . and were thus elevated in the social scale." In Catholicism they have found a new representation of collective identity, which while not elevating their caste status in the eyes of the Hindus, has helped the Mukkuvar to distance themselves from the caste society and affirm a separate collective identity. This has muted the denigration a lowly agrarian caste usually suffers in the purity-and-pollution scale. Affiliation with Catholicism enables the Mukkuvar to affirm their distance from the caste sociey and resist their incorporation into and oppression by the caste structure.

During the Mondaikadu communal clashes of 1982, this Catholic identity was further accentuated for the Mukkuvar. Purportedly a clash between Hindus and Catholics, engendered by the Hindu revivalist organizations and by the actions of an overzealous volatile priest, the clash was more or less confined to Hindu Nadar and Catholic Mukkuvar, in spite of the fact that Catholics from other castes, numerically equal to the Mukkuvar, now live in the district. This period of Mondaikadu communal violence, as the clash between the Mukkuvar and the Hindus was called in the newspapers, also saw an emergence and reinforcement of the collective identity of all the Mukkuvar villages along the coastline of Kanyakumari District. Many villagers, both men and women, never tired of narrating the events of those days; of how villages supported each other, how they were able to supply essential food along the sea route, how bombs were made and petrol and kerosene were supplied to those villages under siege from the Hindu Nadar. A recurrent theme of these narratives was that the clash was primarily between the Mukkuvar and the Hindu Nadar, dismissing the role of other Catholics in the district. The Mukkuvar thus sought to establish their credentials for being more committed Catholics than others. One unassailable argument advanced was that they became Catholics in 1554, long before other groups in the district did (in about 1890). This claim is an affirmation of the separate identity of the Mukkuvar Catholics, who do not want to be submerged under the general rubric of Catholics of the Kottar Diocese. From the middle of 1996, a simmering tension between the Mukkuvar and Nadar priests of the diocese erupted into the demand for a division of the diocese.

An aspect of their collective identity as Catholics and their commitment to forging and strengthening this identity is the pride the Mukkuvar have in constructing and renovating their churches. The churches in these villages were built largely by the contributions of the villagers themselves. The parish priest of Kanyakumari claimed that its imposing church was built by the contribution of six beach seine operators over a period of 15 years. In 1989, the church in Colachel was extended, renovated, and a new bell tower built, at the cost of Rs.1,500,000. The churches in Muttom and Inayam Puthenthurai were being renovated in the early nineties at costs running over Rs.100,000.

The church in Chinnavilai was completed in 1979 with money raised from the villagers themselves. It took five years to complete the building. The village had a small chapel on the beach which collapsed due to sea erosion. The villagers pulled themselves together and built themselves a rather spacious church. Narrations of how each one played a role and the contributions each made, who went and ordered stones, cement, wood, abound in the village talk. The church is their pride and the patron saint, Anthony, to whom the church is dedicated, is their joy. Both the church building and the village saint stand as a symbol of their collective identity as both Catholics and as members of Chinnavilai.

THE HISTORY

The Catholic Church in the Mukkuvar villages presented itself both as the secular administrator—a quasi state (Ram 1991, 34)—and as the formal religious authority. The unique configuration of the Church's secular and religious roles unravels itself through history.

The Mukkuvar were converted to Catholicism during the hectic missionary activities that formed part of the Portuguese colonization of India in the sixteenth century. In the wake of the travels of Vasco da Gama, the Portuguese took over Goa and established a colony there. With the Portuguese, Christianization almost entirely coincided with the state enterprise (Panikkar 1959, 280). Gun and cross were both weapons of dominance. Captains and clerics acted as partners in an enterprise that fused colonization and Christianization (cf. Roche 1984, 41-42). Franciscan friars, for example, fought alongside soldiers in the capture of Goa on 25 November, 1510.

There is a record of Mukkuvar conversion, seemingly the first, which occurred in 1517 at Cochin. A group of Ilavas and Mukkuvar became Catholics following the missionary work of a Portuguese priest, Alvaro Penteado (Mundadan 1967, 90-103). However, the mass Christianization of the Mukkuvar of the present Kanyakumari District and the few contiguous villages, in the present Kerala State, followed that of Paravas, the fishing community on the east coast of southern India.

There are striking differences between the Parava and the Mukkuvar histories of conversion to Catholicism. Though the Paravas (also called the Parathars or the Parathavar) shared with the Mukkuvar social traits such as exclusive settlements, a specialized occupation of fishing, and a corporate economy of the *jati*, they also differed in many important ways. The Paravas had a far more diversified occupational structure. They were not only ocean fishers but also specialized in pearl harvesting. Pearls were a matter of trade interest.

The most striking difference between the histories of conversion of the Paravas and the Mukkuvar is that the Paravas became Catholics by political choice, to throw off the domination of the Moors. Their request to be made Catholics was almost immediately acceded to, while the Mukkuvar request was kept in abeyance until it suited the Portuguese.

The conversion of the Mukkuvar did not occur until the arrival of Francis

Xavier, hailed as the Father of the Catholic faith by the Mukkuvar. Catholicism in the villages on the west coast of Kanyakumari District owes its presence to his missionary work. Although there is some evidence of the presence of Catholicism in the region (Kottar) before the arrival of the Portuguese, the mass conversions of the western coast of Kanyakumari District occurred only when Francis Xavier, the first Jesuit, appeared on the scene. The Mukkuvar flock to the cathedral dedicated to him in Kottar during the annual festival (3 December). They often refer to Xavier as the saint with powers to grant one's desires ("ketta varam tharum kottar saveriar").

THE COLONIZATION

Details of Xavier's conversion program have been gleaned from the accounts of his companions in the missionary expedition, as well as those of the Jesuits who came to the Mukkuvar villages after him (Schurhammer 1977, 460-475). Starting at Poovar, he moved southeast, along the coast toward Kanyakumari. He reached Pallam, but before he could move on to Manakudy, he was called to Goa to accompany a punitive expedition by the Portuguese against the King of Jaffna. The Mukkuvar of Manakudy, the southernmost village on the west coast, adjacent to the Parava village, had already asked Xavier to come to their coast and baptize them. He did not immediately respond to this invitation. But he did respond to a similar request from the Karaiyas of Manar, received around the same time, by sending them a cleric. While Manar was in the general area of Portuguese control, most of the Mukkuvar villages were in the Kingdom of Travancore, within which the Portuguese had as yet no foothold. That Xavier's missionary work kept pace with the Portuguese expansion is hardly a coincidence.

Xavier had not acquired any fluency in the Tamil language. He had learned the Tamil translations of prayers and a sermon by rote and would repeat them a number of times, until his converts were able to learn them by heart. His method of conversion in a village was a two-day operation. On the first day, he collected all the men and boys and from early morning got them to learn the prayers. Once they could recite the prayers, he poured water over them and baptized them. On the next day, he did the same thing with the women. After baptizing all those who accepted Catholicism, he asked the children to bring to a designated spot in the village all images and statues of "pagan" deities, and he burned them. He got his new converts to destroy the village temples and shrines.

Xavier himself personally carried out the baptisms in the Mukkuvar villages, except Manakudy. However, he ensured that his Jesuit colleagues were sent to these villages to consolidate the conversion work.

Under Xavier's direction, each of the Mukkuvar villages was left under the charge of a *Kanakkapillai* and a *Melinchi*. It was the duty of the *Kanakkapillai* to hold regular prayer services, and keep track of newborn babies and marriages. When the missionary priest visited them, every three or four months, the babies were baptized and marriages solemnized. Some further instruction on Catholicism was given, and admonitions and punishment to defaulters were meted out. The *Melinchi*, most probably a corruption into Tamil of the Portuguese word *meirinho* (petty officer), functioned both as a sexton in the village, calling people to worship, and as a law officer, jailing repeat offenders. He was in charge of law and order under the direction of the missionary. Even today, the two offices exist in the coastal villages, though with limited powers. The *Kanakkapillai* is reduced to being a sacristan of the church and the *Melinchi* is simply the sexton.

The missionary expansion in the coastal villages was clearly seen to be Portuguese expansion. The Travancore kings, at least on five occasions (1547, 1572, 1579, 1584, and 1604), withdrew their permission to the missionaries to function in their territories and asked them to leave the kingdom. However, the threat of a breakup of trade and the military strength of the Portuguese made them relent and renew their concessions to the missionaries. The villagers themselves remained Christian mostly by the threat of reprisals from the Portuguese.

The imposition of Catholicism upon the Mukkuvar was achieved through the military power of the Portuguese and the political connivance of the King of Travancore. More than imposing a religious belief and ritual system, Catholicism was the imposition of colonial rule upon the Mukkuvar villages. Catholicism was also maintained by the threat of reprisals from the Portuguese. The immediate political advantage was the foothold the Portuguese obtained within the Kingdom of Travancore. They also had access to two small seaports, in Colachel and Thengapattnam. In contrast to the fishing coast, the control of which also gave control of the pearl trade to the Portuguese, the Travancore coast itself did not offer any direct material advantage. The Catholic missionaries were the outpost of the Portuguese within the Travancore kingdom, which facilitated the trade in pepper and cardamom. As outposts of the colonies, they established their own village administrative structures and strengthened these with the threat of Portuguese military intervention as well as their own punitive measures.

The Jesuits continued the missionary work started by Xavier until the expulsion of the Society of Jesus from the territories of Portugal in 1759. In 1557 a new diocese was set up in Cochin, which included the territory of the Mukkuvar villages. The Jesuits worked south of Quilon, while Franciscan missionaries covered the area north of Quilon.

The Franciscans constantly accused the Jesuits of not adhering fully to the *Padroado* system, the crux of which is the power of the Church to levy taxes and administer the village. The Jesuits' diminishing enthusiasm for the *Padroado* system was linked to political changes in Europe and to the fact that many of the new Jesuit missionaries came from countries other than Portugal. After the edict of expulsion (1759), the Jesuits were replaced by Franciscan missionaries in the Mukkuvar villages. The Franciscans were commited to the *Padraodo* system and reinforced it.

In 1833, Rome established its own organization, called Propaganda Fide, to carry out missionary work, which was to be directly controlled by it. It had begun to send out missionaries to former Portuguese territories. Under the Propaganda

Fide administration, new missionary organizations, the Carmelites, Capuchins, Missionaries of St. Francis de Sales, the Holy Cross Fathers, and Foreign Missions of Milan, appeared on the scene. The coexistence of the two ecclesiastical systems, the *Padroado* and the Propaganda Fide, resulted in a period of confusion.

Quilon was established as a separate diocese on 1 September, 1886. Bishop Ildephonse of Quilon issued a circular on 13 March, 1878, ordering a fish levy in all the villages, for the maintenance of the parish. This arrangement had been approved by his successors. In this the Propaganda Fide followed the *Padroado*.

On 26 May, 1930, the Diocese of Kottar was mapped out and established. The diocese was "entrusted to the native clergy" from its inception, at which time there were 32 priests. Of these, 28 were Indians and 7 were from the coastal villages. One of the first acts of the new bishop, Lawrence Pereira, relating to the parishes was to renew the demand for a fish levy in coastal villages (*Circular of the Bishop, Kottar Diocese, No. 600*, dated 24 April, 1931).

THE TWIN ROLES OF THE CHURCH

The unique configuration of the secular and religious roles of the Church in the Mukkuvar area has its beginnings in the Portuguese *Padroado* system. Even when the system of taxes in the villages has been trimmed, the parish priest is at the heart of the village finances. It is this role that gives the priest and the Church their extensive powers in secular administration. This contrasts sharply with the parishes of the interior, even within the same diocese. In the interior parishes, most of which are Nadar Catholics, generally village affairs have been left in the hands of parish elder *mudutham,* and the priest largely confines himself to religious matters.

The multifaceted administrative roles of the priest in the Mukkuvar villages set up the priest as the local lord and as a spiritual functionary at the same time. A notion common among the priests of the diocese is that the priest is "all in all" in the parish, a status guaranteed by the Church. In contrast to missionary times, particularly after the setting up of the Kottar Diocese, the priest is exposed to increasing and closer control by the Church's bureaucracy. Often the priests find themselves pulled in different directions by the demands and the directives of the diocesan curia, on the one hand, and by the expectations of the villagers, on the other.

In the village the priest is expected, as the President of the village committee, to be the common person, not linked to any faction in the village. As he is educated, conversant with the English language, and has access to both the secular and sacred power centers, he is expected to be the broker in most of the dealings the village has with government departments. He is the spokesman for village affairs to government bureaucrats, the police, *panchayat* or village administrative committee officials, *tahsildar* (a district officer), and the district collector. Government officials approach the priest if they want any programs to be con-

ducted in the village or any information to be passed on to the villagers. The
villagers approach him for help in all sorts of matters. When someone is in trouble
with the police, the priest is asked to intervene. His advice is sought in matters of
long-persisting illness. His recommendation is valued for admission to educational institutions. The priest is pestered with requests to secure employment.
Financial assistance in times of destitution is sought from him. Above all, he is
asked to arbitrate in disputes.

Catholicism came to the Mukkuvar along with Portuguese colonial Catholicism. The Church long continued to discharge functions that properly belonged
to the State. With local-level democracy and participation of the Mukkuvar in
state and national-level politics through affiliation with various political parties,
along with the rise of educated members in the community, the political function
of the Church has been drastically reduced. However, the Church and its representatives remain the official authority in the village. Alongside, there has been
another process. The Mukkuvar have appropriated, adapted, and used the Church
and its trappings in ways they have thought to be beneficial to them. This can be
seen in the constant contestation of the functioning style of the priest, sometimes
in physically violent forms. There have been a number of priests who have had to
leave a coastal village because of the unpleasantness that had developed and
insults that reached beyond the point of endurance. There are also cases where
the priest was driven out of the village or refused entry into the village.

The pulling and pushing which the priests of the coastal region are subject to
is a sign of the uneasy fulcrum on which the twin authorities of the Church rests.
The combination of secular and religious authority has rested on successful and
satisfactory recognition by the larger secular powers such as the kings, the colonizers, and recently, the Indian government departments. The agency of the villagers, in and through the Church, is affirming their own identity distinct from
whatever the caste society of India is offering them.

At the time of the missionization of the Mukkuvar villages, the missionaries
represented the powerful Portuguese colonizers and the consent of the Travancore
king. Indeed, the conversion of the villages themselves was preceded by a pro-
mulgation of the king's wishes. Xavier himself ensured that the Portuguese cap-
tain stationed in Quilon would guarantee the missionaries' work. For the
Mukkuvar, Xavier and his followers represented the sovereign power of the Portuguese, combined with the sovereign power of the Travancore king. In their turn
the missionaries duplicated the sovereign power in their work. The two-days program of conversion, which climaxed in the destruction of native shrines and sacred idols, was a sensational *episodic* intervention, a strategy which affirmed the
sovereign power. The appointment of the *Melinchi* and *Kanakkapillai*, the local
policeman and the village bureaucrat, reinforced the claim to a share in the sovereign power. At the same time the derivative sovereign power which the missionaries enjoyed was not itself omnipotent. The resistance to the power of the
missionaries was strong enough for one of them to plead with the Governor of

Goa to send an army contingent to "put fear into them" (Henriques 1956, 137-190). During their periodic visits, the missionaries dealt with misdemeanors and meted out punishment. The missionaries themselves were not present in the villages to represent the sovereign power associated with them, but their officials were. They exercised the power during these visits. On the other hand, the sovereign power that the King embodied, which was always at a distance except for episodic intervention, had come to be represented within the village itself through the *Melinchi* and *Kanakkapillai*.

The proximity of the agents of the hitherto distant power itself changed the type and strategy of power. The representatives of power were the village chieftain and the family heads. The sweep of power could be taken to be localized and restricted to community custom and the organization of labor. In the first instance, the presence of the missionaries shifted the center of power from the community chieftain to the missionaries' officials. Even today, the village leaders and committee members are those who are in some measure the head of a family group. It is not impossible that at the time of the missionaries some of the *arayans* were chosen to be officials. The crucial thing is that the power they represented was constituted through the derivative sovereign power of the missionaries. However, the proximity of the agencies of power radically changed the methods of the exercise of power. From episodic intervention, which left the internal relations and structures untouched, the strategy took on a disciplinary character.

In the early days the disciplinary power was exercised through officials and in later years by the resident priests themselves. The *Melinchi* and/or the priests rounded up reluctant churchgoers and forced them to attend services and sacraments. Older men recalled with nostalgic affection the Sundays when the priest used to circumambulate the village with a stick in hand, and whip any boy or girl playing truant from the catechism classes. The priests would insist on regular confessions for adults. Public scandals of adultery and extramarital affairs were given public penances; the offender had to hold a life-size cross during the entire Mass on a Sunday. The sermons were focused on errant behavior, and family and private devotions were promoted. The emphasis was on promoting a Christian morality. The disciplinary power supported the power of the priest in administering the village and mobilizing the finances of the village. The power of the priest was accepted because behind the priest was the Church, which, as late as 1954, had access to the King of Travancore and later to the government officials of independent India.

While the exercise of disciplinary power brought a level of dominance by the priests, it also provided the villagers with ammunition to resist them. The very moral principles the priests were inculcating into the villagers became the yardstick against which they came to be measured. When the priests fell short of the morality they preached, they were criticized and in some cases physically manhandled. The rebound of disciplinary morality upon the priests has greatly undermined their authority and the actual power they exercise in the village. Their authority is constantly under scrutiny, and each priest must make his claims to authority in the village credible.

The rise of informed and influential leaders in the village and the attenuation of the influence which the Church had with the secular authorities have only served to further reduce the authority of the priest in the village. The priests themselves, frazzled by the scrutiny of the villagers, want to avoid getting embroiled in the effervescence of the social life of the Mukkuvar. They want to confine themselves to purely pastoral activities and to leave community matters in the hands of the village committee/parish councils. They have no easy escape, as the authority of the committees/councils themselves are challenged by the Mukkuvar and factional conflicts flare up with ease. The priest finds himself in the unenviable position of being expected to exercise his authority and keep the village community together, and of having his credentials as an authority constantly countermanded.

The priest and, consequently, the Church, find themselves in an ambivalent position. On the one hand they are the paramount centers of power in the villages (though not for all) and, on the other, their power is constantly eroded and challenged.

THE APPROPRIATION

For the Mukkuvar themselves, Catholicism gives a distinct identity to their community. This is an identity they have been and are willing to celebrate, not only at village feasts or in the great personal sacrifices they make in constructing their village churches, but, most important, in engaging themselves in an irrevocable way with the priests and the Church, to gain for themselves the control of their destiny.

It is not only the institutional Church that has historically been molded to function in the interest of the Mukkuvar, but their beliefs and practices present a unique configuration of indigenous and official beliefs and practices. Their religion centers on illness, misfortune, and augmenting the fish catch. Not only do these beliefs seem to have an independent existence of their own and to survive outside the direct control of the Church, but they coexist comfortably with the rituals of Catholicism. The Catholic rituals are transformed to suit the Mukkuvar's conception of spirits and demonic deities and accustomed ways of relating to them. The enormous number of Masses said for blessing, for healing, and for the repose of souls suggests poignant links with their concern to ward off evil and to ensure good. In times of illness, a blessing is sought from the priest. Prolonged illness is treated with a long stay at a shrine or the village church. The priest is called to bless the fishing gear, and when there is a lean season for fishing the beach is blessed with a procession of the statue of St. Anthony.

Particularly among the older men and women, and to some extent among the young women, who are involved in the teaching of catechism in the church, there is an understanding of formal theology. These are persons who take an active part in the liturgies and other programs of the Church. They attend the Sunday Masses, as well as occasional Masses offered in the village church, and devotions organized in the church such as the recitation of the rosary, the Way of the Cross, and morning prayers. Their representation of Catholicism is primarily through the formulas they have learned in catechism. In the playing back of the catechism formulas, they also evince a conviction which seems to define their lives. They sum up Catholicism as the membership of believers in a Church which remains united with the Pope and the bishops. Without belief, there is no Church. One has not seen the birth, death, and resurrection of Christ. One believes the testimony of those who were with Him. It is this faith that expresses itself in devotion to God and the saints. A good Catholic should attend Mass and receive Holy Communion and behave as a Christian. Any practice other than sacramental practice is suspect. The prevalent practice of visiting shrines or *kurusadi* and churches and receiving *kanakku* (divination) is strictly errant. The *kanakku* received in these places have been proven false. "Kannakku ketpathu themmalithanam" (To receive divination is harmful). It is the work of the devil (*chattanin velai*). Everything is in the hands of God. Without God's consent, nothing will ever happen, not even a speck of dust will move ("Iraivanudaiya sittham illamal, oru thurumbu kooda asaiyathu").

For minor ailments the villagers make a pilgrimage to neighboring churches dedicated to saints credited with special powers to heal them. Thus, for sore eyes the church of St. Lucy at Puthoor is frequented. They make an offering and pray to the saint, standing in the middle of the church. When suffering from acne, a pilgrimage is made to the church of St. Theresa of Lisieux at Kandan Vilai. In times of persistent misfortune or enduring illness, the villagers make pilgrimages to Edathua, shrine of St. Sebastian and to Velankanni, shrine of Mary. All that the pilgrims could tell me was that these saints have the power; they had no knowledge of, nor did they evince any interest in, the legends associated with these saints or with the shrine.

Nerchai (vows and votive offerings), pilgrimages as the execution of devout promises made to God or a saint in times of misfortune, novenas, living in a shrine or a church during a period of illness are all considered orthopraxis, as these are carried out within the rubric of Catholicism. It is only the rituals or beliefs involving deities of other religions that the "orthodox" Catholics claim to shy away from.

THE *MANTRIKAM*

These "orthodox" Catholics, however, also recognize the existence of demonic deities, evil spirits, and the practice of *mantrikam* associated with them. Two of them claimed that they had been bothered by spirits and were frightened. It was only because of their courage and their Catholic prayers that they had protected themselves. Though they despise astrology, palmistry, and household rituals for warding off the evil eye, they admit that their own household members espouse non-Catholic customs. Though they deny any involvement with the beliefs and practices of *mantrikam*, they steer clear of "haunted" spots and avoid doing things that might make them defenseless against the spirits, and are keen to acquire prayers (*kettu mantram*) that would protect them.

"One Friday evening, my brother and I went to the beach to launch our catamaran. It was past 8:00 pm. We had to pass through the sand dunes to the west of the village. Normally people don't go near the sand dunes at night. Halfway toward the catamaran a small donkey appeared and began to grab at my brother. Thinking that it was only a donkey, I beat it off with the oar I was carrying. After a short distance, it appeared a second time; and I drove it off. When it appeared a third time, I was convinced that it must be a *chatthan* (devil). Immediately, I recited the *kettu mantram* I knew. The *chatthan* left us." The prayer was:

> *O Queen of Heaven,*
> *Reigning over the Hosts of Angels,*
> *From the beginning of the world,*
> *You have the power and grace,*
> *to stand over the head of the Devil,*
> *Exercise your authority and power*
> *over all the devils and consign them*
> *to the depths of hell. Amen.*
>
> *Holy Trinity and Angels of God,*
> *Protect me. Amen.*

"Even though I had beaten back the *chatthan*, I felt uneasy in my mind. I was afraid that it might push me into the river and kill me. So we returned home and took along with us Peechiar. Peechiar was powerful because he knew many *kettu mantram* (prayer-spells). After he reached the catamaran with us, he told us that the devil appeared to him in the form of a bird."

This story was told to me by an "orthodox" Catholic, who vehemently denied any dealings with *mantrikam*. Indeed, he dismissed the magical practices of the villagers as stupid and false. However, not only is he aware of the belief in spirits but the power of the spirits is very real to him, and, in spite of his bravado, he is afraid of them.

This event provides clues into some basic elements of the Mukkuvar popular Catholicism. It situates their world between heaven and hell. Invoking the Queen of Heaven and using a fixed and formalized text makes what appears as a traditional prayer into a spell for one's own protection. While the Mukkuvar appeal to the powers of heaven for protection, they do recognize that the power of the devil is equally strong. To deal with such power one needs to have recourse to someone who has mastery over both worlds. The real goal is to acquire power and not simply be supplicant to heavenly powers.

STELLA

Stella is a young married woman. She is 30 years old. At the time of my fieldwork, she had separated from her husband and was living with her parents. She had had a troubled marriage and was ill treated both by her husband and her father-in-law. She became ill and withdrawn, and after a while she lost the power of speech. It was then that her parents realized that her father-in-law was a *mantravadi* who worshipped Kali, Isakki, and other Hindu deities. The family took Stella to a charismatic prayer meeting at a place called Assisi. She was also taken to churches and shrines dedicated to St. Michael, St. Anthony, and St. Sebastian. They made a vow to offer a human image in silver to the church at Velankanni. Stella's illness was controlled and she had some spells of clarity. However, she recovered more completely only after the family took her to a Catholic *vaidyar*, or shaman, in Thoothur. He divined that some Hindu deities were holding sway over her. He performed some rituals to free her from the clutches of malevolent deities but let the benevolent ones stay with her. The benevolent deities would warn her if someone were planning to harm her or any other member of the family through *mantrikam*. But Stella needed to keep praying regularly; otherwise the Hindu deities would gain ascendancy over her and she would again become possessed.

Stella and her family regarded their behavior as completely orthodox. In their opinion, they had resorted only to Catholic rituals. The *vaidyar* was a Catholic and his prayers were addressed to Catholic saints. He did not invoke any Hindu deities. The fact that the *vaidyar* has no official sanction from the Church is not a matter of consequence to them. Nor do the continued presence of Hindu deities with Stella and her family's grateful acceptance of their "protection" pose any problem for their "Catholic" faith.

The case evidences the strong desire of the Mukkuvar for keeping a Catholic face on their religious practices. This hinges on their identity as Catholics. The religious practices of their own tradition are given a Catholic mantle. The *vaidyar*, the shaman, has Catholic allegiance. He prays (uses spells invoking Catholic saints) to Catholic saints. Neither he nor Stella eschews belief in the Hindu deities. They recognize their power; they do not want to keep away from it but only to mute it. They have no objection to having the benevolent Hindu deities help Stella. The recognition of the power of Catholic saints and the Hindu deities coexists comfortably.

The priests in the area are very much aware of "suspect" religious practices in the coastal villages. However, there are at least two priests with a high reputation for the divination of illness and possession. In the Mukkuvar mind, the priests' function is equivalent to that of the *vaidyar*, but with added sanction.

Since Vatican II, charismatic prayer groups have been encouraged in the diocese. However, the fundamental Catholicism that is characteristic of charismatic groups has not percolated down. Most who attend are occasional users, who consider the charismatic group pretty much in the same way as they would consider a *vaidyar*. A majority of priests, however, adopt the strategy of providing Catholic rituals which they hope will ultimately replace the magical practices. They promote devotions to various saints, novenas, liturgies for healing and blessing, and, of course, Masses for various intentions. However, their attempts are constrained by their own theological training, which does not recognize the existence of divine beings other than the Catholic God and the canonized saints of the church. Schooled in a scientific rationality, they have little empathy with the conceptualization of a spirit world and its interaction with human beings.

The younger priests, the Vatican II generation, are more concerned with the enhancement of the quality of human life. Nearly 50% of the priests of the diocese profess a school of theology tinged with varied shades of Marxist thought. Most others subscribe simply to a more generalized, humanistic thought which recognizes that improvement of the human condition is an essential part of Catholicism. There are hardly 10 among the 140 priests of the diocese who are "diehard conservatives" and who vehemently propound the idea that Catholicism is concerned with the salvation of souls through the practice of pre-Vatican II Catholic morality. Barring the few priests who actually claim to have special powers of divination and healing, the priests ignore the native religious beliefs and practices.

Unhampered by any direct condemnation by the Church, and outside the direct control of the Church, the native religious practices coexist with formal Catholic rituals. Orthodoxy is claimed simply on the grounds of remaining under the broad umbrella of Catholic rubrics. Orthodoxy is lost, according to them, only by participation in rituals involving deities of other religions.

PUBLIC DISCOURSE, PRIVATE THOUGHTS

The public stage of village life is dominated by quarrels. The backstage buzzes with tales of misfortune, suspicions of witchcraft, and quiet tears over hard times. Hostilities and conflicts take on another dimension in the belief and practice of *mantravadam*, or *mantrikam*, generic words used loosely to describe the presence and influence of spirits and deities.

Direct admission of *mantrikam* was rarely forthcoming. However, almost everybody was willing to talk about how widespread *mantrikam* was in the village and was able to provide some detail or other of the belief in, and practice of, *mantrikam*. More often than not, the victims of *mantrikam* were willing to talk about their misfortune, who caused it, how it was divined, and what steps they had to take to find the antidote for it.

An ailment that is not quickly cured or easily diagnosed is a misfortune which is sooner or later linked to *mantrikam*. So are persistent hostilities within a household, between husband and wife, and between parents and children or among siblings. Consistently low catches of fish over a protracted period of time, as well as good catches, are also linked to *mantrikam*. The explanation and practices of rituals of healing and divination offer no systematic and consistent models, which is in itself not surprising. What did surprise me was that in the village, to the extent of my knowledge, there was no one in the Mukkuvar community who could offer me an elaboration on their rather cryptic statements on, and sketchy description of, rituals. One could not escape the impression of an utter and bland pragmatism that seems to imbue their approach to the alleviation of misfortune. Whatever works is right. For instance, an adult male suffering for more than six months with what the doctor diagnosed as cirrhosis of the liver had originally taken a course of treatment with a woman for jaundice (hepatitis); when that did not work he switched to allopathy. This treatment did not work, and by this time he had become convinced that he was a victim of *mantrikam*. He pressed into service two diviners, one after the other, and hosted two performances of rituals in his house. He was told by the diviners that two of his brothers had done *mantrikam* on him. He was given protective charms to wear around his neck. A few months after this, his condition was worsening. He went on a number of pilgrimages to shrines of St. Anthony and spent a few weeks at one shrine. He even went to the parish priest to have Masses said for his recovery. His family organized a votive offering to St. Anthony. He eventually died during my fieldwork. Neither he nor his family and friends were ever sure of what caused this misfortune. In the same breath they would say that the misfortune was brought about by *mantrikam* and deny that his brothers, accused of *mantrikam*, would ever do such a thing, as the brothers were so friendly to each other. To them, his death remained unexplained. The Mukkuvar approach potential remedies for an illness or a misfortune as they would a menu. They choose what is immediately available and try another item if one doesn't work. Their shift from one to another is conditioned by what works and what does not. There is no hierarchy in their approach to finding a remedy for illness or misfortune.

The rituals of healing and divination are performed by a *vaidyar*. All the *vaidyar* that I have identified are male. There are a few the villagers frequent. The *vaidyar* are referred to by the town and village they reside in, and not by name, e.g., Palavakkam Vaidyar, Azhikkal Vaidyar, Vadaseri Vaidyar. The reputation of a *vaidyar* is determined by the number of incantations and spells he knows. These are called *kettu mantram*. There is a strong belief that a knowledge of *kettu mantram* is efficacious in controlling and warding off evil spirits and forces. So too is the belief that the proper *kettu mantram* could enable one to augment one's wealth and ensure prosperity.

Though there were several men in the village who had a reputation for powerful *mantrikam*, particularly for augmenting their fish catch, only one person in the village readily admitted his desire to be a *vaidyar*. He had already acquired the knowledge of a few spells, which he had recorded in a notebook. He also sought me out to share with me, in style, his experience of the spirit world. Later I discovered he considered me to have magical power and was trying to augment his repertoire with my secret knowledge! This was linked to the reputation with which I suddenly found myself saddled. On the first two mornings after my arrival in the village, I went to the beach. The beach was bustling with activity, and most of the fishermen were engaged in beach seine operation. The women fish vendors huddled together in a group waiting for the net to be pulled in. Unable to resist the lure of cool seawater, I waded in and stood for a while among the gently lapping waves. After I returned to the village, the beach seine netted a large catch of *vela*, large snappers. The value of the catch was Rs.50,000. The villagers were happy and, in good humor, ascribed their good luck to me. However, when this kind of catch was repeated the next day, it gave rise to rumors that I must have some magical powers. The villagers had not had such a large catch in some years and to have had two large catches could only be explained by some powers I must have had. Their experience is that after a large catch, there is inevitably a lull in fishing ("Vela patta kadal, verung kadal"). Throughout the fieldwork, when fish catches were low, men and women would beg me to go to the beach and use my powers on their behalf. The reputation that one has power is paramount in defining the people's recourse to him.

The evidence that someone has been performing *mantrikam* are items such as sealed copper tubes, 3-4 cm long and 0.5 cm in diameter, seashell *chanku*, and copper scrolls with inscriptions of *mantram*. These are generally found buried in the ground at the bottom of the front steps or at the four corners of a house. If one could find these items, either at the time of rituals or by accident, and remove them, then danger would be averted.

Mantrikam always involves spirits. The spirit is commissioned to take possession of the intended victim, bringing harm or fortune. The evidence of *mantrikam*, the materials used, do not have any power in themselves. These are objects used in the rituals to commission or decommission the spirits. The powers the *mantravadi* and, by the same token, the *vaidyar* have are derived from the power of the spirits and from the extent to which the specialists have domesticated the spirits or have found favor with them.

JOSEPHAT

Josephat is married and has two children. He is from one of the founding families of the village. He has a reputation as a competent fisherman and as one who manages his affairs well. He does not generally get into village conflicts and is said to be a peaceable man. He believes that *mantrikam* is powerful and that he is himself a victim of *mantrikam*.

After 12 years of marriage, he was possessed by a spirit. Both Josephat and his wife kept referring to the spirit as *muni* and *kadalkanni*. *Muni* is the spirit of an ascetic who has acquired power through his penances but has not attained *moksha*, or ultimate liberation. *Kadalkanni* is the mermaid. Apart from this meager information, I could not obtain from them, or anyone else in the community, any further details of the spirit and its characteristics. Josephat had lost all appetite and would suddenly go quiet. He was listless and visits to allopathic doctors did not leave him any the wiser as to his condition. His family, his mother, his wife, and his father's brother made a vow to go to the shrine of St. Sebastian at Edathua, a pilgrimage center in Kerala, some 150 miles away. The day of the pilgrimage, Josephat developed a high temperature and became silent. He refused to take the medicine for fever and was very irritable. The family forcibly took him to the allopathic doctor and got him some tablets. The family did not want to renege on the vow, so they set out on the pilgrimage. Josephat would not eat or drink anything throughout the journey. He huddled in a corner of the train and slept through the journey.

On arrival at the shrine, Josephat wandered off by himself into the crowd, and it was difficult to keep up with him. He was so weak that he sat on the veranda of a building and refused to go into the church. The family all went into the church to pray. His wife stayed with him. He drank four liters of water at one time. Later, he went into the church by himself. His wife remained with him.

The family stayed that night in the pilgrims' center. Josephat could not sleep in the room. The entire family, along with Josephat, made their beds at the foot of the flagpole. Still Josephat could not sleep. He complained of severe chest pain. He got up and went and sat on the porch of the church. He sat silently for more than half an hour. His wife woke his mother and brought her to him. His mother asked him what was wrong. Josephat replied that he was not her son; her son was at that moment with St. Sebastian. "Those who worshiped me have deserted me now," he said. Then he grew quiet and sat watching the flagpole. Suddenly, he darted to the flagpole, climbed it, and from the top of the pole jumped into the pond next to it. His family began to wail and shout. Josephat was not seen for more than an hour, until he quietly walked out of the water. He seemed to be all right thereafter. The family returned home after the pilgrimage.

A few days after his return, Josephat surprised everybody by demanding a bottle of country liquor (*charaayam*) and a bunch of plantains. He (the spirit) repeated the complaint that those who worshiped him had now deserted him; he was hungry and wanted liquor and plantains. His wife's mother's brother, who had knowledge of *kettu mantram* was called in and he recited the *jebam* (prayers of healing and exorcism) of St. Anthony, St. Sebastian, St. Michael, and Our Lady of Velankanni. Josephat (the spirit) said that there were now four persons around him and repeated his request for liquor and plantains. He also said that Josephat's ancestors worshiped him regularly on the First Friday of the month and he was very helpful to them. He promised that if his (the spirit's) request was fulfilled, he would not give any further trouble and would leave Josephat in seven months' time.

Josephat and his wife went over to Kottaipattanam, a small seaport in the Bay of Bengal, and were operating their mechanized boat. Eight months passed without any incident of the spirit. Again the spirit possessed him. This time the spirit directed his wife to go to a *vaidyar* in Tirunelvely. The *vaidyar* was a Muslim, though he had installed pictures of Catholic saints and Hindu deities in his house. He told them that the only way out was to provide a bottle of liquor and a bunch of plantains every First Friday to the spirit. He also revealed that the spirit was a mermaid, who was acquired by the great-grandfather of Josephat. He assured them that the mermaid was benevolent. From the great-grandfather, the mermaid was bequeathed to the grandfather of Josephat. But the grandfather did not bequeath the mermaid to any of his sons, and the mermaid was without a devotee for nearly 25 years.

Josephat and his wife regularly offered the customary bottle of liquor and a bunch of plantains on the First Friday of the month for seven months. Now they do not make the monthly offerings regularly as they cost them Rs.50, and they make them only when the mermaid acts up.

Josephat also linked the spirit possession to the quarrel he had with his father's brother. When Josephat acquired a boat, he had his father's brother as a shareholder. Later, because there was continuous disagreement on the division of profits, he bought him out. His uncle was angry and set the spirit upon him. He also believed that his father's brother must have had control of the mermaid for some time and could not meet its demands, and must have set it on him.

The entire episode is set in the context of kinship. The mermaid was acquired by kin and hence belongs to the family and was handed down, properly or improperly, to the next generation. The uncle set it upon Josephat when he could not meet its demands for worship and food offerings. The mermaid remains within the kinship nexus. It forced itself upon Josephat, putting him and his family to a lot of trouble. Now that it has at least sporadic worship, it remains quiet. The spirit simultaneously boosts the power of an individual and his family, and becomes a handicap.

THE CATHOLIC HEALER

I was introduced to a Catholic *vaidyar* by one of my informants. He is a regular client of the *vaidyar*. He has been using the services of the *vaidyar* to ensure success in fishing as well as for the cure of a number of illnesses in his household. He believes absolutely in the efficacy of the incantations and rituals of the *vaidyar*. His brother is also a regular client of the *vaidyar*. Moreover, the brother fancies himself as an aspirant to the title of *vaidyar*; and he already has gained a modest reputation for exorcising less powerful *pey* (demons), and for draining poison from scorpion and snake bites and from certain fish stings with spells.

The *vaidyar* lives in Mondaikadu, a village 4 km from Chinnavilai. Mondaikadu is a Hindu pilgrimage center which attracts large numbers of Hindus from Kanyakumari District and southern districts of Kerala. It is dedicated to the goddess Bhagavati. The pilgrimage season is the first fortnight of March when the temple festival is held. Mondaikadu is adjacent to Puthoor, another Catholic fishing village. An irrigation canal and a road separate the two villages. The close proximity of the villages, one Hindu and the other Catholic, has been one of the factors leading to friction between the two. In 1981 there was a communal riot between these two villages, which later spread throughout the district. The *vaidyar* lives in a small colony of *vannan*, the washermen caste. The small community of 20 *vannan* families is Catholic. The *vaidyar* presides over the community. He has persuaded a wealthy Catholic landowner to donate a piece of land on which a shrine to St. Anthony of Padua was built in 1979. Because of the continuing tensions between the Hindu and Catholic communities, work on the shrine has been suspended, but the family of the *vaidyar* has invested some money in putting a thatched roof over the foundation. They pride themselves in having ensured a Mass in the shrine every Sunday for the last five years. The *vaidyar* claims that there are at least three telling cases of miraculous cures obtained by devotees who spent a night in the shrine. The *vaidyar* hopes that within a few years the shrine will become famous throughout the district. Though he evidenced a lot of interest and pride in the shrine, he strongly denied that he treated his clients there. He vaguely suggested that the shrine was somehow an extension of his spiritual powers.

The *vaidyar* is in his fifties and sports a flowing gray beard. He is 5 feet 6 inches tall. He is lean to the point of being gaunt. I met him in his house. He was sitting in an easy chair on the front veranda of his house. He was wearing a clean white *dhoti* (loincloth) and a cream-colored full-sleeved shirt. He had turned up the sleeves a couple of folds. His appearance suggested the respectability associated with a high-caste male with modest wealth.

The *vaidyar* portrayed himself as having been a hardworking man all through his life. At the age of 12, he said, he would rise early, at 4:30, go to the canal to wash clothes for three hours, return home for a meager breakfast, go to the school in a town 7 km away. On his return from school, he would go to the canal to help his parents finish the washing. He had to do his share of work at home to be allowed to continue his studies.

His interest in *mantrikam* was aroused when he witnessed healing rituals and exorcisms performed at his home. He discovered that there were books available on *mantrikam,* which he purchased and studied. He gave the title of one such book: *Pitambra Jalam.* Though he was born into a traditional Catholic family, he began to practice healing rituals and exorcisms in the manner of Hindus. As was demanded by the rituals he worshiped the Hindu deities while at the same time maintaining his affiliation to the Catholic Church. It was only much later that he came by some palm leaves containing the *jebam* (prayers) written by Veeramanunivar, a Catholic priest, a few centuries ago.

He had been using the dual system, the Hindu and the Christian, of healing and exorcism for a while. He was sure, however, that his reputation as a *vaidyar* was built up through his practice of the Hindu rituals of exorcism. He gave up the Hindu practice some seven years ago at the insistence of the then parish priest, Fr. Narchisan. The *vaidyar* told me that the arguments of Fr. Narchisan convinced him of the error of his ways, particularly the argument that he was flirting with danger for his own soul and the future of his family. He knew for himself, as the parish priest had pointed out, that the demonic deities he was invoking for the rituals would not just leave him or his descendants, even if he wanted to leave them. He knew that the only way he could make a clean break with the demonic deities was to "gift" them away—ceremoniously hand them over to another practitioner (*tarai vaarthu koduthal*). The *vaidyar* is now being treated for diabetes. He connects the onset of diabetes to his "mistake."

He gave a number of explanations for the development of diabetes in a person. One explanation was that it was because of the "heat" of the body—an idea from folk medicine. The other was from the Western medical system—genetic inheritance. The third explanation was moral—failure of the kidneys due to excessive sexual activity with many women. However, he is convinced that in his case, the diabetic condition is the result of his "mistake."

He is not very clear about what the "mistake" is. At one time he was referring to the "mistake" of practicing Hindu rituals and remaining a Catholic—apostasy of his Christian faith. At another moment he was referring to "mistakes" in the Hindu rituals, both in the practice of exorcism and in the final "gifting" away of his deities. He spoke at length about his diabetic condition. His illness is incongruent with his status as healer and diviner, and it was a blemish on what otherwise would have been an unsullied reputation as a healer and diviner with extraordinary powers. He was at pains to explain his illness as somehow connected to his practice of rituals of healing. By tracing his illness to his own "mistakes," he succeeded in creating the impression that he himself was the cause of his illness, albeit unwittingly; the important thing was that he knew the cause, and the cause was none other than himself. As long as he knew why and how he became ill, he was in control of the situation, even if he had not yet remedied his condition. My informant, who had taken me to him, was utterly convinced that this was so.

He traced the Christian tradition of exorcism and healing to Veeramanunivar. Veeramanunivar is Fr. Joseph Constantine Beschi, a Jesuit missionary who came to South India in the seventeenth century. He followed the example set by Robert De Nobili, another Jesuit, discarded his European clerical dress and adopted the saffron robe of a *sanyasi* (wandering ascetic). He had, in an attempt to acquire competence in the local culture, set himself to master the Tamil language. He acquired sufficient fluency in it to have been able to compose a full-length heroic epic on the life of Christ. Though I had known of Veeramanunivar, and of his reputation as a Christian poet and the forerunner of prose in Tamil (the historians of Tamil literature accord him the credit for writing the first novelette in Tamil, the first prose work in the language), it was only the *vaidyar* who claimed Veeramanunivar as a *mantrik* and composer of incantations and spells.

The Catholic *vaidyar* claims that Veeramanunivar composed a number of *jebam* in poetic verses. He composed these prayers because he saw that Catholics were turning to the *mantrikam* (magical practices) of the Hindus in times of trouble and were praying to the Hindu deities for healing.

Two of the *jebam* composed by Veeramanunivar are very powerful. One is addressed to St. Anthony and the other to Michael the Archangel. These are called

Antoniyar Jebam, and *Mikkelandavar Jebam* respectively. The *Antoniyar Jebam* is so strong as to have power over even the most terrible demon (*koduramana pey*).

Antoniyar Jebam should be recited with total concentration. One must control the five senses, keep the mind focused on the mental image (*rubam*) of St. Anthony, and recite the prayer verses 21 times. If one does this correctly, the figure (*saayal*) of St. Anthony will appear before one. The *saayal* is unstable, similar to a cloud of smoke; however, the shape of St. Anthony becomes clearly discernible. When the *saayal* appears before one, a strong feeling of power (*akrosham*) develops within oneself. It is at this moment that the power of *jebam* is at its highest. Whatever questions one puts to the *saayal* in this state, one gets the "correct" response; it is not necessarily the response that one would desire, nor one that could be thought up. One has no control over the response. The response is given by the *saayal* and one just speaks the words as given. One must keep one's mind focused on the *saayal* and keep reciting the *jebam*. One should never allow the senses to move away from the prayer. This is the phase of divination. By the question and responses one comes to know who caused the illness, by what method, and for what reason.

The *vaidyar* continues the incantation "without a break." He is simultaneously tying a knot, in a thread which he holds in his hand, at the rate of one knot per incantation. Any time after the 21st incantation, the first symptoms of the uneasiness of the spirit that has taken possession of the client will become evident. The spirit is a *pey*, a Hindu demonic deity such as Vadai, Ishakki, or Vannaramadan. The client starts to yawn. Sometimes the yawning will be so long that one wonders when the client is going to stop. As the incantations continue uninterrupted, the spirit will start screaming to leave it alone (*ennai viddudu*). One must not respond to the spirit, but must turn a deaf ear to it and keep on reciting *jebam*. After a while it will get tired and will let out a final ear-piercing scream: "I am leaving." Then the spirit will leave the client, his/her house, and the village. This is exorcism proper.

A variation in the exorcist's ritual is to give a coconut to the client and ask him/her to hold it. As the incantations continue, the coconut progressively becomes heavier, to the point that the client cannot hold it up any longer and drops it on the floor. The *vaidyar* then takes the coconut, which now imprisons the spirit, and disposes of it in an unfrequented spot outside the village.

The final part of the ritual is to ensure protection of the client from further attack by the spirit. The *vaidyar* takes a handful of water and splashes water hard on the face of the client. Then the *vaidyar* ties the thread which he has been knotting as he recites the *jebam* around the neck of the client. He leads the recitation of an Our Father and The Creed in which the members of the household join in. The ritual is now complete and the client is "cured"; the outward symptoms of illness which the client was suffering begin to disappear, and the spirit that caused the illness has now been exorcised.

The *vaidyar* described further the magical ritual for ensuring a large catch of fish. The ritual is done at night on the beach. He states that the recital of the

Antoniyar Jebam 21 times will ensure a large catch. He said that St. Anthony has a special relationship with fish. He recalled an incident in the life of St. Anthony of Padua. In one of his journeys, he came to a seaside town and began to preach in the public square. The crowds laughed at him and heckled him. St. Anthony left the town square, went to the beach, and began to preach to the fish to show that the fish were more sensible than the people of the town. The fish are supposed to have gathered around St. Anthony and stayed still throughout his sermon. Because St. Anthony had demonstrated his power over fish during his lifetime, it followed that the incantation to him would be efficacious in ensuring a large catch of fish.

The ritual is done in this manner. The *vaidyar* takes some seawater in a clay pot and throws a handful of beach sand into it. He then starts the recitation of the *Antoniyar Jebam*. Simultaneously, he knots a thread which he holds in his hand: one knot at the completion of a single recitation. Anytime after the 21st recitation, an image appears in the water of a particular type of fish in a *mandal* (a group of large fish playing on the surface of the seawater). The *vaidyar* concludes the ritual with the recitation of the Our Father and the Creed, hands over the knotted thread to the client to take with him on the fishing expedition, and empties the contents of the pot into the sea. The fishing expedition will invariably be successful, the *vaidyar* claimed, and my informant agreed with him, citing cases when he had made good catches after such a ritual. The village gossip also has it that my informant regularly returns with a good catch even when others come away with little or no catch, all because he indulges in *mantrikam*. However, there were others in the village who had organized such rituals with various *vaidyars* but had had nothing to show for it.

The *vaidyar* does not normally accept any cash payment for his divination and exorcism services, even though the performance of a healing ritual may well take the best part of the night and leaves him exhausted. He believes that accepting cash payment would somehow reduce his powers, as such a practice reneges on the promise which he made to his teacher Aasaan. However, he accepts gifts such as fruits and clothing. But for services in performing the ritual for a large catch of fish, he accepts cash payment which may be anywhere between Rs.1,000 and Rs.5,000.

Though the *vaidyar* gave me a detailed account of the "Catholic" ritual for ensuring a good catch of fish, he added, almost as an afterthought, that the Hindu rituals involving incantations to *pathirakali* and *vairavan* (goddess and god images in angry, destructive [against evil] form) are far more efficacious. The *saayal* of the Hindu deities are fearful to behold. If one is frightened at their appearance, one will be marred for life—one will become insane or chronically ill until one wastes away and dies. The trick is to concentrate on the recitation and not to lose control over one's senses. Because the ritual is fraught with danger for the one who performs it, one accepts a large fee.

The *vaidyar* allowed me to tape the interview. When I asked him to recite the *Antoniyar* and *Mikkelandavar Jebam*, he hesitated. He closed his eyes for quite a while. He agreed to recite it on condition that I did not record the recital. However, I later succeeded in getting a version of the incantation from the brother of my informant. The version I have is very similar in structure and content to the one recited by the *vaidyar,* as far as I can remember.

> *St. Anthony, you who reside in the heart,*
> *come near.*
> *Wheel of victory in one hand, the seven*
> *worlds in the other, come to this place.*
> *Break down every barrier and come close to me.*
> *Cut down Siva and Parvathi,*
> *break into bits, spear, plate and staff.*
> *Annihilate Ganapathi, Balasubrmanian,*
> *Kalyani, Kali, Neeli*
> *Mahadevi, Bhagavathi,*
> *Thanumalayan, Murugan.*
> *I bind all foes,*
> *evil spirits,*
> *and the host of devas.*
> *This is not my binding,*
> *but that of St. Anthony.*
> *With a six-cornered figure,*
> *I bind them all.*
> *I bind the four directions, the eight corners*
> *This is St. Anthony's binding.*
> *I recite the prayer of St. Anthony.*
> *I invoke the three persons of the Trinity,*
> *I invoke the three armies of Angels,*
> *St. Anthony, come and help me. Amen Yesu.*

In the *jebam* St. Anthony is represented as one with absolute power over all things. He can break down all the barriers, and bind and neutralize the demons and deities of the Hindu pantheon. The Hindu deities mentioned in the *jebam* are the resident deities of the large temples of the region: Trichendur, Suchindram, Kanyakumari, and Mondaikadu. Lumping the Hindu gods and goddesses together with the demons and the evil spirits of suicides and unfortunate and gruesome deaths, the *jebam* draws the line between good and evil sharply along the division of Christianity and Hinduism. There is a significant absence of any mention of devils from the biblical and Christian tradition, e.g., Lucifer, Beelzebub.

The core of the prayer is "to bind." By binding, the forces and causes of misfortune are contained and neutralized. Once the spirit deity possessing the client has been effectively contained, the *vaidyar* then orders it to leave the client. He speaks as though he is speaking to another person now under his authority. The spirit may not immediately oblige him. At this point, he shouts at it as one would shout at a recalcitrant underling. Once bound, the *vaidyar* treats the spirits as he would treat another ordinary human being.

THE SEA

For the Mukkuvar fishermen the sea is the center of life. As they wake up in the morning, their first thought is the sea, the strength of waves, direction of wind, types of current. They come on to the beach and look at the sea to gauge its condition.

The fishermen claim that the sea is their property (*chothu*). It is their property because only they have the knowledge of the sea; it is they who are blessed with the bountifulness of the sea; it is they who wrestle with it to make their fortunes; it is their life that is inexorably tied with the seasonal changes of the sea.

For the Mukkuvar the sea is alive. The sea currents, waves (*ummalam*) are all signs of its life. The force of wind rising from the sea is generally stronger than that rising from the land. The sea wind is stronger because sea is stronger, alive and not inert like land.

The sea has moods. In monsoon season, June to September, the waves are high, the sea is in turbulence, and they break on the beach with a ferocity that sends a rumbling tremor through the village. The sea is angry and violent. The sea rises and moves onto the beach, erodes and eats away the land, sweeps away fishermen's dwellings. *Kadaladi* is both a challenge to the fortitude and ingenuity of the fishermen as well as a threat to their lives. Once fear of the sea seizes one's heart, one must stop putting out to the sea in times of *kadaladi*. At other times, the sea is quiet, sleepy like a lake (*kulam*).

> "The sea is our property [*chothu*]. Our wealth is in the sea. We make our wealth with the fish from the sea. All our wealth is below, in the sea. Above, on the ground, we have nothing."

The sea is claimed as the property of fishermen. It is there, with all its bounty hidden in its bowels, dispensing its riches according to its whims and fancies.

The sea is not just a common resource; the fishermen claim the sea as their property. It is their property because only they have the knowledge of the sea; it is they who are blessed with the bountifulness of the sea; it is they who wrestle with it to make their fortunes; it is their life that is inexorably tied up with the temperamental changes of the sea. This collective ownership of the sea also precludes any individual exploiting the sea at the expense of others. Various protocols or *paadu* have been developed over the years.

The monsoon sea, turbulent and ferocious, as well as throwing up the chance of a large and lucrative catch, defines what the sea is for the fishermen. The sea is a thing at once "fascinating and tremendous."

> "The sea is a god. No one can stand against the sea. No one can live having opposed the sea. Even if one is a villain, one cannot oppose the sea. There

is no response to the 'sea beating' [*kadal adi*—breaking of waves]. Even a slight beating by the sea can kill. The sea is large; the largest in the world. One can oppose another human being, but not the sea."

"The sea is strong. It has all the power. No one has an answer to its small movement. No one can predict its moods. Hence we pray as we enter the sea and make the sign of the cross on our forehead:
I hear the single peal of the church bell. I come,
the breaking sea [*thumbu kadale*], to meet Jesus, my Heart, my
Solace.
Do not suffer my soul to be lost
Have mercy on me, Jesus."

The prayer has a strong resemblance to prayers said at bed. The single peal is the way the church bell is tolled to announce a death in the village. In death the Christian goes to meet the Savior. The fisherman goes to meet the sea. Going to the sea is like going through death. The sea, which is a god, is also threateningly awesome.

CONCLUSION

The sea is the root metaphor for Mukkuvar social construction. The sea is both benevolent and malevolent. They tend to view every person and institution in a similar way. Everything is an embodiment of both benevolent and malevolent power. This dual perception is ascribed to religious practices, personages, and even to a religious system. The popular religion of the Mukkuvar embraces both aspects of power and constantly strives to maintain contacts with both powers in solving life problems.

The sea is obviously central in the religious life of the Mukkuvar as we have outlined it. We have seen how the Mukkuvar have built up their social identity around the Church. From the *Padroado* system they have inherited a close integration of their social and religious identity around the Church and the parish priest, who is the acknowledged head of the community in every way. They welcomed this identity by becoming Christians willingly. In this manner they set themselves apart from the Muslims and Hindus around them. Their social identity as fisherpeople also sets them apart from other Christians in the area.

But the way in which they live this Christian identity is very particular. Officially and publicly they maintain their Christian identity. But in practice, when they have to face problems either with fishing in the sea or with sickness or social disharmony they feel free to have recourse to other gods and goddesses and other ritual technologies that they consider effective. There is an inclusive spirit that integrates not only their own traditional religion but also the traditional religion of their neighbors, whether Hindu or Muslim. The Christian saints are given a certain primacy. But the power of the other spirits or divinities, either for good or evil, is recognized. Their cosmos is filled with good and evil powers with whom they constantly negotiate through ritual in the pursuit of survival and well-being.

While various rituals like fasting, pilgrimage, and offerings are used, the primacy of place goes to the incantation that can tie or dominate the power of the one who can do evil or cause damage. These incantations are known only to the ritual specialists and are the source of the influence of these people in society.

The religion of the people is then seen as a system of belief and practice that they have constructed. The context is their life and work as fisherpeople. They live in a cosmos inhabited by good and evil powers. They have traditional ways of relating to these forces and of making use of them for their own benefit. They have integrated the Catholic system into their traditional one, giving it a certain primacy. Their awareness of being Catholic, even when it is strong, does not deter them from carrying on their complex religious practice. One can say that in their experience, religion is for life, not vice versa.

THEOLOGICAL QUESTIONS

This selective description of Mukkuvar Catholicism raises a number of interesting theological and missiological questions. What role does religion play in determining the identity of a people? How does official Catholicism relate to popular religiosity? How do people relate to the religions of their neighbors at a popular level? What about the problem of syncretism? How do they tackle the problem of evil? Are the people slaves to superstition and magic? Is popular religion liberative and in what way? How does religion relate to social change? We do not have space to discuss all these questions here. But we shall take up some of them.

RELIGION AND IDENTITY

When we talk about identity with regard to a great religion like Roman Catholicism we tend to imagine that such identity is determined by the creed, code, and cult laid down by the official heads of the Church. But what we see among the Mukkuvar is that they build up their special socioreligious identity. The context is their life as fisherpeople. This situation of life not only distinguishes them from others around them; it also determines what their needs are, needs which religion is supposed to meet. The Mukkuvar are proud of their identity as Christians. Their ancestors asked for baptism. They know that this identity distinguishes them from the inlanders; they are thus free from the caste system under which they would have been oppressed otherwise. It also sets them apart from the Muslims who are also involved in fishing and in sea trade.

They experience and assert this identity in multiple ways. They acknowledge the parish priest as the supreme head of the village, both socially and religiously. They construct their own churches. They are faithful to the sacramental practices

demanded by the Church. They are attached to the saints as powerful interces-
sors. They accept them as superior to other powers, whether good or evil. They
will be ready to die for their faith, if necessary.

But what is important to them is not some abstract universal creed, which they
have no problem in professing, but what the religion, particularly its ritual, has to
do with their day-to-day life. The support of religion for life is gratefully appreciated, even welcomed. But their interest is centered on life, not religion. Though
they would not make such a distinction today on their own, we can say that they
are Mukkuvar first and Roman Catholic Christians afterward. Anything that is
detrimental to their basic identity will probably be resisted, either openly or in a
hidden manner.

CATHOLICISM AND TRADITIONAL RELIGION

Mukkuvar Catholicism also gives us one example of what happens when a
great religion meets a popular or traditional religion: Roman Catholicism claims
the conversion of the total person. We saw above how St. Francis Xavier, after he
baptized the Mukkuvar, asked them to bring all their idols and burn them in
public. This is the ideology. But one does not get rid of a tradition so easily. What
actually happens is that people continue, in practice, to preserve elements from
both religious traditions. If the great religion does not approve the traditional
one, the people might continue to practice it in parallel fashion, unbeknownst to
the officials of the great religion. Sometimes the officials may be aware of the
traditional religious practice and tolerate it, provided the people are also faithful
to the practices of the great religion. In the awareness and practice of the people
what seems to happen is a certain integration of two levels of religion: cosmic
and metacosmic. There is a level of religion that caters to the basic needs of
people living in the world, like food, health, and community. It deals with their
relationship to the cosmos and to others. This is cosmic or traditional religion.
The metacosmic religion deals more with ultimate goals and realities of a transcendent world. It deals more with meanings than needs. Every metacosmic religion is linked to a cosmic one. When a metacosmic religion spreads to different
areas it relates to the different cosmic religions that it encounters, either officially or unofficially.

Among the Mukkuvar, the metacosmic level of religion is identified with the
priest and the official Church. It is accepted and followed. People are even forced
to be faithful to the Sunday Eucharist and other public religious observances.
Some of the elite in the village, like teachers and catechists, are knowledgeable
about the doctrines of the Church. This religion is focused on God and Jesus
Christ. But in practical life people feel that they depend on the sea, which acquires a divine aspect in their eyes with its ability to be bounteous and to be
disappointing, but always powerful. They also depend on various other spirits
who have the power to do harm or good. Some are evil; some can do good but
also evil if they are not propitiated; others do only good. In day-to-day life the

Mukkuvar learn to negotiate with these through various sorts of rituals, some-times seeking the help of ritual specialists. Some of these cosmic religious prac-tices are not openly acknowledged. But, in practice, there is an integration in life of need-based rituals with more official ones that refer to more transcendental realities. The high God is acknowledged as a transcendent point of reference. But in day-to-day life one deals with lower beings—saints and good and evil spir-its—that have a certain power in specific areas and for specific purposes.

AN INCLUSIVE SPIRIT

Such an integration of the cosmic and the metacosmic is not foreign to offi-cial Roman Catholicism, which has built a flourishing popular religious practice around devotion to Mary and to various saints, who are deemed to have special powers in certain areas of life. Roman Catholicism also has an interest in exor-cising the spirit of evil, seen as responsible for various calamities, especially in relation to health and relationships. This is what we have called cosmic religios-ity.

When the Mukkuvar become Christians, they integrate this cosmic dimension of Christianity with the cosmic dimension of their own traditional religion. They see no reason to disbelieve in the spirits with whom they have been more familiar so far. After all, these spirits are related to their own geography and history. While they accept the saints of Christianity as historical persons with special powers, the spirit world is no less localized and contextualized. Christian spirits like St. Michael and other angels as well as devils are also accepted.

This vast array of spiritual beings can coexist because they have different functions and cater to different needs. Utimately they are all subject to the su-preme God. While God is approached through the priest, the others can be ap-proached either directly or through ritual specialists, who are lay—even if these do appreciate and seek official approval when forthcoming.

Once the world of the spirits is opened up in this manner, it is possible to integrate within it the spirits of the religious traditions of the neighbors, Hindu and Muslim. The integration, however, takes place around a basic Christian iden-tity. This is assured in many ways. The Christian saints and spirits can be ap-pealed to openly, while the other spirits are approached only in an unofficial, secretive manner, when it is absolutely necessary and unavoidable. The incanta-tions cited above show that the Christian saints and spirits do have an upper hand over the other spirits.

INTEGRATION OR SYNCRETISM?

Normally, theologians looking at a phenomenon like this would think imme-diately of labeling it syncretistic. Syncretism means an indiscriminate mixing of symbol systems. Are the Mukkuvar syncretistic?

When does mixing become indiscriminate? For someone who is looking at ordinary religious practice from a metacosmic standpoint, even the integration of the cosmic and the metacosmic would look like syncretism. With a certain insistence on the "word" and on reason, the symbolic world is suspect. The people at the cosmic level feel at home in the symbolic world of the spirits. Similarly, the metacosmic stresses the transcendent in religion and somehow looks down on popular, need-based religion. I think that these presumptions of the elite who place themselves at the metacosmic level to look down upon and condemn the cosmic should be challenged.

Others are open to the symbols that come from the Jewish culture of the Bible or from the Greco-Roman culture of the liturgy. But the symbols that have their source in other cultures and religions are seen as unacceptable. In the context of a changed, more open attitude to other religions and cultures, I think that a blanket condemnation of all other symbols is not appropriate.

I think that what we see here is a conflict of criteria. The elite theologians base themselves on intellectual and theological criteria. But the people are interested in concrete results. The nature of a ritual is judged, not by its conformity to an official model, but by its efficacy in bringing about the result hoped for, like health of mind and body, a good catch, or a safe return from the sea.

I think that we must not look at and compare the different symbolic worlds, but rather the experiences and meaning systems that underlie these symbolic worlds. We may then discover that behind the symbols there is a similarity of life situations and experiences which the symbols seek to objectivize and make available for ritual handling. We need not exclude abuses, whether conscious or unconscious. But such abuse has to be proven, not taken for granted.

SOCIAL CHANGE

It was suggested above that some of the younger clergy are more interested in liberating the people from their "superstition," and focusing their attention more on their economic and sociopolitical problems. I think that the liberative zeal may be inadequate, if not misplaced. It is necessary to liberate the people from those who exploit them: middlemen traders, people with mechanical fishing instruments that despoil the sea, people who deprive the poor. But by the side of such injustices the fisherpeople will always face the uncertain bounty of the sea that will always remain a challenge, which can be met only through symbol and ritual. As long as life does not become devoid of mysteries and as long as the problem of evil has not disappeared, what we term "popular" religiosity will continue in some form or other.

Popular religiosity has many liberative elements too. Through it people are able to handle, in symbolic ways, the basic problems that they encounter in life, which even "modern science" cannot handle. In doing so they are much more in touch with nature, with the sea, and with the community. Popular religiosity also offers a space for the laity and for women. This has to be encouraged rather than discouraged. A certain promotion of metacosmic religiosity may highlight the role of the priest and the religious while downgrading the laity. This may be counterproductive for real social transformation. A growing political awareness in a democratic order is making the people question the dominant role of the priest in the community. This could be an opportunity to encourage the participation of the laity in the life and organization of the community. In recent years there has been a movement to organize the people in Basic Christian Communities. These communities could build up people's participation in the Church. Any effort at social change must take seriously the contribution that popular religiosity can make for people's self-affirmation and development, solidly rooted in their living context.

I do not think that popular religiosity by itself is an agent for social change. But it is pointing to the real needs of the people and their ways of handling them. Any social change will have to start with the people and make them agents of their own transformation. Popular religiosity and its cultural roots will have to play an important role in this process.

We can say in conclusion that the need of the hour is not to liberate the people from their popular religiosity and to integrate them in some presumed universal metacosmic order. We must try rather to transform it from within. As they have done in the past, the people again will construct their own new social and religious identity based on their living context. They will do so by integrating different sociocultural and religious elements that are available to them without worrying about their source, provided they are effective for their purpose. The people should have the freedom to do so, because what is important are not the symbols and rituals but the relationships they mediate between the Ultimate and the people as relevant to their life.

7

Hong Kong

Catholicism among the Laity

KIT-MAN LI, KA-HING CHEUNG,
and KUN-SUN CHAN

INTRODUCTION

Wai Bing was a Catholic. She was dissatisfied with what she called the "style" of the Catholic Church, and therefore she was not a whole-hearted participant in church activities. This impression changed when she moved to Tuen Mun and joined the parish in that district. She found that the parish played an active part in fighting for the benefits of grassroots people in the district. This stimulated her to care more about social issues. She became an active member of the Justice and Peace Group. After the June 4 incident of 1989 in Tiananmen Square in Beijing, Wai Bing shifted her focus of concern to Chinese issues. She became a member of the China Concern Group in the parish. Her growth in faith was closely linked with her participation in social issues and social action, both as a Catholic and as a member of a Catholic group.

Wai Bing considers herself to be Chinese. She was not identified with British colonial rule. She agreed that China should resume its sovereignty over Hong Kong. However, she was afraid that the political change of 1997 could endanger individual freedom and that religious freedom could also be hampered. In the end, Wai Bing is positive about the future of Hong Kong. She joins pilgrimage trips to mainland China every year to show her concern about the Chinese Catholic Church and

*get to know more about it. She thinks that sharing the experience in
mainland China helps her face the future.*

*Siu Lun studied in a Catholic secondary school in his youth. He felt
that he believed in God, but he did not want to be baptized into the
Catholic Church so soon. He wanted to experience and understand
more about life before he decided. He married and had a daughter. The
family moved to Tuen Mun when Tuen Mun was at the height of the
district's development. Siu Lun was an ordinary middle-class person.
He got up early, went to the city for work, and came home late at night.
Later on he began to have health problems. He felt extremely insecure
and was very frustrated. He went to the Tuen Mun parish and talked to
the priest about his problems. The priest prayed for him and eventually
his problems were solved. Siu Lun felt that it was God's will to let him
experience this hardship and that it was God's blessing which helped
him go through it. He thanked God. From then on, he attended Sunday
Mass with his family regularly.*

Wai Bing and Siu Lun are among the common people who are Chinese, come
from the middle and lower middle classes, grew up in Hong Kong, enjoyed the
material prosperity resulting from Hong Kong's economic development, and developed a sense of belonging here. They moved to Tuen Mun from the city to
improve their living environment in the late 70s and early 80s. It was around this
period that they joined the Tuen Mun Catholic parish.

The Tuen Mun district, which is located in the northwestern part of Hong
Kong, is largely the product of the Hong Kong Government's New Town Development Plan and Public Housing Plan in the 50s. Between the late 70s and mid
80s it quickly expanded and has now become a large modernized "new town."
About 7% of the entire population live there. The Catholic parish of this district
was established in the 70s. Its membership quickly expanded with that of the new
town itself and constitutes about 1% of the population of the whole district.

Tuen Mun is a new town whose residents are mainly middle- and lower-middle
class families. It is distant from the urban area on the Kowloon side. There are
only two main roads linking the district with these urban centers. Most breadwinners must travel a long distance to their workplaces every morning. Transportation is always a major problem for the residents. Also, due to the government's
lack of detailed planning on resource development, many social problems have
arisen. An insufficient supply of schools for students, lack of recreational facilities, marital problems, and juvenile delinquency all followed as more and more
people moved into the area. Social programs and actions emerged rapidly. These
contributed to the construction of a sense of community among the residents
living in the district. This social background helps us understand why the sense
of community is also quite high among Catholic parishioners in Tuen Mun.

The changeover of the sovereignty of Hong Kong on July 1, 1997, had a big
impact on the Hong Kong community. Some people fled to other places to escape

this political reality. Many others had no choice but to stay behind and face it. Many Tuen Mun residents, mainly because of their material background, are among them. Whether or not the future of Hong Kong is as gloomy as some people may expect, the social awareness of many is greatly raised. This becomes an important factor affecting the political development of Hong Kong and a vital resource for rebuilding the sense of community of the society.

In this case study, we try to understand how lay Catholics in the parish maintain and express their Catholic identity within this social context. We specifically want to understand how Catholic identity is expressed in liturgy, conflict resolution in the family, and participation in social and political affairs. We believe that profound value issues are comparatively more explicit in these areas.

Concerning the methodology of this case study, we have employed several methods of data collection. We have carried out documentary research, field visits, and participant observations to investigate the general background of the parish and the normal operation of parish activities. We have done personal interviews and focus group interviews with different categories of people. These include regular and irregular Sunday Mass attendants, members of some functional groups and Small Faith Communities in the parish, and priests and sisters working in the parish in the past or at present. This research was carried out between December, 1994, and September, 1996. We also conducted a telephone questionnaire survey in September, 1995, and a self-administered questionnaire survey in August, 1996. In the former survey, we successfully contacted 240 respondents from a sample of 462 people who were at the age of 18 or above and were selected randomly from a list of all registered members of the parish. In the latter survey, we sent out 977 copies of a questionnaire to all the Catholics who were at the age of 15 or above at all the Sunday Masses held in the parish in an assigned week. In the end we received 664 valid responses. The following analysis is based on the qualitative and quantitative data we collected through all these methods.

LITURGY

In this section, we shall explore how Catholicism is sustained through liturgy within the parish. Several questions will be asked. First, Hong Kong underwent drastic changes in the past 150 years. It has now developed into a highly modernized society. Does this mean that people have become more pragmatic and rationalistic, so that liturgical practices recede in importance in Catholic lives today? Second, as Hong Kong society becomes more modernized, people become more affluent and educated. They become more knowledgeable about events happening around them. Their expectations toward what they can do and achieve in liturgy greatly increase. Does this affect the attitude of Hong Kong Catholics toward liturgy? Do they expect to know more about these liturgies and have more control over them? Vatican II produced a renewed conception about liturgical practices in the Catholic Church. The council made some positive responses toward the participation of lay Catholics in liturgy. How has the Hong Kong Diocese been affected? Third, Vatican II evaluates the inculturation of Catholic faith into indigenous cultures positively. To what degree has the Hong Kong Catholic Church achieved this goal in the past two decades? Fourth, the Chinese government regained control of Hong Kong on July 1, 1997. This political transition has pushed Hong Kong citizens to pay more attention to and participate more actively in politics. In this context in which the political consciousness of the general citizenry has been greatly aroused, does Catholic liturgy become more sensitive and responsive to politics, or does it remain purely religious and concern itself only with Catholics' private lives?

THE SIGNIFICANCE OF LITURGY FOR ORDINARY LAY CATHOLICS

It is understood by the official Church that Sunday Mass and other Masses held on special occasions during the year are a key element which functions to sustain Catholics' own religious faith. They are also a central element which sustains the internal solidarity of the Catholic community. A Catholic is generally understood to be not only a follower of Christ Jesus but also a member of the Church. A Catholic has an obligation to join a parish and attend Sunday Mass. The Church does not condemn those who rarely attend Mass, but it would consider them as leading imperfect Catholic lives and needing assistance and improvement. This understanding of Catholic identity has so far not been challenged. In practice, however, it often happens that some ordinary lay Catholics do not go to church regularly. Nor do they always register in a new parish when they move from one district to another. Nowadays, it is generally estimated that only about 26% (or one-fourth) of all Catholics who have registered in the parishes of the Hong Kong Diocese attend Sunday Mass regularly (see Ha 1991, 531 for a recent official figure). This rate is only a crude estimation because parish records of church membership are often not updated regularly. There are also no statistical data showing how many Catholics have not registered in any parish.

As far as Tuen Mun parish is concerned, the parish priest, who is a Hong Kong Chinese, is assisted by a pastoral team in looking after the activities within the parish. This pastoral team includes the parish priest, three other priests (one is a Hong Kong Chinese, another is Mexican, and the third is French), and a sister (who is a Hong Kong Chinese). The parish priest estimates that in 1995, the parish had a membership of about 4,000 Catholics and that an average of about 1,000 attended Sunday Mass in the parish every week. That amounts to some 25% of the parish membership. This accords with the statistics of the diocese. However, our telephone survey conducted in Tuen Mun parish in 1995, indicated that 47.7% of the respondents attend Sunday Mass every week and another 23.4% attend at least once a month. Given that the response rate of our sample was only 51.9% and that our survey may overrepresent a bit the actual Sunday Mass attendance rate of lay Catholics in Tuen Mun parish, we think that it is still reasonable to estimate that the actual attendance rate is slightly higher than 25%.

In our survey conducted in 1996, we find that 46% of the respondents agree or strongly agree that Catholics who regularly take part in Sunday Mass, prayer, and Scripture reading can be considered to be fulfilling their Christian duty, compared with 37% who disagree or strongly disagree with this view. This indicates that many lay Catholics perceive that regularly attending Sunday Mass fulfills their duty as Catholics. This does not imply that fulfilling one's duty is the only meaning of attending Sunday Mass. For these Catholics, it may contain some other meaning. What meaning does Sunday Mass have for lay Catholics? In the same survey, we discover that those Catholics who attend Sunday Mass regularly concern themselves mainly with the relationship of this liturgy with their spiritual growth and personal daily practices. Sociologists suggest that liturgy strengthens social solidarity. The official Church also aims for liturgy to have this effect—to strengthen the sense of community among Catholics. However, for these Catholics, this function is of very low priority. We shall discuss one implication of this situation later.

When the respondents are asked what aspects need to be strengthened in their parish, spiritual growth and personal daily practices remain their major areas of concern. Of course, some of them still care about how to incorporate more social, cultural, and political elements into their Sunday Mass, such as "respond to social affairs" and "have greater concern for China."

THE ORGANIZATION OF LITURGY IN THE PARISH

Liturgical practices in Tuen Mun parish involve the routine participation of many lay Catholics. They are performed in a very organized way. In fact, Vatican II has had a great impact on the reform of liturgy in the Hong Kong Diocese. After the promotion of the Council, the diocese made some attempts to indigenize Catholic liturgy. The most popular vernacular language in the society, Cantonese, is increasingly used in Masses. There are also adjustments in the content of Masses to make them more relevant and responsive to the day-to-day concerns of local lay Catholics. Classes and seminar sessions are conducted to teach lay people the structure and meaning of different liturgies. This reform indeed has its cultural significance, and we will come back to this issue later. Due to this reform, ordinary lay Catholics are more informed about liturgy. They are therefore more capable of actively participating in it. Indeed, the Church also invites lay people to participate in the performance of liturgy.

In Tuen Mun parish, the pastoral team come together once a week to discuss and plan their work. In the early 80s, several lay Catholics were invited by the parish priest to form a liturgy group to assist the priests in the preparation and performance of the liturgy. In the late 80s, this group expanded into a liturgy committee composed of representatives from several other newly formed parish groups. They include lectors responsible for preparing the Scripture passages to be read during Mass. The group also allots some time in their meetings for Bible study. A choir, divided into two subgroups, is responsible for leading the congregation in singing hymns. Members of an altar servers' group arrange the schedule for the servers to assist the priests at Mass. Representatives of these groups come together once a month for training in liturgy and to plan their work.

Besides these groups, a women's association is responsible for arranging for ushers—to collect the offerings during Mass. A men's group is responsible for cleaning the church hall and keeping order in the parking lot before and after Mass. So we can see that many lay people are responsible for liturgical roles and participate in the celebration of Mass. We can also see many other lay Catholics contributing their efforts in the preparation of these Masses.

It is worth discussing the Liturgy Committee in some detail here to see the contribution made by the laity of the parish in formal liturgies and the amount of input they can have to inject new elements into the liturgy. The Liturgy Committee is a very functional group in that it is focused on planning and performing liturgy, mainly Sunday Mass. In the past two years, they also spent the first quarter of each monthly meeting for training or reflection about the parts of the Sunday Mass and their religious meaning. The Mexican priest is in charge of this discussion. This knowledge is very important for the Mass servers, who are expected to know exactly what to do and how to enter fully into the spirit of the liturgical service. The remaining part of the meeting is for planning and checking their preparation.

In fact, the Liturgy Committee has planned that the priests presiding at Sunday Masses explain to the congregation the meaning of some parts of the liturgy as they take place. This helps to deepen lay Catholics' understanding of Catholic liturgy, which is so desired by the official Church.

The activities of the Liturgy Committee and its subsidiary groups are monitored by the Mexican priest through his presence as supervisor in the monthly meetings of the committee. This does not necessarily impair the active part played by lay Catholics in liturgy. In fact, in Tuen Mun parish, the priest grants the committee members a large amount of liberty in their functioning. Moreover, though the issues at the discretion of the Liturgy Committee are limited mainly to the songs to be sung, Scripture readings, the materials to be used, and some division of labor among themselves, there is still space for committee members to suggest new elements and make innovations. This can, in effect, make the liturgy become more resonant with the life situations of the lay Catholics in the parish and respond more readily to their needs. At present, the committee members do have this leeway in preparing Masses on some special occasions such as the Masses on some Chinese festivals and the Mass commemorating the June 4 Tiananmen Square incident.

However, the dynamics of power now existing in the parish constitute an obstacle which subtly and effectively makes innovation unlikely. Age and seniority are very important factors in defining the authority of the members of the Liturgy Committee and the legitimacy of their ideas and suggestions. Members of older age are generally more realistic and cautious about new things than younger members. They do not reject all possibilities of innovation, but they are very slow and cautious in experimenting with new things. This situation contributes to the pressure and tensions felt concretely by committee members of younger age. This happens not only in the Liturgy Committee but also in the parish as a whole.

When discrepancies in understanding and expectation arise, conflicts may emerge among committee members. However, these conflicts are normally covered up; it is considered an impediment to the unity of the parish to let them become manifest. In some cases, these conflicts emerge along the matrices of age and seniority. Those who are younger and lower in seniority are in weaker power positions. Their general response is to escape from confrontation by keeping silent or withdrawing from participating in further debates and/or actions.

In fact, some of the younger members of the Liturgy Committee have the general feeling that their opinions are seldom considered seriously. This may be one reason why some of them are frequently absent from committee meetings. Within the Liturgy Committee, most of the younger members feel the same way. New ideas are rarely raised in the committee for discussion and experimentation.

The gap between older and younger parishioners was revealed by the young people in the parish. Most young people interviewed expressed an unwillingness to work with their seniors in the parish, senior meaning not the priests and the nuns but the laypersons who are older and have been active in the parish long before them. They do not want to work on the same project with them, because they feel that the "seniors have more history in the parish. They need to be given a lot of face, and be respected. They have their set ideas which they think are better. They may ask you for opinions and assistance. But in the end, they insist in doing their own thing and reject your ideas." Also, "we like to take a parish project, and carry it out from beginning to end, all by ourselves." Like parents expressing concerns about their children, most adults in the parish we interviewed lament the lack of youth in the parish and the lack of youth participation in parish activities. The problem seems clear: as with problems in the family, the adults have not listened enough to the young people, and the young people have not tried to understand the adults.

This analysis does not imply that very few innovations have been made in Tuen Mun parish. When lay parishioners have some suggestions about parish liturgies, the normal channel is to share them with members of the Liturgy Committee, letting the latter bring them out at their discretion in their regular meetings. Or parishioners can even join the committee themselves. However, given the present state of power dynamics in the parish, we cannot expect the committee to play a more influential role.

Therefore the pastoral team, and the parish priest in particular, are decisive factors for the innovations in liturgy. Tracing the history of the parish, it can be seen that the parish did experiment with something new here and there, however fragmented and unsystematic this was. But in most cases, these innovations were brought about by the parish priests themselves. While some of them were then institutionalized, many simply faded away as priests left the parish and other priests came to pick up the pastoral work.

In general, the priests concentrate the leadership of the parish in their own hands. They especially want to keep control over the performance of liturgy in the parish. They understand that the liturgical services performed in the church are the official worship of the Church. They do not want any distortions to appear in these liturgies. They want to make sure that any experimentation does not violate the principles laid down by the Diocesan Liturgical Commission. Notwithstanding this, the priests themselves sometimes do introduce new elements. This is more true of those priests who have a more progressive attitude toward liturgy. In fact, the priests have a certain degree of liberty and authority as to what deviates from diocesan principles and what does not. So we see that the priests are the center of local liturgy, and movements to introduce innovations into liturgy come from them. Input from lay Catholics remains minimal.

LITURGY AND PUBLIC CONCERNS

In the above analysis, we mentioned that liturgy is a central element of Catholicism. We also pointed out that, in regard to the meaning of liturgy, ordinary lay parishioners concern themselves mainly with the relevance of liturgy for their spiritual lives and personal daily practices. However, it is too hasty to conclude that, for these people, Catholicism is purely a private religion (cf. Casanova 1994, Part 1, for the concept of private and public religion).

Many people living in Tuen Mun are quite dissatisfied with the district's environment and public facilities. They are politically more active than people living in other districts. In the past ten years or so, they have organized social actions to fight for improvements in the public facilities in the district. Also, the members of Tuen Mun parish generally believe that the church should play a role in social policy and politics, and especially in the period before July 1, 1997, when Hong Kong was preparing itself for its reunion with mainland China. Against this social background, we asked the respondents in our 1996 survey which aspect of social ministry they thought should be given more attention in their parish. It is to our surprise that 30% of the respondents suggested that the parish should give more attention to internal church development. In fact, on the issue of social ministry, Tuen Mun parishioners have less interest in social issues and social action than in social services. They have the least interest in politics.

In the same survey, we discover that it is likely that those parishioners who suggested that the parish should give more attention to internal church development also suggested that the parish should strengthen its response to family and individual daily lives through the Sunday Mass. Also, it is likely that those parishioners who suggested that the parish should give more attention to social issues and social actions also suggested that the parish should strengthen its response to social affairs. This indicates that what the parishioners expect from the parish is closely associated with what they expect from liturgy. Our statistics also indicate that those parishioners who expect from the parish and its liturgy a greater emphasis on social affairs are a small minority in the parish.

In Tuen Mun parish, some lay Catholics who are active in social and political action are quite dissatisfied with other parishioners' lack of interest in these things. They expect the parish to do something to strengthen the social awareness and social responsibility of all the parishioners. The parish has indeed acted in this regard. According to our observations, in Sunday Mass, the priests frequently try to bring out this message in their homilies. The prayers of the faithful often mention social and political issues. Tuen Mun is one of the three parishes in the Hong Kong Diocese which hold a Mass service on June 4 to commemorate the 1989 patriotic democratic movement in mainland China.

What more can the parish do? This is a question asked by those who want to promote participation in social and political affairs in the parish. Related to this, in general, the parishioners think that Sunday Mass is chiefly about worshiping God. This and additional spiritual and personal concerns have priority over other concerns. For most parishioners, these concerns are not only central to Catholic liturgy, they are also central to their daily lives. Comparatively speaking, promoting participation in social and political affairs among parishioners is only subsidiary, though this goal is not unimportant.

Some parishioners who are not very conscious of, or do not bother very much about, the social or public characteristics of Catholicism would ask what liturgy such as Sunday Mass has to do with social and political affairs. They would say, "If the Catholic Church should do something in society (and that is certainly the right thing to do), let those interested form organizations, committees or groups to achieve this purpose. When these people come to liturgy, they still must recognize that liturgy is about worshiping God. Do not let anything else interfere with this purpose." However, we can ask whether such a prioritization of spiritual and private matters as distinguished from public matters is problematic. According to our observations, the parishioners in Tuen Mun have generally not yet probed deeply into this issue.

LITURGY AND CULTURAL DIALOGUE

How does Catholicism respond to Hong Kong Chinese culture? In Hong Kong, the Chinese lunar year cycle definitely has an influence on Catholic liturgy. So, besides basic liturgies for Sunday and Easter and Christmas Masses, there are Masses on Lunar New Year's Day, Ching Ming, and Chung Yeung.

The Lunar New Year is a great festival for all Chinese. It symbolizes the beginning of a new lunar year. It brings in new hopes and energies. On Lunar New Year's Day, people wear festive dresses, visit parents and relatives, exchange gifts, and say words of blessing to each other. Catholics attend Lunar New Year's Mass before they visit their relatives and friends. They decorate the church. They dress up festively and come to church to give thanks to God and receive blessings from the priest. The message of the priest's homily usually revolves around the topics of giving thanks to God, reviewing the year's plans, and caring for people who need help.

An interviewee told us that the priest who served as a pastor in Tuen Mun parish in the early 80s was enthusiastic about reviving Chinese culture in the church. Under his leadership, the parishioners erected a monument in the yard of the parish church and put fruit, flowers, and candles before it on Lunar New Year's Day so that every parishioner attending Lunar New Year's Mass could stop there for a few minutes to pay respect to their ancestors and pray for them. However, an Italian priest came and took over his work in the mid-80s. His focus of interest was on something else, and this practice was dropped. Here we see how important the parish priest's role is in maintaining innovative practices in liturgy.

Ching Ming is a festival when Chinese families come together to pay respect to their ancestors. Originally, at the Chung Yeung festival, people followed the custom of climbing up mountains to escape from any bad luck that might come to them that day. Gradually, more and more people also spend this day to go to the graves to pay respect to their ancestors. This is especially true when they do not have time to do this at Ching Ming. So the social cultural meaning of Chung Yeung gradually has merged with that of Ching Ming.

The Catholic Church responds positively to respect for ancestors and holds Masses on both occasions. In Tuen Mun parish, parishioners prepare a board before Masses and put on it the names of those people who passed away and for whom they want to show their respect during Mass. Toward the end of each Mass, the priest places the board by the altar. He says a few words praising the spiritual meaning of commemorating and paying respect to our ancestors. He then lights candles and asks everyone to bow before the board and pray for our ancestors.

Besides this blending of Catholic liturgy with Chinese culture, Tuen Mun parish also tries to make Mother's Day and Father's Day two major themes of the Sunday Mass. On those days, the parish priest invites some mothers and fathers to give witness before the homily on how God cares for them in their family lives.

Besides the blending of Catholic liturgy with Chinese festivals, there are other traces of subtle influence of Chinese culture on Catholic liturgy. We see that Catholic faith is deeply mixed with the practically oriented Chinese mentality of the ordinary lay Catholics in Tuen Mun parish. In our survey conducted in 1996, we found, first, that 56% of the respondents agree or strongly agree with the statement "It matters not what God one worships. What is most important is to be a person of virtue"; 21% of them disagree or strongly disagree, and 19% are neutral. We do not know what "one" means for these respondents. It may mean all other people they may meet, no matter what religious faith they have. It may also mean the respondents themselves. If the latter is the case, it means that more than half of these Catholics emphasize not their loyalty to God, but the practical effect of their religious commitment. If the former is the case, it means that they have a reconciliatory and accommodating attitude toward other people. They care more about their moral quality than about their religious background. This attitude is also expressed by Vatican II. On the whole, both cases have a close affinity with the practically oriented Chinese mentality.

Second, 58% of the respondents agree or strongly agree with the statement "Catholics can take part in the traditional Chinese custom of offering incense/

joss-sticks to ancestors." Only 18% disagree or strongly disagree with it, while 19% are neutral. There exists a significant positive statistical correlation between the responses given by the respondents to this statement and the above one.

Through personal interviews we discover that many lay Catholics in the parish do not care much about traditional popular religious cosmologies. Many of them still offer incense to their ancestors, mainly for two reasons. They agree that they should pay respect to their ancestors, and offering incense is one way of expressing that respect. Furthermore, like other Chinese, these Catholics like harmony and unity and dislike conflict and discrimination. They do not mind following traditions and customs as long as this helps maintain human social relationships and keeps things in harmony, and as long as one can do this nicely without severely contradicting one's own core principles. This whole attitude is in line with the reconciliatory and accommodating attitude expressed by Vatican II as well as the practically oriented character of Chinese mentality.

However, there are areas in which Chinese culture may clash with Catholicism. In the same survey, we asked the respondents whether they employed traditional popular Chinese methods (such as geomancy, casting lots, and palm-reading) to help solve their problems. No respondents said that they did these frequently. But 13% of our respondents said that they sometimes did them; 30% said they rarely did them. Only 55% said that they never did them. This result reveals something which may make members of the official Church feel uncomfortable given that those traditional methods carry cosmologies and value-orientations which have their origins in Buddhism, Taoism, and traditional popular religions. These cosmologies and value-orientations may contradict the Catholic principles.

The parish priest in Tuen Mun told us of his experience when he was invited to lead a funeral liturgy in a village. Before the liturgy, the priest had been in contact with the family of the deceased Catholic about the Church's viewpoint. He had made clear what they could do and what they could not at the funeral, which was specifically Catholic. However, at the scene, the priest discovered that before he came, the family had finished some traditional popular ritual practices. When his part came, they put all the things aside but put them back afterward. So what they promised the priest was only not to do anything unacceptable to the Church within that part of the funeral liturgy which he performed. For the priest, these family members were not enthusiastic followers of Catholicism. They probably became Catholics simply because their parents were Catholics. At least, this kind of cooperation shows their attempt at reaching a minimum understanding with the Church. The Church should not demand too much as long as no apparent contradictions emerge. The only thing he can reasonably do in situations like this is explain to the participants the Church's viewpoint and ask them to respect it.

In fact, similar practices sometimes happen among lay parishioners. Why do some parishioners, after they have become Catholics, still keep their old traditional ritual practices? They are aware that these practices carry cosmologies and value-orientations which may contradict their Catholic faith, and they practice them deceptively. It seems that such people still lack a sense of security after their conversion and that Catholicism does not give them the kind of promises or assurance that they want. But why? Does this reveal that Catholicism cannot meet some of its followers' aspirations and needs, or that these "unfulfilled" aspirations and needs are indeed false ones? In the latter case, the Church still needs to understand better what is deeply embedded in these aspirations and needs and do something in response. It is inadequate simply to stick to a modernist and rationalistic attitude and judge such persons as superstitious and unrealistic.

The same thing may happen in the practice of offering joss-sticks to ancestors. Believing in traditional popular religious cosmologies, some people may fear that their ancestors will starve if no one burns joss-sticks to them. Some people of younger generations may also accept this understanding. However, a young parishioner rejected it in an interview. This young lady therefore faces a problem. She knows very well that offering joss-sticks makes no sense except to show respect to ancestors. But her non-Catholic parents and relatives do not have the same understanding. She rejects this practice, but feels cut off from the tradition and history of her family. She feels confused and uneasy. There are other parishioners who judge in their consciences that there is no problem in keeping this practice as long as they know what it means for them. Here, we see that the issue is left to the individual's own deliberation. But one's conscience is sometimes not entirely clear. Very few parishioners have asked the priest or anyone else for clarification and guidance. The issue remains unclear.

Does this mean that the Catholic Church needs to promote cultural dialogue? So far the Catholic Church relies heavily on the Diocesan Liturgy Commission to do this. Members of the commission are seen as experts in this area, and others just wait for their guidance.

Hong Kong people are generally pragmatic in value-orientation. They lack interest in cultural reflection and dialogue. They are exposed to various cultural influences usually in subtle and unconscious ways, but they lack awareness of and do not reflect on these influences. Now Hong Kong has changed its political status from being a British colony to a special administrative region of China. Culture will certainly be an important issue to be dealt with. Cultural awareness and reflection become more and more important. In this context, if the Catholic Church can raise the cultural awareness of ordinary lay Catholics and facilitate their participation in cultural reflection and dialogue, it will not only benefit the Church itself in its task of inculturation. It will itself become a social witness. The Church will play a pivotal role in promoting cultural reflection and dialogue in the wider society. This is badly needed in the present era of Hong Kong development.

CONFLICT RESOLUTION IN THE FAMILY

Patterns of communication in the family in Hong Kong vary, where the traditional is present alongside the modern. There seems to be a gradual transition from the traditional to the modern. Traditional communication is based on a strong emphasis on responsibility and duty, and authority by seniority. Modern communication is based on a strong emphasis on individual rights and freedom. Both seniors and juniors are individuals in their own right, equal in all respects, particularly after the age of 18.

In Tuen Mun, because of its geographically segregated location from the urban areas, the problem is aggravated. Breadwinners leave for work early in the morning and come home late at night. Children have very little waking time to be with their parents, particularly with their fathers. Traditional family ties are breaking down. For various reasons, child abuse has become a serious problem in Hong Kong, and Tuen Mun tops the list.

CONFLICT RESOLUTION AND CULTURAL VALUES

There is a Chinese saying which goes like this, "In a harmonious family, everything is filled with vitality." Another one says, "Harmony makes for good business and prosperity." Under this perspective, conflicts are seen to be detrimental to business and the well-being of the family, and so need to be avoided or suppressed. There is strong evidence of the existence of this kind of mentality among the parish Sunday Mass attendants in Tuen Mun. In our 1996 survey, when asked what attitude they would adopt in facing conflicts in the family, with each allowed to make no more than three choices, 45% said they agreed that "conflicts are not good. Family members need to accommodate each other. If each person can refrain from saying harsh words, the whole family will be at peace."

However, the very extreme traditional approaches to conflicts did not attract many adherents: only 2% agreed that "the man is the master of the family; he makes all the decisions." On the other hand, about 16% said they agreed that "no matter how old a junior is, no matter how unconvinced he/she is, he/she has to obey the one who is senior." Wai Man is one of them.

Wai Man, aged approximately 25, baptized about four years ago, now works as an accountant. His parents sell fish in a housing estate market. When it comes to making decisions, it is the father or the elder brother who has the say. Wai Man, being the youngest son in the family, has no say at all. Seniority counts. His father is more willing to listen to the elder brother. He said, "Being the father, he has a special dignity, and we have to give him face." According to Wai Man, they generally have peace and harmony in the family.

Under British rule, Hong Kong has been exposed to Western influence for over 150 years. Hong Kong people, including Catholics resident in Tuen Mun, are also exposed to modernization. One component of this is handling conflicts based on principles of equality and rationality. Among parish Sunday Mass attendants, 57% said they would "not evade the issue, but discuss it rationally. Listen to whoever has sound reasoning, giving no regard to age or seniority." This is the most preferred choice. Of those surveyed, 12% adhered to the so-called democratic principle of "rule by majority; the majority opinion is the most authoritative opinion"; while only 1% adhered to the crude capitalist principle of "whoever has more money, has the biggest say."

There is a discrepancy between theory and action, between beliefs and practices. When asked what they would actually do in situations of family conflicts, only 29% said they would "face the issue, and reason things out calmly." The rest said they would "accept and tolerate" (30%), "leave the scene of conflict"(14%), or "blame the other party"(23%).

During an interview, Min Yee recalled with pain and bitterness her experience four years ago when she was a 21-year-old young woman. She was slapped in the face by her mother because the mother did not like to hear her talk back. "My mother was a traditional kind of parent. She felt even if you are thirty or forty years old, you are still her daughter, and she has the right to have control over you, and to beat you, even to death. She was proud to tell her friends afterward that, at my age, she was still able to slap me in the face. But I was already twenty-one. They just don't understand. I am already a grown-up person, and I have a job."

Min Yee did not fight back. "Basically you can't win. My mother doesn't have good health. If we argue too much, she gets very sick, and I am the one to feel the pain. So I keep quiet."

Min Yee goes to work very early in the morning. After work, she goes out with her friends. She will not come home until about midnight. She takes a shower and then goes to bed. That is to keep away from her parents. "Going out with friends every night makes one tired. Sometimes I want to be home and be myself. But what can I do? I don't want to quarrel with my mother, and I don't want to hear her unending quibbling."

A study of the mean ages of the respondents reveals that those who identified more with principles of equality and rationality have a mean age of 36.5, while those who identified with the principle of keeping harmony and avoiding conflicts have an older mean age of 40.7. When asked what they would do in actual practice, those who chose "to tolerate" have an older mean age of 41.5, and those who chose "to face the issue squarely, reason things out calmly" have a younger mean age of 39.3; those who chose to "leave the scene of conflict" have a still younger mean age of 34.7.

We have not been able to compare the results of this study with any other previous study that dealt with a similar topic and population. We do not have evidence about the actual trend. Our guess is that modern thought is gaining ground in the hearts of the young. The trend is toward an increasing incidence of modernity emphasizing principles of equality and rationality.

Our own personal interviews revealed that households having independent-minded young people living with traditional parents who demand obedience and respect from the young are fertile grounds for conflicts. We have cases where the young, when not being allowed "to face the issue squarely" with their parents, chose to avoid their parents completely, leaving early in the morning and returning late at night.

An interesting phenomenon was observed in a group meeting of a Small Faith Community (this is a community made up of six to ten families, or members of families, who gather to pray, read the Bible, share problems, encourage and sometimes counsel each other, comfort one another in times of stress, and sometimes also organize assistance to elderly neighbors by cleaning their homes or doing shopping for them). In this meeting, women aged between 40 and 55 expressed extreme dissatisfaction at being caught in the middle between the old and the young. Being daughters of traditional parents, they have to defer constantly to the authority of their own parents and parents-in-law. Being mothers of the new generation, they have to play the game of modern democracy, listening to the young, and making decisions in accordance with a democratic process. These mothers have a strong feeling that they live in two worlds, and get the worst of both.

CONFLICT RESOLUTION, CULTURAL VALUES AND CATHOLIC IDENTITY

In situations of conflict in the family, does faith come into the picture? If so, in what way? Does Catholic faith help to reinforce traditional cultural patterns of passive acceptance, encourage modern rational behavior, or pose a new model?

When asked what helps them most when they have to confront conflicts in the family, and given not more than three choices, the largest percentage (43%) of respondents said they find prayer most helpful. The mean age of this group of respondents is slightly above the average, at 41.0. But do they pray before, after, or during the conflict? What do they pray for? How do they pray? Do they pray singly or together with those with whom they have the conflict? These questions are not answered. Only a small group of respondents (6%) said they found the Bible helpful in resolving family conflicts. They are at a mean age of 45.0.

During personal interviews, we came across women, members of Small Faith Communities, who during quarrels with their husbands, kept silent, went into their own room, and started to read the Bible and pray. For them, this has three purposes: (1) it helps them stop the quarrel immediately; (2) it helps them calm down; (3) they let God come into the scene and allow themselves to be inspired by their Christian faith. We do not know how common this kind of experience is among those who said they find prayer helpful.

When asked if their faith has any impact at all on how they deal with conflicts in the family, 7% said "rarely," 1% said "not at all," and 6% "don't know." The rest (86%) replied in the affirmative, either "yes often" or "yes sometimes." Among those who answered in the affirmative, 62% said their Catholic faith "reminds them to be forgiving, accepting, and tolerant toward neighbors." This often means submissiveness and forgivingness even before any arguments take place. If we compare this figure with the 45% who identify with the attitude of "harmony and mutual accommodation" where the faith factor is not included, this 62% shows a disproportionate influence of the Catholic faith toward accepting and forgiving, rather than facing conflicts and promoting change under the guiding principle of reason. This may be interpreted as reinforcing traditional authority structures and passive acceptance of the status quo.

Min Yee recalled how in her primary school days, she was beaten by her mother because she got only 85 in mathematics. Then she had to go to confession and confessed the sin of hurting her mother's heart because she didn't do well in mathematics. From the way she told her story, it seemed that the priest hearing her confession did little but reinforce her need to be obedient to legitimate authority.

When faith was not a factor for consideration, 57% of the respondents said they identified with the attitude of "not evading the issue, and rationally discussing the whole issue"; 29% said they would in actual practice "directly face the issue, and reason things out calmly." But when asked the kind of impact faith exerts in family conflicts, only 15% said their Catholic faith reminds them "to face the issue squarely, saying yes for yes, and no for no." This shows that only a minority of Catholics draw inspiration from their faith to face conflicts in life directly and rationally, based on truth and justice. Is this a diminishing or expanding minority? There is no clear evidence to show that this minority represents the younger generation of Catholics. On the contrary, statistics show that this minority has a mean age of 39.3 while the majority portion has a mean age of 38.8. In this regard, the future development of Catholic identity is unclear.

The 20% who said their Catholic faith helps them see their own faults more clearly reveals a Catholic faith that encourages self-criticism. We are not sure whether this is taken as rationally seeing their own faults, and so helps communication, or as being overdemanding on oneself, and so misses the whole point.

In summary, the Catholic identity itself seems to be going through a process of change since Vatican II. It can be variously perceived as: (1) reinforcing the traditional Chinese mentality of passive acceptance and deference to authority (currently the dominant influence); (2) encouraging self-criticism (this is on a smaller scale); (3) reinforcing the modern mentality of facing issues squarely and reasoning things out calmly (this is on an even smaller scale).

It is difficult to tell whether the avoiding of extremes in both traditional and modern approaches is due to the traditional wisdom of staying in the middle or to the influence of the Catholic faith.

THE IMPACT OF POLITICAL TRANSITION

Data collected on this specific topic are extremely limited. The little that has been obtained was through in-depth interviews.

The majority of those interviewed had no plan at all to emigrate in order to seek social and political security after the changeover of the sovereignty of Hong Kong on July 1, 1997. The sister who now is working full-time at Tuen Mun parish said from her pastoral experience in three parishes in the New Territories that this is the parish where fewest Catholics emigrate. In other parishes in city areas, particularly in areas inhabited by the middle and upper middle class, it has been quite well accepted that large numbers of people emigrate, including many Catholics. This sister's comment is that most people in Tuen Mun are from the lower middle class. Only very few of them have enough resources or connections overseas to be able to emigrate.

The one family that we interviewed that decided to emigrate certainly was very concerned with family unity. They decided that either all stay or all go. They do not accept, as many have done already, that the husband remains in Hong Kong to continue his job, and the wife and children reside in the country of adoption. Another family had a unique situation in which both the husband's and wife's brothers and sisters have all emigrated. Their parents were left behind in Hong Kong to be taken care of by the couple. The burden of 1997 and emigration in this case has been laid on the shoulders of those who opt to stay. Some are very rational and pragmatic. One young man, a trained accountant, said he would concentrate on his professional development, paying little attention to controversial issues in politics. One woman said she encouraged her son who had finished his secondary education and was unable to get into university to take any course he could to advance himself in educational institutions, while such courses were still available (cf. Cheung, Ka-Hing, et al. 1995).

As far as the parish is concerned, the major focus of development is either on reaching out to people in the new town of Tuen Mun in an effort to promote evangelization, or on building unity and harmony within the parish community. Little effort has been spent that directly responds to the anxiety of people related to the changeover of July 1, 1997. The only program that may connect the thinking of some Catholics with that of political transition is that of promoting Small Faith Communities. One active woman member of a Small Faith Community commented thus:

"We are apprehensive of the future, particularly in the area of religious freedom. We are not sure if we will be able to attend Sunday Mass after 1997. We have been told by priests that, after 1997, priests may not be around to say Sunday Mass and help the spiritual life of the laity. Laypeople must learn to pray together and read the Bible on their own, and help and encourage each other in the Small Faith Communities in order to sustain their faith."

At the diocesan level, it didn't seem that there was an active coherent response to family issues as 1997 drew near. The Diocesan Priests' Council and Pastoral Council meets regularly about once a month to discuss various Pastoral issues. The family, however, has seldom been on their agenda.

THE GENDER ISSUE

Do women respond differently to faith and family conflicts than men? According to research data, when it comes to family conflict, Tuen Mun Catholic men, more than women, seek assistance from spouses (42.5% versus 28.8%), from priests (12.8% versus 10.9%), and from colleagues at work (7.3% versus 5.6%). On the other hand, more women than men pray when they are in a family conflict situation (46.2% versus 36.1%), seek assistance from brothers and sisters (22.5% versus 11.9%), from nuns (2.2% versus 0.5%), and from social workers and counselors (4.1% versus 1.4%).

Conceptually, women identify more than men with the attitude that conflicts are normal in life (60.3% versus 48.9%) and that the way to face conflicts is not to evade them but to reason things out (57.5% versus 56.0%). On the other hand, men more than women identify with the attitudes that conflicts are not good and should be avoided (47.1% versus 43.3%), that seniority in age gives one more authority (19.6% versus 14.4%), that majority rules (14.2% versus 11.3%), that men decide (2.7% versus 1.9%) and that whoever earns more decides (1.8% versus 1.0%).

When asked what course they took in practice in the face of family conflicts, more men than women said they reason things out (32.3% versus 27.7%) and tolerate (35.5% versus 26.5%). On the other hand, more women than men said they leave the scene of conflict (15.1% versus 11.4%) and blame the other party (26.0% versus 16.8%).

As seen from the above statistics, the gap of incongruence between conceptual identification and actual practice is more pronounced in women than in men. Why is this the case? Is it because, in cultural, economic, and sociopolitical hierarchies, including the family hierarchy, women are often found to occupy much inferior and disadvantaged positions? In an unequal and irrational structure favoring men, do women have to fight and act irrational in order to be heard and defend themselves? Are women so culturally socialized that against their own wishes, they have to act submissive and mild and tolerant in order to be perceived as gentle, kind, and graceful? Or do most women believe that there is a positive value in acceptance, understanding, kindness, and forgiveness, and, above all, in imitating Mary the Mother of God; that this is truly the way to change, but they are frustrated by men who hold power and refuse to change? These are questions that must be further explored.

In the question of faith and family conflict, more women than men claimed to be influenced by their Catholic faith (89.3% versus 79.8%). A larger percentage of women than men have the understanding that faith teaches them to be more tolerant and forgiving (64.2% versus 56.6%), whereas a smaller percentage of women than men said they would face the issue and reason things out (14.3% versus 17.5%).

The actual experience of women in the parish is not entirely negative, however. Women in the parish often assume positions of responsibility, in the Small Faith Communities, the Liturgy Committee, the Hospital Visitation Group, the Concern for China Group, the Justice and Peace Group, and so on. These experiences either provide opportunities for learning and leadership, or for the women concerned to be exposed to a wider social sphere.

Mrs. Lee, 45, born into a family in which women were thought to be a financial loss to the whole family and thus inferior, was thrown into a dustbin by her father but later salvaged by her mother. She was often beaten by her father in childhood. She learned to tackle problems and communicate through force and violence. More than once, she came to the Small Faith Community meetings black-eyed, after having fights with her husband. Through sharing and discussion at the meetings, she learned to be purposefully silent, and tactfully choose right moments for bringing up issues for discussion with her husband, instead of getting into a hot argument or being suppressed into silence. She also learned to express her feelings and communicate with her children in a nonaggressive manner.

These figures pose a serious concern. There seems to be a much bigger contradiction in women than men between their values identification and their faith. Conceptually women are more inclined toward equality and rationality, but in practice they are more prone to acting submissively and irrationally. How can they cope with this contradiction? How do they manage to stay in a church that constantly asks them, against their own wishes, to be more tolerant and forgiving in situations of conflict?

OFFICIAL CHURCH PRESENCE AND CONFLICT RESOLUTION IN THE FAMILY

At the diocesan level, the Church has issued pastorals and spoken in Sunday homilies on the importance of the family and the formation of faith in the family. But there has never been a commission that is exclusively dedicated to the family apostolate.

The Hong Kong Catholic Marriage Advisory Council was established as an independent nonprofit social welfare institution in the mid 1960s by a group of laypeople supported by several Jesuit missionaries. Its precise purpose was to provide marital counseling service to the married, premarriage training, and training on natural family planning to those who wanted to regulate pregnancies. Caritas, the official arm of the local Catholic Church entrusted to provide social services, also has a department of family service and family life education that provides marital counseling and premarriage training. Both the Catholic Marriage Advisory Council and Caritas are being subsidized by the Hong Kong government. Their services are open to the public, irrespective of religion.

There is one Italian missionary, Fr. Giampietro, who over the past three years or so has gone to different parishes encouraging Catholic couples to live out their Christian faith in the family. There is an independent lay organization supported by two local priests and a local sister, set up in 1996 with the specific purpose of strengthening the marital bond. The targets are mainly Catholic.

Over the past ten years or so, the diocese, in response to new needs and new situations, with or without taking 1997 into consideration, has decided to build several new churches, mainly in the New Territories, and set up a number of new institutions. These include the Committee for the On-going Formation of the

Clergy, the Committee for Promoting the Cardinal's Pastoral Exhortation, the Diocesan Commission for Hospital Pastoral Care, the Diocesan Commission for Pastoral Services to Filipino Migrants, the Diocesan Commission for Pastoral Services to the Disabled, the Diocesan Commission for Pastoral Services to Vietnamese, the Diocesan Committee for the Formation of the Laity, the Diocesan Youth Commission, the Hong Kong Catholic Commission for Labour Affairs, the Hong Kong Diocesan Sacred Music Commission, and the Pastoral Office for Overseas Chinese Catholics. But there is no Diocesan Family Commission, or any other institution, that has a pastoral orientation to the needs of Catholic families, helping them to integrate gospel values into their family lives. To our knowledge, there has never been a pastoral letter issued by the Bishop of Hong Kong specifically on the question of family and family ministry.

The promotion of Basic Christian Communities (which are also called Small Faith Communities here) in the diocese is the closest there is to family ministry. But here, the family is not at the center of attention, and not enough energy has been invested into the whole Basic Christian Community movement to make it look like a serious ministry.

To what extent do ordinary lay Catholics find the priests and nuns and the communities of the parish helpful when they are in trouble, and what kind of assistance do they give the family in times of conflict? According to data from our survey in 1996, only a small percentage of our respondents (from 2% to 12%) answered that they found people in the Church, including priests, nuns, Small Faith Communities, and laypeople, helpful when they had family problems. The Church does not seem to be present through its institutional representatives in the family lives of the faithful. The Church is not seen to be accompanying the faithful as they face conflicts in life, particularly in the family. For most ordinary lay Catholics, Church presence in their family life is marginal.

For those Catholics who experience significant Church presence in their family lives, the Church offers, through its institutional representatives, a sympathetic ear to listen to their problems and to give emotional support. There is no evidence that contact with the Church reinforces psychological dependence on clerics.

The Church also offers opportunities for training, for learning to handle conflicts positively. This is particularly the case for members of the Hospital Visitation Group and some Small Faith Communities. Catholics learn, directly and indirectly, to listen, to ask questions more confidently, to feel that they are equal and full members of the family, and to turn conflicts into opportunities for deepening understanding. In a very concrete and positive way, the Church is offering assistance to the laity to confront deteriorating family relationships.

Unfortunately, these positive experiences are very rarely channeled back into the larger community, either through special sharing sessions, sharing/witnessing during Sunday liturgies, or write-ups in the monthly parish newsletter. Very little conscious effort has been made by the parish leadership to integrate the life of the parish with the family life of parishioners. The parish is centrally identified with the Sunday liturgy, and the liturgy is identified with worship. The meaning of worship still has to be clearly defined.

Interviews with priests working in different parishes reveal two basic approaches to family conflicts: counseling and the pastoral approach. In the counseling approach, the priest either takes on the counselor's role himself or refers the case to a professional social worker or marriage counselor. In the pastoral approach, the priest almost always listens, explains the Church's teaching on marriage, and encourages dialogue and reconciliation, particularly in the case of marital conflicts.

What happens when reconciliation is not possible? Different priests respond in different ways. Some priests insist on the principle of nondissolution of marriage, that what God has joined together no one can put asunder. One simply must try to make it work. With faith, nothing is impossible. Some priests advise Catholics to assess the whole situation objectively, take into full consideration the teaching of the Church on marriage, and arrive at a decision according to the dictates of one's conscience. Other priests accept the fact of the dissolution of marriage and try to maintain a pastoral relationship with both parties, hoping that assistance can be offered when needed.

It is quite evident that in the diocese there is no one coherent approach and practice among official Church agents as regards family issues. In the extreme case of divorce, this divergence makes it possible for Catholics to maintain their Catholic identity while adopting different approaches to handling family conflicts.

PARTICIPATION IN SOCIAL AND POLITICAL AFFAIRS

In the preceding part, we see that the Church stresses a balance between witnessing to truth and justice and witnessing to reconciliation and forgiveness. To strike such a balance, the question of civic and national responsibility is a focus of attention of the Church. Back in 1984, soon after the signing of the Sino-British agreement over the future of Hong Kong, the Cardinal issued a pastoral letter asking Hong Kong Catholics to affirm their triple identity as Hong Kong people, Chinese, and Catholic. The pastoral emphasized that Catholic identity did not contradict civic and national identities; indeed, it enhanced them and raised them to a higher level of participation.

The question of justice and prophetic participation was also given attention, particularly in encouraging Catholics to register as voters and to take active part in voting in the 1991 and 1995 direct elections of the Legislative Council. However, the stance taken by the diocese in the issue of the Election Committee set up by the Preparatory Committee to elect the Chief Executive and the Provisional Legislative Assembly of the Hong Kong Special Administrative Zone gave many people the impression that the Church was accommodating to the future political power (cf. Yuen 1997)—though some people may argue that there is evidence that the Church is shifting its position toward a somewhat opposite direction in the present period, when the problem of Hong Kong's political sovereignty is settled and Hong Kong has become a Special Administrative Region of the People's Republic of China. Moreover, although the Church openly supported the democratic political system, witness within the life of the Church to democratic values of equality and participation seems to be lacking. Although much progress has been made in absorbing laypeople into positions of responsibility in diocesan commissions and offices, in essence, it is still a Church run by clerics. In this part, let us see how this situation of the diocese matches the situation of a local parish.

BACKGROUND

In the pastoral letter mentioned above, the Cardinal acknowledged that the Hong Kong Catholic Church needed to enhance its prophetic role so that it would have a more balanced position between performing this role and playing its role as a servant in society. The Cardinal did not elaborate what he meant by the servant and prophetic roles of the Church in that pastoral. It is generally understood in the Church that fulfilling the Church's servant role in society mainly includes providing social services to people needing help—visiting hospital patients, visiting prisoners, and so forth. Fulfilling its prophetic role mainly includes showing concern over social issues at the policy and/or political level. At the policy level, examples of social action include signing petitions urging the government to change a particular social policy on education and public housing. At the political level, examples of social action include signing petitions urging the government to introduce a more representative form of democracy to Hong Kong and urging the Chinese government to release prisoners of conscience.

During the 90s, Hong Kong people have been experiencing enormous societal changes, which include democratization in the political sphere (e.g., the introduction of direct elections in the Legislative Council in 1991), and the return of sovereignty back to mainland China on July 1, 1997. The issue about the servant and prophetic roles of the Church has become a major concern among Catholics. More specifically, at the parish level, how do the lay Catholics in Tuen Mun respond to these political changes? Will Tuen Mun parish become more politically active or will it stay out of politics? Will the lay Catholics become disoriented? Does Catholicism provide the parish spiritual support and help enhance participation in political affairs? What support does the Catholic parish at Tuen Mun provide for the lay Catholics who actively participate in political affairs? Moreover, as the national identity of lay Catholics is undergoing a process of reconstruction because of the change of political sovereignty in 1997, how is Catholicism related to this process?

The Tuen Mun parish has a relatively long history of social action. For example, during the first district board election in 1982, the previous parish priest gave explicit support and assistance to some candidates who stood for election, e.g., putting up posters, delivering propaganda materials, and encouraging parishioners to vote for particular candidates. Certainly, this does not mean that the whole parish would also support these particular candidates. However, influence was exerted on some parishioners, and due to the explicit posture of the parish priest, some parishioners were motivated to be more concerned about politics.

This phenomenon is quite unusual even to date, because the Catholic Church of Hong Kong today does not allow Catholic priests and groups and committees inside the Church to express their personal views concerning a particular political party or candidate in elections. This is to uphold the principle of the separation of Church and State; the Church also seeks to strengthen its prophetic role in society and social participation among ordinary lay Catholics at the same time. In other words, although the lay Catholics are encouraged to participate in social and political affairs, the Catholic Church should not participate in politics directly. Moreover, some priests in the diocese worry that if the Church participates in politics directly, divisions among Catholics may be created along different political lines. This is seen by them as undesirable because it would contradict the unity of the Church.

It may be widely agreed among Catholics that the Church (as a religious community) should not participate in politics directly. However, a problem arises when political discussions are not encouraged within the Church. For example, on the issue of the election of Legislative Councilors in 1991 and 1995, the Church generally avoided giving clear messages concerning particular social and political issues, such as whether all the seats in the Legislative Council should be filled by direct election. It may be argued that this is because the Church is trying to stay out of political disputes. However, this may also give the impression that political disputes among lay Catholics should be minimized. And the way to minimize political disputes is to avoid giving any clear political standpoint in public. This has a negative effect on the Church's attempt at strengthening social participation among ordinary lay Catholics. Should a certain amount of political disputes in public be allowed and tolerated if genuine political discussion is to be promoted inside the Church?

Interestingly, we notice that in Tuen Mun during the elections more parishioners supported the democratic parties which stand on the side of grassroots people and defend the degree of liberty Hong Kong people have been enjoying than the political parties with business background and the pro-Communist Chinese political parties. In the telephone survey conducted in Tuen Mun parish in 1995, 53.7% of the respondents said that they supported the Democratic Party (which was seen by many people as a political party that fights for freedom and democracy in Hong Kong), whereas only 2.6% supported the Democratic Alliance for the Betterment of Hong Kong (which was generally recognized as taking a pro-Communist Chinese political stance). This might be a result of the political culture among Tuen Mun residents, because some members of the Democratic Party were very popular in Tuen Mun. However, this creates a problem for lay Catholic groups in the parish. Because these groups are constrained by the principle of the separation of Church and State, they cannot openly support the Democratic Party as Catholic groups. In effect this constraint hinders the possibility of open discussion among lay Catholics concerning their views about different political parties and candidates, since open discussion does not and cannot lead to any collective action. Voting and other kinds of political participation thus become merely a matter of personal deliberation and decision.

ATTITUDES TOWARD POLITICAL PARTICIPATION

Before discussing further the role of lay Catholic groups in political participation and illustrating in more detail the above constraints felt by lay Catholic groups, let us take a look at the attitudes of lay Catholics. As noted before, one major societal change in Hong Kong was the introduction of direct elections in choosing the members of the Legislative Council in 1991. First, we will look into ordinary lay Catholics' voting behavior as it was shown by the surveys we did in September 1995 and August 1996.

The 1995 survey was conducted just after the September 17 Legislative Council Election. In the survey, it was found that 81.7% of the respondents had registered as valid voters in the election. Furthermore, 71.9% of those validly registered had actually voted in the election. So the voting rate was 58.7% among our respondents, given that this rate is normally a bit overrepresented in interview surveys. This was a high voting rate compared with the 35.8% overall rate in Hong Kong. What was the cause of this high voting rate? Of the valid respondents, 87.6% said that the Christian faith required them to vote in order to fulfill their civic obligation. However, we do not yet have adequate information to judge whether the Hong Kong Diocese was successful in inviting Catholics to participate in voting.

With respect to political party identification, we have just pointed out that 53.7% of the respondents identify with the Democratic Party. Even though there is such a high rate of political identification, the parish cannot support a particular political party or candidate openly due to the principle of the separation of Church and State mentioned above. This creates a difficult situation for some active parishioners, especially if they want to play a more active role in mobilizing others to be concerned about political affairs or collaborate with any political party.

This difficulty can be seen more clearly in our 1996 survey in which 45% of the respondents agree or strongly agree that the Hong Kong Catholic Church cannot support or criticize a political party openly, 27% remain neutral, and only 23% of the respondents disagree or strongly disagree. In other words, only a minority of the respondents agree that the Hong Kong Catholic Church can support or criticize a political party openly. At the same time, however, 69% of the respondents agreed or strongly agreed that the Hong Kong Catholic Church should express its opinion concerning Hong Kong's political development during the transition period around 1997. Moreover, 72% of the respondents agree or strongly agree that the Hong Kong Catholic Church should express its opinion concerning Hong Kong's democracy. For some Hong Kong Chinese, the Democratic Party is a symbol of democracy. Thus, it is not unusual for some people to collaborate with the Democratic Party in order to strive for democracy. Although it may be difficult to conclude whether the lay Catholics in Tuen Mun also see the Democratic Party as a symbol of democracy, they clearly show strong support for the Democratic Party in their personal political orientations. And we also notice that some of them have a strong desire for democracy. Thus those who have a strong urge for democracy but do not agree that the Church (as a religious community) should openly support the Democratic Party have to find an alternative way to express this collective need. Parallel with this, the diocese should find a way to express its positive stance toward democracy without at the same time collaborating with the Democratic Party. However, how this can be done remains unclear in the present political scene.

Another interesting result of our surveys is that 39% of the respondents agree or strongly agree that different lay Catholic groups should be allowed to support or criticize particular political parties, because this is an expression of political pluralism in the Catholic Church. This compares with 25% who disagree or strongly disagree and 26% who stand neutral. In fact, the official Church does not encourage Catholic groups to participate in politics. Some parishes set close restrictions on political participation among Catholic groups. Now it appears that 39% of the respondents in Tuen Mun hold an attitude which seems to contradict the principle set by the official Church that the Hong Kong Catholic Church should not support or criticize particular political parties. It is not clear what the cause for this "inconsistency" is, as there is not enough information for explanation.

The above statistics indicate that a diversity or ambiguity in attitude toward their political participation exists among ordinary lay Catholics. This ambiguity can also be seen in the Justice and Peace Group of the Tuen Mun parish. In name, this group is concerned with fighting for justice and peace in society. This may require a lot of social action. However, in reality, the group does not initiate or participate in many social actions. This may be due to the constraint exerted by the principle of the separation of Church and State. For example, before the Legislative Council Election in September, 1995, the Justice and Peace Group did a lot of work to raise the consciousness of the parishioners so that they would vote on Election Day. In order to encourage the parishioners to participate in voting, a talk was organized to help them understand their responsibility to vote. However, the Justice and Peace Group was obliged not to support any particular political party or candidate standing for election. Furthermore, it was unable to find an alternative way to encourage political discussion in the parish. Thus the group could do nothing beyond consciousness-raising.

The frustration behind this self-restraint on the part of the group members can be seen in the following example. Just before the Legislative Council Election in 1995, some parishioners were asked whether they would vote on Election Day. They said that they would certainly go to vote. However, when asked whom they would vote for, they did not know. Some of them even did not know who the candidates were, or their background and policy positions. This shows clearly that knowing the obligation to vote does not necessarily imply the ability to choose a suitable candidate. In order to arrive at a thoughtful decision, it is better for one to discuss and share opinions with other people. This kind of discussion and sharing seems to be lacking in the parish. One possible cause of this situation is that public space needed for political discussion has not been promoted in the parish. In order to avoid political disputes inside the Church and with the outside, the Church does not allow the clergy and lay Catholic groups to express their views about particular political parties or candidates. This may in effect limit the public space for political discussion inside the Church.

As we have mentioned in the section on liturgy and public concerns above, in the survey conducted in 1996, lay Catholics were asked whether the parish should concentrate on social services, social policy, or political participation, as ways of responding to societal needs during the next five years. This can indicate the degree of importance they place on political participation. The response to this question was quite diverse. Only 4% of our respondents agreed that the parish should concentrate on political participation. One-third of them said that all three forms of social or political participation were the same in importance. Another one-third said that the parish should concentrate on the Church's internal affairs before responding to social or political affairs. This diversification in their responses seems to indicate that the role of the Church in society was still unclear in ordinary lay Catholics' minds. It is not clear whether the Church should set social participation or its own internal affairs as a priority. Furthermore, this result may indicate that for a significant proportion of these Catholics (about 30%), the Church is the center of their religious faith. For them, it is necessary to concentrate on the Church's internal affairs before participating in other social affairs.

HONG KONG IDENTITY, CHINESE IDENTITY

From July 1, 1997, onward, Hong Kong has become a Special Administrative Region under the rule of the Chinese Communist government. For many Hong Kong Chinese, this creates a great deal of anxiety, accentuated for many by their memory of the June 4 incident in Beijing. Many Hong Kong Chinese feel the need to reflect upon their Hong Kong identity and Chinese identity. The Tuen Mun parishioners are no different.

In the telephone survey we did in the parish in September 1995, we discovered that 57.2% of the respondents agreed that they identified themselves as more Hong Kong than Chinese, compared with 25.8% who disagreed. Furthermore, 19.8% agreed that they would give up their Chinese identity if being Chinese involved lowering their living standards, compared with 59.5% of those who disagreed; 47.8% agreed that they would give up their Chinese identity if being Chinese involved giving up their human rights and freedom, compared with 40.9%

of those who disagreed. While both material success and the development of human rights and freedom are cherished by most Hong Kong people, these figures show that a significant percentage of the parishioners are willing to sustain their Chinese identity by giving up some of their material gains, whereas a much lower percentage of them are willing to give up their human rights and freedom for the same purpose.

The identification with China indeed varies according to age and generation. We have interviewed some young parishioners who joined the pilgrimage to Sancian Island and Guangdong Province in the summer of 1995. The trip was organized for the youth of the parish; the parish priest and a sister were among the four organizers of the trip. The organizers hoped the trip would be a good opportunity for these young Catholics to get in touch with China and their national identity. Most of these young Catholics were born in Hong Kong. How do they perceive life in mainland China? How do they perceive their own national identity?

As can be seen from the sharing session after their pilgrimage to China, their feelings toward China are rather inarticulate. When asked by the parish priest what they felt and what their deepest impressions were from the trip, most of them did not say anything. They might have had some scattered memories. They mentioned an old man they met in an old church, their visit to a Catholic village, the physical setting of a hotel where they had stayed, the sister whom they spoke to, and so on. But they could not articulate their feelings associated with these events. In general, the trip did have some impact on these young Catholics. Some of them found out that the social situation and living conditions in mainland China were not as bad as what they had expected. Some said that China and its people had been strangers to them before the trip, but during the trip they came across familiar things and kind human faces. These "surprises" and new discoveries motivated them to know more about China.

Studying the China Concern Group in the present research gives us a better understanding of the (re-)constitution of the Chinese identity in the face of the Chinese takeover of Hong Kong in 1997. This is because the China Concern Group was set up in Tuen Mun parish after the June 4, 1989 incident, which had an enormous impact upon Hong Kong people. It was difficult for Hong Kong people to understand how the Chinese government could crush the democratic movement in such a brutal way. Adding to this the fact that Hong Kong was to be reunited with mainland China in July 1997, many Hong Kong people developed a deep sense of doubt and deep distrust toward the Chinese government. Thus immediately after the June 4 incident, the parishioners in Tuen Mun organized some activities such as prayer meetings and a commemorative Mass, to pray for China.

As recalled by its core members, the aim of the China Concern Group was at first to study the social and political conditions of mainland China. They invited several scholars and organized some courses on the economic and political development of China. However, they soon found out that this aim was too ambitious for them and that they were incapable of doing something meaningful in this area. So they switched their target to understanding the Catholic Church of China and exploring what they can do for it. As the zeal of the parishioners gradually cooled down, the group contracted to a size of about eight regular members. The number of people joining their monthly prayer meetings also dropped significantly. At present, the major activities of the group include (1) organizing pilgrimages to China at least once a year, open to all parishioners (and holding preparatory meetings and report sessions after the trips); (2) making regular contacts with some religious people in China whom they meet in the pilgrimages; (3) giving material support to some seminarians in mainland China; (4) organizing monthly prayer meetings; and (5) organizing the annual June 4 commemorative Mass. They found that doing these things was more appropriate as they were within their abilities. Also, they had more satisfaction in doing them than in what they tried before. They said that their faith in God was stronger after seeing how faithfully Catholics in mainland China practiced their religion under difficult political conditions.

How much influence does this group have on the (re-)constitution of the national identity of the Tuen Mun parishioners? Most members of the group are core, active members of the parish. They have many informal contacts with other parishioners. Some members of the group told us parishioners outside the group sometimes show their concern and support for the group by inquiring about its progress. They sometimes give money and ask them to send it to those religious in the mainland who need material support.

Why are the group members so concerned about the Catholic Church on the mainland? Their answer is simple. They identify with the Catholics in China in a double sense. The Catholics in China are both Catholic and Chinese. This double identification gives the group members a sense of closeness and familiarity with the Catholics in China because they share a common faith and a common national identity. When the group members shared with us their experiences in the pilgrimages, they were enthusiastic. They had much to say about the breakdown of barriers between human beings from radically different social and political settings, the development of new mutual understanding, and deep reflection about their faith.

The group members are indeed very realistic about their achievement. They see that politics is a very sensitive issue in China. Therefore, during their pilgrimages in China, they deliberately avoid this topic or swiftly cover up any political tone when they talk with people there, especially in the presence of Chinese officials. To their surprise, they found that some religious in China were more open and willing to talk about politics than they had expected.

Indeed, the group members developed greater internal solidarity in these trips. In their normal meetings in the parish, they spend most of their time organizing activities and making plans. It is during these trips that they share their religious experiences deeply with each other. All these experiences give the group members the energy to maintain the group's functioning. There is no doubt that they treasure their pilgrimages very much. When asked about their group, they usually talk about these trips.

When asked what made them Chinese, the group members answered without hesitation that they were born Chinese. They treasure the richness of Chinese tradition and culture. Most of them have no doubt that they are Chinese: their skin is yellow and their eyes are dark—though one member considers herself more Hong Kong than Chinese. When we pushed further to ask why they thought they were by nature Chinese, they could not answer. They only reaffirmed their previous answer. They were only persuaded later that they needed to articulate more clearly what they mean by being Chinese. They accepted that they had never reflected on this issue deeply before. As they often said, they like doing concrete things rather than reflecting on their beliefs. Like many other Hong Kong Chinese, they are practical people.

The members of the China Concern Group did have some worries about the loss of religious freedom in Hong Kong after 1997, even though they all know very well that the Chinese government has assured people that they will retain this freedom after Hong Kong is taken over. This worry has been typical in the parish.

Do parish priests have any positive influence on lay Catholics in social participation? It seems that the parish priests' personalities are a decisive factor. For instance, the present parish priest in Tuen Mun is not an authoritarian person. He allows lay Catholics in the parish to have a lot of freedom. He is willing to help the Catholics respond to social or political issues when necessary. For example, after the June 4 incident, the parish priest gave the parishioners support when they wanted to do something for China, such as holding commemorative Masses or prayer meetings. Now the June 4 memorial Mass is held every year. There is also a prayer meeting for China on the first Friday of every month. In his homilies during Mass, the parish priest urges the lay Catholics to be concerned about social or political affairs. However, perhaps due to his personality, he seldom gives concrete directives concerning social services or actions. He would rather ask the lay Catholics to decide for themselves how they should respond to particular social or political issues. He thinks it is not appropriate for him to decide how each person should respond to these issues.

CONCLUSION

Several points can be drawn as a conclusion to the above analysis of our case study. First, if we look at Catholicism in terms of how it is experienced and expressed in the actual life-practice of lay Catholics, we see that identity issues are involved, and Catholic identity interweaves one way or another with culture and sociopolitical conditions. Diversity arises in Catholic liturgy, ordinary lay Catholics' family lives, and their participation in social and political affairs. It also is present in the ways these aspects of Catholicism interact with social and cultural conditions. In our case study, we do not perceive the existence of any "Golden

Rule" which can guide lay Catholics in how to face all the matters arising in different aspects of their daily lives. If it exists at all, this rule is surely highly abstract and thin in content. We cannot avoid going into detail to understand how Catholic identity is maintained in the different contexts of daily life.

Second, as Western society becomes more and more modernized, human social relationships become more and more individualized. Traditional ethical religions may become more and more privatized. Does the same concern apply to Hong Kong? Hong Kong has become highly modernized in the past three to four decades. There are signs that individualism has become more and more a prominent value among younger generations. However, we do not see any apparent sign that Catholicism is becoming more and more privatized. It is instead moving slowly in the opposite direction.

Catholicism has always been more like a private religion among Hong Kong Chinese. By this we mean that private and spiritual matters are the major concern of ordinary Catholics. Social and political matters are comparatively secondary and subsidiary. They are perceived as an extension of Catholic faith, a social expression which enhances it, rather than a core element of it.

To express this point in another way, it has frequently been stressed among Hong Kong Catholics that liturgy is the climax and source of Catholic living. Everything concentrates on the Mass, where all Catholics come together to glorify God and receive God's blessings. Catholics should treasure their religious experiences in the Mass. They should get some training to be sure they know how to participate in the Mass. Comparatively speaking, the encounter with Jesus in daily social practice, including participation in society, is much less frequently mentioned. This mode of thinking can be reflected in some parishioners' view, which we have mentioned above, that the Church should take care of its internal matters before it considers the goal of strengthening its participation in society.

This private image of Catholicism has been changing, though slowly, since the 70s. After Vatican II, and after the Diocesan Convention in 1970-71 in response to it, the Hong Kong Catholic Church identified strengthening its social role and participation in society among lay Catholics as an important target of development. To achieve it, the Diocesan Justice and Peace Commission was established in 1977. The Church has also urged parishes to establish justice and peace groups and encourages lay Catholics to show more concern about social and political issues, and actively participate in elections.

As we have indicated, the Catholic Church is strengthening its role in society, but it also faces some difficulties. A serious difficulty is that, while lay Catholics take greater part in social action and election issues, their participation remains individualized. As a result, they lack deeper reflection and mutual support. To deepen its participation in society, the Church must tolerate internal differences in political viewpoints and allow more space for internal dialogue on social and political matters. The Church needs to reconsider its understanding of the relationship between itself and the State. These become urgent tasks as Hong Kong is now facing major social and political changes.

The third point we would like to raise here concerns inculturation. In the past 150 years or so, Hong Kong has become more and more modernized and has at the same time been exposed to the influence of Western culture. However, we can still find imprints of Chinese culture in different aspects of daily social life. We have mentioned how the Chinese mentality is expressed in Catholic liturgy and the family lives of lay Catholics. In these areas, we perceive a mixture of Catholic, Chinese, and modern secular values which subtly exert their influence. In many cases, very little articulation has been attempted to make the influence of these values more explicit, and deal with the confusions and contradictions among them. It is important to see how the self-identity of Catholicism is maintained when articulation and clarification are attempted in the effort to face such confusions and contradictions.

Hong Kong people have lived with these confusions and contradictions for a long time. In an era where they must return to their mother nation politically, socially, and culturally, and where cultural shock is deep, they can no longer ignore them. Nor can the Catholic Church. The Church has always claimed that it would not leave Hong Kong people behind and it would face the challenge of the unknown future with them. Can it do something which is pivotal in cultural reflection and dialogue? Having lived in an environment which was colonial in political status and pragmatic and materialistic in value-orientation, Hong Kong people have in general had low cultural awareness. Recent social and political changes have pushed them to face this deficiency. Under the teachings of Vatican II, the expression and experience of the Catholic faith should not be confined within the Church, but should be extended to the wider society. The Church certainly needs to do something in response to this deficiency and set an example for society based on its faith, hope, and love in God.

Part Two

THEOLOGICAL REFLECTIONS ON THE STUDIES

1

"I Have Become All Things to All People..."

KOSUKE KOYAMA

The project "Forging Vital Christian Identities: Popular Catholicism in the Emerging Global Church," which led to this book, offers a new vision of ecumenism. Ecumenism begins with our thanksgiving to the Holy Spirit who, in sovereign freedom, creates the people of God. "For most people, however, theological work and episcopal/papal ministry are not the common ways of participating in the religion," and "Popular Catholicism is . . . a different way of relating to reality and of living the Christian gospel," writes Orlando Espín (Espín 1997, 111 and 144). These words of the Latin American theologian make us anxious as well as hopeful. "Forging Vital Christian Identities" is the theme integral to *ecclesia semper reformanda*. It places us on the stormy sea with St. Paul on his missionary journey. "I have become all things to all people, that I might by all means save some" (1 Cor. 9:22), wrote the apostolic forger of Christian identity.

In this popular Catholicism study we are led to examine carefully our accepted scheme that places official Catholicism at the center and popular Catholicism in the outer circle. As this rethinking begins we realize that our subject, the official and popular experiences of Catholicism, touches upon our understanding of the gospel itself. The faith expresses itself in two modes; the priestly official and the popular. The former is concerned to maintain the *right doctrine* and liturgy, while the latter seeks the *immediate cure* from the power of evil that affects physical and spiritual well-being. "Their religion centers on illness, misfortune, and augmenting the fish catch" (Mukkuvar Catholicism). "Popular Catholicism is the complex of beliefs and religious practices (sacramental, devotional, problem solving and social change related) of Catholics who belong to the popular sectors of society" (St. Lucia).

The two modes are organically related, though the relationship involves tension and even conflict. The presence of the two modes is discernible, in varied intensity and forms, from the beginning of the Christian faith, including the religious history of the biblical Israel. No official institutional expression of faith is possible without the input of the wisdom and experience of the people. On the other hand, without the presence of right doctrine, Catholic identity will disappear from popular Catholicism. The popular is democratic. The official is hierarchical. Catholicism has shown the "ability to hold things together in tension with one another," says Avery Dulles (Schreiter 1997, 128). "The Church is slowly adjusting structurally," according to the Dagbon paper.

The official teaching of the Catholic Church is readily available in the documents of Vatican II (1962-1965, with 4 Constitutions, 9 Decrees, and 3 Declarations) and the *Catechism of the Catholic Church* (English edition 1994, with 2,865 concise statements). Papal encyclicals and the teaching office of the Church (magisterium) give authoritative instruction on "matters of faith and morals." Or some may study the Canon Law (revised in 1983 under Pope John Paul II), which records the historical and theological substance of the Catholic faith in one of the most solemn legal languages humankind has ever known. In it, pastoral concern for the "right teaching" and the hierarchical institution of the Catholic Church are intimately related. It is the bishops who maintain and defend the right teaching of salvation.

The official pronouncement of the faith—coherent, consistent, and precise—impresses us. It proceeds from page to page quickly and without obstacle. Popular Catholicism cannot share this comfort because "many of the Dagomba customs go against the Church's teaching and tradition." How can the Catholic faith be expressed in the strong culture of divination? "Ideally Christians should go to their priests instead of their diviners. But they do not." How about polygamy, witchcraft, and "bad death" (Popular Catholicism in Dagbon)? It is far easier to discuss the various forms or merits of inculturation than to deal concretely with persons who visit diviners and not priests. When people go to diviners, do they lose their Catholic identity? The Tanzania paper reports that a certain Helena says: "My problems have diminished and even my income has increased. . . . Because of this I see no reason to leave this group no matter what the bishops say." Has she lost her Catholic identity?

Surely Catholic identity does not disappear easily just as one loses one's pocketbook. Identity is personal and multidimensional. It is a breathing reality, an invisible spiritual connection. First, if a person says, "I am a Catholic," to that extent he or she is Catholic. Such a personal statement must be respected. It implies that he or she feels a spiritual connection with Catholicism expressed in both official and popular manners.

Secondly, it is always possible to have "a unique configuration of indigenous and official beliefs and practices. . . . The Catholic rituals themselves are transformed to suit the Mukkuvar's conception of spirits and demonic deities" (Mukkuvar Catholicism). "As regards well-being, health, and healing, the institutional Church provides many avenues" (St. Lucia). The consideration of Catholic

lic identity must be directed to both official and popular Catholicism. Schreiter writes: "Consistent failure in communication must raise questions about how the message is being sent, and not just about the capacity or sincerity of the receiver" (Schreiter 1997, 130). Catholic rituals transformed to suit the Mukkuvar culture are still Catholic rituals. They have not become something else. Liturgy that is alive is always open to the possibility of transformation.

Thirdly, the interest of the people in a virtuous life, inspired by the Confucian tradition, does not threaten Catholic identity (Hong Kong). Catholic identity has the capacity to embrace the Asian ideal of the virtuous life. Interreligiously, the consideration of this "capacity" has become one of the most challenging theological issues for official Catholicism. In this connection I have noticed that popular Catholicism moves interreligiously with greater ease than does official Catholicism. Is it because it is an "underground tradition" (St. Lucia)?

Fourthly, the spiritual connection to official Catholicism has a sacramental dimension. Participation in the Mass celebrated by the priests confirms Catholic identity. This connection is there throughout the world, even under the strong global influence of the West where religion has largely been reduced to the category of consumption (Schreiter 1997, 88).

THE RELEVANCE OF THE PAULINE AXIOM TO OUR THEME

"I have become all things to all people," says the apostle Paul. This reveals the inner passion of apostolic ecumenism. Catholicism is an organic body made of both official and popular Catholicism. The study of the relationship between the two manifestations teaches us vital lessons on Christian identity in the world as we move into the third millennium of Christianity. The Catholic identity of official Catholicism would be incomplete without the incorporation of popular Catholicism. "I have become all things to all people"—what a striking way to express the apostolic (missionary) identity! It is paradoxical. The apostolic "I" is established by becoming "all things to all people." The ecclesiastical "I" is affirmed in self-denial. The same theological note is heard: "Whenever I am weak, then I am strong" (2 Cor. 12:10).

First, there is bound to be a gap between the official teaching and the down-to-earth human experiences in a given particular historical context. The gap is cultural, educational, and theological. How do the people of a traditional fishing community (in which 42.42% are illiterate) in South India experience the God of Catholicism (Mukkuvar Catholicism)? Mukkuvar's naked human stories come closer to the kind of stories we read in the New Testament gospels than do the documents of Vatican II. The New Testament image of Jesus seems to be on the side of popular Catholicism. Jesus' language, Aramaic, is the common language of Galilean peasants.

Biblical scholars write:

The mortal struggle between Jesus and his opponents has elements not only of Galilean versus Judean, of the poor versus the rich, of the

charismatic versus the institutional, of the eschatological versus the this-
worldly, but also of the laity versus the priests (Brown, Fitzmyer, and
Murphy 1990, 1319).

It would take a great deal of scholarly work to unpack these few lines. But my
perception that there was a serious conflict between Jesus of the powerless people
and the power-people of the official religion may not be far off from the historical truth. This conflict scheme cannot be directly applied to our theme. "The laity
versus the priests" here does not correspond directly to "popular Catholicism
versus the official Catholicism." Historical and theological situations have significantly changed since the day of Jesus. There is no "mortal struggle" between
official Catholicism and popular Catholicism. There is a creative dialogue as
given in the following quotation:

> Christian rituals often remain formal, neither spontaneous nor particu-
> larly Asian. There is a gap between leaders and ordinary believers in the
> Church. . . . The church has created a powerful priestly class with little
> lay participation. . . . We need a new hermeneutic suitable for the Asian
> idiom (Gaudencia and Arévalo 1992, 337).

Since the official church understands the theological value of the Pauline saying, and claims to stand in the tradition of the apostles, the Pauline saying is more
directed to official Catholicism than to popular Catholicism. It is important for
the official theology to maintain the quality of the paradox: "whenever I am weak,
then I am strong." On the other hand, popular Catholicism expresses itself through
"all things." Its identity is "multi-cultural" (Chile). The sacrament of Baptism is
validly there even if it can be "stolen" (St. Lucia)! These "all things" will become
Christian if the apostolic church, by the grace of God, "becomes all things to all
people." Official Catholicism has found, and will find, that some elements of
popular Catholicism can be appropriately incorporated into the official liturgy of
the church.

"A new hermeneutic suitable for local idiom" points to the need for the
contextualization of theology, in the parlance of the World Council of Churches.
The seven case studies provide useful information for the foundational work on
the contextualization of theology. A theological comment on the Tanzanian Marian
Faith Healing Ministry—"Mary takes the place of ancestors in African religiosity. She is a powerful ancestress of the faithful and of Tanzania, her family or clan
before God"—takes us deep into the theology of contextualization. Evidently
one of the most important contributions of this project is calling theologians'
attention to the great reality of popular Catholicism. Theologians of the Eastern
Orthodox and Protestant traditions can learn from this study a great deal about
"the theology of Christian identity," which is what contextualization tries to
achieve.

Secondly, the drift of this discussion does not diminish the importance of the official church's concern for right doctrine. Catholics number 981 million, 16.9% of the world population of 5,800 million (*Encyclopaedia Britannica 1997, Book of the Year*). These global Catholics are touched, influenced, and instructed by official Catholic teaching in untold ways. Without the leadership of the official church how can this vast multitude forge and maintain the Catholic identity in today's world? Feed my 981 million sheep—it is a task of cosmic proportion! It requires great skill of communication and organization. To be human is to be institutional. Sexuality, kinship, and family are institutions. Community, from village to such complex nations as the United States, cannot function without institutional organization. Religion, too, is institutional, even for the solitary recluse and the Quakers. The most anti-institutional voice is not free from its own institutional life. Catholicism represents a great historic hierarchical institution. The question is not about the validity of the institution itself, but what kind of institution it is. The question is not whether there is or should be institutional authority, but what kind of institutional authority it is. Institutionalism is different from institution. Authoritarianism is different from authority. Christian theology rejects institutionalism and authoritarianism. In the Pauline axiom we do not detect institutionalism and authoritarianism.

In this context I wish to introduce a paragraph from Biblical scholars:

> Since we are ill-informed about popular Jewish-Aramaic religious practices and vocabulary in early 1st cent. AD Galilee, it is wiser to speak of what is "strikingly characteristic" of Jesus (e.g. "Abba," "Amen, I say to you"). Similarly, in dealing with the deeds of Jesus, it is better to speak of the "sort of things Jesus did" rather than to claim that a particular narrative describes exactly what Jesus did at one particular time (Brown et al. 1990, 1318).

How seriously should we take this advice? Institution yearns to have complete knowledge. To have complete knowledge means a possession of full security and authority. This advice indicates the possibility of honest elasticity. The spirituality represented in the "sort of things Jesus did" will make us more open and understanding about practices of popular Catholicism. It frees us from both legalism and literalism in neither of which is to be found the element of the paradox of the apostle Paul.

Thirdly, pluralism rejects legalism and literalism. The present project has illuminated our understanding of pluralism. Pluralism has been discussed from the hidden (and treacherous) perspectives of paternalism, colonialism, and imperialism. It cannot genuinely function if understood within these frameworks. Pluralism is neither the third position after exclusivism and inclusivism, nor the hybrid between them. Theologically speaking, pluralism is a witness to the generosity of God. The apostolic generosity—"I have become all things to all people"—points to the possibility of theological pluralism. Are there many truths or one truth perceived in many ways? Theological pluralism, which is basically pastoral, is relatively free from such metaphysical questions. It can respond to either possibility pastorally. Popular Catholicism, being in physical proximity to the broken reality of the world, perceives truth differently from the official Catholicism that can maintain a certain physical distance from such worldly reality. It is helpful to discern the presence of the generous God in the confusing religious experience of popular Catholicism. In order to discuss pluralism sensibly one must be well informed of human brokenness.

The normative is an institutional concept which is subjected to a system of institutional authority. That which is normative may change. I accept the view that "the historical and the relative are identical" (Troeltsch 1901, 85). For example, the normative idea *of extra ecclesiam nulla salus* has gone through significant changes through the centuries (Dupuis 1997, 84-109). The historical fact that it was the 16th-century Jesuit, Francis Xavier, who brought the gospel to Japan for the first time points to the ambiguity of relativity in history. Why did not the gospel come to Japan in an earlier century? History is replete with such temporal relativity. The official Catholic doctrine of the Bodily Assumption of Mary was pronounced in 1950. That doctrine endorses the view of Troeltsch.

For Christians, the Christian scriptures are normative. This is a confessional truth. I find popular Catholicism functioning actively without much "Bible study." Acquaintance with the scriptures requires literacy and an economic investment of time. I find the verb "listen" in the following solemn statement significant in view of the vast Catholic population who practice popular Catholicism. Illiterate peoples can listen to bishops who speak in the people's language:

> The sacred synod consequently teaches that the bishops have by divine institution taken the place of the apostles as pastors of the Church, in such ways that whoever listens to them is listening to Christ and whoever despises them despises Christ and him who sent Christ (cf. Lk. 10:16) (*De Ecclesia*, #20, p. 100).

The above quotation is, however, not referring to the alleviation of the difficulty relating to illiterate Catholics. It is addressing the heart of the hierarchical structure of the church. Even in the moment of being "out of step with the official teaching" popular Catholicism understands this authority structure emotionally and communally. It accepts it in practice. It is here, in this emotional connection, that Catholic identity is "officially" established among the people. "Masses are offered for all kinds of intentions" (St. Lucia). In the time of affliction, often "the person seeks out a Catholic priest to request a Mass to be celebrated in the home of the person and attended by family, friends, and neighbors" (Peru).

Finally, there is obviously a difference between the language of the *Catechism of the Catholic Church* and the language with which the Aymara people talk about "health and illness and the process of building and roofing a house" (Peru). This does not diminish the importance of the *Catechism*. What I want to say is something that is hidden here. Some traditional Christian symbols are losing their relevance for the needs of today's peoples. It is possible that the symbols so dear to official Catholicism, and the attendant explanations of them, may not be so meaningful to popular Catholicism. What are they? Can we name them? Humanity yearns to have a new image or experience of the Christian faith. What kind of "form of Christ" *(morphe,* Gal. 4:19) will appear when the language of the *Catechism* and the language of the Aymara people are united?

2

A Feminist Perspective
on Enigmas and Ambiguities
in Religious Interpretation

IVONE GEBARA

INTRODUCTION

When we speak of religion, we speak of a tapestry of which we can see only the external design, the interwoven threads, and the material bulk that impresses our senses. But the interwoven threads conceal many hidden stories; their roots are fed by a variety of elements that are not clearly visible either to the outside observer or to the adherent who lives them out. Religious experience is usually an obscure tapestry, especially when we make the effort to understand it. This "obscure" character gives it an apparent opacity that suggests it cannot be analyzed in the same way other human activities can. More than in the case of any other kind of experience, we find ourselves faced with the deep mystery of the human person: his or her desires, fears, and hopes.

What are we to say, then, of the great variety of peoples' and cultures' religious experience? What are we to say of the diverse ways in which the various Christian traditions have moved into different parts of the world? What are we to say of Catholic styles of action as they have been interwoven with the various forms of power and resistance? What should be our criteria in examining them, and what do we want them to tell us? With what tools should we analyze their integrity and their faithfulness to Tradition? In today's world, are we not finding our analytical tools to be somehow fragile?

These and other questions show how complex is the task of understanding the phenomenon of religion, and especially popular religion as it relates to the official character of our doctrines.

My intention in these pages is not to critique the excellent articles and research the authors have done. I must say I've learned a great deal from the various situations they describe and the reflections that accompany them. They all bear witness to the serious work of many people who have spared no effort in giving the best of themselves in this excellent collective task. My only concern is to dialogue respectfully, to raise a few questions, and to share some of my own viewpoints regarding the "sacred" ground that our feet walk together.

I'm sure many of my remarks are already to some degree implicit in some of the reflections I have received. Nonetheless, I feel the need to set them forth in general terms so that they will not be overlooked in subsequent studies.

My observations arise from my own situation. I am a woman and a Latin American philosopher and theologian; and I have been influenced by feminism, ecological concerns, and Liberation Theology. I live in a poor neighborhood in northeastern Brazil, and I travel often to different parts of my own country and the rest of the world giving talks and doing consultations. My experience is at the same time global and regional, and it is marked by both the richness and the limitations of this twofold presence. Often what I perceive in my everyday relationships challenges my more intellectual reflections; in particular, it challenges the expectations I have regarding the behavior of the people with whom I live and work. Often I wish that all I learned in books and universities, as well as my own "ruminations" on the world—which have come from my own experience and ideas as well as those of groups I interact with—could also be present in the world of the poor. This is not the case, however. Living in the world of the poor as just another neighbor is a constant invitation to avoid construing everyday life according to my own taste. Everyday life relativizes our understanding of it, constantly inviting us to reexamine our analyses.

Meanwhile, I continue to analyze the world around me; but I often do so from the outside, and with aims that differ from those of the various actors I observe. This is my work and my mission, although I am aware of its limitations.

It is on the basis of this personal situation, then, that I will make a number of comments on the texts. My comments have arisen as I've read the material and as it evoked questions I was already asking myself.

FIRST OBSERVATION

To be consistent with what I said in my introduction, I'd like to begin by once again relativizing the role that intellectuals, whether men or women, play in analyzing religious phenomena—and most especially as it is expressed in popular settings. I fully agree that our observations and analyses are important and valuable, but the reality lived out by the great multiplicity of human groups always goes beyond what people tell us or what we are able to observe on our own. What I'm saying is that there are always realities that are not accessible to our observers' eyes and ears. The "world we observe," especially if we are involved in it, always surprises and surpasses us. And besides this, the simple fact of picking this group rather than that one already shows a selectiveness that, while it is undoubtedly necessary, is partial and fraught with limitations.

Along the same lines it is necessary to recall that observers already have power: the power of knowledge and that of possessing analytical tools. Furthermore, they make their observations, do their interpretations, and publish their results with precise objectives in mind, even if those objectives happen to be the improvement of the life situation of those observed. This means that every analysis, and in fact every research project, is filtered through a kind of "strainer" or "sieve."

Anyone who carries out a study does so from a position of power over those studied. The researcher is not in a position of direct control over people's lives, but he or she does represent the power of analysis, and research often supplies data to power holders. A research project always has some objective, even if it does not have an immediate and direct influence on the lives of those studied.

In this sense I would call to mind that above and beyond his or her social or ideological position, the researcher's sex as well as his or her gender position and analysis will have an influence on the way the study is focused and also on its outcome. It is very common for male researchers and analysts, even when they have respect and concern for all people, to fail to deal directly with the issues that affect women's lives. In concrete terms, this means that "women's" variables are not always present within the purview of their observation and analysis.

In the specific case of the research projects done for this study, women's participation was very limited. Furthermore, the issue of feminism in its various cultural manifestations seems to have been overlooked by the researchers. Surely some of them would argue they found nothing significant to report in this area, and in some cases that might even be true. In others, however, there is undoubtedly a "gap" in the researcher's or analyst's training. The style of perceiving human relationships reveals that he or she has yet to deal with the reality of power relations between the sexes, which express themselves at all levels on which human life is shared. A patent example of this is the absence of any mention of feminism or a gender perspective in the introductions to some of the case studies.

"Today a new epoch for Christianity is dawning in which the many perspectives of the world's culture are coming to play a part in forming a new 'World Church.' Living 'Christ's way' has been interpreted on a monocultural model as one language and culture, one view of the world, but this is now changing rapidly" ("Ghana: Popular Catholicism in Dagbon").

Can we not add that analyses, teachings, and Christian language have also been "monosexual," and that changes have been slow and half-stifled?

"We are faced not just with a new economy but also with a new culture that is being born out of the transition to a postindustrial society" ("Chile: Identity and Diversity in Urban Popular Catholicism").

Once again, there is no mention of the new feminist culture emerging on all continents, the importance of which is underlined even by some postmodern thinkers. This omission unquestionably affects the overall results.

Once again, then, I see the study's results as partial—not only because data and analysis are always partial, but also because the analysts were not sensitive enough to gender issues, to the social construction of gender, or to the reality of gender-based power relationships. They probably assumed that these constructions are part of the overall culture, without understanding the complexities which that culture both reveals and hides in the specific case of hierarchical relationships between men and women. Their failure to perceive differences in the ways religious doctrines and beliefs affect men and women seems to me an illustration of the problem I'm raising. During the current stage in the history of all peoples, the gender issue is of fundamental importance. "Gender," in this context, does not necessarily refer to feminism: it refers to socially constructed, sexually based power relationships in all cultures.

While the domination suffered by women in the various groups surveyed is very clear, even with respect to Marian devotion and cases of witchcraft, there seems to be little interest in analyzing this phenomenon or, most especially, in looking at women's understanding of their own lives. Their situation of oppression and the cases in which they have achieved some degree of autonomy always seem to have been revealed through analyses done by "others"—in general, by male interpreters.

SECOND OBSERVATION

A second observation has to do with a form of philosophical idealism that is found in the Roman Catholic Church's official doctrine, and which many of us researchers adopt almost without realizing it. By an idealistic vision I mean the particular Platonic or Aristotelian (in other words, Greek) frame of reference we find in Christian, and especially Catholic, theology. This frame of reference upholds the existence of eternal, atemporal truths and sets them over against the historical truths present in the variety of world cultures. Christian theological construction, even of the more liberating sort, is framed within this idealistic tradition; and it often bases the hope that inspires us upon such constructions.

I'm not saying that the Greek idealist vision is good or bad; neither am I denying that in the past it helped theologians develop an understanding of Christianity that was helpful in building up the life of many communities. Rather, I am looking at its current historical repercussions and addressing its conscious or unconscious role in legitimizing sexist, racist, and classist hierarchical patterns. It is in this precise sense that I refer to idealist theological constructions.

From this perspective, one often has the impression that the Gospel is regarded as a supracultural reality, a kind of "truth" that stands above and beyond all cultures. And the most interesting thing of all is that this "supracultural" truth is not only presented as the Christian contribution to all of humanity; it is disseminated from within the centers of power.

It is precisely because this message is regarded as "supracultural" that one can speak of "inculturation," even if we broaden its meaning, analyze it, or criticize it. The term "inculturation" stands within the framework of an idealistic-dualistic worldview that has marked not only theological writing but also the daily living out of the Christian faith. It is as if the "essence" of Christianity, to use a classical philosophical term, were grounded in predefined truths, predetermined hopes, and paths that have already been marked off. To some degree, this dual structure appears to have been adopted in different cultures because of difficulty in responding to certain immediate and pressing problems.

The hierarchical magisterium is the guarantor that this path will be respected and followed. Its authority is also legitimated by the same idealistic principles.

The term inculturation, which has come into use since the 1970s, has tended to be applied by central Catholicism to peripheral Catholicisms. Despite the existence of positive and fruitful intercultural dialogue, all the talk about grasping "seeds of the Word" in the various cultures really cloaks a form of superiority of some over others. This might be the reason why Fr. Nkwera rejects the term inculturation. "What I do, that is making people be aware of the demons' existence and their influence on humanity and teaching people how to combat the demons is not an example of inculturation," he says. "This is teaching them true faith in God, not culture" ("Tanzania: Marian Faith Healing Ministry").

Above and beyond philosophical considerations and value judgments regarding his work, Fr. Nkwera defends himself against the imposition of "inculturating" discourse. In this perspective, popular Catholicism seems to reject certain forms of control; rather, it affirms the autonomy of popular religious expression.

Meanwhile, following the same line of reasoning, both "official" and popular Catholicism appear to uphold the existence of atemporal and acultural truths. Historically, this has led to behaviors that have impeded the recognition of contextualized discernment, differentiated needs, and a multiplicity of religious expressions.

In a certain sense, to speak of a revealed truth that is above and beyond all cultures might conceal the competition and "turf wars" that are so characteristic of human behavior. "Supracultural" revealed truth could authorize intervention in other cultures: after all, this is not just another ideology or cultural value; it is "something" that has come directly from God. To continue to affirm, even indirectly, that what is essential to Christianity is its "supracultural" grounding is to go on insisting on its superiority vis-à-vis the variety of religious expressions born of the great multiplicity of human cultures.

In this sense, albeit within a more open and ecumenical stance, we still continue to reproduce the traditional, idealistic, hierarchical model.

THIRD OBSERVATION

My third observation regards the poverty of the study's research and analysis with regard to the influence of the natural environment on respondents' religious questions and answers. The South American, Caribbean, Asiatic, and African populations all retain the deep bonding with nature that is integral to their culture. This does not seem to have been given sufficient consideration in all the research projects, although it was mentioned as an element in the lives of the Mukkuvar fishers and in the Pilcuyo Aymaras' relationship with the earth.

If this study's objective is to foster the growth of missionary action in the various churches, I think that in this time of serious destruction of our ecosystems, special attention to the topic could contribute to the broadening of our own understanding of Christianity.

Are we not challenged to broaden our understandings of salvation, which remain extremely anthropocentric and continue to be marked by a kind of virility cult, and to open ourselves to a wider perspective that could include ecosystems as well? I remember, for example, the importance of the Pachamama for several Spanish-speaking groups in the Americas, especially the Aymaras. The topic, which is of such great significance for these peoples, nevertheless seems to be obscured not only by official Catholicism, but to some degree also by a more open and critical Catholicism.

The belief that the natural world is worthy of worship and reverence has been regarded as something that is characteristic of primitive peoples, whom we should treat with respect and sympathy. But even today their beliefs are not taken as a real challenge to our churches' official doctrines. On the contrary: our official beliefs are regarded as more "evolved" and reasonable, and are considered to be a challenge to those of indigenous or native peoples. Reciprocity seems to be a word that has no real historical content, or else it is understood one-sidedly.

References to the mystery of physical nature, with its visible or its unseen power, appear a few times in the text; but in the light of the kinds of groups that were surveyed I think its importance should have been underlined more strongly.

There is often an implicit suggestion that "gods" with human faces can be more helpful in the people's salvific processes. There is a distrust of impersonal forces or of customs and practices that elude the traditional Catholicism that is still regarded as official.

The problem here is not only religious but political, since it involves forms of domination and power. It is also ideological, because it involves ideas that have turned into certitudes and are often accepted dogmatically, whether subtly or otherwise.

FOURTH OBSERVATION

My fourth observation touches on an issue I think is fundamental to all religions: the reality of evil and of people's vulnerability to it. This problem also needs to be approached from a gender perspective; but up until now it has not been well enough appreciated by the various Christian communities. This shortcoming is very common in the research projects carried out for this study.

Evangelization and inculturation seem always to be on the side of the good, a good that is invariably "salvific," positive, and equally valid for men and women.

Evil, for its part, is always done by men and women; but from a cultural perspective women seem to have a greater vulnerability to evil. This becomes quite clear in the discussion of witchcraft cases (Ghana); and even devotions to the Blessed Virgin (Tanzania), where the number of women practicing these devotions is greater than that of men.

The analyses fail to point out that Catholicism has often upheld this understanding of women as vulnerable to evil, and has done little to denounce the evil to which millions and millions of women were and still are victims. Catholicism has functioned as a consolation, but also as a means of controlling behavior and of encouraging self-regulation on the part of individuals and groups.

At the same time it is important to recognize that Christianity has opened up spaces that have often allowed women to escape the kind of domestic prison in which patriarchal structures have attempted to confine and constrain them. Churches and temples were the places to which many women turned in seeking to ease their pain. The churches were also places where they learned to band together and fight for their social and civil rights. In some cases the churches have even supported feminist struggles, but they have never been a forum for criticizing the hierarchical structures found in religious institutions.

As we know, Christianity has simultaneously extolled and oppressed women. The most common ideology was one that enjoined them to be submissive as homemakers and obedient to the orders of fathers, husbands, and brothers, while at the same time exalting motherhood or consecrated virginity. It is common enough to hear well-intentioned male discourse underlining the blessed character of woman as giver of life. But that character, or characteristic, can often be used as a shield or a buffer in power conflicts between men and women. In fact, both men and women are givers and receivers of life. For historical and cultural reasons, women have taken on a greater role in domestic, nurturing, and cleanup tasks, but this does not mean they are the only givers of life. Insisting on this could conceal difficulties in recognizing not only the mechanisms that have oppressed women, but their liberation processes as well; it could also uphold an idealization of the feminine image as connected especially with motherhood.

FIFTH OBSERVATION

Despite the great diversity of human experiences, and especially of religious experiences, it is important to mention points of convergence within that diversity. These points of convergence reveal a common grounding, a kind of anthropological "constant" that is present in the great variety of human cultures.

Examples would be fear in the face of pain, suffering, violence, and death; the creation of myths that explain good and evil; and appeals to mysterious powers, especially in times of danger. All of these point to a grounding in some shared experience. This is how I understand the similarity among religious motifs from one culture to another. In my view, this similarity should be reworked in missionary practice, responding to the challenges posed by the variety of cultures we encounter.

Depending on the challenges posed by different historical situations, and on the experiences of encounter or of conquest lived out by the various peoples, the components of differing religious traditions may be assimilated or they may enter into conflict with one another; in some cases they may even undergo a loss of meaning. To point out this rather simple and direct pattern of mutual influence among religions would be one way of reaffirming the value and integrity of every religious approach to the world. Once again, the term "inculturation" needs to be reexamined in the light of a multiplicity of religious perspectives.

From a feminist point of view, the insistence on the term inculturation also appears to assign special importance to an ideal of conduct and behavior that was originally established by the male tradition, but which seeks to become normative for all human groups regardless of their sex or their cultural traditions. While our tradition has always spoken of equality, there has likewise been a continual tendency to regard women as "inferior" humans. It is more than enough to examine Christianity's teachings and the history of its treatment of women. In the last analysis, what is it exactly that is to be inculturated? Is it love, justice, and the spirit of Jesus? Whose is the task of inculturation, and what is it that is to be inculturated? Where do we get the "eternal" or "genuine" contents that are to be inculturated? Are they neutral? Are they exempt from human conflict, from the conflict that characterizes all our relationships, or specifically from gender conflicts?

I understand and am sensitive to the importance of the term inculturation in some African countries. I realize how reflection on inculturation has led to the creation of a more autonomous Catholicism that is more respectful of African cultural traditions. I am aware of the degree to which, in the name of inculturation, African communities have been able to "marry" their traditions to the white Catholic traditions brought by the colonizers. But these realities do not invalidate the reflection I am proposing here. Rather, they open the possibility of broader and more critical reflection in the light of both the present and the future.

SIXTH OBSERVATION

This final observation has to do with certain social roles women play in popular religion, both as active and as passive subjects. I want to emphasize these issues in order to underline the importance of contributions based on women's experience.

Whether women play an active or a passive role in religious life is related to their sociocultural standing. While it is not always explicitly acknowledged, the submission of women is apparent in the texts of all the studies presented here. This is evident in the research done in Pilcuyo, Peru: complementarity and reciprocity between men and women are not achieved in practice, despite the fact that they are held up as an ideal in some Aymara cultural expressions. The subordination of women to men, manifested in a higher rate of illiteracy and in the virtual absence of political activity among Aymara women, shows that the ideal of equality is far from being realized. In a different context, the same subordination appears in Hong Kong, especially in the limitations placed on parish liturgical organization. The subordination of the laity to the clergy becomes clear, but the subordination of women to men is equally evident. The kind of domestic work women do at home is simply continued in the church context.

I was struck by the fact that in Hong Kong, Bible reading and the practice of prayer often encourage women to keep quiet and avoid conflict with their husbands.

Once again we can see that religious practices can legitimate either situations of oppression and slavery or the achievement of freedom and autonomy. It all depends on individuals' levels of consciousness and the specific courses of action that are open to them.

Rather than go on farther, I will once again call to mind the importance of using gender analysis to understand situations of injustice that are based on neither race nor social class. Gender relationships emerge as a setting in which subtle injustices very often arise, and religion often plays a role in legitimating these injustices.

CONCLUSION

I would like to conclude this quick reflection by underlining the importance of dealing with traditional pastoral and theological issues in the light of new frames of reference. Among these, I think feminist and ecological struggles should be regarded as fundamental for any analysis. They should also be basic reference points in the renewal of our theologies, our pastoral practice, and the exercise of power in the churches. These are the new and challenging paths in our search for "life in abundance" and for communion among all living beings.

3

Popular Catholicism in the Emerging Global Church

Convergence and Synthesis

LAMIN SANNEH

It seems increasingly to be the case that Catholic popular identity is being formed and forged by people rubbing shoulders with one another in a church that is increasingly non-Western in membership and in the wider society that is increasingly diverse. For example, according to the study done in Ghana, this process is being worked out in terms of mutual interpenetration with Muslims and traditional religionists. It has created a lively context for expressions of Catholic popular piety, with ethnicity, language, regional differences, and the forces of modernization all playing a role. Into this picture the state has sometimes stepped to deal with issues at the flashpoints of intercommunal suspicion and enmity.

In the Tanzania study led by Dr. Christopher Comoro, popular Catholic identity is being forged in the dynamic setting of a strong charismatic movement, the *wanamaombi* movement, led by Fr. Felician Nkwera, whose authority is connected to a vision he is claimed to have had of the Blessed Virgin. The *wanamaombi* movement displays all the great themes that have identified traditional African religious life and practice, although the special circumstance of the movement occurring inside the Catholic Church transforms what would have been a local ethnic cult into a contested facet of the global church. The perennial themes of visions, prophecy, prayer, and healing are compressed into a charismatic Catholic spirituality defined by Marian piety and by overtures to an otherwise unresponsive church.

In the Hong Kong study a small minority of Chinese Catholics are poised on a critical threshold as they brace themselves for the consequences of absorption into mainland China, and what that would mean for their faith and identity. Representing a mobile, Western-educated community, Hong Kong Catholics have resolved to maintain their triple identity as Chinese, Catholic, and Western, and resolved eventually to participate fully in public life in Communist China. One issue the Hong Kong Christians confront immediately is how they will be perceived by the rest of mainland Chinese Catholics; how much, for example, a shared Catholic identity transcends or does not transcend the experience of Western assimilation and a common ethnic identity. Will Hong Kong Catholics value their success as Western entrepreneurs more than their Christian or ethnic ties with mainland Chinese Catholics? The fast-developing political situation has concentrated the minds of Hong Kong Catholics because of the perceived threat to their identity, status, and position following the lapse of Western control over Hong Kong. In the past, Hong Kong as a British Crown colony offered these Catholics direct and immediate access to the West, while after 1997 they have to proceed on the basis of their being fully a part of a Communist-led China. While it may be said that such uncertainty has not disheartened Catholics or destabilized structures in the church, it has nevertheless inserted a certain ennui into discussions about the future role of Chinese Catholics.

The situation among the Mukkuvar Catholics in South India as reported by Fr. Francis Jayapathy offers a contrast in the sense of no imminent loss of identity, status, or position, yet a similarity in terms of a minority Catholic community living in the midst of Hindus, Muslims, and others and destined to remain a minority, whatever the level of contact or conflict with the wider society. However, the fact that these Indian Catholics are the heirs to the ethos bequeathed by the state-and-church arrangement fashioned by the Portuguese in India under the *Padroado,* and the fact that religious and cultural pluralism has struck deep roots in the society, together imply, among other things, that local Catholics are free of the minority complex more typical of suppressed and persecuted minority groups elsewhere. This freedom, with discernment to match, expresses itself in commitment to fairness and impartiality in their dealings with the official church so called, and with government officials. It expresses itself in the pride local Catholics take in the church being a central focus of community life and social engagement.

The Mukkuvar fisherfolk use their Catholicism as a shield against incorporation into caste stigmatization and as a protection against caste oppression. They take pride in their historical roots in the sixteenth-century missions of Xavier and his companions, even though the history of Catholic expansion there was connected with military suppression, colonial subjugation, and local political intrigues. However, Mukkuvar Catholicism has evolved into a unique blend of local church and state interests, with the priest, for example, becoming a president of the village committee and a spiritual functionary at the same time. The priest represented the church, and the church had direct access to the king of Travancore and to government officials. The villagers had an interest in both church and state, and so played an active role in the church to promote their interests on the state level.

Visits to shrines and other pilgrimage centers mark the religious life of Mukkuvar Catholics. Such popular religious practices help to soften the line between "orthodox" Catholics and the village faithful. Individual stories of such village Catholics are redolent with accounts of divination, saintly mediation, libation and offerings, exorcism, healing, and evil spirits. It is appropriate that the Catholic Mukkuvar fisherfolk should consider the sea as a metaphor of life and faith, imposing but sustaining, invincible yet not unyielding, distant and approachable at the same time. So is God.

Fr. Patrick Anthony reports of the vigorous interface between Catholicism and popular religious practices of the majority Catholic population of St. Lucia who descended from blacks transported there from Africa and elsewhere. At one stage of its history, St. Lucia changed hands some thirteen times between the British and the French, resulting in a mixed heritage for the island people. Catholics continue to mix Catholicism with popular religious customs, customs that have been traced to their origin in Yoruba country. Thus have funeral, benevolent, and spirit societies exerted a powerful influence on Catholic piety, producing an accommodation in which language, culture, and religion are blended in a lively creolization that has penetrated all ranks of society.

Sr. María José Caram describes Aymara rituals in Peru that have survived concerted attempts at suppression and external explanation, and in so doing have preserved the distinctive voice of the people. Such rituals are also connected with the people's stories whose retrieval, then, becomes an important part of the process of religious and cultural revitalization and of self-affirmation. Aymara society and the people's identity still bear the marks of the impact made on them by incidents of political violence, land fights, communal tension and discord, and the advent in the 1920s of aggressive proselytization by American Seventh-Day Adventists. The challenge the Aymara face is similar to that faced by Catholic communities in many Third World places, namely, the need to establish against external and internal pressures a vital and articulate connection between their cultural identity and Catholic piety.

Dr. Cristián Parker G. of Chile reflected on the implications for Chilean Catholics of the transition recently made from military rule to democratic civilian rule, a transition that has been marked by increasing modernization, the coming of the media culture, and rampant consumerism. Consequently, old cleavages have been reawakened and new ones created, such as those between modernity and tradition, urban and rural, popular culture and elite privilege. The great imbalance between urban concentration, say, in Santiago, with 33% of the total national population, and rural districts indicates a disproportionate concentration of the country's resources in the urban sector. The social dislocation that is the inevitable consequence of such cleavages has produced or exacerbated the problem of youth delinquency, drug abuse, and urban malaise. Thus a majority Catholic country is being fragmented by secularism and being riven by an economic system that thrives on competitive individualism.

MARGINALITY AND TRANSFORMATION

It is necessary to make explicit what at present is implicit in several of the studies, and that is the compelling connection between the slavery of an earlier era and the poverty and injustice of today's world. For example, the St. Lucia case study makes reference to the population descended from African slaves, while Mukkuvar Catholics recall the days of Portuguese colonialism. Whatever the historical origins of these populations, the terrible misery to which the poor are subjected reduces them to the status of slaves. As was the case with slavery, the poor of today are denied their basic human dignity and civil rights. The popular idea that the creation of wealth will bring about a gradual amelioration of the plight of the poor shifts the attention from the oppressed to the oppressors, from the victims to the beneficiaries. It brings to mind Hegel's contention that the "problem" of slavery was that the more perfect the slave the more *enslaved* the master became, an explanation that subordinates the reality of slavery to speculation about the slave master's mind. In that logic the slave masters are left with slavery as their ultimate alibi, to be blamed for their moral lapse but not for their being enriched by it. Accordingly, the parable of the Good Samaritan would be better adjusted to read: "A man was attacked, dragged, put in chains and sold. Two philosophers came upon him but passed by on the other side, with one saying to the other, 'We must go and find the person who would buy such a poor slave. He needs enlightening.'"

This top-down view of the world ill serves the cause of the poor and the afflicted, and what is needed is for the whole superstructure of abstract justification to undergo a radical shakedown, for the whole mental attitude to undergo a shift in moral consciousness and open the way for the emergence of a new ethic based on a bottom-up view of the world. About two centuries ago it took such a moral revolution to upset the pillars of the old slave establishment and to allow ex-slaves and ex-captives to take command of their own destiny. As Cardinal Lavigerie of the White Fathers put it in the 1860s, people came to be committed "to wage against [slave traders] a relentless and unceasing warfare." Lavigerie emphasized in his missionary method that a church would emerge in Africa only through Africans themselves, with missionaries in the meantime constrained to adopt African manners and customs in language, dress, food, and lodging. "To succeed in the transformation of Africa . . . the first requirement is to train Africans chosen by us in conditions which from the material point of view leave them truly Africans," he wrote. Thus former victims would rise to become masters of their own lives.

No less a heroic struggle is indicated for our age with regard to the poor and oppressed whose faith in the face of overwhelming odds remains astonishing, if not always recognized. What happened with the breaking down of the continuity of the old world structural tradition, with the collapse of the intellectual scaffolding for slavery and the slave trade, requires repeating with the dominant structures of power and wealth. Under the spell of the earlier collapse, confidence in the advantages of political genealogy, and the tradition-tempered etiquette of fealty and deference to which such confidence felt entitled, was shaken. The warrior ethos of the lord-man relationship that distinguished the earlier epochs was no longer adequate to the awakened expectations of a culture of personal freedom, social activism, and religious empowerment. Human motivation ceased to be a function of political pedigree, lineage distinction, gender status, civic pride, national glory, and military grandeur and became instead an issue of the striving for human freedom, equality, justice, and social involvement. On and off the cotton and sugar plantations, for example, slaves and former slaves were led in their religious meetings by spirit-filled witnesses, often with women and children cast in prominent roles. The experience spilled over into the larger society where self-help projects strengthened it.

Accordingly, it is not enough to speak of this kind of change simply as human progress, since, as the Annales school of historians contended, progress can just mean what is latest in the round of struggle for power and influence, or what the successful public relations machine of the dominant class of a particular age puts out for popular consumption, as C. S. Lewis observed of the writers of the Renaissance. Progress in that sense is in fact another name for a conservative social order. *Plus ça change, plus c'est la même chose.* Rather, we should speak of this progress as a shift in values and orientation that called people away from a defense of the top-dog perks of privilege, breeding, rank, and order, to a search for equality, freedom, and justice—in effect, to a commitment to the ethics of good news for the poor, release for captives, and liberty for the oppressed. It is what Walzer (1965, 128) called "a substitute establishment, 'in which things were compassed, which legally were never conceived.' " We may, therefore, call it progress provided we allow for the fact that it was streaked with the spirit of the outcast and the downtrodden as well as by the sweetness and light of the enlightened among the favored classes, and provided also we reject the indifference to the conditions of suffering and injustice of the underdog, and the disregard of the values of other cultures, that the progress tradition in the West has tended to foster. In any case, with the epochal shift of antislavery went a corresponding challenge to reshape and adapt the old and once-valuable tools of structural analysis and reconstruction and place them at the service of the community of ex-slaves, ex-captives, and their counterparts today among the dispossessed and forgotten of economic and political structures.

CONCLUSION

To return, then, to the issues of vital Christian identities, all the particular cases presented suggest that at the close of the twentieth century, the Catholic mind is being formed by a religiously and culturally pluralist world, by the secular political and economic pressures of the new international order, by the factors that correspond to the search for national and communal identity and the building of a better life for people. One may, therefore, speak of rank-and-file Catholics entering the church and attempting with uneven gifts of mind and heart to indwell the Christian story by bringing with them their own personal stories, stories that are still emerging but always vital. They wish to tell those stories in the life-affirming setting that God's story in the Bible provides, especially the story of Jesus and his Blessed Mother. One finds, consequently, that although Third World Catholics have joined their stories to the story of God in Scripture and tradition, and commendably done so in many cases with courage and imagination, they would wisely leave the end of the larger story of the journey in faith in God's hand. The inclination of the so-called official church to demand a final reckoning by opposing all forms of popular religiosity and imposing standard rubrics conflicts with the narrative character of faith, always dynamic, often lacking in foresight but in turn abundantly armed with hindsight and grasping after what has grasped it. Catholic identity in this milieu is a multifaceted phenomenon, intentionally Catholic in diversity and radically local in expression and self-understanding.

What has been said of the irruption of world Christianity may with modification equally plausibly be said of popular Catholicism in the non-Western world. Popular Catholicism is a genuinely multicultural phenomenon, thriving profusely in the idioms of the peoples' languages and cultures, marked by a lively cross-cultural and interreligious sensibility, unburdened by the heavy artillery of doctors and councils, and undaunted by material poverty. In situation after situation, we find fresh energy and intelligence being devoted to the production of new hymns, music, artistic and liturgical materials, to the creation of fresh categories for doing theology, to the retrieval of threatened or neglected cultural resources, to the application of faith to public agenda issues, and to the promotion of solidarity, sharing, and partnership.

Such activity, lamentably sluggish or timorous in some threshold areas, exhilarating and galvanizing in others, has, in all its variegated forms, signaled a crucial shift from Christianity's Euro-American dominance, from its missionary and colonial burden and controversy, to matters pertinent to local potential and possibility.

We sense in all of this the dawn of a new dispensation, a fresh, if at times uneven, point of departure for the Apostolic heritage, a galvanizing hope born of proven confidence that we can move beyond Day One of the missionary landing to enter new spheres, carried there by the momentum of the "inculturation" of the Gospel. All things considered, this movement in World Christianity represents a landslide change in the old order, an axial shift of mass and direction.

POSTSCRIPT

I was struck by the theme of evil which persists in one form or another in several of the studies. It has prompted the following reflection as a postlude.

Grappling with evil, with what political correctness allows us with felicitous ease to call poverty, has been the matrix of popular religiosity. Official religious spokesmen and spokeswomen, perhaps, are focused on the efficacy of grand theological categories which are the *metier* of religious scholars who expound the subject in terms of ideas of God. Popular religiosity, instead, is preoccupied with evil to an extraordinary degree, preoccupied, that is, with evil's concrete manifestation in the lives of ordinary people, in their homes, their work and lack of work, all around them in poor drainage, unlit dwellings, refuse dumps, the smoke and fumes of dilapidated neighborhoods, evil as the normative power that drives capitalist greed. Real life lived in terms of the power and ubiquitousness of evil does not beg questions, does not split hairs. For the poor, the hungry, the suppressed, the ill-clad and neglected, the game of analysis gives way to life-and-death issues: $2 + 2 =$ a concrete sum of four, or better, five loaves of bread. Grappling with evil has marked the lives of the vast majority of humanity: it has sobered people, centered them concretely, connected them vitally to each other in solidarity, filled them with a passion for truth and justice. Knowing evil in so many of its manifestations, what else can such people fear except our indifference?

4

Toward a New Ecumenism

Churches of the People

MICHAEL AMALADOSS, S. J.

Popular Catholicism is very much alive. It is even flourishing. This is the message of the stories that we have heard from seven different places in the world. Caught between the secularizing forces of rationalist and materialist modernity, promoted in the name of scientific progress, and the domination of the official/ elite Church, with its insistence on orthodoxy and conformity, the people have held on to their religious ritual and social practices, which satisfy their needs in life and work. They experience in them the roots of their own identity as a people. They show that religion is for the people, and not vice versa. When they are not able to celebrate them openly, they find many subtle ways to live them. They are clamoring for understanding and dialogue. They also challenge the influence of modernity on the official/elite perspectives and practices.

SEVEN DIFFERENT STORIES

The seven stories that we have heard show that people live this experience in different ways in different contexts.

For the community of Tuen Mun in Hong Kong, their Christian life is centered on the Sunday liturgy and the experience of the parish. They seek in their Christian faith a support for their moral life, both as individuals and as family groups. While the efforts of the official Church to adapt the liturgy to the Chinese cultural context is still hesitant and limited to some gestures like venerating the ancestors and celebrating the festivals of the Chinese temporal cycle, the people continue to find their traditional religious practices helpful, especially in crisis situations like death and bereavement. As Catholics they have no direct, certainly no concerted, impact on sociopolitical life.

The Mukkuvar of the southwestern coast of India find in Christianity a social bond that unites them as a community and sets them apart from the surrounding populations, hierarchically organized in a caste order. Their life revolves round the Church, with the priest having also a social and political role in the village. Their religiosity centers on the sea and their daily encounter with it as fisherpeople. They have adapted their Christianity to their own life and social needs. Their cosmos is full of spiritual beings, good and evil. Their rituals provide them the means to harness the power of these spirits for their own ends. Mary and some popular saints like St. Anthony are adopted into this cosmic network. Ritual specialists cater to their various needs: with regard to fishing, health, and social relationships. They have constructed their identity around Christian praxis, distinguishing themselves even from other groups in the Church. The introduction of modern technology in the form of mechanized boats and of education may diversify the social roles of people in the community. But the Christian identity of the community remains strong.

In Tanzania, the Wanamaombi have built up a community around prayer, particularly through the intercession of Mary. In a context of increasing poverty and marginalization, prayer caters to the needs of the poor—physical, psychic, and spiritual—and often takes the form of exorcism. The community is strengthened by mutual help in need and solidarity. They stand for traditional values and do not hesitate to take concrete options in politics in favor of "good" Christian politicians, though their own intervention is limited to prayer. They remain attached to the Church and the Eucharist. Even if the present authorities in the Church have virtually excommunicated them, they affirm their belongingness, claiming to be loyal to a more universal tradition, which, however, they have "domesticated" to suit their own needs. Their cosmovision does not, as a matter of fact, contradict the traditional vision of the Roman Catholic Church.

For the small groups of Dagomba Christians in Dagbon, northern Ghana, Christian life itself is an adventure. They live an ambiguous existence among a people who have interiorized a tradition of domination and who have recently combined it with Islam. They are admired because they know how to pray, they love and help their neighbors even if they are not Christian, their women are freer and more respected, and, finally, they seem to have access to European (missionary) education, health facilities, and resources. But still they are a marginalized minority in a largely Muslim milieu. The Church itself is far from becoming African. So the people have recourse to traditional rituals to meet the needs of individual and social life. Belief in witchcraft is still strong and widely prevalent, whatever its implications for the rights of the people, especially women, accused of being witches. Divination is so popular that even some priests tend to take on the role of diviners.

Someone who has only a superficial contact will think that the people of St. Lucia in the Caribbean are like Catholics everywhere. The rites of passage like Baptism, First Communion, and Marriage are not only religious but also intensely lived social celebrations. Pious practices like novena Masses abound. But a closer look shows a different picture: the possibility of Baptisms being stolen and wombs being tied; the activities of the sorcerers (obeahman) and of the healers (gadè); people in touch with the spirit world. While efforts have been made to adapt the liturgical celebrations to the local culture, perhaps the cosmovision of the people and their deeper spiritual needs are yet to be taken seriously.

The Aymara of the altiplano of the Peruvian Andes are a deeply religious people. Their relationship to God as an ever present reality is almost mystical, affecting their whole life and manifesting itself in their various religious practices. Their belongingness to a particular religious tradition like the Catholic or the Adventist Church seems secondary. Their main concern is "walking and being well in life." Making offerings to Pachamama (Mother Earth) or lighting candles to the saints are related to the generation, restoration and promotion of life. Diviners and healers (yatiris and qolliris) have an indispensable social function. Rituals spell out a set of mutual obligations that relate them to their protector spirits. Rituals surround their quest for health and their affirmation of their identity, expressed in the construction of their own houses. All these rituals are not seen as contrary to their identity as Catholics. They are loyal to the institutional and sacramental structures of the Church. The Catholics, as opposed to the Adventists, feel even freer to practice their traditional rituals. The Aymara have succeeded in constructing their religious identity on the basis of their religiosity by integrating the saints and sacraments of Roman Catholicism.

The urban Catholic community of San Joaquín in Chile has withstood the inroads of globalizing modernity. Popular Catholicism here takes various forms. Some remain loyal to the popular devotions of the Church. Others are more faithful to traditional practices that relate in ritual and symbol to a world of spirits. Still others are more secularized but attached to self-help practices that go under the name "new age." However, people live together in a religiously pluralistic world. Though people have taken readily to the market culture of a globalizing economy, they have not abandoned their religious sense. Their belongingness to the Catholic tradition as manifested in their participation in its official rituals like the Mass and in their devotion to the saints has not interfered with their traditional or new age cosmovision, whose rituals meet very different needs of life. Many people will take a sick person both to the medical doctor and to a traditional healer, because they feel that modern medicine has no cure for the "evil eye." Modern individualism has not eroded the social relationships characteristic of families and other primary groups. People are also socially aware and their popular religiosity may favor hidden structures of resistance to social injustice by providing alternate sources of meaning and empowerment. In short, the Chilean experience questions the supposition that modernity is necessarily secularizing.

AN AFFIRMATION OF IDENTITY

What is common to all these seven stories is the affirmation of their identity as Catholic by the peoples themselves, though the reasons for doing so may be different. Most of them like the Mukkuvar, the Aymara, the St. Lucians, the Chileans, and the Tanzanians have inherited a tradition that they see no reason to question. The Mukkuvar are proud of it. The Aymara affirm it in the face of alternatives like Adventism. The Chileans defend it in the face of modernity. The Tanzanians cling to it even in the face of rejection. The St. Lucians cannot imagine an alternative. The Dagomba in Ghana choose it in spite of the odds against it. The Chinese in Hong Kong are looking forward to defending it, under greater Chinese hegemony. A certain religious pluralism seems to be a factor everywhere, except perhaps in St. Lucia. While this pluralism is accepted in places like Chile and Peru, the Christian identity seems a largely private matter for the Chinese. For the Mukkuvar, Dagomba, and Tanzanians, their Christian identity is something that needs to be defended against other religious believers who seem to be hostile. Nowhere is the Catholic identity seriously contested or doubted, either by themselves or by others. Even in Tanzania, where the Wanamaombi are virtually excommunicated, it seems more a question of power and authority than of identity.

The tension with the official Church seems extreme in Tanzania. In other places people combine their traditional rituals with official practices in their own way. Their popular cosmovision seems to merge well with the traditional Roman Catholic vision. But such similarity does not always eliminate tension, because some representatives of the official Church have interiorized a modern/elite cosmovision which looks on popular religious practices as "primitive." The official Church is on the whole tolerant. This tolerance has a negative character, however. That is to say, the official Church pretends not to notice what the people are actually doing, provided they take part in the official rituals. This gives rise to parallel religious practices. But the tolerance of the official Church goes hand in hand with an unwillingness or hesitation to adapt or contextualize its own rituals in the various cultural and human situations. Irrespective of official policy and, perhaps because of its immobility, it is the people who construct their own identity by integrating rituals around their life-needs. Except in the case of Hong Kong, the identity they claim and assert is not merely religious, but globally social.

We can fully understand this attitude of the people only if we analyze a little more deeply how the people live their popular religiosity. Let us therefore look at various dimensions of popular Catholicism in a phenomenological way without attempting to evaluate them at the moment. With the previous seven stories as our background, I can dispense with offering concrete examples to illustrate these dimensions.

THE DESIRE FOR A GOOD LIFE

When we look at popular Catholicism what strikes us most is the people's quest for a good life. They are not interested so much in salvation in the other world after death. They want life before death. Their prayers and rituals therefore are focused on material abundance and human and social well-being. People pray for a good harvest, a good catch of fish, a good job for their children. They are not concerned in the abstract about development. Their search is for tangible benefits that improve their quality of life here and now. They do not understand delayed benefits as a reward for sacrifices in the present.

A good life also involves a healthy life. Many of the rituals of popular religiosity are for healing. Sickness is understood in a broad way to include both physical and psychological illnesses. People seek healing not only from fever but also from depression, whatever may be the cause of that depression. A breakdown in family and/or social relationships is also lived as a sickness, an emotional burden that might cause depression and unhappiness. Lack of strength to perform one's tasks can also be seen as an illness. Death, of course, is the greatest loss. So one tries one's best to ward it off and to take every possible preventive step. Health for the people is not absence of physical illness, but a sense of holistic well-being at physical, personal, and social levels.

WARDING OFF EVIL

Evil is whatever is detrimental to health and a good life. Sickness of all kinds, lack of success in work, absence of rain, a bad harvest, a poor catch of fish, tensions in the family or among the kin in the village, accidents, and sudden death—these are some examples of evil that can afflict a person. People do not accept the experience of evil without a cause and the cause must be personal. So whenever there is an experience of evil or limitation that is considered abnormal—prolonged or repeated illness, an accident or sudden death of a young person, unforeseen or undeserved misfortune—it is attributed to the evil eye, witchcraft, sorcery, or possession. These involve some personal agency. It may be others acting independently or through special ritual agents, or spirits of the dead or other suprahuman spirits good and evil. It is not that people are not aware of natural causes for sickness. They have their herbal medicines. But because of their integral approach to life they refuse to see sickness as merely physical. Human and suprahuman agency require appropriate remedies. Through the mediation of ritual they try to activate the spirit world to act in their favor. Sometimes evil, if foreseen, can be prevented through an appropriate action. At other times propitiation may be needed. Protection or healing is also promoted through various intercessory rituals like vows and pilgrimages.

THE WORLD OF THE SPIRITS AND ANCESTORS

It is in struggling with the problem of evil in their lives that people become acutely sensitive to the world of the spirits. Their awareness of the divine pervades their whole life as well as the world in which they live. They may often believe in a high creator, God. But God's presence is mediated to them through a world of spirits. The divine is never far away. This spiritual world is as real to them as the cosmos in which they live. The world, their own lives, are experienced as a battleground between evil and good spirits. Rituals are ways in which the power of helpful spirits can be harnessed for one's own purposes. To call these rituals magic is to misunderstand them. Rituals do not have an automatic efficacy. Their effect is always mediated through some personal spiritual agency. It is a search for empowerment in a game of power. The power of an evil spirit is always countered by a more powerful spirit. The difference between good and evil spirits is not as clear as we would like. Sometimes a good spirit can harm someone as a punishment for being or doing evil. It will turn favorable if it is appropriately propitiated. When the spirits get involved in interhuman conflicts their role may become very ambiguous. The people seem to be aware of an ongoing cosmic conflict between good and evil in the world in which they are caught up. But at the same time there is a desire for life and a deep sense of hope that evil can be successfully countered.

It is in the context of the spirit world that we must evoke the reality of the ancestors. Death is not the end of life. Human and family relationships continue into the next life and the elders continue to be close to and to look after their descendants. People feel empowered by the closeness of their ancestors. They are a source of strength. It is precisely because an untimely or accidental death may prevent one from becoming an ancestor that people try to avoid such a death at all costs.

This cosmovision of spirits and ancestors merges easily with the Catholic Christian cosmos with its angels, devils, and ancestors in the form of saints. Mary and other popular saints take over the task of protective spirits. The spirits are the concrete mediations of the divine for the people. They may not have an awareness of God as a person, set apart from them, to whom they can directly relate.

THE SACRAMENTAL AND COMMUNITY DIMENSION

Since the spirits are not accessible to the senses, the people relate to them through a world of symbols and symbolic actions. The rituals which they employ are not magic but rather symbolic actions which embody their relationship with the divine. Some anthropologists speak of ritual technologies. The religiosity of the people is therefore rich in its sacramental dimension. Materials like blessed water and oil, and gestures like the imposition of hands are used. The people also celebrate the sacraments of the official Church, though they may give them added meanings which the official ministers may not recognize or approve. Their own traditional rituals are Christianized by the use of symbols like the cross and the images of the saints or of prayers like the Lord's Prayer and the Creed. Sanctuaries as special places which manifest divine power are popular and become places of pilgrimage where one comes to request favors, to fulfill one's vows, and to give thanks. People feel free to use the services of unofficial ritual specialists for nonsacramental rituals. They are chosen because of their special knowledge or demonstrated closeness to the spirit world.

Popular religiosity is celebration of community. No one is involved in it alone, especially when it is a question of life cycle or seasonal rituals. Intercession on behalf of others is common. Apart from cases when a ritual specialist is involved in a power-play with the spirits, the rituals offer an occasion to be in communion with the family, the community, and the ancestors.

WARINESS OF MODERN IDEOLOGIES

Popular Catholicism may employ the rituals of traditional religion. But popular Catholics are not tied down by tradition. They are open to modernity and are ready to make use of its discoveries and techniques when necessary. They appreciate the benefits of education and the job opportunities that it brings. But they distinguish between the techniques of modernity and its secularizing and materialist ideology. Their own deep wisdom, in contact with nature and life, protects them from such ideology. As poor people at the bottom of the economic scale, they are familiar with the unjust structures that come with economic development and modernization. As a matter of fact, some of their rituals may actually be used to protect themselves from the evils of economic globalization.

The women seem to play a special role in the phenomena of popular Catholicism. They may form the majority of the actual participants in its various manifestations. The proportion of women who are possessed is certainly greater, and they are more often accused of being witches. Some of the ritual specialists too are women. One of the reasons for this may be that their close association with life and its reproduction makes them specially sensitive to its burdens and challenges.

TENSION BETWEEN THE POPULAR AND THE OFFICIAL

Hearing the various stories of popular Catholicism in its different dimensions we notice, on the one hand, the close relation that its cosmovision has with that of traditional Catholicism and, on the other, a certain tension that leads the people to keep their practices hidden and parallel. What could be the reasons for this tension?

Mission in the past, especially in the colonial period, meant not merely preaching the Good News of Jesus, but also the transplantation and imposition of the doctrinal, organizational, and ritual structures in which the Gospel had been embodied in the culture and society of the missionaries. The Good News of the Kingdom proclaimed by Jesus found expression in his own Jewish culture. Later it was lived and developed successively in the Greek and Latin cultural contexts. It also took on the cultural particularities of the various peoples that responded to the Gospel in the course of history. The missionaries therefore bring with them a Gospel loaded with a variety of cultural baggage. They also confuse the Gospel with its various cultural expressions. Rather than free the Gospel from these cultural embodiments and encourage the incarnation of the Gospel in a new culture, they impose the Gospel with all its cultural trappings. The poor who receive the

Gospel, who are often objects of economic and political colonialism, are not free to respond to the Gospel in their own way. So they accept the structures that come with it. They try to integrate some of it, giving it new meanings in their new context. They tolerate some of it without real involvement. They continue their own traditional rituals, either openly or secretly, according to circumstances to cater to their own real needs. In this manner they also affirm their own cultural and social identity. Some of these activities may involve a mild, hidden element of protest.

The Church, being a highly organized body with an undue focus on its institutional dimensions, imposes itself without adverting to the cultural identity and needs of the people and without listening to their aspirations and dreams. Provided its institutional framework is accepted and respected, at least outwardly, it may ignore or even tolerate other practices. It may hope that these latter will progressively disappear. In some cases, as in Tanzania, the institutional Church may be more interested in maintaining its authority and power and condemn practices that otherwise do not conflict with its own devotional tradition.

The official Church, even in its sacraments, seems to affirm an otherworldly salvation, somewhat spiritualized and related directly to the transcendent God. The other needs of the people related to their ongoing life in the world, their work and their social relationships were always catered to by popular rituals and devotions that were unofficial or semiofficial. These dimensions of popular religiosity were decried by the Protestant tradition. This is one reason that official Roman Catholicism tends to tolerate, if not encourage, practices of popular Catholicism. The people, for their part, while they accept the ritual/sacramental structures of official Catholicism, feel that they do not meet adequately their other real needs which they seek to meet by calling upon the world of the spirits and by using the various ritual technologies.

THE OFFICIAL CHURCH AND MODERNITY

After the Second Vatican Council, the Church seems to have developed in directions that take it further away from popular Catholicism. The post-Vatican liturgical reform stressed rather the word and gave less importance to the symbol, thus making the official liturgy even less attractive to the people. The Church may also have interiorized the cosmovision of the secularizing ideology of modernity that rejects anything that is not under the control of science and technology, as far as life in this world is concerned. This is certainly out of step with the cosmovision of the people, not only of the poor who are described in these stories, but also of the middle classes and of the rich who do not see science explaining all the experiences in their life and in their world, nor meeting all their personal, social, and spiritual needs. In this process, the Church may be ignoring its own popular and sacramental roots. Finally, some of the younger clergy, guided by a certain ideology, may be more interested in promoting economic development and political liberation than a project of holistic well-being. While the people appreciate this necessary concern, they do not see it as explaining their more integral experience of life in all its complexity.

The stories of the people indicate that, in spite of the attitudes adopted by official Catholicism, the people continue to assert their Catholic identity, but face and solve problems in their own way. People seem to have integrated their traditional religion with Catholicism in creative ways, which may not always meet the approval of the official Church. What are we called to do in such a situation today?

Before answering this question we must become aware that, in the period after the Second Vatican Council, the attitude of the Church to other cultures and religions has become more positive; that this has brought about a change in the way the Church looks at its task of mission; that the Church has also a more positive appreciation of popular religiosity and its liberative potential. Let us briefly explore this change in awareness before we go on to ask ourselves how best we can respond to the phenomena that these stories have presented to us. Though at the level of popular religiosity the distinction between religion and culture is not clear and adequate, in contemporary theological reflection and discussion, one tends to explore the areas of cultures and religions separately. I shall also do so for the sake of greater clarity. We shall see later how they interact mutually.

THE CHURCH AND CULTURES

It is commonly said that at the Second Vatican Council the Church became aware of itself as a world Church with a multiplicity of peoples and cultures. Its very first document on the liturgy bears witness to this. The Church asserts the need of adapting the liturgy to the different cultures of the world. The reason given is the promotion of full, conscious, and active participation of the people in worship. In order to achieve this, the Church asserts its power to change the liturgical rites:

> The liturgy is made up of unchangeable elements divinely instituted, and of elements subject to change. The latter not only may be changed but ought to be changed with the passage of time . . . The Christian people, as far as is possible, should be able to understand them with ease and take part in them fully, actively, and as a community (Constitution on the Sacred Liturgy, 21).

The Council also suggests various structures to promote appropriate adaptations according to various cultures, even to the extent of allowing the emergence of new ritual families:

> Even in the liturgy the Church does not wish to impose a rigid uniformity in matters which do not involve the faith or the good of the whole community. Rather does she respect and foster the qualities and talents

of the various races and nations. Anything in these people's way of life which is not indissolubly bound up with superstition and error she studies with sympathy, and, if possible, preserves intact. She sometimes even admits such things into the liturgy itself, provided they harmonize with its true and authentic spirit (ibid., 37).

Provision shall be made, when revising the liturgical books, for legitimate variations and adaptations to different groups, regions and peoples, especially in mission countries (ibid., 38).

In some places and circumstances, however, an even more radical adaptation of the liturgy is needed (ibid., 40).

I have given these long quotations from the Council because they deal with ritual, which is one of the principal manifestations of popular religiosity. Secondly, if the Church is so open to adapting and even to changing its own official rituals, it should be much more open to adopting/adapting other rituals that express a people's way of life.

CATHOLICITY AND COMMUNION

This openness to the different peoples and cultures of the world is further emphasized and broadened in the document on the Church:

Since the kingdom of Christ is not of this world (cf. Jn. 18:36), the Church or People of God which establishes this kingdom does not take away anything from the temporal welfare of any people. Rather she fosters and takes to herself, insofar as they are good, the abilities, the resources and customs of peoples. In so taking them to herself she purifies, strengthens and elevates them. . . . This characteristic of universality which adorns the People of God is a gift from the Lord himself whereby the Catholic Church ceaselessly and efficaciously seeks for the return of all humanity and all its goods under Christ its Head in the unity of his Spirit (Dogmatic Constitution on the Church, 13).

I would like to point to two important affirmations here. First of all is the assertion of a certain transcendence of the Kingdom of Christ with reference to all cultures so that it can welcome and integrate all cultures. Secondly, such a welcoming of all the cultural riches of the peoples of the world is not an option but an obligation, as a concrete manifestation of the task of the Church by virtue of its catholicity, to gather all things in Christ (cf. Eph.1:10). The catholicity of the Church therefore is manifested in a multiplicity of local Churches.

This multiplicity of local Churches, unified in a common effort, shows all the more resplendently the catholicity of the undivided Church (ibid., 23).

Here we have the vision of the Church universal as a communion of local Churches. This supposes that the Church is really rooted in each local people with their culture.

The document on the Church in the modern world develops further the relationship between Gospel and culture. It adverts to the pluralism of cultures as the product of humans and its link to the Gospel:

> In his self-revelation to his people culminating in the fullness of manifestation in his incarnate Son, God spoke according to the culture proper to each age . . . The Church has been sent to all ages and nations and, therefore, is not tied exclusively and indissolubly to any race or nation, to any one particular way of life, or to any customary practices, ancient and modern. The Church is faithful to its tradition and is at the same time conscious of its universal mission; it can, then, enter into communion with different forms of culture, thereby enriching both itself and the cultures themselves (Pastoral Constitution on the Church in the Modern World, 58).

The Church's dialogue with different cultures is presaged by God's own dialogue with them in the course of history.

The link between Gospel and culture is evoked again at the Bishops' Synod on Evangelization in 1974. The postsynodal document, *Evangelii Nuntiandi,* while it is not very positive to human cultures and stresses more the need for evangelizing them, does acknowledge the pluralism of cultures. The Gospel can relate to every culture because it is above all cultures (20).

INCULTURATION OR GOSPEL-CULTURE ENCOUNTER?

Around the same time as the Synod on Evangelization, a new term to indicate the relationship of Gospel and culture appears, namely, "inculturation." Inspired by the paradigm of the mystery of incarnation in which the Word of God becomes flesh in a particular human society and culture, theologians speak of the need for the Gospel to impregnate every culture in order to transform it. Though this term is widely used, even by official circles, today, some theologians feel that it is a theological vision which does not really represent what actually happens in the field. Inculturation evokes the Word of God in its purity incarnating itself in the cultures that it encounters. But the Word of God that we have is already inculturated. We have the Good News presented to us in four Gospels that reflect the life and culture of four different communities. The Gospel brought by the missionary today is further conditioned by the various cultures through which it has been handed down in history.

It is such a Gospel conditioned by various cultures already that the missionaries proclaim to a new people. The people who have the Gospel proclaimed to them have already their culture, animated by a religion. What happens then is an intercultural and interreligious encounter. This can only be a process of dialogue. In and through this dialogue a local Church emerges. The agents that build up this local Church are the local people. The missionaries proclaim the Word. They try their best to translate and adapt it to the cultural and social condition of the people. But it is the people who interpret the Gospel to discern its challenges for them here and now and who respond to it through their faith affirmation and life, ritual and celebration. Their response is certainly mediated by their culture and is the genesis of the local Church. Unfortunately, much of the current discussion about inculturation speaks about it as an ethereal Gospel entering into and transforming cultures. The focus is on the missionaries and what they do, which does not go beyond translation and adaptation. The attention is on the proclamation of the Word in diverse cultures by the missionaries (Church) and not on the diversity of the people (Churches) who respond to the Gospel from the depth of their cultural and social situation and are really the sources of pluralism and richness. That is why I think that today it is better to talk about Gospel-culture encounter than about inculturation.

OPENNESS TO OTHER RELIGIONS

Another related area where there has been a growing openness in the Church is its attitude to other religions. Before the Council, while the Church accepted the possibility of God's salvation reaching out to individuals who are true to their conscience, the other religions were considered variously as devilish, the manifestation of human effort, or the fruits of revelation in nature, if not a mixture of all three elements. The Council, however, in its Declaration on the Relation of the Church to Non-Christian Religions, strongly affirmed that God is the common origin and goal of humanity. It recognized in other religions "a ray of that truth that enlightens all men" (2). Rejecting "nothing of what is true and holy in these religions," the Church encouraged Christians to dialogue and collaborate with the members of other religions and "to acknowledge, preserve and encourage the spiritual and moral truths found among non-Christians, also their social life and culture" (2).

In its Declaration on Religious Freedom, the Council affirms that human persons, because of their inherent dignity, have "a right to religious freedom" (2). They also have the right to search for truth in religion in a social way as appropriate to human beings (3).

A CALL TO INTERRELIGIOUS DIALOGUE

The Church's attitude to other religions becomes much more positive in the years after the Council, especially in the teaching and practice of John Paul II. During a visit to Madras, India, in November 1985, he calls the leaders of other religions to dialogue and collaboration and sees it as a spiritual activity in the presence of God:

By dialogue we let God be present in our midst; for as we open ourselves in dialogue to one another, we also open ourselves to God ... As followers of different religions we should join together in promoting and defending common ideals in the spheres of religious liberty, human brotherhood, education, culture, social welfare and civic order (John Paul II 1986, 598).

In October 1986 he calls the leaders of various religions to come together in Assisi to pray for peace. This symbolic gesture is an acceptance that the believers of other religions can pray and that their prayer is effective. It is significant that among those invited were leaders of traditional religions from Africa and North America. In December of the same year, explaining and defending his gesture before the Cardinals, he not only declares that all authentic prayer is from the Holy Spirit, but also affirms a profound unity in the divine plan for humanity:

There is only one divine plan for every human being who comes into this world (cf. Jn. 1:9), one single origin and goal, whatever may be the color of his skin, the historical and geographical framework within which he happens to live and act, or the culture in which he grows up and expresses himself. The differences are a less important element, when confronted with the unity which is radical, fundamental and decisive (John Paul II 1987, 56).

John Paul II even goes further in his appreciation of other religions when, in his encyclical *The Mission of the Redeemer,* he discerns the presence and action of the Spirit in them:

The Spirit is at the very source of man's existential and religious questioning, a questioning which is occasioned not only by contingent situations but by the very structure of his being. The Spirit's presence and activity affect not only individuals but also society and history, peoples, cultures and religions (1990, 28).

Our attitude to the members of other religions can only be dialogue, which respects both the dignity of the others as human and the presence and action of the Spirit in them. This attitude of dialogue is reserved not only to the so-called great religions but also to the traditional religions. This was made clear in 1988 by the Pontifical Council for Interreligious Dialogue (Arrinze 1988, 102-106).

INTRACOMMUNITY DIALOGUE

When looking at the phenomena of popular Catholicism we see this interreligious dialogue taking place, not between two religious communities, but within the same community. When the Gospel is proclaimed to a community, the Gospel encounters another religion that has so far animated the life of this community and its culture. In the past the aim of mission may have been to destroy this religion completely and replace it with Christianity. The new believers would be expected to abandon their religion, its beliefs, and rituals to embrace the new faith. But if their original religion is no longer considered evil or merely human, but contains also the work of the Spirit, even if it may be mixed up with elements of human imperfection and even sin, then one is called to dialogue with it and integrate whatever is not evil, whether human or divine. What is called for is not a substitution of one religion by another but an integration. It is from such a point of view that we are called to rethink easy accusations of syncretism hurled at peoples' efforts at such integration and examine these phenomena more carefully. Theologians today are not only open to syncretistic phenomena, but even consider it inevitable and necessary in a multicultural and multireligious situation (Amaladoss 1996).

THE COSMIC AND THE METACOSMIC

Such an integration of religious elements is very complex and rare between the "great" religions. People very rarely abandon one great religion for another. But the integration of a popular religion with a great one seems to be necessary and constantly happening. Aloysius Pieris distinguishes between cosmic religions rooted in a particular place and culture and metacosmic soteriologies. According to Pieris, a cosmic religion

> represents the basic psychological posture that the *homo religiosus* (residing in each one of us) adopts subconsciously towards the mysteries of life... These mysteries relate to cosmic forces—heat, fire, winds and cyclones, earth and its quakes, oceans, rains, and floods—which we need and yet fear. Such forces serve as ambivalent symbols of our own subconscious powers, symbols freely employed in ordinary speech and in sacred rites, expressing our deepest yearnings... In our cultures these natural elements and forces merge into the mysterious world of invisible powers that maintain the cosmic balance... Rites, rituals, and a class of mediators form the constitutive elements of this religiousness (Pieris 1988, 71).

We can recognize many of the elements of popular religiosity in this description.

The metacosmic soteriologies, on the other hand, lead to a transphenomenal beyond, justifying the existence of a certain spiritual elite. They have scriptures and theologies. Pieris suggests that these metacosmic soteriologies are never found in themselves, but always integrated with one or more cosmic religions, which give them a social and cultural base. We have in this manner a twofold level of religious experience.

A NEED FOR INTEGRATION

In the first centuries the Church integrated easily with the various local cosmic religions and gave birth to different religious families. But in recent centuries, in the context of colonial domination, the missionaries sought to suppress the local cosmic religions and impose, together with the Gospel, the cosmic religious elements in which the Gospel was already embodied in their own tradition in the forms of rituals and customs. The people, of course, were not ready to surrender their own cosmic religious rootedness, even when they embraced Christianity. So the result was a parallel religiosity. Side by side with official Catholicism, the people built up their own parallel religion, often Christianizing it in many ways. In recent times the missionaries, coming from a progressively secularizing society, had no use for any cosmic religion, even of their own culture. So they imported, together with the Gospel, a minimum of sacramental ritual. The people felt the need, not only to fill out these sacramental rituals with local social and cultural color and substance, but also to continue to practice other rituals that responded to their personal, social, and cultural needs that were ignored by the official ritual. The task today is therefore to promote an authentic integration of cosmic and metacosmic elements in each people. This can be done only through an intracommunity dialogue which is intercultural and interreligious, which is carried on by the people themselves. The question then is how to form, free and animate the people for this dialogue.

MISSION AS DIALOGUE

In the context of the growing positive view of other cultures and religions, evangelization itself has come to be seen as dialogical, particularly with regard to cultures and religions. Jesus proclaimed the Good News of the Kingdom as a promise of freedom and fellowship, love and justice in a new community of people. His own life and mission were experienced as an ongoing struggle with Mammon. Over the centuries mission came to be seen as directed primarily against other religions, from which people had to be rescued. This happened because of an overemphasis on Baptism as a sacrament of saving souls from hell. Becoming a member of the Church is to be saved from hell. I think that today the focus of mission is changing again to what it was at the time of Christ. The Good News is a call to conversion from Mammon to God, because no one can serve two masters. This struggle between God and Mammon finds its traces in all religions and cultures, as also in the Church itself, unfortunately. But the cultures and religions are also marked by the presence of the Spirit. The missionary challenge therefore is not primarily to substitute cultures and religions by a Christian culture and religion, but to fight against Mammon in dialogue and collaboration with other believers and all people of goodwill. In the process the cultures and religions too will be transformed in the power of the Gospel. It is this dialogue that will lead to the emergence of a local Church where a well-integrated popular Catholicism will find its rightful place in the Church and where the metacosmic aspects of Christianity will themselves be authentically and fruitfully (evangelically) rooted in the local cultures and religions.

A POSITIVE ATTITUDE TO POPULAR RELIGION

After a period in which popular religiosity was either patronized as the religion of the poor or dismissed as syncretistic or tolerated as remnants of primitive societies which would eventually disappear, in recent decades the official Church has shown some interest in harnessing its positive elements. *Evangelii Nuntiandi* speaks of the importance of popular religiosity. But by preferring to call it popular piety it seems to focus more on popular devotion than on the kinds of religiosity that our stories have evoked for us. It does not avoid a patronizing tone, speaking of being sympathetic to it and of directing it (48). One has the impression that the peoples and their cultures are not really respected. The document's attitude to other religions is not positive either: it only sees them as "arms raised up to heaven" unable to establish "a true and living relationship with God" (53).

The bishops of Latin America who gathered in Puebla show a more positive appreciation of the people and their religiosity:

At its core the religiosity of the people is a storehouse of values that offers the answers of Christian wisdom to the great questions of life. The Catholic wisdom of the common people is capable of fashioning a vital synthesis . . . This wisdom is a Christian humanism that radically affirms the dignity of every person as a child of God, establishes a basic fraternity, teaches people how to encounter nature and understand work, and provides reasons for joy and humor even in the midst of a very hard life . . . The people's religious life is not just an object of evangelization. Insofar as it is a concrete embodiment of the Word of God, it itself is an active way in which the people continually evangelize themselves (Puebla 448, 450).

The bishops go on to spell out various pastoral strategies. In spite of the reference in the passage cited above to the people evangelizing themselves, they speak of the task of the Church and of its pastoral agents to evangelize popular religiosity.

THE PEOPLE AS SUBJECTS

We note here a tension that we should look at a little more closely. When I spoke above about the situation when the Gospel is being proclaimed, I suggested that while the missionary proclaims the Gospel, it is the people who interact with it and become or build up a Christian community. The missionary is a facilitator, a minister (servant) of the process. The people are the agents. The dialogue is between the cosmic religion of the people and the metacosmic soteriology of the Gospel. Even when such a dialogue is not officially permitted, the people do it all the same and integrate the Gospel into their life and culture in their own way. The popular Catholicisms that the seven stories have narrated to us are such spontaneous efforts of the people. They are in a way unforeseen and unintended by the missionaries. But then we have a tension within the Church community between the "people" and the official group. Even if the popular and the official forms of religion are seen as two poles of one continuum that is recognizable as Catholic, the poles can cause tension. The people at the official pole look at the popular pole in a disdainful, if not patronizing, way as superstitious. The people at the popular level look at the official pole as inadequate to their needs, if not alienating from life.

This tension is aggravated when those at the official pole also interiorize certain attitudes of modernity that dichotomize this material, historical world from the divine. They consider themselves the "elite" and look down upon the people as "primitive" or "prescientific." Their cosmovision distances itself even from the traditional cosmovision of the official Church which believes in the world of the spirits. Thus, when the "official" become also "elite," they move further away from the "people."

In this situation one can see the need for a twofold dialogue. On the one hand, the people must be allowed and enabled to actualize a creative dialogue between their popular culture/religion and the Gospel, leading to a new synthesis or integration through which the religion/culture of the people is really evangelized. This interior dialogue, on the other hand, takes place in the context of a dialogue between the people and the ministers/missionaries who are at the official/elite pole.

AN ATTITUDE OF *KENOSIS*

If we, as missionaries, place ourselves at the elite/official pole, what does this dialogue demand from us? In the era of the colonial type of mission we simply imposed on the people a ready-made belief and ritual system to which the people had to conform, at least outwardly. For their own reasons, which I shall not go into here, the people did conform outwardly, but carried on with their own rites in unofficial settings. To move from a method of mission as imposition or conquest to mission as dialogue requires two things. First of all we should learn to distinguish the Gospel from its various cultural embodiments which we take for granted. We must learn to identify the element of the Good News from the cosmovision that we have inherited consciously or unconsciously. We must not take for granted that our cosmovision is necessarily better than, superior to, or more adequate than the Gospel. Ultimately, experience will be the criterion, not scientific ideology. If I can still evoke the incarnational paradigm of Gospel-culture encounter, just as the mystery of incarnation involved a *kenosis,* a self-emptying of divine form and power by the Word of God, we too must empty ourselves of our cosmovisions and cultural prejudices as well as of our attitude of superiority and domination. We can let the Word of God act with its own power, without arrogating to ourselves that power. We must really be ministers, servants of the Gospel, mediating the Good News and not importing and imposing any particular culture(s) in which it may, at the moment, be embodied. This does not mean that we carry a disembodied Gospel. But in the context of an ongoing dialogue with another religion/culture, we must be able to liberate the Gospel from its cultural conditionings through interpretation, done in collaboration with the people. The Gospel itself will be further read and interpreted in the living context of the people. In the process the people are giving it a new expression in their language, culture, and context. If the Gospel itself needs such reinterpretation and reexpression, it goes without saying that ritual and organizational structures should follow the same path. This was indicated by the Second Vatican Council with regard to the liturgy.

Secondly, such an attitude of *kenosis* goes hand in hand with an attitude of respect for the people as humans with their proper dignity, which will also extend to their cultures/religions. Authentic dialogue will be mutual prophecy, but also mutual learning, in an atmosphere of mutual respect. We should therefore be able to go beyond a patronizing attitude that we often find in official documents where the Church is going out to evangelize the peoples and their cultures. The people become objects. By the term "Church" we normally mean ourselves as the elite/official group in the Church. As the Bishops of Latin America indicated, the people evangelize themselves. We proclaim the Gospel and mediate the Word of God. But it is the people who dialogue with that Word in the context of their own experience of God and evangelize themselves. The people are agents. They are not passive recipients, but active creators. The people show constantly this capacity in all the stories that we have heard, even if their creative agency is not always acknowledged and appreciated by the elite/official pole in the Church. The people are not insensitive to the forces and ideology of modernity. But they react to them and integrate them in their own way which does not lead to a secularized universe.

THE KINGDOM AS THE HORIZON FOR DIALOGUE

The dialogue that I am proposing is not open ended. The horizon in which the dialogue is taking place is always the process of evangelization. The point of reference and the criterion of control remain always the Gospel. In the concrete the criteria that will guide prophecy are the values of the Kingdom of God which Jesus proclaimed. Jesus announced the coming of the Kingdom in history. He proclaimed God's unconditional love for humanity. He witnessed to it by his miracles of healing and exorcism and his empowering of the poor and the marginalized whom he befriended. He gave a new commandment calling people to love and serve one another as he himself loved them even unto death. He invited people to a new community rooted in God. George Soares-Prabhu has described this new society to which Jesus called humanity:

When the revelation of God's love (the Kingdom) meets its appropriate response in man's trusting acceptance of this love (repentance), there begins a mighty movement of personal and societal liberation which sweeps through human history. The movement brings *freedom* inasmuch as it liberates each individual from the inadequacies and obsessions that shackle him. It fosters *fellowship,* because it empowers free individuals to exercise their concern for each other in genuine community. And it leads on to *justice,* because it impels every true community to adopt the just societal structures which alone make freedom and fellowship possible . . .

The vision of Jesus summons us then to a ceaseless struggle against the demonic structures of unfreedom (psychological and sociological) erected by mammon; and to a ceaseless creativity that will produce in every age new blueprints for a society ever more consonant with the Gospel vision of man. Lying on the horizons of human history and yet part of it, offered to us as a gift yet confronting us as a challenge, Jesus' vision of a new society stands before us as an unfinished task, summoning us to permanent revolution (Soares-Prabhu 1981, 601, 607).

The Church itself is the sacrament—symbol and servant—of this Kingdom, toward which it is on pilgrimage and by which it is constantly challenged. The mission of the Church is to promote the Kingdom and to build up the Church-sacrament as its servant.

This vision of the Kingdom challenges all cultures with their cosmovisions and sociopolitical structures and all the religions with their rituals and ministerial structures. It remains the criterion that will guide every intercultural and interreligious dialogue in the context of evangelization. The pilgrim Church has always been tempted to set its own limited and historical realization of the Kingdom as the criterion. The attitude of *kenosis* I have suggested above involves also the surrendering of such pretensions.

Though the dialogue between popular and official Catholicism must take place in each particular historical and social context, with their rich diversity, after listening to the seven stories we can venture to indicate some common and general areas that will emerge in the course of such dialogue. We shall first of all look at the positive points and then consider the elements that need to be challenged to conversion or change in the name of the Gospel.

A HOLISTIC VIEW OF LIFE

Popular Catholicism has a holistic view of salvation. Its concern is for health and well-being. Its rituals for healing are focused not only on the body but also on the psyche, the spirit, and the community. Sickness is not lived only as a physical malady. Its psychological and social causes are also sought for and tackled. The rituals for healing make use of the body and of the cosmic elements. The human individual is so much a part of the community that some anthropologists speak of it as the social body. Life is integrated with and sensitive to the cosmos. Life's activities revolve around the temporal and seasonal cycle. The earth itself is laid out in a sacred geography with its places of special divine manifestation. Pilgrimages and special rituals surround such holy places. The whole of life acquires a sacramental dimension. Symbols in the form of dreams and divination mediate divine-human communication. Symbolic actions of the community—rituals—structure individual and social life.

Contemporary official/elite Catholicism seems to have lost such closeness to the cosmos. Salvation is envisaged as something spiritual and otherworldly. The cosmos has become a material object to be dominated and exploited by science and technology. Dichotomies between the body and the spirit, between the human and the divine, between the human and nature, between the individual and society structure contemporary thinking and action. When a person is sick, the healing methods and rituals of popular Catholicism cater to the whole person in all his/her aspects: medicinal herbs, prayers of intercession, symbolic rituals, exorcism when thought necessary, the involvement of the community, at least of the immediate family. In contemporary society there is a diversification of responsibilities between the medical doctor, the counselor, the social activist, and the spiritual father/mother, the focus often being, rather exclusively, on the medical doctor. The doctor may try to heal the symptoms, but not handle the possible psychological and social causes of the sickness. Traditional Catholic rituals did have such a holistic approach. Though the official Church is not formally opposed to them, in practice the elite leadership among the ministers tend to empty the rituals of their symbolism and their holistic impact, influenced not by the Catholic faith, but by contemporary secularist-materialistic ways of looking at the human and the world.

MODERN, WITHOUT BEING MATERIALISTIC

The stories have shown us how people can live and adjust to the modern world, use its new technologies, and profit by its new industrial and commercial possibilities for development, without adopting its secularizing and materialistic/atheistic ideology. While for the contemporary elite, ecological destruction seems inevitable and necessary, for the people, the cosmos has not lost its sense of mystery and its symbolic power of mediating the divine. For the Mukkuvar the sea continues to be a maternal divine presence, generous in its bounty, but awesome in its power over their lives. For the Aymara, the earth is the benevolent mother—the *Pachamama*—that one is always grateful to. The urban slum dwellers in Chile can be in the "modern" world without succumbing to its secularizing forces.

Among the people, then, religion is for life in the world and in community. It does not isolate or alienate them through a spiritualistic and otherworldly focus. They find the sacraments meaningful and necessary. They do not feel the need to substitute symbols with discourse: the symbols communicate much more than what words can ever express.

SENSE OF COMMUNITY

Popular culture has a sense of community. It is not individualistic. It discourages competition. The wider family is very important to them. The human person is never alone. Its rituals are always communitarian. Its sense of community reaches out to the ancestors. The ancestors do not disappear into thin air after death. They continue to be close to their children, taking care of them, helping them and protecting them. Life is their gift and remains an enduring link between generations. To venerate the ancestors is to feel their closeness, power, and concern. It is enabling and comforting. The celebration of one's relationship with the ancestors is common and current among people everywhere, especially in the Far East and in Africa. Traditional Catholicism has its belief in the communion of saints. These are evoked and prayed to in every sacramental celebration, especially in the Eucharist. But it is not a living experience for many "modern," elite Catholics. For them death is lived as a severance, a disappearance. Fewer and fewer people believe in a life after death.

Together with a sense of community goes a strong sense of equality and of sharing. Many celebrations among the people are thinly veiled ways of sharing wealth and well-being. The assertion of equality may even take violent forms, forcing people to share their goods. For the individualistic and competitive spirit of modernity, such a quest for equality may be upsetting. But it affirms a value that the modern world has lost. Solidarity and mutual help are seen as values of the Christian community in Ghana. Communal celebrations are a way of life in St. Lucia. Many Tanzanians are attracted to the community of Wanamaombi for their sense of solidarity and mutual help. The Mukkuvar see people who become rich either through the use of mechanized boats or through industrial or government jobs as destructive of the community. They have not come to terms with the growing inequality among them. The community sense of the Aymara is self-defensive and protective of their identity. It is the experience of family and community that·protects the urban slum dwellers of Chile from succumbing to the inroads of modernity. The New Religious Movements in Africa and Latin America promote this sense of community which the official/elite Church has lost or is not encouraging sufficiently. The promotion of Basic or Small Christian Communities seeks to revive this community dimension of Christian life.

COMMUNITY AND AUTHORITY

Another aspect of life in community among most tribal peoples, or people at a level of popular culture, is a certain experience of the democratic spirit. Problems are encountered, discussed, and solved in common. Leadership is often collective. Authority is exercised in the name of the community. The people feel that they are agents and are responsible for their life. Ritual specialists may have their role, but they do not dominate social life. The Church's organizational structures, with their strong hierarchical order, have always felt uncomfortable with this. This is one of the areas where there is tension in popular Catholicism. In practice people tend to live in different worlds. In a mission situation, given the paucity of ministers, this tension may not always be acute, as in Peru. Among the Mukkuvar the priests functioned as absolute leaders of the community, not for religious, but for other sociological and political reasons. This is now changing. In Tanzania, the power of ecclesiastical authority seems to be affirmed for its own sake against a group which is threatening to become another religious power center. But everywhere, in the religious sphere, while people respect and benefit by the special powers of the priest as a ritual specialist, they feel free to assert their independence in other complementary areas of religious practice.

BUILDING A LOCAL CHURCH

If, as we have seen above, the people are to be the agents of their own evangelization, then the official Church must find some way in which the people can be enabled and empowered to be evangelizers. The ministers of the Church remain what they ought to be, namely, servants and facilitators, not dominating leaders of the community. One of the positive and attractive features of the New Religious Movements is precisely the sense of freedom and agency that ordinary people seem to have both in celebration and in witnessing. In popular Catholicism today, people seem to have this freedom and agency only in parallel ritual structures. The aim of evangelizing mission then will be to enable the people to become subjects of life and celebration in the Church, not merely objects of the clergy's ministrations.

When people become Church in this manner, then we will have a truly local Church. The stories that we have heard show us that, on the one hand, people exercise their rights to contextualize their faith in their life, culture, and cosmos. But, on the other, the people value and preserve their link to the universal Church. The Chilean Catholics may have their special shrines and rituals. But they relate to the priest and value the Eucharist. The Aymara, while preserving their local cultural identity, wish to signify their relatedness to the wider identity of the Church by building a church in a central place. The Wanamaombi in Tanzania may be excluded at the moment by the local Church, but they still hope to be vindicated by the wider Church to which they continue to affirm their loyalty. The St. Lucians may have their private rituals, but they surround and nourish official ones like Baptism, First Communion, novenas, and Eucharist. For the Mukkuvar the priest is an essential point of reference, and their relationship to the wider Church is a guarantee of special identity in a world surrounded by Hindus and Muslims.

What these phenomena point to is that the current tension between the official and popular Catholicism indicates the unwillingness of official Catholicism, in recent centuries, to become authentically local under the guise of protecting the unity of the Church. In spite of the openness of the Second Vatican Council, the recent document *The Roman Liturgy and Inculturation* insisted that the unity of the Roman Rite must be protected in any efforts at inculturation (Congregation for Divine Worship and the Discipline of the Sacraments 1994). A Roman Cardinal suggested during the special Synod for Africa that African Christians have to be a little Semitic, a little Greek, fully Roman, and authentically African. What our stories of popular Catholicism show is that people, as subjects, spontaneously and almost unconsciously "inculturate" the Gospel, while remaining loyal to its universal significance. People, as in Chile, Hong Kong, and India, have even shown that they can withstand the forces of contemporary economic and cultural modernization and globalization in asserting their local identity. It is the elite that seem easy victims of globalization.

A COMMUNION OF LOCAL CHURCHES

We need therefore to continue the efforts started at the Second Vatican Council, not only to see the universal Church as a communion of local Churches, but to actualize this vision by enabling the people to build up authentic local Churches. This is not the place to elaborate the role of tradition in the process. But we can say that the tradition that must be preserved is the tradition of the Gospel, of the Word of God, and not its particular cultural expressions in history. The New Testament itself is a model of diverse cultural embodiments of the Gospel. While it remains the source to which every Christian community should return to discover the Word of God, this Word always needs to be liberated from its cultural embodiments, interpreted in the living context of people and reexpressed in their cultural idiom in their life and celebration.

To speak of the universal Church as a communion of local Churches also involves the promotion of a relationship of dialogue between the local Churches and not of domination of any Church over the others. Such a dialogue supposes that each local Church may highlight and develop one or another element or aspect of the Gospel in a special way and that every local Church can learn from the other. One could rather speak of the mutual sharing of riches among the Churches. One purpose of mission is precisely to promote such sharing among the Churches and thus promote the gathering of all things in Christ. In the light of such a Catholic vision of communion we can say that the official Church or "missionary" should be open to learn from and share the riches of popular Catholicism. What we have said above about the holistic view of salvation, the sense of closeness to nature, the experience of community of popular Catholicism are precisely the elements that today's official Catholicism would do well to learn, to free itself from the many alienations that it is suffering from and to promote a holistic life.

Through such an ongoing dialogue between the local Churches one would discover the universal Church concretized in the local and as the communion of the local Churches. Such a vision and experience can be a real antidote to the prevailing destructive thrust toward economic, political, and cultural globalization aided by commercial and communicational networks. It will also be a defense against temptation for the Church to follow similar globalization policies, either in the name of promoting and preserving unity, or in the name of effectiveness in facing a globalizing world situation.

A WIDER ECUMENISM

A closer look at popular Catholicism also shows a spirit of ecumenism operative in it, sometimes in ambiguous ways. In itself it is an attempt to integrate the cosmic religiosity of the people with the metacosmic soteriology of Catholicism. Already here one can see a certain ecumenism operative. But besides that, the Aymara in Peru seem united in their common cosmic religiosity even if they are denominationally divided into Roman Catholic and Adventist communities. The Christians in Ghana are noted for their openness to help even the majority Muslims around them. For the Christians in Hong Kong, their Christianity is rather private and they seek to collaborate with all people of goodwill in pursuing political and cultural goals. The Mukkuvar have an ambiguous relationship with their neighbors. While their Catholicism distinguishes them in a defensive manner from the surrounding Hindus, the Hindu gods and spirits are very much alive in their lives. They tend to identify the great Hindu gods as evil spirits. But they are open to harness the power of other spirits, sometimes perceived as neutral. They do not hesitate to use the services of Hindu ritual specialists for this purpose. In India, for instance, it is well known that many Christian sanctuaries attract devotees from other religions. Similarly Christians are not averse to profit by the divine power that they may experience in other religions. Such crossing of boundaries can be shocking only to those who consider that everything that is not Christian is evil and devilish. But if the Spirit of God is present and active also in other believers then the borders between religions do become porous. Discernment is always necessary, but exclusion is not the only option. It is in this context that one must evaluate the possibilities of participating in the symbols and rituals of other religions. People do seem capable of reaching out to the significance and reality behind symbols or of reinterpreting symbols in new historical and cultural contexts or of conflating symbols with similar meanings.

In the world today, torn apart by different forces, peace between religions is seen as necessary to promote peace among peoples. At the official level, the religious leaders seem to believe in the efficacy of dialogue among intellectuals. Even in the field of ecumenism between the Churches such dialogues and agreement among officials do not seem to lead anywhere. Perhaps we could learn from the spontaneous and pragmatic ecumenism we see among these people to promote fraternity and community in life among believers of different religions.

From the point of view of evangelization and of the Kingdom not everything is positive and praiseworthy in popular Catholicism. There are also some areas of concern.

ENCOUNTERING EVIL

What strikes us most when we read these stories is the experience of evil in its many forms, which is the reverse of their quest for healing. People feel the need to find a cause for any problem or sickness that they consider abnormal. The purpose of this search for a cause is pragmatic. In the pursuit of healing and wholeness they wish to counter and neutralize the source of evil. Though people are not unaware of natural causes, they search for some personal agency in cases considered unusual. Such personal agents to whom people attribute evil (suffering) or sickness fall into three broad categories: witches with whom we can also count people who are supposed to cast an "evil eye"; evil spirits, either acting on their own or sent by sorcerers; and neutral or good spirits/gods who send sickness or misfortune either to punish or to claim attention. Diviners are often used to help in the search for or to identify the causes. In the case of witches, they may be identified and expelled from the community, or even killed. The spirits are exorcised by countersorcery or other means of exorcism—for example, by the power of the Holy Spirit. The neutral or good spirits are propitiated.

Belief in spirits, good and evil, and in possession by them belongs to a particular cosmovision. The official Church is favorable to belief in evil spirits and has official exorcists and rituals for their use. A certain elite may claim to disbelieve in them. This is a clash of cosmovisions. We shall take up this point later.

The Church must certainly condemn the use of sorcerers to cause evil. Sometimes a person will use sorcery to harm people who are thought to have harmed him- or herself in some way. For similar reasons accusations of witchcraft or the "evil eye" are hurled against others. A twofold approach here seems necessary. On the one hand, sicknesses may be psychosomatic and may be caused by tensions in personal or social relationships. Accusations of witchcraft or sorcery may be a symbolic way of handling this situation. In a Christian community, in the context of the sacrament of reconciliation, we can make an effort to acknowledge open conflicts and surface hidden tensions and solve them in a human way through dialogue, conversion/repentance when necessary, and forgiveness. We should promote peace among people as a way of promoting healing in the community. Similarly, people who do not conform or who are handicapped in some way are often accused of being witches. In such cases there must be an effort to defend their rights and dignity as humans and to integrate them into the community. In the absence of such a community reconciliation process, symbolic ways of handling the problem will continue.

More fundamentally, the stories of Job and Jesus can be used to educate the people: suffering is not always deserved; suffering may be permitted by God for our good; God can bring good out of evil; suffering willingly accepted can be redemptive and so can be made meaningful. We can also help the people by broadening their scientific knowledge so that they can understand that many illnesses and accidents that they consider abnormal, and for which they seek some personal agency, may have natural causes.

CREATION AND REDEMPTION

In Christianity there is always a tension between creation and redemption. Some traditions emphasize a continuity between them, while others stress the discontinuity. I think that in the past, official Catholicism has emphasized rather the discontinuity, especially in relation to other cultures and religions, stressing that in Christ all things have been made new. In recent years there has been an effort to see what is positive in cultures and religions and see them as the work of the Spirit of God. Recent ecological reflection has also made us sensitive to a spirituality of creation. This approach would rather stress the continuity. An approach that either empties creation of its mystery or considers creation as essentially imperfect and even evil, affected of course by the sinfulness of humanity, will certainly have to be abandoned. But on the other hand, creation may be so glorified that redemption is seen merely as fulfillment, and not as conversion leading to a transcendence and to creative newness. While the contemporary elite may need a spirituality of creation, popular Catholicism may be so integrated with the cosmos and creation that it does not sufficiently value history, change, creativity, and newness. Retelling the story of the Bible, especially the story of Jesus and his paschal mystery helps the people to develop a deeper and firmer commitment to history as a process or transformation in the power of the resurrection.

Looking at the figure of Jesus dying and rising, people can also grasp the possible meaning of suffering in their lives and its creative possibilities. This will help them not always to look for people to blame it on. Or even if they can clearly see someone to blame, they will be ready to forgive and love rather than think of revenge. The command of Christ is to love even our enemies. In popular Catholicism the passion of Christ seems to have a particular place. People seem to discover in Jesus someone who not only suffers like them but does so undeservedly. But people do not seem to be attracted equally to the event of the Resurrection. An active belief in the Resurrection can help them to find in their suffering not merely a burden that they undergo passively and with resignation, but the seed of new life.

One can describe this shift in awareness in spatial terms. Though people believe in a transcendent God, their normal transactions are with spirits and ancestors to whom they relate rather at the horizontal level. I think the story of the Resurrection will open a space for transcendence and transformation. The danger is that in official/elite circles one tends to push this transformation into the future. The integration of popular and official Catholicism should lead to making the transcendent not horizontal but imminent. It is present here and now, but it makes present a different dimension that takes our reflection beyond causes and effects.

THE CHALLENGES OF SOCIAL CHANGE AND THE SPIRITS

Before we finish our extended reflection on popular Catholicism I would like to focus, rather briefly, on two questions, to clarify the issues rather than to offer solutions. These are: popular religiosity and social change, and the world of the spirits.

SOCIAL CHANGE

The people whose stories we have listened to are the poor who are oppressed and marginalized in many ways in their societies. Sometimes one thinks that the rituals of the people are alienating insofar as they blame their suffering on the spirits and sorcerers rather than on the real social-structural causes. This would be to take a superficial view of the situation. People do distinguish between personal suffering and social injustice. The very affirmation of their separate identity in the midst of an oppressive situation is a way of self-defense. The preservation of the identity and culture of the Aymara in spite of more than 400 years of exploitation and oppression is an amazing example of self-protection and survival. The Christians in Hong Kong, who are perhaps a small minority, show their political options by commemorating Tiananmen every year, even if they are not actively involved in politics in any organized way. The Mukkuvar's Catholicism is an affirmation of difference from the surrounding Hindus of castes socially higher than themselves. This separate identity is jealously guarded even against Christians of other castes. They also agitate against the mechanized boat owners of today for their unjust exploitation of the sea. The Wanamaombi pray for good Catholic politicians against the prospects of conflict and corruption. The Christians in Ghana affirm a democratic spirit that enhances the role and rights of women. The St. Lucians are sensitive to the effects of trade liberalization on their banana industry. The Chilean urban dwellers are active in community organizations and trade union movements.

The rituals of popular Catholicism reveal countercultural aspects with regard to the increasing hegemony of a new global secularizing culture through their affirmation of local identity and culture. They also successfully withstand the pressures of official Catholicism to conform, irrespective of their real life-needs. The rituals and prayers can also be seen as the "weapons of the weak" (Scott 1985). People are neither unaware nor accepting of their oppression. But being powerless at the moment, they can only manifest their opposition in symbolic ways, in prayer and ritual. These symbolic elements may also nourish and sustain their hidden protest.

RELIGION AND REVOLUTION

This hidden religious protest of the weak cannot, however, lead to real social transformation, unless it becomes an element in a sociopolitical movement that can profit by favorable circumstances. The Mukkuvar, historically, found their freedom from local oppressive forces, not only by becoming Christian, but by finding an alliance with Portuguese forces in the process. The Wanamaombi prayer for peace and protection against Muslim power may become effective because there are already leading Christian politicians in the field. The Christians in Ghana can use the democratic process to upset the traditional domination of the Dagomba chiefs. The Chileans can depend on their democratic organizations. A clearer example of the phenomenon would be the liberation of the Philippines from the domination of the exploitative dictatorship of Ferdinand Marcos. The popular religiosity of the people supported them in the struggle. But it would not have succeeded without a general mobilization of the people and the support of the rebel army, not to speak of the not so hidden denial of support of the United States to Marcos.

The countercultural elements of popular religiosity can therefore become liberative only when other sociopolitical circumstances are favorable. Religion by itself does not bring about a revolution. When people are totally oppressed and feel utterly powerless, then they tend to become millenarian. They wait passively for a miraculous intervention by God. Communalists, who use factors like religion and ethnicity for political ends, then seek to use the power of popular religious feeling as a political weapon, especially against other religious groups. Religious fundamentalism alienates people from society and misdirects their enthusiasm toward religious fanaticism. But where there are ongoing movements for change and hope is alive, religion can become messianic in the sense of being committed to transforming society and history. The task of mission is to keep a healthy messianism alive so that, in the power of the risen Christ and of the Spirit, people become agents of their own transformation.

A CLASH OF COSMOVISIONS

The cosmovision of popular religiosity with its belief in spirits is another area that requires some reflection. The official Church does believe in the spirits—in angels and devils. The former Archbishop of Lusaka, Msgr. Milingo, is an active exorcist in Rome and in Italy, in spite of the active discouragement of the leaders of the Italian Church who frequently deny him the use of their churches. While he is not encouraged, he is not condemned. There are also official exorcists in some dioceses like Turin. Charismatic or Pentecostal movements are quite prevalent in the Church. Therefore the cosmovision of popular religiosity is not against official orthodoxy.

On the other hand, the tendency of the modern elite, in or outside the Church, would be to disbelieve in spirits, good or evil, in the name of a scientific spirit. But the physical sciences do not have anything to say about human experiences that transcend the merely material and physical. If we believe that humans are spirits-in-bodies, then we must be open to phenomena that cannot be objects of study by the physical sciences.

Some think that the world of the spirits could be symbols and projections of powers. The symbolic way may be the only way of reaching out to these levels as depth psychologists like C. G. Jung have found. Sufficient evidence of cases of extrasensory perception, telepathy, and telekinesis have been recorded over the years. Some psychologists consider them to be the effects of an altered state of consciousness. But such altered states of consciousness seem to unleash powers that are not available to ordinary humans. People who function in such altered states are not conscious in the normal sense. They do not know what is happening to them or what they are doing. If individuals can have such altered states of consciousness we need not exclude the possibility that they can also interact with others at such unconscious levels. Such interactions may cause experiences which an individual feels without being able to account for it. The Asian traditions of Hinduism and Buddhism seem to explore this realm through their practices of meditation. The Buddhist masters often speak of sending out good vibrations into the world. If good vibrations are thought to be effective in some way, bad vibrations may also be effective in the contrary direction.

Spirits, if any, could eventually act on human beings through these levels of their personality. I think that the new age movements are efforts to explore this world-in-between of human powers beyond the reach of ordinary science through techniques which Asian, Hindu, and Buddhist masters have developed and perfected over the centuries. I would therefore suggest that the cosmovision of popular religiosity does not deserve rejection but deeper study. Abuses and manipulations like sorcery and witchcraft must certainly be done away with. But we should not let science deprive us or the people of dimensions of the human that science cannot know and control.

Similarly, modern science seems to persuade some people that phenomena that are the presence of the divine in the world—miracles—are not possible. To approach experiences of popular religiosity with such an a priori is not proper.

I would suggest therefore an openness in this area that is not dogmatic. We may have our own cosmovisions. But we should not rush to condemn the cosmovision of others. On the contrary other cosmovisions can challenge some of the simplistic and reductive presuppositions of the ideology of scientific modernity. A naive belief in the all-knowing character of science can also be a superstition—that is, a belief without a foundation.

SYNCRETISM OR SYMBIOSIS?

Popular Catholicism is often accused of syncretism by the official/elite people in the Church. Syncretism can be described as the indiscriminate mixing of elements from different religions. The people themselves are not aware of being syncretistic. While not denying the possibility of syncretism in some cases, much of the phenomena of popular Catholicism is the effort of the people to combine beliefs and rituals from two different religious traditions in their own way. Being at the cosmic and metacosmic levels they do not really clash with each other. In the mind of the people their cosmic rituals meet needs of life and society that are not attended to by official Catholicism. It may seem like parallel religiosity from the point of view of the official Church. But for the people they operate in different realms and do not clash with each other.

Aloysius Pieris distinguishes between syncretism, synthesis, and symbiosis. While syncretism is a haphazard mixing of religions and synthesis is a rational, artificial mix, symbiosis comes out of a dialogue in which each religion discovers its identity, grows through integration, and affirms its identity-in-relation-ship. It is not one religion absorbing another. Neither is it simply two religions mixing together to form a third one. Given the cosmic-metacosmic dialectic, it can really be two poles in tension enriching each other and forming a complex identity.

CONCLUSION: NOT ONLY THE POOR

The stories that we have reflected on have spoken about the popular religios-ity of the poor. This, however, should not give us the impression that "popular" in the sense of "unofficial" religiosity is limited to the poor or that it is not present among the rich or the elite. Pilgrim centers like Lourdes or Medjugorie do not attract only the poor. People who throng charismatic prayer groups belong rather to the middle class. The New Religious Movements are as active among the rich as among the poor. The United States is said to have 5,000 of them. In a secular-ized, individualistic, and competitive world, people search for meaning in sym-bols and security in rituals that mediate the divine. People who have little faith in the Transcendent still seek to transcend their human limitations in new age move-ments that employ various self-help techniques to achieve altered states of con-sciousness. Others seek security in the stars. Though everything is predetermined, knowledge gives the possibility of preparing oneself to cope with the inevitable. The new age movements represent the popular religiosity of the secularized who do not believe in the Transcendent.

Compared to these types of secular religiosities or substitute religions, popu-lar Catholicism can be a force for change and integration. The faith of the people is neither fatalist nor militant. But it is rooted and committed to search for per-sonal and community well-being here and now. The task of mission is to enable them in the Spirit to build the Kingdom that Jesus proclaimed and which is God's promise and gift to all peoples. In the process, the Church will discover itself, not as an institution with a power structure, but as the peoples of God, affirming their diverse identities, but united in communion.

Bibliography

Aguilar Arce, Marcelino, and Pedro Mercado Ventura. 1991. *La realidad educacional en las comunidades campesinas del Lago Titicaca*. Licentiate Thesis, Universidad Nacional del Altiplano, Puno, Peru.

Albó, Xavier. 1996. "The Aymara Religious Experience." In *The Indian Face of God in Latin America*, edited by Manuel M. Marzal et al., 119-167. Maryknoll, NY: Orbis Books.

Allpanchis vol. 10, "Mito y Utopía en los Andes." Cusco, Peru: Instituto de Pastoral Andina, 1977.

_____vol. 20, "Religión, Mito y Ritual en el Perú." Cusco, Peru: Instituto de Pastoral Andina, 1982.

_____vol. 31, "Religiosidad Andina." Cusco, Peru: Instituto de Pastoral Andina, 1988.

_____vol. 32, "Religiosidad Andina." Cusco, Peru: Instituto de Pastoral Andina, 1988.

_____vol. 40, "El Poder De Lo Sagrado." Cusco, Peru: Instituto de Pastoral Andina, 1992. .

Alomia Bartra, Merling. 1990. "Los comienzos de la actividad educacional adventista." Mimeograph. Biblioteca del Colegio Adventista del Lago Titicaca.

Amaladoss, Michael. 1989. "Popular Religions: Some Questions." *Vidyajyoti* 53: 357-368.

_____1990. *Making All Things New: Dialogue, Pluralism and Evangelization in Asia*. Maryknoll, NY: Orbis Books.

_____1991. "The Challenges of Mission Today." In *Trends in Mission: Toward the Third Millennium*, edited by Jenkinson and O'Sullivan, 359-397. Maryknoll, NY: Orbis Books.

_____1992. *Becoming Indian: The Process of Inculturation*. Rome: Centre for Indian and International Studies.

_____1996. "Syncretism and *Kenosis*." In *The Agitated Mind of God: The Theology of Kosuke Koyama*, edited by Dale T. Irvin and Akiintunde E. Akinade. Maryknoll, NY: Orbis Books.

Aman, Kenneth, and Cristián Parker. 1991. *Popular Culture in Chile: Resistance and Survival*. Boulder, CO: Westview.

Anthony, Patrick A. B. 1977. "A Case Study in Indigenization." In *Out of the Depths*, edited by Idris Hamid, 185-215. Trinidad: St. Andrew's Theological College.

_____1985. "The Flower Festivals of St. Lucia." *Culture and Society* Series no. 1. Castries, St. Lucia: Folk Research Centre.

_____1988. "The Encounter between Christianity and Culture: The Case of the 'Kélé' Ceremony in St. Lucia." *Bulletin, Secretariatus Pro Non Christianis*, 23/3 (69): 287-300.

_____ed., 1995. *Theology in the Caribbean Today 1: Proceedings 1994*. St. Lucia: Archdiocesan Pastoral Centre.

Arrinze, Cardinal. 1988. "Pastoral Attention to African Traditional Religion." *Bulletin of the Secretariat for Non-Christians*, 23.

Arroyo, Gonzalo, et al. 1992. *Por los Caminos de América . . . Desafíos socio-culturales a la Nueva Evangelización*. Santiago: Paulinas.

Barker, P. 1986. *Tribes and Languages of Northern Ghana*. Accra: Ghana Evangelism Committee in association with Asempa Publishers.

Bayly, S. 1989. *Saints, Goddesses and Kings: Muslims and Christians in South Indian Society, 1700-1900*. Cambridge: Cambridge University Press.

Berger, Peter et al. 1973. *The Homeless Mind: Modernization and Consciousness*. New York: Random House.

Bosch, David J. 1991. *Transforming Mission: Paradigm Shifts in Theology of Mission*. Maryknoll, NY: Orbis Books.

Bourdieu, Pierre. 1971. "Genèse et structure du champ religieux," *Revue Française de Sociologie* 12: 295-334.

Brown, L. V. 1982. *The Indian Christians of St. Thomas: An Account of the Ancient Syrian Church of Malabar*. Cambridge: Cambridge University Press.

Brown, Raymond E., Joseph A. Fitzmyer, and Roland E. Murphy, eds. 1990. *The New Jerome Biblical Commentary*. Englewood Cliffs, NJ: Prentice Hall.

Bühlmann, Walbert. 1986. *The Church of the Future: A Model for the Year 2001*. Maryknoll, NY: Orbis Books.

Burkhart. G. 1974. "Equal in the Eye of God: A South Indian Devotional Group in Its Hierarchical Setting." *Contributions to Asian Studies* 5: 1-14.

———1976. "On the Absence of Descent Groups among Some Udaiyars of South India." *Contributions to Indian Sociology (N.S.)* 10: 31-61.

Campredon, Gabriel. 1992. *Luis Dalle: un hombre libre*. Lima, Peru: Tarea.

Caplan, L. 1980. "Caste and Castelessness among South Indian Christians." *Contributions to Indian Sociology (N.S.)* 14: 213-238.

———1980. "Class and Christianity in South India: Indigenous Responses to Western Devotionalism." *Modern Asian Studies* 14: 6435-6471.

———1983. "Popular Christianity in South India." *Religion and Society* 30: 28-44.

Carrier, Hervé. 1993. *Evangelizing the Culture of Modernity*. Maryknoll, NY: Orbis Books.

Casanova, José. 1994. *Public Religions in the Modern World*. Part 1. Chicago and London: University of Chicago Press.

Cassidy, F. G., and R. B. Le Page. 1967. *Dictionary of Jamaican English*. London: Cambridge University Press.

Catechism of the Catholic Church. 1994. Washington, DC: US Catholic Conference.

Catholic Bishops Conference of Ghana, Justice and Peace Commission (Rt. Rev. Peter K. Sarpong, Chairman). 1984. *Inter-Tribal Conflicts in Ghana*. Kumasi, Ghana: Cita Press, Ltd.

Center for Mission Research. 1994. *"Forging Vital Christian Identities: Popular Catholicism in The Emerging Global Church." Grant Application to The Pew Charitable Trusts*. Maryknoll, NY.

CERC-UAHC. 1997. (C. Parker and Associates). *Forging Vital Christian Identities: "Popular Catholicism in the Emerging Global Church," Chile Case Study, San Joaquín—CHILE, Final Report*. Santiago: Centro de Estudios de la Realidad Contemporánea, Universidad Academia de Humanismo Cristiano.

Cheung Ka-hing, Peter. 1987. *A Reflection on Society and the Catholic Church in Hong Kong* (in Chinese). Hong Kong: Catholic Institute for Religion and Society.

Cheung, Ka-Hing, Kit-Man Li, Kun-Sun Chan, and Shing-On Leung. 1995. *Ninety-Seven, Family, Religious Faith: The Value-Orientations of Hong Kong Catholic Women* (in Chinese). Hong Kong: Catholic Institute for Religion and Society.

Conferencia Episcopal Latinoamericana (CELAM). 1992. "Secunda Relatio" de la Cuarta Conferencia Episcopal Latinoamerica Santo Domingo. Bogota, Colombia.

Congregation for Divine Worship and the Discipline of the Sacraments. 1994. *The Roman Liturgy and Inculturation*. Rome.

"Constitution on the Sacred Liturgy." 1966. In *The Documents of Vatican II*, edited by Walter M. Abbot. New York: Herder and Herder.

Cooksey, Brian. 1994. "Who's Poor in Tanzania?" In *Poverty Alleviation in Tanzania*, edited by M. S. D. Bagachwa. University of Dar es Salaam Press.

Correa, Jorge, and Luis Barros Lezaeta, eds. 1993. *Justicia y marginalidad, percepción de los pobres*. Santiago: CPU.

Darmuzey, Phillippe. 1994. "EU-St. Lucia Cooperation." *The Courier* 148 (November-December): 33-36.

Davis, Br. Paul. 1994. *Fr. Nkwera, Disposer of Demons*. (Private printing).

De Backer, Roger. 1994. "Country Report/St. Lucia: Weathering the Economic Storm." *The Courier* (November-December): 21-28.

Debray, Régis. 1996. *El arcaismo postmoderno: Lo religioso en la aldea global*. Buenos Aires: Manantial.

"Declaration on the Relationship of the Church to Non-Christian Religions." 1966. In *The Documents of Vatican II*, edited by Walter M. Abbot. New York: Herder and Herder.

"Declaration on Religious Freedom."1966. In the *The Documents of Vatican II*, edited by Walter M. Abbot. New York: Herder and Herder.

De Ecclesia: The Constitution on the Church of Vatican Council II Proclaimed by Pope Paul VI November 21, 1964. 1965. Glen Rock, NJ: Deus Books, Paulist Press.

Dery, Peter P. 1989. "The Challenges and Prospects of Education in Northern Ghana." In *Development Through Adult Education in Northern Ghana*, edited by R. A. Aggor. Northern Easter School, Legon: Institute of Adult Education, University of Ghana.

Dhananjayan, A. 1966. *Totemism and Fishermen Folklore*. Palayamkottai: Abidhaa Publications.

"Dogmatic Constitution on the Church." 1966. In the *The Documents of Vatican II*, edited by Walter M. Abbot. New York: Herder and Herder.

Dollfus, Olivier. 1985. *El reto del espacio andino*. Lima, Peru: Instituto de Estudios Peruanos (IEP).

Dretke, J. P. 1970. "Islam in Africa Project—Ghana Area Adviser's Report: 10 March, 1970" (unpublished MS).

Dupuis, Jacques. 1997. *Toward a Christian Theology of Religious Pluralism*. Maryknoll, NY: Orbis Books.

Dussel, Enrique. 1986. "Popular Religion as Oppression and Liberation: Hypothesis on Its Past and Present in Latin America." *Concilium*, August, 1986: 82-94.

Eades, J. S. 1994. *Strangers and Traders: Yoruba Migrants, Markets and the State in Northern Ghana*. Trenton, N.J.: Africa World Press, Inc.

Eagleson, John, and Philip Scharper, eds. 1979. *Puebla and Beyond: Documentation and Commentary*. Maryknoll, NY: Orbis Books.

Espín, Orlando O. 1997. *The Faith of the People: Theological Reflections on Popular Catholicism*. Maryknoll, NY: Orbis Books.

Evangelii Nuntiandi: On Evangelization in the Modern World (Apostolic Exhortation of Pope Paul VI). 1976. Washington, D.C.: U.S. Catholic Conference.

Fernandes, W. 1981. "Caste and Conversion Movements in India." *Social Action*, ISI, New Delhi 31: 261-90.

Forrester, D. B. 1977. "The Depressed Classes and Conversion to Christianity 1860-1960."

In *Religion in South Asia: Religious Conversion and Revival Movements in South Asia in Medieval and Modern Times,* edited by G. A. Oddie. London: Curzon Press.

_____1979. *Caste and Christianity: Attitudes and Policies on Caste of Anglo-Saxon Protestant Missions in India.* London: Curzon Press.

Gaudencia, Rosales B., and C. G. Arévalo, eds. 1992. *For All the Peoples of Asia: Federation of Asian Bishops' Conference Documents from 1970 to 1991.* Maryknoll, NY: Orbis Books; Quezon City, Philippines: Claretian Publications.

Ghana. 1964. *1960 Population Census of Ghana, Special Report "E": Tribes in Ghana.* Accra: Census Office.

Ghana Evangelism Committee (GEC) 1988. *Northern Regional Church/Evangelism Survey: Facing the Unfinished Task of the Church in the Northern Region.* Accra: G.E.S Box 8699.

Gonja Traditional Authority. 1984. *Gonja Traditional Authority's Reply to the Justice and Peace Commission of the Catholic Church of Ghana's Paper on Inter-Tribal Conflicts in Ghana Part One: Northern Sector.* Mimeo.

González, José Luis. 1987. *La Religión Popular en el Perú, Informe y Diagnóstico.* Cusco, Peru: Instituto de Pastoral Andina.

González, José Luis, Carlos Rodrigues Brandão, and Diego Irarrázaval. 1993. *Catolicismo Popular: História, Cultura, Teologia.* São Paulo and Petrópolis, RJ: Vozes.

Goody, Esther. 1973. *Contexts of Kinship.* Cambridge: Cambridge University Press.

Goody, J. R. 1971. *Technology, Tradition and the State.* London: Oxford University Press for the International African Institute.

Grebe, María Ester et al. 1971. "Enfermedades populares chilenas. Estudio antropológico de cuatro casos," *Cuadernos de la Realidad Nacional* (Santiago), N. 9, Septiembre: 207-238.

Gutiérrez, Gustavo. 1990. *La verdad nos hará libres.* Salamanca, Spain: Sígueme. Available in English as *The Truth Shall Make You Free: Confrontations.* Maryknoll, NY: Orbis Books, 1990.

Ha, Louis. 1991. "Catholicism in Hong Kong." In *The Other Hong Kong Report 1991,* edited by Sung Yun-wing and Lee Ming-kwan, 527-541. Hong Kong: The Chinese University Press.

Hamid, Idris. 1973. "Theology and Caribbean Development." In *With Eyes Wide Open,* edited by David Mitchel, 120-133. Barbados: CADEC.

_____ ed. 1977. *Out of the Depths.* Trinidad: St. Andrew's Theological College.

Haughton, Rosemary. 1979. *The Catholic Thing.* Springfield, IL: Templegate.

Healey, Joseph G. 1981. *A Fifth Gospel: The Experience of Black Christian Values.* Maryknoll, NY: Orbis Books; London: SCM Press.

Healey, Joseph, and Donald Sybertz. 1996. *Towards an African Narrative Theology.* Naoribi: Pauline Publications; Maryknoll, NY: Orbis Books.

Henriques, Henricus. 1956 (1558). "Letter to the Superior General." In *Documenta Indica IV (1557-1560), Monumenta Missionum Societatis Iesu IX,* edited by Josephus Wicki. Rome: Monumenta Historica Societatis Iesu.

Hervieu-Léger, Danièle. 1989. "Tradition, Innovation and Modernity." *Social Compass* 36 (1): 71-81.

Hillman, Eugene. 1993. *Toward an African Christianity: Inculturation Applied.* New York: Paulist Press.

Hodgson, Dorothy. 1997. "Embodying the Contradictions of Modernity: Gender and Spirit Possession among Maasai in Tanzania." In *Gendered Encounters: Challenging Boundaries and Social Hierarchies in Africa,* edited by Maria Grosz-Ngate and Omari Kokole. New York: Routledge.

Holland, Joe, and Peter Henriot. 1983. *Social Analysis: Linking Faith and Justice*. Maryknoll, NY: Orbis Books.

Hoornaert, Eduardo. 1997. *Os Anjos de Canudos: Uma revisão histórica*. Petropólis: Vozes.

Houtart, François. 1989. *Religión y modos de producción precapitalistas*. Madrid: IEPALA.

Hsu, Francis L. K. 1981. *Americans & Chinese: Passage to Differences*. Chapters 9-10. Honolulu: University of Hawaii Press.

Hyun Kyung, Chung. 1996. "The Wisdom of Mothers Knows No Boundaries." In *World Council of Churches, Women's Perspectives: Articulating the Liberating Power of the Gospel*, 28-35. Geneva: WCC Publications.

Impulsados por el Espíritu. Documento Pastoral de los obispos del Sur Andino. 1995. Cusco, Peru: Instituto de Pastoral Andina (IPA).

Instituto de Pastoral Andina (IPA). 1990. *Problemática y perspectivas de los jóvenes del Surandino*. Taller sobre Diagnóstico y Planificación de la Pastoral de Jóvenes. Cusco, Peru.

———— 1996. *Memoria de la Consulta Ecuménica*. Cusco, Peru.

Iyer, Anantha K. 1981 (1909). *The Cochin Tribes & Castes*, vol. 1. Madras: Higginbotham & Company.

Jenkinson, William, and Helene O'Sullivan, eds. 1991. *Trends in Mission: Toward the Third Millennium*. Maryknoll, NY: Orbis Books.

Johansson, Cristián. 1990. "Religiosidad Popular entre Medellín y Puebla: Antecedentes y Desarrollo." *Anales de la Facultad de Teología* 41, Santiago de Chile: Pontificia Universidad Católica de Chile.

John Paul II. 1986. "Address to Non-Christian Leaders." *Origins* 15.

———— 1987. "Address to the Cardinals of the Roman Curia." *Bulletin of the Secretariat for Non-Christians*, 22.

———— 1990. *Mission of the Redeemer*. Boston: St. Paul Books & Media.

Jolicoeur, Luis. 1994. *El cristianismo aymara: Inculturación o culturación?* Cochabamba, Bolivia: Universidad Católica Boliviana.

Joseph Irudhya Xavier, Ma. 1994. *Puniflia Pazhamapukkathikal*. (Tamil). Palaymkottai: St. Xavier's College.

Kakar, S. 1982. *Shamans, Mystics and Doctors*. Delhi: Oxford University Press.

Kalemera, Jason. 1993. *Huduma za Maombezi in Its Historical Perspective*. Dar es Salaam, Tanzania.

Kassimir, Ron. "The Politics of Popular Catholicism in Uganda." Paper presented at conference on "East African Christianity," Madison, Wisconsin, August 23-27, 1996.

Katanga, J. 1994. "Stereotypes and the Road to Reconciliation in Northern Ghana," *Uhuru* 6, (9): 19-22.

Kirby, J. P. 1986. "God, Shrines and Problem Solving among the Anufo of Northern Ghana." *Collectanea Instituti Anthropos*, no. 35. St. Augustin, Germany: Anthropos Institute.

———— 1992. "The Anthropology of Knowledge and the Christian Dialogue with African Traditional Religions," *Missiology* July, 20 (3): 323-341.

———— 1993. "The Islamic Dialogue with African Traditional Religion: Divination and Health Care." *Social Science and Medicine* 36 (3): 237-249.

Kirwen, Michael C. 1987. *The Missionary and the Diviner: Contending Theologies of Christian and African Religions*. Maryknoll, NY: Orbis Books.

Klausen, A. M. 1968. *Kerala Fishermen and the Indo-Norwegian Project*. London: Allen and Unwin.

Kremser, M., and K. R. Wernhart, eds. 1986. *Research in Ethnography and Ethnohistory of St. Lucia*. Horn-Wien: Ferdinand Berger & Söhne.

Ladouceur, P. 1979. *Chiefs and Politicians: The Politics of Regionalism in Northern Ghana*. London: Longmans.

Lanternari, Vittorio. 1982. "La religion populaire. Perspective historique et anthropologique." *Archives de Sciences Sociales des Religions* 53 (1): 121-143.

Levine, Daniel H., ed. 1986. *Religion and Political Conflict in Latin America.* Chapel Hill: University of North Carolina Press.

———1992. *Popular Voices in Latin American Catholicism.* Princeton: Princeton University Press.

Levtzion, N. 1968. *Muslims and Chiefs in West Africa: A Study of Islam in the Middle Volta Basin in the Pre-colonial Period.* Oxford: Clarendon Press.

Li, Kit-Man. 1996. "The Change of Sovereignty and the Problem of Identity among Hong Kong Catholics." In *Church Responses to Rapidly Changing Society—Conference Proceedings*, edited by Ka-Hing Cheung, 477-495. Hong Kong: The Catholic Institute for Religion and Society.

"The Living Tree: the Changing Meaning of Being Chinese Today." *Daedalus* 120 (2) 1991: special issue.

Luzbetak, L. J. 1988. *Church and Culture: New Perspectives in Missiological Anthropology.* Maryknoll, NY: Orbis Books.

Maduro, Otto. 1992. *Mapas para la Fiesta: Reflexiones latinoamericanas sobre la crisis y el conocimiento.* Rio de Janeiro and New York: Centro Nueva Tierra.

Magesa, Laurenti. "Reflections on the Marian Faith Healing Ministry, Response to First Draft." 1997. Unpublished document.

Maroz, Cecilia Loreto. 1994. "L'affrimation des intérêts dans l'étude des faits religieux au Brésil" *Social Compass* 41 (3): 355-365.

Marx, Karl, and F. Engels. 1979 (1844). *Sobre la Religión.* H. Assmann, R. Mate, eds. Salamanca: Sígueme.

Marzal, Manuel. 1986. "Análisis etnológico del sincretismo latinoamericano." *Cristianismo y Sociedad* 24 (88): 27-40.

McCoy, R. 1988. *Great Things Happen.* Montreal: Society of Missionaries of Africa.

McGilvray, D. B. 1983. "Mukkuvar vannimai: Tamil caste and matriclan ideology in Batticaloan, Sri Lanka." In *Caste, Ideology and Interaction*, edited by D. B. McGilvray, 34-97. Cambridge: Cambridge University Press.

Mundadan, A. Mathias. 1967. *The Arrival of the Portuguese in India and the Thomas Christians under Mar Jacob, 1498-1552.* Bangalore: Dharmaram College.

Muzorewa, Gwinyai H. 1995. *The Origins and Development of African Theology.* Maryknoll, NY: Orbis Books.

Neil, Stephen. 1966. *A History of the Christian Alission.* London: Penguin.

Newall, Venetia. 1978. "Some Examples of the Practice of Obeah by West Indian Immigrants in London." *Folklore* 89: 29-51.

Nkwera, Fr. F. V. 1996. *Kanisa, Serikali, Msikiti na Uchaguzi Mkuu Tanzania, 1995.* Dar es Salaam: MFHM.

———1997a. *MFHM Messages and Testimonies, 1969-1994.* Dar es Salaam, Tanzania: MFHM.

———1997b. "Written Comments on the First Draft of Paper on the MFHM, Popular Catholicism of African Independent Church," Riverside, Ubungo, Dar es Salaam, February 6.

Ossa, Manuel. 1997. "Reflexión Teológica." In CERC-UAHC (C. Parker and Associates), 1997, *Forging Vital Christian Identities: "Popular Catholicism in the Emerging Global Church," Chile Case Study, San Joaquín—CHILE, Final Report.* Santiago: Centro de Estudios de la Realidad Contemporánea, Universidad Academia de Humanismo Cristiano.

Pace, Enzo. 1995. "Tendencia y corrientes de la sociología de las religiones." *Sociedad y Religión*, no. 13. Buenos Aires.

Panikkar, Kavalam Madhava. 1959. *Asia and Western Dominance*. New York: Macmillan.

Parker G., Cristián 1992a. "Fe popular urbana y campo cultural: las lógicas en juego." In *Por los Caminos de América . . . Desafíos socio-culturales a la Nueva Evangelización*, edited by Gonzalo Arroyo et al., 113-187. Santiago: Paulinas.

_____1992b. *Animitas, Machis y Santiguadoras en Chile*. Santiago: Rehue.

_____1994. "The sociology of religion in Latin America." *Social Compass*, 41 (3): 339-354.

_____1996. *Popular Religion and Modernization in Latin America: A Different Logic*. Maryknoll, NY: Orbis Books.

"Pastoral Constitution on the Church in the Modern World, Gaudium et Spes." 1965. In *Documents of Vatican II*, edited by Austin P. Flannery. Grand Rapids, MI: William P. Eerdmans, 1975.

"Pastoral Constitution on the Church in the Modern World." 1966. In *The Documents of Vatican II*, edited by Walter M. Abbot. New York: Herder and Herder.

Paul VI. 1976. *Evangelii Nuntiandi. On Evangelization in the Modern World*.

Pieris, Aloysius, 1988. *An Asian Theology of Liberation*. Maryknoll, NY: Orbis Books.

Plath, Oreste. 1981. *Folklore Médico Chileno*. Santiago: Nascimiento.

Plissart, X. 1983. *Mamprusi Proverbs*. Tervuren, Belgium: Musée Royal de L'Afrique Centrale, no. 11.

Porcile Santiso, María Teresa. 1995. *La mujer, espacio de salvación: La misión de la mujer en la Iglesia, una perspectiva antropológica*. Madrid: Publicaciones Claretianas.

Pro Mundi Vita. "Popular Religions." 1988. *Pro Mundi Vita Studies* Nov.: 1-51.

Puebla Final Document. *Conferencia General del Episcopado Latino-americano*, 1979. *La evangelización en el presente y en el futuro de América Latina (Documento de Puebla)* Conferencia Episcopal de Chile, Santiago, Chile. In English, found in John Eagleson and Philip Scharper, eds., *Puebla and Beyond: Documentation and Commentary*. Maryknoll, NY: Orbis Books, 1979.

Ram, Kalpana. 1991. *Mukkuvar Women: Gender, Hegemony and Capitalist Transformation in a South Indian Fishing Community*. London: Zed Books.

Read, Margaret. 1966. *Culture, Health and Disease*. London: Tavistock.

Robertson, Roland. 1992. *Globalization: Social Theory and Global Culture*. London: Sage.

Roche, P. 1984. *The Fishermen of the Coromandel: The Social Study of the Paravas of the Coromandel*. New Delhi: Manohar.

Salado, Domingo, and Jesús Tapuerca. 1996. *Inculturación: Nuevo rostro de la Iglesia*. Coban, Guatemala: Textos Ak Kutan Centro Bartolomé de Las Casas.

Santo Domingo Final Document. *Conferencia General del Episcopado Latinoamericano, 1992. Nueva Evangelización, Promoción humana, Cultura Cristiana, Jesucristo ayer, hoy y siempre (Documento de Santo Domingo)*, Conferencia Episcopal de Chile, Santiago, Chile. In English, found in Alfred Hennelly, ed., *Santo Domingo and Beyond*. Maryknoll, NY: Orbis Books, 1993.

Scherer, James A., and Stephen B. Bevans, eds. 1992. *New Directions in Mission and Evangelization: Basic Statements 1974-1991*. Maryknoll, NY: Orbis Books.

Schreiter, Robert J. 1985. *Constructing Local Theologies*. Maryknoll, NY: Orbis Books.

_____1997. *The New Catholicity: Theology Between the Global & the Local*. Maryknoll, NY: Orbis Books.

Schurhammer, Georg. 1977. *Francis Xavier: His Life, His Times. Vol. 2, INDIA 1541-1545*. Rome: The Jesuit Historical Institute.

Scott, James C. 1985. *Weapons of the Weak: Everyday Forms of Peasant Resistance*. New Haven: Yale University Press.

_____1990. *Domination and the Arts of Resistance: Hidden Transcripts.* New Haven: Yale University Press.

Senge, Peter. 1990. *Fifth Discipline: The Art and Practice of the Learning Organization.* New York: Doubleday.

Sereno, Renzo. 1948. "Obeah: Magic and Social Structure in the Lesser Antilles." *Psychiatry* 11: 15-31.

Shorter, Aylward. 1988. *Toward a Theology of Inculturation.* Maryknoll, NY: Orbis Books.

Simmons, Harold. 1963. "Notes on Folklore in St. Lucia" in *IOUANALOA: Recent Writings from St. Lucia*, 41-49. Department of Extra Mural Studies, University of West Indies.

Skalnik, Peter. 1983. "Chieftaincy and State, The Dragging History of the Nanumba-Konkomba Conflict." *Ghana Newsletter* no. 17, November.

Soares-Prabhu, George. 1981. "The Kingdom of God: Jesus' Vision of a New Society." In *The Indian Church in the Struggle for a New Society*, edited by D. S. Amalorpavadass, 579-607. Bangalore: National Biblical, Catechetical and Liturgical Centre.

Soneira, Jorge Abelardo, et al. 1996. *Sociología de la Religión.* Buenos Aires: Docencia.

Staniland, M. 1975. *The Lions of Dagbon: Political Change in Northern Ghana.* Cambridge: Cambridge University Press.

Stirrat, R.L. 1992. *Power and Religiosity in a Post-Colonial Setting.* Cambridge: Cambridge University Press.

Stott, R. W., and R. Coote, eds. 1980. *Down to Earth: Studies in Christianity and Culture—Papers of the Lausanne Consultation.* Grand Rapids, MI: W. B. Eerdmans.

Süess, Paulo. 1986. "The Creative and Normative Role of Popular Religion in the Church." *Concilium* 206 (July): 122-131.

Tait, David. 1961. *The Konkomba of Northern Ghana.* London: Oxford University Press, Published for the I.A.I.

_____1963. "A Sorcery Hunt in Dagomba." *Africa* 33 (2): 136-147.

Tanzania Gender Networking Programme (TGNP). 1993. *Gender Profile of Tanzania.* Dar es Salaam.

Tau, Siu-kai, and Hsin-Chi Kuan. 1988. *The Ethos of the Hong Kong Chinese.* Hong Kong: Chinese University Press.

Tönnies, Ferdinand. 1955 (1895). *Community and Society.* New York: Routledge.

Tornos, Andrés. 1992. "La perspectiva del análisis cultural." In *Por los Caminos de América: Desafíos socioculturales a la Nueva Evangelización*, edited by Gonzalo Arroyo et al., 211-217. Santiago, Chile: Paulinas.

Troeltsch, Ernst. 1901. *The Absoluteness of Christianity and the History of Religions.* Richmond, VA: John Knox.

_____1931. *The Social Teaching of the Christian Churches.* London: Allen and Unwin.

Urbano, Henrique. 1992. *La tradición andina o la memoria del futuro.* Cusco, Peru: Centro Bartolome de Las Casas.

Valveçius, A. 1995. "Le Nouvel Age ou l'éternel retour du même." *Nouvelle Revue Théologique* 117: 694-709.

Van den Berg, Hans. 1990. *La tierra no da así no más: ritos agrícolas en la región de los aymara cristianos.* Cochabamba, Bolivia: Universidad Católica Boliviana, Temas Monográficos, Yachay.

Van Nieuwenbore, Jacques, and Berma Klein Goldewijk, eds. 1991. *Popular Religion, Liberation and Contextual Theology.* Nijmegen, Netherlands: Nijmegen Catholic University.

Venner, Dwight K. 1989. "The Saint Lucian Economy in the 21st Century." In *St. Lucia:*

10th Independence Anniversary Souvenir Magazine. Castries, St. Lucia: Voice Publishing Co.

Villavarayan, J. M. 1956. *The Diocese of Kottam.* Nagercoil: Bishop's House.

Vrijhof, Pieter H., and Jacques Waardenburg, eds. 1979. *Official and Popular Religion: Analyses of a Theme for Religious Studies.* The Hague: Mouton.

Walcott, Derek. 1976. *Sea Grapes.* London: Jonathan Cape.

Waliggo, John. 1986. *Inculturation: Its Meaning and Urgency.* Nairobi: St. Paul.

Walzer, Michael. 1973 (1965). *The Revolution of the Saints: A Study in the Origins of Radical Politics.* New York: Atheneum.

Weber, Max. 1958. *The Protestant Ethic and the Spirit of Capitalism.* New York: Charles Scribner's Sons.

_____1964 (1922). *Economía y Sociedad.* México: Fondo de Cultura Económica.

Wijsen, Frans. 1993. *There Is Only One God: A Social-Scientific and Theological Study of Popular Religion and Evangelization in Sukumaland, Northwest Tanzania.* Kampen: Uitgeverij Kok.

Williams, Joseph J. 1932. *Voodoos and Obeahs: Phases of West India Witchcraft.* London.

World Bank. 1995. *World Development Report, 1995.* Oxford: Oxford University Press.

World Council of Churches. 1996a. *Women's Perspectives: Articulating the Liberating Power of the Gospel.* Geneva: WCC Publications.

World Council of Churches. 1996b. *Conference Message and Acts of Commitment. Conference on World Mission and Evangelism.* Salvador, Brazil.

Yuen, Mary M. Y. 1997. "The Catholic Church in Political Transition." In *The Other Hong Kong Report 1997*, edited by Joseph Y. S. Cheng, 505-528. Hong Kong: The Chinese University Press.

Contributors

Thomas Bamat is Research Director at the Center for Mission Research and Study at Maryknoll, New York. A sociologist (Ph.D. Rutgers) and lay missioner, he has worked in South America as well as the U.S. Among his publications are articles on religion and politics, books on human rights and new religious movements in Ecuador, and a coedited volume on life in Brazil's agrarian reform settlements, *Qualidade de Vida e Reforma Agrária Na Paraíba* (Imprell, 1998).

Jean-Paul Wiest is former Research Director at the Center for Mission Research and Study at Maryknoll, currently on assignment in Shanghai, China. A historian (Ph.D. University of Washington), he has specialized in Chinese history, Catholic mission history, and oral history methods. In addition to numerous journal articles and book chapters, he wrote *Maryknoll in China: A History, 1918-1955* (M.E. Sharpe, 1988), and coedited *The Catholic Church in Modern China, Perspectives* (Orbis, 1993).

Cristián Parker Gumucio is a Research Associate and Professor at the Institute for Advanced Studies, University of Santiago de Chile, and Assistant Director of the Center for the Study of Contemporary Reality (CERC) at the Academy of Christian Humanism University (UAHC). A highly respected sociologist of religion (Ph.D. Catholic University of Louvain), his works on religion and culture include *Popular Religion and Modernization in Latin America* (Orbis, 1996).

María José Caram directs the Andean Pastoral Institute (IPA) in Cuzco, Peru. A Dominican sister and a theologian (STL, Civil and Pontifical Theology Faculty, Lima), she has focused on popular religion among the indigenous peoples of the altiplano. Among her recent works is an article on identity, faith, and the impact of globalization, "Identidades Creyentes en Tiempos de Cambio," in volume 50 of the Peruvian journal *Allpanchis*.

Patrick A. B. Anthony is former director of the Archdiocesan Pastoral Centre in St. Lucia, the Caribbean regional president of the World Association for Christian Communication, and editor of *Theology in the Caribbean Today.* He holds a master's degree from Catholic Theological Union in Chicago and is a doctoral student at the University of the West Indies, St. Augustine, Trinidad. His writings include "The Encounter between Christianity and Culture," in Kremser and Wernhart (eds.), *Research in Ethnography and Ethnohistory of St. Lucia.*

Vincent Boi-Nai is former Provincial of the Divine Word Missionaries in his native Ghana and a member of their General Council in Rome. He studied at Catholic Theological Union, Chicago, received a doctorate in field education from Andover Newton, and directed the program for learning ministry from another cultural perspective at the Tamale Institute of Cross Cultural Studies. His article "Witchcraft Mentality: A Personal Reflection" appeared in *Divine Word Missionaries,* Summer 1998.

Jon P. Kirby is a Divine Word missionary and founder director of the Tamale Institute of Cross Cultural Studies in northern Ghana. He studied theology in Chicago and holds a

Ph.D. in social anthropology from the University of Cambridge, UK. Kirby has published extensively on the connections between African traditional religion and problem-solving, probing the implications for human development and Christian ministry. His monograph on Dagomba religion is soon to be released by Regnum Books, Oxford.

Christopher Comoro is Head of the Department of Sociology and Anthropology and a Senior Lecturer at the University of Dar es Salaam, Tanzania, as well as director of its medical sociology research unit. A social scientist with a Ph.D. from Carleton University in Ottawa, he has published on issues of demography and democratization, as well as health and AIDS. He is an adviser for religious studies at the Open University of Tanzania.

John Sivalon is the Regional Superior for Maryknoll's Africa Region, and a Senior Lecturer in the Department of Sociology at the University of Dar es Salaam. He received his Ph.D. in Sociology and Theology from the University of St. Michael's College in Toronto, and has published articles on education, politics, and religion in Tanzania. An adviser for religious studies at the Open University of Tanzania, he is currently working on a book on urbanization and religious consciousness.

Francis Jayapathy directs the Folklore Resources and Research Centre at St. Xavier's College in Palayamkottai, India, where he also serves as a professor. A Jesuit and a social anthropologist, he has completed work for a Ph.D. in the School of Oriental and African Studies, London School of Economics, UK, and is currently preparing a full-length book on popular Catholicism among the Mukkuvar fisherfolk.

Kit-Man Li is an assistant in the Department of Applied Social Studies at the Hong Kong Polytechnic University. He obtained an M.A. in Philosophy from the Institute of Advanced Chinese Studies in the People's Republic of China, and a Ph.D. in sociology from the University of Leicester, UK. He is now completing a book called *Western Civilization and Its Problems: A Dialogue between Weber, Elias, and Habermas.*

Ka-Hing Cheung is Editor in Chief of *Kung Kao Po*, a Catholic weekly newspaper in Hong Kong, and Executive Director of the Catholic Institute for Religion and Society there. He holds an STL from Propaganda Fide in Rome, and an M.A. in Comparative Asian Studies from the University of Hong Kong. Among his writings are a study on the value orientations of Catholic women and *The Subject, Community, and Social Consciousness of Hong Kong Catholics* (CIRS, 1989).

Kun-Sun Chan, a graduate student in the Department of Applied Social Studies at the Hong Kong Polytechnic University in Kowloon, HK, has been a Lecturer at Hong Kong Shue Yan College. He received his M.A. in Sociology from the University of Kent at Canterbury, UK, and is currently working on a research project about social welfare organizations in Hong Kong.

Kosuke Koyama is Professor Emeritus of Ecumenical Studies at Union Theological Seminary in New York. A native of Japan and a graduate of Princeton Theological Seminary, he has also taught theology in Thailand and New Zealand. His works include collections of meditations and *Mount Fuji and Mount Sinai: A Critique of Idols* (Orbis, 1984). A 25th anniversary edition of his acclaimed *Waterbuffalo Theology* is being published this year by Orbis Books.

Ivone Gebara is a Brazilian philosopher and theologian who lectures worldwide today. For seventeen years she was a professor at the Theological Institute of Recife. Everyday life in her impoverished neighborhood in Camaragibe in Brazil's northeast helps her to link her intellectual work with the experiences of the oppressed, especially women. Her most recent book is *Teologia Ecofeminista* (São Paulo: Olho da Água, 1997), published in Uruguay in Spanish as *Intuiciones Ecofeministas.*

Lamin Sanneh, trained as a historian of religion, was born in Gambia and educated on four continents. A naturalized U.S. citizen, he taught at Harvard and is currently at Yale University. He has authored over a hundred articles and books on religion and historical subjects. His books include *The Crown and the Turban: Muslims and West African Pluralism* (Westview, 1996) and *Encountering the West: Christianity and the Global Cultural Process* (Orbis, 1993).

Michael Amaladoss, currently Professor of Theology at Vidyajyoti College of Theology, Delhi, India, has served as President of the International Association of Mission Studies, and as Assistant to the Superior General of the Society of Jesus. Among his most recent works are *Life in Freedom: Liberation Theologies from Asia* (Orbis, 1997) and *Beyond Inculturation: Can the Many Be One?* (Vidyajyoti and the Indian Society for Promoting Christian Knowledge, 1998). He has also published some two hundred articles on subjects such as contemporary mission, interreligious dialogue, liturgy, music, and Indian theology.

ABOUT THE CENTER FOR MISSION RESEARCH
AND STUDY AT MARYKNOLL

Popular Catholicism in a World Church is the fruit of collaboration between researchers in various local churches and the Center for Mission Research and Study at Maryknoll (CMRSM), a research and educational institution that shares the charism and traditions of the Catholic Foreign Mission Society of America (Maryknoll).

Through exploration of the meaning and contexts of Chrisian mission both in the past and in the contemporary world, CMRSM seeks to assist Christians in their mission to share the Gospel of Jesus Christ in ways that are informed, culturally and spiritually sensitive, and relevant to local economic, social, and political challenges. CMRSM gives particular attention to mission outside the continental United States. In so doing, it offers persons within the United States resources for understanding and participating in the Church's worldwide mission. To these ends, the Center collaborates ecumenically with persons of other faiths and ecclesial traditions, promotes and participates in systematic research, offers lectures and programs of study, and organizes consultations of scholars and other persons knowledgeable about Chrisitian mission in its many facets.

For more about Maryknoll and the Center for Mission Research and Study, visit our website at: http://www.maryknoll.org.

Of Related Interest

The New Catholicity
Theology between the Global and the Local
Robert J. Schreiter, C.PP.S.
ISBN 1-57075-120-X

The most important single resource in print on how the local theology movement has given new shape to a classic notion — "Catholicity." An amazing synthesis of social, scientific, theological, and common sense insights into one of the deepest traits of Christianity in our time.

"For those of us who are seeking a theological path that avoids both a homogenizing globalism and a relativizing localism, Schreiter is a wise and reliable guide. May his brand of catholicity flourish."
—*Richard Mouw, Fuller Theological Seminary*